Supply Chain Management in the 21st Century

Supply Chain Management in the 21st Century

with European applications

Jan Renaud

Amsterdam University Press

Note to the image on the cover page:

Already in 2014, the largest e-commerce retailer in the world, Amazon Inc, filed an application for a patent at the United States Patent and Trademark Office (USPTO) envisioning an innovative distribution system. In the application document (U.S. patent 9,305,280 filed by Amazon Technologies Inc.) they describe a large airship (zeppelin) serving as a floating fulfillment center in the air, accompanied by a fleet of drones transporting packages from the airship to the destination address on land. Although this innovative distribution system is still in a research phase, and far from being operational, it is one of the many innovations taking place in the organization of Supply Chains.

Cover design: Gijs Mathijs Ontwerpers, Amsterdam
Lay-out: Crius Group, Hulshout

ISBN	978 94 6372 987 1
e-ISBN	978 90 4855 614 4
DOI	10.5117/9789463729871
NUR	780

© J. Renaud / Amsterdam University Press B.V., Amsterdam 2022

Table of Contents

Foreword

Synopsis

Supply Chain Management in the 21st Century is a textbook written for final-year Bachelor students in business and management sciences, but it also fits into programmes for MBA students. The book is a useful supplement to curricula of industrial and production engineering students who are considering a career in the field of production planning, procurement, inventory management, and Supply Chain Management in business organizations, public administration entities, and not-for-profit organizations. Every subject in the book starts from the basics and develops the theory and models up to an intermediate level. To be able to follow the text, the basic requisites are an elementary background in mathematics, statistics, and spreadsheet skills.

The didactical approach

The book pursues a blend of theoretical concepts and models alongside practical applications. Supply Chains in the 21st century are faced with challenges that hardly existed in the previous century. Technological advances in the field of Information Technology, autonomous vehicles used in distributions centres, an exponential increase in online shopping and the organization of last-mile deliveries, the Covid-19 crisis, and smart infrastructure, just to mention a few, are impacting supply chain operations and performance significantly in the 21st century. Many of these new developments are discussed in this book.

The scope and the level of the book strike a balance between introductory qualitative textbooks about Supply Chain and operations management, on one side, and specialized papers published in scientific journals, such as *Supply Chain Management, Journal of Supply Chain Management*, and academic publications of similar standing on the other side.

The learning approach of the book is based on a blend of theory and exercises. The theory discusses the structure and methodology that are needed to solve practical exercises. The problem-solving, in turn, highlights the value of a consistent theory. Most of the quantitative exercises in the book are presented and solved in spreadsheet format. Several models are discussed and worked out in detail, showing the scope and limits of the model. For mathematically interested readers, formal mathematical proofs have been subsumed in a digital mathematical appendix that will be posted on the book's corresponding website.

Supply Chain is a broad field that generates ever more scientific research and papers, each of which zooms in on increasingly specialized topics. It is therefore impossible to address the full range of subjects making up the field of Supply Chain and business operations, and the scope of the book had to be reduced by making choices. The selection of topics I have pursued offers a coherent general picture of the main fields in Supply Chains, whereby quantitative models are preceded by qualitative descriptions, sometimes taken from real-world situations.

No textbook on Supply Chains in the 21st century would be complete without a chapter about revenue management, and this book is no exception. A final chapter is dedicated to the alignment and coordination of individual Corporate Social Responsibility policies of firms working together in a Supply Chain to create a shared Supply Chain CSR and sustainable Supply Chain policy.

The aim of this textbook

Besides the topicality of global Supply Chains in the 21st century, a field that overlaps with the realm of many business jobs, including financial, accounting, and IT, many textbooks about supply chain and business operations management are either predominantly descriptive or qualitative in their approach, or they are highly quantitative with a focus on mathematical modelling. This book aims to fill a gap and take an intermediate stance between the two approaches.

Another reason for writing this book is that many textbooks are based on US Supply Chain examples, while the number of books with a European perspective is limited. Although the differences in abstract Supply Chain models are small and globally applicable, the institutional framework for companies and Supply Chains working in the United States and Europe are different. Case descriptions and illustrative examples are therefore taken primarily from European institutions and companies.

The book will include some topics that are not commonly found in supply chain textbooks: a description and analysis of infrastructure assets and their impact on logistics operations, and the increasing problem of congestion occurring at all levels in a Supply Chain using basic concepts of queueing theory in distribution planning.

Quantitative problems for each chapter will be posted on the book's corresponding website. The problem set will be expanded over time and adjusted when necessary. The quantitative exercises can be solved with MS Excel and its mathematical and statistical function library as well as the Add-in Solver.

For instructors who prescribe the book for their course, the Excel files with the examples shown as screenshots in the book will be made available. They will also have access to most standard solutions to the questions and problems.

All endnotes at the end of each chapter, containing references as well as more details, extensions, and some entertaining anecdotes about specific subjects and important players in the field of Operations Management, have been consolidated in a separate instructor's manual. That manual will be made available for instructors who prescribe the book for their students.

The author welcomes suggestions from instructors and users that can improve the quality of a future edition of the book.

Chapter distribution and learning objectives

The last column indicates whether the learning objective is solely discussed in descriptive terms (D) or supported by quantitative models (Q) and/or in Excel format (Ex)

Chapter 1. Introduction to Supply Chains
Learning objectives chapter 1
After having studied chapter 1, the student will be able to explain:

– The fast growth of global Supply Chains and value chains in the 21st century	D
– Fundamental structures and pyramidal base models of Supply Chains of mass consumer goods	D
– The pivotal role of Customer Response Time in Supply Chain problems	D
– Classification of production processes and the growth of mass customization	D
– The asset flows in a Supply Chain and their mutual relationship	D
– The different layers and nodes in a Supply Chain network	D
– The bullwhip effect and the streamlining of order flow in a Supply Chain	D
– The digitalization of the economy and its impact on distribution systems	D

Chapter 2. Demand Forecasting
Learning objectives chapter 2
After having studied chapter 2, the student will be able to explain:

– The added value of collaborative demand for the performance of a Supply Chain	D
– The difference between qualitative and quantitative forecasting methods	D
– The structural and random components of a forecasting model	D
– The centred moving average forecasting model	Q/Ex
– Forecasting with linear regression and binary variables	Q/Ex
– The Holt-Winter forecasting model	Q/Ex
– When and which forecasting model is appropriate for which data structure	D

Chapter 3. Capacity planning and location decisions
Learning objectives chapter 3
After having studied chapter 3, the student will be able to explain:

- The different capacity concepts for organizations and their relevant   D
  cost components
- The relation between capacity planning and production planning   D
- The decision tree as a decision support tool for capacity investments   Q
- Optimization models for integrated capacity and distribution planning Q/Ex
- Qualitative factors for the selection of a location for new capacity   D
- Gravitation model for finding an optimal geographical location for   Q/Ex
  capacity
- The Hoteling model explains the geographical concentration of   D
  competing retailers

Chapter 4. Production planning
Learning objectives chapter 4
After having studied chapter 4, the student will be able to explain:

- The interrelation between products, production processes, and produc-   D
  tion planning
- How one product can be produced by different combinations of   D
  production factors
- Some common levers to match production to demand: inventory;   Q
  overtime; and subcontracting
- Basic models for production planning at the lowest cost in spreadsheet Q/Ex
  format
- The Bill of Materials and Enterprise Resource Planning   D

Chapter 5. Inventory policy under certainty conditions
Learning objectives chapter 5
After having studied chapter 5, the student will be able to explain:

- Classification of different inventory assets in relation to production   D
  and sales
- Classification of costs associated with keeping inventory   D
- The Economic Order Quantity base model and the reorder point in an   Q/Ex
  inventory cycle
- The EOQ model with marginal units and with all-units quantity   Q/Ex
  discounts
- The minimalization of inventory cost with a coordinated inventory   Q/Ex
  policy in a Supply Chain
- The impact of joint orders on total inventory costs   Q/Ex

Chapter 6. Inventory policy under uncertainty
Learning objectives chapter 6
After having studied chapter 6, the student will be able to explain:
- The relation between the Cycle Service Level and the fill rate to benchmark inventory policy — Q/Ex
- The calculation of safety stock when demand follows a normal distribution and lead time is constant — Q/Ex
- The calculation of safety stock when both demand and lead time follow a normal distribution — Q/Ex
- The impact of centralization of inventory on the total inventory costs — Q/Ex

Chapter 7. Procurement, inventory risk-sharing, and the Cycle Service Level
Learning objectives chapter 7
After having studied chapter 7, the student will be able to explain:
- Cost of understocking and overstocking and the optimal Cycle Service Level — Q/Ex
- The main components of procurement policy in private companies — D
- The main components of public tenders for procurement by public agencies in the EU — D
- The concept of Total Cost of Ownership — D
- Supplier selection and negotiation strategies for procurement — D
- Instruments for risk-sharing between producer and retailer: buyback contracts, revenue sharing contracts and quantity flexibility contracts — Q/Ex

Chapter 8. Asset Mobility and Infrastructure
Learning objectives chapter 8
After having studied chapter 8, the student will be able to explain:
- The main asset flows in a Supply Chain: goods, persons, information, and financial flows — D
- The trade-off between inventory and logistics — D
- The relation between transportation modes, infrastructure, and Customer Response Time — D
- The five major transportation modes for goods: water, road, rail, air, and pipeline, with main cost components and travel time — D
- Institutional features of infrastructure assets for different transportation modes — D
- Travel modes for persons in a service Supply Chain — D
- Information flows and data traffic in a Supply Chain with its supporting infrastructure — D

–   The impact of congestion on infrastructure assets on lead time and   D
    logistical performance
–   The distribution configuration for the last-mile delivery   D

Chapter 9.   Optimization of transportation and distribution planning in
networks
Learning objectives chapter 9
After having studied chapter 9, the student will be able to explain
–   The network patterns of infrastructure assets and their impact on   D
    distribution and logistics planning
–   The use of the shortest-path algorithm and the travelling salesman for   Q/Ex
    logistics planning
–   Various distribution configurations from supplier to business   D
    customers
–   Typical features of distribution configurations for online and offline   D
    consumer purchases

Chapter 10.   Revenue Management and Capacity Usage
Learning objectives chapter 10
After having studied chapter 10, the student will be able to explain
–   How dynamic pricing can improve the occupancy rate of capacity   Q/Ex
–   How an overbooking policy with uncertain demand can lead to   D
    improved capacity utilization
–   How to calculate the optimal number of overbookings when demand   Q/Ex
    is normally distributed
–   How vertical price agreements in a distribution chain affect the   Q/Ex
    reseller's price
–   The pivotal role for the price-reaction curve in the determination of   Q/Ex
    the optimal retailer's price

Chapter 11.   Queueing Management in a Supply Chains
Learning objectives chapter 11
After having studied chapter 11, the student will be able to explain
–   How queueing theory helps to understand and model delays in a   D
    Supply Chain
–   How delays are an element of the broader phenomenon of risk propaga-   D
    tion (chain reactions) in a Supply Chain
–   The economic and psychological aspects of waiting lines   D
–   Different queueing disciplines in a waiting line   D

– The role of the Poisson distribution and Exponential distribution for waiting line management	Q/Ex
– The determination of structural parameters to benchmark waiting lines	Q/Ex
– A specific queueing model for a Supply Chain: Jackson networks	D

Chapter 12.   Sustainability in Supply Chain
Learning objectives chapter 12
After having studied chapter 12, the student will be able to explain:

– The main components of Sustainability and Corporate Social Responsibility	D
– Complications to transform a sustainability policy of a single corporation into a sustainability policy of an entire Supply Chain	D
– How Blockchain technology has the potential to advance sustainability in a Supply Chain	D
– How a Supply Chain can be extended by integrating the after-sales phase	D
– Drivers and management of consumer waste: an inverted Supply Chain pyramidal structure	D
– Institutional dimensions of consumer waste management	D
– **Case:** the global food supply chain: *the Tragedy of the Commons*, food waste and food loss and models for sustainable management of biological resources with the concepts of *carrying capacity* and *maximum sustainable yield*	D/Q /Ex

1   An Introduction to Supply Chains in the 21st Century

An introductory Supply Chain case: The evolution of the supermarket sector in the Netherlands

The food retail industry, with the supermarket chains as main players, is a good example of understanding the different dimensions of and relations within a Supply Chain. This sector can be characterized as a well-organized industry with a long-standing, highly competitive environment. Over the years, the Dutch food retail sector has experienced spells of merger waves and acquisitions. It has a well-developed logistics and distribution system, and is fertile ground for new marketing techniques. It is a major source of jobs in the Netherlands. It uses sophisticated inventory management systems, invests in IT, is expanding in the 21st century in online sales, and is endowed with many other features of modern businesses models.

Prior to World War II, most grocery stores were privately owned family businesses, ubiquitous in European cities and towns, and offering a limited product assortment that met the basic needs of their customers in the field of food and drinks. The inflow of food from outside the country was limited: no Chilean wine; no Italian Pasta; no Spanish jamón, although many spices arriving from colonial areas were sold in the grocery stores. Most stores had an loyal group of customers who belonged to their catchment area. Moreover, the store manager was close to the customer and able to detect consumer satisfaction with his products quickly. Most stores were supplied directly by food manufacturers without the physical interface of distribution centres. Already by the end of the nineteenth century, single grocery stores were starting to expand their assortment with meat, bread, vegetables, fruit, dairy products like milk and butter, spirits, and others. The enactment of the trademark law enabled entrepreneurs to run several stores under the same trademark, with a similar product assortment and store layout. One of the oldest food retailers with an established brand name in the Netherlands is Albert Heijn. Named after the Dutch entrepreneur who founded it, in Zaandam, in 1887, today it is the largest supermarket chain in the Netherlands and is currently part of the Ahold-Delhaize concern.

A typical innovation introduced by supermarkets was self-service. Customers could walk freely through the store space, mostly arranged in aisles, and pick the food and household items they needed from the shelves, depositing and moving them in a shopping trolley. In the old service system, the customer waited in front of a counter and asked the shop assistant to pick the items from the shelves. In a modern supermarket layout, the checkouts are located close to the store exit.

Especially after the creation of the European Economic Community, on 1 January 1958, a new flow of foreign food entered the assortment of Dutch supermarkets; at the same time, Dutch supermarkets opened new stores abroad. The assortment expanded with a large portfolio of foreign food, including Italian pasta and Greek produce, thus the creation of the single European market resulted in a boost to foreign products penetrating the Dutch food market.

In the 1980s, two large German supermarket chains entered the Dutch food retail market: Lidl and Aldi. The last two decades of the 20th century saw a wave of acquisitions. Many familiar brand names, such as Konmar, De Boer, Edah, Bas van der Heiden, and more than 40 other brand names, disappeared from the supermarket landscape as they were consolidated, integrated, reorganized, or absorbed in other larger food retail chains. Achieving economies of scale to withstand the competition was a driving force. At the same time, supermarkets continued to expand their supply thereby outcompeting smaller, more specialized food shops: the supermarket added vegetables and fruit sections, displacing many independent greengrocers in the process (430↓ between 2008 and 2017, according to CBS 2018 Statline). They added meat sections, outcompeting many small independent butcher shops (405↓ between 2008 and 2017, according to Statline), and sections of bread and other cereal products, taking custom from many small independent bakeries (10↓ between 2008 and 2017, according to CBS 2018 Statline), as well as sections of dairy products. Despite this, the number of stand-alone specialized cheese shops actually increased, reaching 100 stores between 2008 and 2017 (CBS 2018 Statline). Specialized liquor stores fared less well, with many customers now shopping in the supermarkets' dedicated alcoholic drinks aisles (110↓ between 2008 and 2017, according to CBS 2018 Statline).

The 21st century has seen an increase in the number of foreign supermarkets establishing themselves in the Netherlands. There are now, for example, more than 75 Polish supermarkets, a growing number of Asian supermarkets – so-called tokos – and rising numbers of Turkish supermarkets as well as supermarkets from other countries. Each has its own assortment of national and local dishes and food. All supply is organized under a single roof, saving shopping time for consumers who no longer need to walk from one small shop to the next one.

Another typical feature of supermarkets is the supply and replenishment of store locations – often on a daily basis (especially fresh food). The twenty-first century saw a growth in the establishment of new distribution centres (DC) or the expansion of existing DCs. They are spread throughout the Netherlands to optimize the distribution network and use state-of-the-art Information Technology and robotization for handling the movement of goods within the DC (intrafacility). Simultaneously, lorries designed with customized layouts, like cooling systems, were introduced so that the goods could be transported from the DCs to individual retail locations.

Focusing on the Dutch supermarket landscape in 2017, according to data disclosed by the Dutch Central Bureau of Statistics (March 2018, CBS), there are approximately 6,000 supermarket stores offering direct employment for more than 300,000 people, and many more indirect jobs, such as accountants taking care of store administration, marketing, IT firms, and other companies whose major clients are supermarkets.

The Dutch supermarket sector entered the twenty-first century consolidated – with fewer food retail brand names – but with more brick-and-mortar stores (185↑ between 2008 and 2017, according to CBS 2018 Statline) operating under the same brand name than a couple of decades before. Adding non-food items to the store shelves, especially medicines, detergents, and personal care products, means the modern supermarket is closer to a hypermarket.

The table below shows a ranking for supermarket chains controlling more than 100 stores in the Netherlands in 2017. It is based on both the number of brick-and-mortar stores operating under the same or related trade name or label – an indicator that is more interesting for Supply Chain analysis than market share – and the number of distribution centres (DCs) supplying these stores.

Store Label	Parent/ owner company	Approximate # of stores	# of DCs & purchase organization
1. Albert Heijn	Ahold-Delhaize	971 stores (includes 81 AH to Go and 37 AH XL)	7 (online excluded & own procurement)
2. Jumbo	Jumbo Group Holding	626 stores	7 (own procurement)
3. Aldi	Siepman (Süd) & Markus Foundation (Aldi Nord)	501 stores	9 (own procurement)
4. Lidl	Schwarz Gruppe	425 stores	7 (own procurement)
5. Plus	Sperwer Group	263 stores	6 SuperUnie
6. Spar	Sperwer Group / Sligro Food Group (<= 100%)	260 stores (other brand names like Attent included: 500)	1 (SuperUnie)
7. Coöp	Coöp Supermarkets	294 stores (including related brands)	2 (SuperUnie)
8. Dirk van den Broek	Detailresult Group	121 stores	1 SuperUnie

Data taken from: http://www.distrifood.nl/formules, corporate websites, and Wikipedia.

Supermarkets operate not only in a strongly competitive environment, but also within a tight institutional and regulatory framework. They are subject to European Union food directives and to national food safety laws, which include standards that ensure food does not compromise consumer health. Supermarkets are also subject to public regulatory laws and require, among other things, a municipal permit to open a store within a municipality's boundaries. Many Dutch municipalities have a spatial planning and zoning policy as well as a retail policy, which allows them to set limits and conditions on the number of supermarkets in specific city areas, and even to pursue a spatial spread of supermarkets where each store serves a particular catchment area. This regulation imposes limits on the number of retail locations within a city or town and also affects the competition within a city (intracity competition).

If a supermarket applies for a permit, local residents, as well as incumbent competitors in the geographical area of interest, can submit objections to the establishment of the newcomer. This can lead to a review of the proposed supermarket location by either the municipality or the supermarket itself.

Another feature of the organization of the food retail industry is the deployment of franchising. The franchisee running a supermarket under a well-recognized protected brand name is an entrepreneur. He or she bears most of the business risk of the supermarket using the franchised formula licenced by the franchiser. The franchisee pays a fee to the franchiser and must abide by the conditions set out in the franchise contract.

Generally, customers will not be able to distinguish from the appearance of the outside or inside of a store whether the supermarket is an affiliate (branch) owned and controlled by the parent company, or a franchised store run by an independent entrepreneur. There is an interesting issue, however, regarding competition in a franchising situation. According to European anti-trust regulations, vertical price restraints are not permitted, with some exceptions. The franchising company cannot force the franchisee store to sell products at a predetermined price, nor can it impose a minimum price. This means that, as an entrepreneur, the franchisee can deviate from the recommended consumer price issued by the franchising company. However, this prohibition on vertical price agreement does not apply to affiliate stores that are owned by the parent company. In that case, the parent company has more control over the price setting of the products sold.

Another remarkable feature shown in the table above is the sourcing or procurement organization: with the exception of the first four supermarkets in the table, the remaining chains are members of a purchasing cooperative called "SuperUnie". On behalf of its members, this cooperative negotiates prices and conditions with major food manufacturers, such as Friesland-Campina, Unilever, Coca-Cola, Heineken, etc. Combining purchasing power is a way to negotiate lower prices and get quantity discounts from the manufacturers and is an established part of their sourcing policy.

A last distinctive feature of the supermarket landscape is the rise of online sales in recent decades. The scope and size of online sales differ per supermarket chain. Albert Heijn has a fully rigged online organization with a website containing a detailed product database, digital payment facilities, a network of distribution centres dedicated to online sales, and is equipped with a fleet of vans for transportation to customer locations and managing other ingredients necessary for online sales. The last issue to address is the proximity of food retailers, mainly supermarkets, to their customers. The map below shows the density of supermarket locations in the Netherlands.

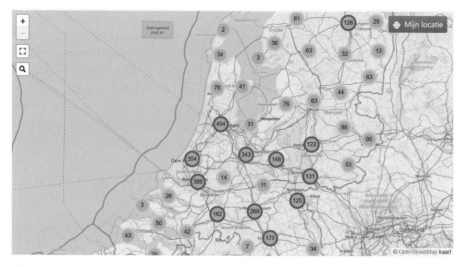

The map shows the situation in 2014. The greener the area the higher the density of supermarkets.
Not surprisingly, supermarkets follow customers. Major cities have the highest supermarket density while rural, sparsely populated areas, like the northern part of the Netherlands, have very few supermarkets. Supermarket sales remain heavily dependent on the physical proximity of the customers, although online sales are growing. Around 2017, the number of supermarkets in the Netherlands exceeded 6000 locations, approximately 1300 of which are concentrated in the four major cities and its agglomerations (Amsterdam, Rotterdam, The Hague, and Utrecht)
Source: https://www.allesupermarkten.com/kaart/

We conclude this industry case by expanding the scope and placing the Dutch food retail industry in a global perspective with comparative data to benchmark the Dutch supermarket industry against globally operating supermarket chains. However, it should be noted that such comparisons face the claim of comparing apples with pears. Let us therefore start with some conceptual terms. In English-speaking countries, a distinction is made between supermarkets, hypermarkets, and convenience stores. These conceptual differences refer to the product assortment and the size of a store, expressed in the square metre floor space of its premises.

A **hypermarket** is generally larger in square meters than a supermarket and contains a bigger non-food section in the total product assortment – although this is not yet as diversified as department stores like HEMA. Many hypermarkets – and this they have in common with the extra-large supermarkets (XL) – are located in city fringes provided with car parking facilities.

A **convenience store** is generally smaller than the other two and focuses on quick purchases by consumers who have no time to do extensive shopping. These stores also serve to remedy unexpected shortages, e.g. when a family discovers in the evening they have run out of coffee. Convenience stores generally have smaller product assortments – often also fast food and snacks, but also non-food items – than super- and hypermarkets, have longer opening times during the evening (and sometimes nocturnal opening times), and are located in (densely) populated areas: the customer must be able to reach the store in a relatively short time. Their products are often slightly higher priced than the same product sold in hyper- and supermarkets. Taking this classification into account, the approximate global ranking in terms of the number of locations (stores) is displayed below:

CBA	Hungarian-based supermarket chain owning around **5200 stores**. One of the largest in Central and Eastern Europe.
BIM	BIM is a Turkish retail company with operations mainly in Turkey. It has **over 8255 locations** in several countries
Ahold Delhaize NV	Overall, the company has **6556 stores** in 11 countries. The merger with Belgian Delhaize in 2016 added approximately 3400 stores worldwide
Tesco plc	This UK-based company has nearly **6970 stores** worldwide. It employs some 460.000 people and is one of the UK's top employers.
Lidl Owned by Schwarz Gruppe	Lidl headquartered in Germany operates **more** than **11,000 stores** in Europe and has recently expanded to the US.
Aldi Owned by Siepman (Aldi Süd) and Markus Foundation (Aldi Nord)	Aldi is the other large German discount supermarket chain and has approximately **12,400 stores** in 18 countries.
5. Carrefour	French multinational retailer Carrefour owns supermarkets, hypermarkets, and convenience stores across the world, with operations in more than 30 countries. The company has nearly **12,225 locations**.
3. Wal-Mart Walton Family owns 51% of the Wal-Mart shares	Wal-Mart Stores (United States) employs 2.3 million people, which makes it the largest private employer in the world. It operates hypermarkets, discount department stores, and grocery stores in 28 countries and has around **11,500 locations**.

| 2. **SPAR** | SPAR has around **13,110 locations** in 42 countries. This **Dutch** multinational operates stores of different types, divided in sub-brands. It has hypermarkets under the *Interspar* name, mid-sized supermarkets under *Eurospar/Superspar*, and small stores called Spar Express, designed for gasoline stations and small sites like university campuses. |
| **1. 7-Eleven** owned by the **Japanese** company Seven & I Holdings Co | 7-Eleven is the largest convenience chain in the world with over **71,100** locations in 18 countries. Most locations are in East Asia. |

Data taken mainly from https://en.wikipedia.org/wiki/List_of_supermarket_chains#Multinational retrieved on January 4 of 2022.

As described above, the food retailer's industry shows some features that are not only typical for the food retail industry, but which also touch basic Supply Chain features and management of firms operating in other industries. Some of these common features are:

1. Location decisions and institutional constraints on establishing stores and distribution centres
2. Inventory Management
3. Logistics and distribution network: modes of transportation for moving goods from DC to store or the customer in case of online sales.
4. Vertical pricing policy: price coordination between the manufacturer, retailer, and between a franchiser and its franchisees
5. Sourcing or procurement policy

Each of these issues will be discussed in more detail in theory and practice in one or more chapters of this book.

The importance of global Supply Chains (SC) has grown rapidly due to globalization

The creation of a common market in Europe, with the establishment of the European Economic Community on the 1 January 1956, has not only promoted global free trade agreements, it has also given a boost to a persistent upward trend in the trade of goods and services between many countries of the world. Economies that were historically disconnected from each other have established step-by-step economic and trade connections, whereby the world economy, and especially the European Union, are now configured as a densely interconnected network of economic relations without precedence in history. Many unexplored countries, which, for centuries were mainly the working grounds for missionaries and, under colonial rule, served as sourcing areas for raw materials, have become recipient countries of western investments. Countries like Cambodia, Laos, and Vietnam, to mention a few in East Asia, East African countries like Kenya and Tanzania, and Ghana and Ivory Coast in West Africa, along with most South American countries, have seen a major inflow of foreign investment, with a major economic boost in the 21st century. While this globalization process did not always go hand in hand with the necessary respect and observation of international law, human rights, and sound environmental practices – indeed, serious abuses by companies and international public agencies have been reported over the years – most of recipient countries did receive benefits and have experienced economic progress.

The increased transparency and speed with which information about corporate abuses disseminates over the world in the 21st century, due to the internet and social media, have made many international companies aware that increasing profits at all costs and without any ethical reference is no longer an acceptable way of running a company. Many companies have recalibrated their business model by implementing ethical codes and environmental practices. These codes of ethics are extended to their foreign operations and incorporated in their Supply Chain relations. We will discuss this issue in more detail in a later chapter about Corporate Social Responsibility (CSR) and sustainability in Supply Chains.

Economic globalization also triggered a chain process whereby companies started to set up manufacturing facilities abroad. Consequently, the physical distance between the place where goods are manufactured and where they are marketed became ever larger. This geographical separation of production, storage, and actual sales created an immense coordination problem for large companies: how to get the right product in the right place at the right time in the right quantities and with the right quality.

Customers are more demanding than half a century ago and this pressure is not only true for end-consumers but also, and perhaps even more so, for companies selling products and assets to other companies, so-called *Business-to-Business* (B2B) transactions. The economic landscape in the EU and in other industrialized countries has been reshaped. Nowadays, the production volume of the manufacturing industry in the European Union is lower than it was several decades ago because many manufacturing activities have moved to low-cost countries. On the other hand, the service sector has experienced strong growth since the second half of the 20th century and especially in the 21st century. At the same time, the supply of physical goods in shop stores and online webshops in the EU is considerably larger than several decades ago. This raises the question of where all these products are made and how they end up in the store premises where they are sold or delivered to the customer's home address. That is where we touch the core of Supply Chain Management. While there are many different definitions of

Supply Chain Management, in this book we will use that set out by the Council of Supply Chain Management Professionals (CSCMP):

> "Supply Chain Management encompasses the planning and management of all activities involved in sourcing and procurement, conversion, and all logistics management activities. Importantly, it also includes coordination and collaboration with channel partners, which can be suppliers, intermediaries, third-party service providers, and customers. In essence, Supply Chain Management integrates supply and demand management within and across companies. Supply Chain Management is an integrating function with primary responsibility for linking major business functions and business processes within and across companies into a cohesive and high-performing business model. It includes all of the logistics management activities noted above, as well as manufacturing operations, and it drives coordination of processes and activities with and across marketing, sales, product design, finance, and information technology."
> **Source:** Wikipedia quoting from www.cscmp.org

As the above definition shows, Supply Chain Management is a very broad concept and encompasses many different business functions and processes directly, including inventory management, procurement, and logistics, but it is indirectly related to virtually all other business functions, including finance and Human Resources.

Although many Supply Chain activities and models have been developed for application in business companies, virtually all the SC models discussed in this book can be made suitable for application by public entities and not-for-profit organizations. Many government departments and agencies, such as the police, firefighter's departments, the army, and agencies in charge of building and maintaining infrastructure, can directly benefit from many Supply Chain concepts used by business organizations. This is also true for many semi-public and not-for-profit institutions: hospitals; educational institutions; museums; operators of public transport; and many more. Every organization of whatever type confronts at least small-scale Supply Chain problems.

Even though the Supply Chain concepts and models discussed in this book cannot be transposed on a one-to-one basis to public institutions, there are recognizable common traits as well as evident differences. A typical difference, for example, is found in the field of procurement for public and semi-public agencies carrying out public and legal tasks in the European Union. They are subject to the complex and extensive EU public procurement regulations.[1] Public entities cannot pursue their optimal Supply Chain configuration and select the suppliers who best fit their needs with the same degree of freedom as businesses who are not bound by public procurement regulations.

Supply Chain concepts can also benefit companies and organizations operating in the service industry, taking into account the specific nature of services,[2] which, in many cases, means that inventory, such as a lawyer's oral plea, or a sports event, cannot be kept for later consumption. By contrast, other kinds of services, like architectural design, translation agencies, and video game developers, a certain degree of work-in-process can be accounted for as inventory.

Information and communication are of paramount importance for optimizing business planning and require a high-quality internal and external infrastructure for information exchange. Information has become one of the main flows through a Supply Chain and we will discuss this topic in more detail later.

For a Supply Chain configuration to become a success factor it must be designed and embedded in the corporate strategy, also called *strategic fit*.[3] Most medium-sized and large companies have either an implicit or explicit strategy that sets their long- and mid-term business goals. These goals are normally set at the central corporate level and then communicated to the operational business and other organizational units. An effective corporate strategy channels and aligns all business processes and units towards achieving the corporate objectives. Designing a new Supply Chain configuration, or reorganizing an existing one to adapt to a changing environment, is never a standalone process but should be based on the goals and principles set out in the corporate strategy.

Besides the strategy, which frames and aligns business operations, another factor of influence is the company's code of ethics and its broader Corporate Social Responsibility (CSR) policy, which for some companies is part of their strategic plan. Both of these put constraints on the possible Supply Chain configurations. If, for example, the code of business ethics declares that the company will not do business with suppliers using child labour, an SC manager cannot negotiate long-term delivery contracts with such suppliers, even when these suppliers offer the lowest price or have the fastest delivery time.[4] Or, if, say, a company sets a strategic objective to become highly responsive to customer demand in Germany, it is not very efficient to dispatch orders for German customers from their distribution centres in Australia. Setting up a distribution centre in or close to Germany is a more efficient solution to providing its local customers with a fast response time. A strategic plan sets parameters within which the Supply Chain configuration will be optimized.

Nowadays, most strategic corporate programmes include the concept of "added customer value". That is to say, the goods or services must add value to the customer, especially if the customer is a company. It also applies to end-consumers to make them more satisfied with the firm's products.

The ultimate source of long-term economic survival for any company is its customers or end-consumers, who are the bottom line of all business processes.

The final customer is the driver of demand. This holds for Business-to-Business relations (B2B), where companies or organizations are the main customers, and individual end-consumers alike.

In most Supply Chains, manufacturers making consumer products do not usually sell directly to final consumers, but rather sell to either wholesalers or retailers. The retailer is an important intermediate level in an SC because retailers have face-to-face interaction or serve as a direct interface with the end-consumer. Not only in brick-and-mortar stores, but also for online firms who sell most products via their webshop on the internet. Webshops receive online questions from consumers, they observe which products are in vogue, and online reviews give them information about the level of satisfaction consumers are experiencing with their products. Customer satisfaction is also measured by the number of products returned by the consumer.

Any marketing campaign for a manufacturing company is dependent on the cooperation of the retailers. When a manufacturing firm, like a car maker or food producer, does not have its retailers – in this case, the network of car dealers or food retailers – aligned with its objectives, all sales and marketing efforts can result in failure and even financial loss for the manufacturing company. We will discuss several incentive schemes to align retailer and manufacturer interests in the chapter about revenue management.

Organizational resources and assets

Some start-ups begin with an idea or a product concept, perhaps a material product or a new service. Some one-person start-ups have no other resources than that – an idea – and lack tangible assets and (sufficient) money and have no organizational structure to build upon. Existing companies, depending on their size and track record, have built up a collection of corporate assets or resources over time.[5] Some of the firm's assets can be found on their balance sheet and financial statements, but not all of them. Assets accounted for on a balance sheet have very generic names, which makes it difficult to discover qualitative differences among similarly labelled assets of different companies. A common label on the balance sheet is "non-current assets", which are subclassified as either tangible or intangible assets.

A tangible asset group encompasses, among other things, *Plant, Property, and Equipment* (PPE), and intangible assets encompass many different items, including patents, copyrights, databases, software, and information. Other asset groups are referred to as current assets and consist of Cash and Bank, Inventory, and Accounts Receivable. Having lots of assets does not necessarily mean that the firm is a high-value company. If the assets do not contribute harmoniously and efficiently to creating added value products for customers, they are close to useless. Assets acquire value if they contribute to making and marketing valuable products. Although tangible assets are necessary, they are not the only decisive resource for success. By far the most important resource of any organization is the human resources (HR): the skills; motivation and morale; creativity; and learning abilities of employees.

At the organizational level, the important drivers for success are a company's intangible resources, such as its organizational capabilities, its flexibility to adapt to changing market conditions, the ability of leadership to manage complex business processes, and the skills to set up and maintain sustainable relationships. All organizational skills are, ultimately, rooted in each employee working for the organization, and business organizations are no exception to this rule. The quality of employees is the most important success factor of any company. In many cases, they are institutionalized in rules, protocols, regulations, corporate culture, and corporate ethics.

Another intangible corporate asset that is a key driver for success is a well-performing Supply Chain design and configuration. Once an SC has been designed and becomes operational, the company must dedicate resources to maintaining its SC and keep it sufficiently flexible to respond to new challenges of the environment and a dynamic market. The modern Supply Chain approach is different from the traditional vertical business pillar. The traditional view of a product flow was top-down. At the top were suppliers of raw materials (minerals, grain, iron, etc.) who sold to the manufacturing industry. They transformed raw materials into products and sold these to either wholesalers or directly to retailers. The consumer was the last stage and purchased from the retailer. This classical pillar-based model has been extended and upgraded over the years to models encompassing many more stakeholders, all of whom are now part of a Supply Chain.

A frequently used classification of corporate Supply Chain activities is the distinction between *upstream* and *downstream* activities. The closer an activity is to the end consumer the more downstream it is; the closer it is to the stage of raw materials acquisition and processing the more upstream it is. This classification of Supply Chain activities reflects itself in the profile of the professional skills of employees. Upstream activities concentrate on manufacturing processes and the employees in this area have mostly engineering or technical qualifications and backgrounds. Moving downward to the downstream activities, the share of employees with marketing, sales, and logistics backgrounds goes up. Corporate Research and Development (R&D) divisions generally operate closer to the production stage than to the selling and marketing activities, although important information about customer preferences and product complaints move upward as input from downstream activities. Sales representatives maintain face-to-face contact with customers and the information they receive is transmitted upward to the production and R&D level where it is used to improve product features and production planning.

The vertical spinal downward flow of goods in an SC is complemented by a parallel upward movement of money from one SC stage to another. When the firms working at the different levels in the supply chain are independent companies, this upward money flow forms the basis for value added tax calculations (VAT).[6]

The modern Supply Chain approach can best be described as a network of vertical, horizontal, and even diagonal relations between SC partners. This network features not only a one-way flow of goods, but also reversed flows are observed: consumers sending back purchased goods to the retailer that did not meet their expectations or that they do not like. This return flow has grown dramatically in the 21st century, particularly for online shops, driving up logistics costs and lost revenues.[7] At the same time, the sustainable movement and environmental regulations press companies towards recycling activities. This requires some retailers and manufacturers to take back products dismissed and discarded by consumers, reversing the logistics flow of goods from consumers back to the store or the DC.

Another resource – considered by some to be the most important resource or production factor of the 21st-century economy – and particularly relevant for a global Supply Chain is *information*. Information and information sharing among all SC partners is a crucial issue and sometimes a critical success factor in Supply Chain performance. Information gathering and sharing are directly linked to the quality of Information Technology a company uses, e.g. real-time data availability and so-called Big Data. This topic will be discussed in more detail in other chapters.

Designing and managing a Supply Chain requires the use of metrics

Familiar sayings among business consultants are: "*You get what you inspect, not what you expect*" and "*A strategy without metrics is just a wish. Metrics not aligned with strategic objectives are a waste of time*". Both quotes refer to the need for quantifiable goals expressed in terms of metrics: business activities and processes must be measured in numbers to evaluate them.

Using quantitative approaches and models to analyse business processes has a relatively long tradition. They are part of Management Science and Operations Research, whose methods and scope expanded quickly after World War II. Supporters of a quantitative approach to business processes believe that a scientific approach by organizations and management is the best way to succeed and progress. Supporters of these quantitative schools go beyond the traditional tools of diagrams and philosophical reflections about the essence of business organizations and the best way to manage them.

Mathematical and statistical models have been developed to support management decisions for controlling, planning, and optimizing business processes. Specific models are available to guide Inventory Management, Logistics, Capacity planning, Production planning, Human resource planning, Demand Forecasting, Queuing management, Project Management, Job assignment, Statistical Quality Control, Decision Trees, and other operational fields. One of the oldest models in scientific management was the Economic Order Quantity model (1913), which was joined by the extremely powerful application of Linear Programming for solving business problems after World War II. With the entry of ever faster computing capacity and the development of more efficient software algorithms, these days the more extensive and complex business problems can (only) be solved with the aid of different types of mathematical programming, i.e. non-linear programming, integer programming, network programming, stochastic programming, Monte Carlo simulation, and others. These tools have also found their way into the design of Supply Chain operations. Parallel to the growth of the internet, the 21st century has seen the rise of Big Data.[8] Big Data has found its place in the toolkit of management scientists and is becoming commonplace in decision support systems to improve decision-making quality.

Metrics refer to measurable and quantifiable units to benchmark business processes and business units both in cross-section and over time (*time series*). Metrics are also part of quantitative models used to optimize business processes and assess organizational performance.[9]

To give an example, when a company's corporate strategy targets a growth policy and the firm wants to evaluate its growth, the firm or its business consultant is confronted with the problem of growth metrics. That is to say, growth can be measured by hundreds of different parameters: by total revenues; by revenues per employee; by profit; by the number of employees; by square metres of floor space; by the number of facilities, and so on.

Depending on its choice of benchmark, the same company can grow on one metric (profit) and decline on another metric (# of employees, because employees were fired to achieve cost savings and thereby increase profit, to give one example). The selection of a specific metric is the first step, applying the selected metric consistently over time is even more important: if, for example, a supermarket pursues international expansion and decides to benchmark its growth using the number of stores opened each year, consistency is needed, i.e. this benchmark must be used year after year. Using revenues as a metric for growth in one year and switching to store numbers the next year makes benchmarking close to useless. Some basic units for metrics refer to *what* is measured and *where* it is measured.

In Supply Chains, standardized concepts for metrics include, among others, *Stock Keeping Unit* (SKU) and *Point of Sale* (POS).

An SKU refers to a specific item stored in a specific location, and it is the most disaggregated or lowest level of inventory and sales. Units stored in the same SKU are supposed to be indistinguishable from each other and fully homogeneous, although they are tagged with different series numbers. An SKU for a distribution centre can be different to that of wholesalers or for local stores. Beer brewers can have an SKU of a pallet with trays of beer cans, to be shipped to supermarket chain distribution centres, which place their orders quantified in the number of pallets. The distribution centre can send separate trays of beer cans to local stores, which place orders quantified in the number of trays. Their SKU is thus a tray of beer cans. The supermarket store sells individual cans to consumers. Their SKU is a single beer can that is inventoried on the store shelves.[10]

Point of Sale is the place and time where a retail transaction is completed. A checkout point in a shop is a POS, a vending machine in an office premise is a POS, and the website of an online company can be a POS for online purchases, once the customer has confirmed his or her purchase online and the company has accepted the order.[11]

Product and production process

A production process is defined as: "The processes and methods used to transform tangible inputs (raw materials, semi-finished goods, subassemblies) and intangible inputs (ideas, information, knowledge) into goods or services".[12]

The output of a production process is a product, and the quality of a product depends, to a high degree, on the quality standards applied in the production process. If a production process is well managed and controlled, meeting high standards to achieve top-quality products, the end products of the production process will generally also be good quality. Quality is not only measured by technical, safety, and health standards, but is also expressed in terms of customer satisfaction.

Different products require different production processes and, even for a single product, more than one production process can yield the same end-product. This fact can be useful for implementing flexibility in production and distribution planning. Each production process has its duration, its specific process steps, other unique features, and costs. The design of a production process has direct consequences for the selection of the associated SC configuration and SC partners.[13]

A manufacturing company will select suppliers of raw materials and ingredients offering a quality that matches the quality standards of its end product. The raw materials and components must be available at the necessary moment and in the right quantity when the production commences according to the planning.

Production engineers and planners distinguish different categories of production processes. One of them is *mass production*, where the same product is manufactured in large to very large volumes. Mass production is typical for many consumer products, ranging from basic foodstuffs to smartphones. Mass production requires a Supply Chain flow of raw materials as well as human resources planning matched to this production model. In some cases, mass production is continuous and the end products – or intermediate products – come out in an uninterrupted flow at the end of the process. Drinking water from the tap is a good example.

Another process is *batch production*. This is a manufacturing technique in which the product in question is created, stage by stage, over a series of workstations until reaching completion.

Products at the end of the production line – those for both mass production and batch production – are provided with serial numbers or tags, which serve to trace and identify a product during the production process and once it has left the manufacturing facility on its way towards the final customer.[14]

The third process is *job production*. Job production refers to mostly custom-made products for individual customers or small-batch production. Housing construction with a unique architectural design, tailor-made clothing, and, in the service industry, business consultants working on firm-specific issues, or professional painters who go from one job to the next, are examples of job production.

Today, an increasing number of tangible products are manufactured as assemblies composed of *modular* components. The main parts that make up the end product are made or supplied as modular units and then assembled on a production line or at a workstation to create the final product.

A laptop computer, for example, consists of many different components, but each component or module is a finished part: the keyboard; the screen; the hard disk or SSD; the graphics card; the circuit board with the microprocessor; the battery, and many more.

All those units can easily be assembled and connected by either clicking them into a slot or a predesigned frame, thus replacing traditional methods, such as welding components one by one onto a circuit board. If the laptop breaks down and the defective component has been identified, e.g. the battery, it can be removed from the frame structure and replaced with a new one. If a valuable component breaks down, that component can be sent back to the manufacturer for repair, while the consumer can continue to use the laptop with a replacement battery. Another advantage of modular production is the possibility of *mass customization*. Customers can decide, within the limits set by the manufacturer, which components they want as part of their product.[15]

The technological development to customize products is expanding its scope to more and more products: bicycles; cars; houses; clothing; home furniture; 3D printing, and many more are offered as customizable products and sometimes not even for much higher prices than the standardized (non-customized) model. Each of the three classes of production processes mentioned above requires a Supply Chain configuration neatly matched to the specific properties of the process. Many Supply Chains are centred around one large core company with many suppliers who serve many different customers. This gives rise to a network of relations and processes among all SC partners. Supply Chain analysts categorize these relations as either *Supplier Relationship Management* (SRM), *Customer Relationships Management* (CRM), or *Internal Supply Chain Management* (ISCM).

All these relations need to be managed, controlled, and coordinated to ensure that they harmoniously contribute to achieving the strategic objectives. This process of smooth coordination among all partners of a Supply Chain is neither simple, nor self-evident. There are abundant examples, some extensively reported in media and others studied in scientific literature, where different stakeholders in a group or a process do not pursue the common objective but strive to achieve their own narrow-minded individual interests. This phenomenon is an example of agency problems or the so-called prisoner's dilemma. The outcome of an agency problem in a Supply Chain is suboptimal performance, a considerable loss of efficiency, and a waste of valuable resources for the Supply Chain as a whole, as well as for its partners.

We will encounter several examples of suboptimal results stemming from agency problems or the unaligned interests of individual SC members in other chapters. The most important players in a Supply Chain of consumer products are the suppliers of raw materials or product components, the manufacturing plants of the company, the distribution centres, and the retail network for sale to the final consumers.

The basic architecture of mass production and distribution

Manufacturing companies focus either on mass production for global consumer markets or customization, where each unit is produced according to the customer's preferences, or somewhere in-between. Nearly all products sold in local store outlets are mass-produced: even cars, cell phones, furniture, and complete houses can become mass-produced by using prefabricated building components. The core of successful mass production is the standardization of the product and the production process to achieve lower unit costs creating economies of scale.

Most costs of mass production are incurred at the stage before the actual mass production: in the design; the development; the correct set-up of all machinery; and the training of workers to give them the necessary skills and knowledge to carry out their work well in the production process. If a pharmaceutical company, for example, is working on a new medicine for a disease suffered by many patients, the bulk of the costs are incurred in the research phase, in the clinical trials necessary for approval, the set-up of all machinery for production and packaging, official registration of the medicine and other related activities. If the first batch of medicines meets all the standards and all resources or assets are set up correctly, the production process becomes a repetitive operation, where all units go through the same production steps to yield the same final output. Marginal production costs drop quickly. For mass products, high costs are incurred in the process of obtaining the first good units and the (re)production costs for larger volumes drop gradually afterwards.[16] An important activity in mass production is sampling for quality control and supervising the process to ensure that it works properly, according to the plan.

In customized – or tailor-made – production, each product (car, house, suit, furniture) is manufactured according to the preferences of the customer. This increases unit costs and leaves less space for standardization. Another feature of mass production and its global distribution to final markets is that production is concentrated in a few manufacturing facilities and production volumes occur in large numbers.

From these manufacturing plants, the products are distributed to a larger number of distribution centres located closer to the end-market than to the location of the manufacturing plant. In the plant, production batches are prepared in volumes matched to the demand of the distribution centres and then shipped to them. From the DCs, they are either shipped to another DC – for example, the DC managed by a retail chain – or they are divided into smaller quantities to supply a wider network of local stores, department stores, hypermarkets, or pick-up points in the region covered by the DC for supply.

Consumers finally go to local stores to buy the product and bring it home, which is the final destination of the product where consumption takes place. For online purchases, the local retail level with brick-and-mortar stores is partially bypassed in the Supply Chain and the products are directly shipped from a DC to the final consumer's home address. In recent years, a trend has been observed of increasing numbers of retail stores also selling online. The Covid-19 pandemic has given a strong boost to online sales by retailers.[17] In Chapter 9, we will discuss in more detail the differences in the distribution configuration for online and offline sales. Graphically, a mass production–distribution network can have the simplified structure shown below.

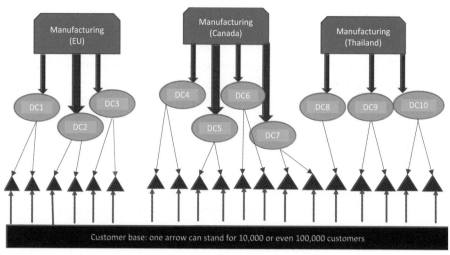

can represent 100 or even 1000 retail stores replenished periodically by one of the DCs.

The network shown above has consequences for the organization of the logistics process. Transporting mass products from a manufacturing site to a DC requires a large carrier capacity (e.g. a cargo train with many trailers or a container ship). Transportation from the DC to local retail stores takes place in lower volumes and can be done via road in lower capacity lorries.

The last stage to get the product to the final customer – the so-called last-mile delivery – can have a number of variations: the customer can go to the shop by car, public transport, scooter, bicycle, or even walking. For online purchases, the distribution process follows different steps: most online products go directly from the DC of the webshop to the customer's home address or to a pick-up point where the customer can fetch the order. The distribution process of mass products starts with large volumes at the top and gradually breaks down into smaller lots, moving downward in the Supply Chain, reaching the individual customer at the final stage, in some cases reaching the most remote areas of the world in individual units. We will return to this issue when discussing last-mile delivery in the chapter about infrastructure and logistics.

We can also describe this process in geographical terms: the SC process branches out, stepwise, starting at a few manufacturing sites via distribution centres moving to a globally spread consumer base. The economies of scale achieved at the production level are gradually lost during the downstream movement to distribution centres and further downstream to local stores to get the product closer to the final customer. In the chapter about logistics, we will revisit this basic Supply Chain structure and match it to an appropriate logistics network.

Moving in an opposite direction to the product flow is – besides the money flow – also the demand for information and order flow. The face-to-face contact with the final customer frequently takes place at the local store level, which is generally the Point of Sale. The local store manager will combine and aggregate the demands of his customers and send orders to the distribution centre(s).

Managers in the distribution centres receive orders coming from many different stores and prepare the ordered products and make them ready for dispatch. At the same time, the DC manager will keep track of its own inventory and send orders to either the manufacturing companies or to other DCs who sell the products. Production planning at the manufacturing site can be based on orders received (*pull process*) or triggered by the demand forecast for the corporate products (*push process*). Part of the production planning involves the allocation of production batches over several plants, if the company operates more than one plant and the capacity of a single plant is insufficient – or not available due to other activities – in order to meet demand. The procurement managers of the manufacturing plant will organize the purchase of raw materials, parts, and intermediate products so that execution runs smoothly.

Source: https://media.insiders.nl/maa/files/image/encigroeve-eighty8things-hr-26_190185433.jpeg

The ENCI (ENCI = First Dutch Cement Industry) was established in 1926 to make the Netherlands less dependent on foreign cement imports. ENCI extracts marl (raw material of cement) and manufactures cement under a government concession from a marl quarry located south of the city of Maastricht, close to the Belgian border. Their main plant for cement *production* is located inside the quarry site (see image). Parallel to the quarry runs a road and the Maas River is equipped with berths for mooring and loading special cement vessels.

Liquid cement is directly loaded into a concrete mixer truck or a ship. From there, the cement is transported to construction and building sites all over the Netherlands. Bags of dry and prepackaged cement are shipped to, among others, DIY stores for direct sale to consumers. A supply chain characteristic of ENCI, as well as other mining companies, is having its production facilities close to the extraction sites. This keeps the distance and lead time for moving raw materials with specialized vehicles to the manufacturing plant short, and keeps shipping costs relatively low. The upstream part of the supply chain activity is geographically concentrated in and around the quarry, while downstream activities are spread over a largely branched network of customers.

However, on 1 July 2018 marl extraction in the quarry stopped and the cement furnaces ceased operations in 2020. The quarry will be converted into a nature reserve.

Demand, orders, and the bullwhip effect

Demand is defined as "the quantity of a commodity or a service that people are willing or able to buy at a certain price".[18] Demand and orders, although closely related, are not the same thing. An order is a formal request to a supplier to deliver a certain quantity of goods under specified conditions (number, quality, brand, and others). When an order is accepted by the receiving party, the selling company, it becomes a legally binding contract. Order sizes are generally based on actual sales, estimated forecasts, and the inventory policy of the firm placing the order. The demand that is not materialized in orders is demand foregone. The most common example of this is the stock-out, a situation where the customer enters the shop to buy an item that is not in inventory and the customer goes to the competitor to buy the same or similar product.

A store manager can either overestimate future demand for, let us say, Christmas time and order too many units with the consequence that some units will remain in stock unsold. These items will have to be deeply discounted after the sales period or discarded. He can also underestimate demand and order too few with the consequence that some customers go home unsatisfied and buy it somewhere else. In the last case, demand and order size do not match.

A distribution centre receiving orders from local store managers has no direct knowledge about real demand, they only observe the orders coming from the many local stores. The order sizes that the distribution centres send to the manufacturing facilities are mostly a combination of the aggregated downstream orders they have received, an estimation of future orders, and their particular inventory policy. The manufacturer receives a wide range of different orders from DCs and wholesalers and will, in turn, plan for the procurement of raw materials and other items needed for the production process.

An empirical observation in many Supply Chains is that the *variation* in order size originating at the retailer level, moving upstream in the Supply Chain to the manufacturer, tends to *amplify* itself, the further upstream in the chain it gets. This phenomenon is called the *bullwhip effect*.[19] Besides the gap between demand and orders, other factors also contribute to the bullwhip effect. Common bullwhip causes are a lack of communication, order batching (combining orders phased over time into one large order), price variations, and free return policy.

The aforementioned causes can be subsumed into behavioral causes and operational causes. The latter encompasses forecast errors, lead time variability, quantity discounts, trade promotion, forward buying, and anticipation of shortages. The former refers to the psychology of procurement managers. Measuring the bullwhip effect precisely is complex, because all partners in the Supply Chain must share their part of demand and order data, which requires full commitment and transparency by all SC partners.[20] Several measures have been proposed and implemented to counter the bullwhip effect in a Supply Chain, some of which will be discussed in the chapters about Inventory Management.

Facility location and Customer Response Time

Many consumer goods can be qualified as fast-moving consumer goods. These are products with high inventory turnover, short shelf-time, often prepackaged in the factory, sold in large volumes while the profit margin per unit is low. Because of the large quantities sold, total profit can be high. These goods are repetitive in the sense that they are repurchased once they have been consumed and basic consumer goods are usually less sensitive to the boom and bust of business cycles than non-basic goods. Many foodstuffs, drugs, care products, and other standardized products serving the basic needs of people belong to this category. Nowadays, many electronic devices and household products are also considered fast-moving consumer goods.

Their main physical points of sales are supermarkets, hypermarkets and convenience stores, vending machines in public places, and online stores. Retail stores and online companies selling these products do *not* compete on product properties – which is the expertise of the manufacturing company – but rather on price, Consumer Response Time, and after-sales service. For brick-and-mortar stores, this means that they need sufficient inventory to meet the consumer demand – a consumer looking for a carton of orange juice in supermarket A will go to neighbouring supermarket B, if supermarket A has run out of orange juice.

This also holds for online shops when it takes too much time for the ordered product to be delivered. The time elapsing between ordering a product and receiving it is called the *Customer Response Time* of the supplier and many companies use the response time as a competitive tool to distinguish themselves from their competitors. A similar argument applies to the location decisions of brick-and-mortar stores: if the customer has to travel one hour to get orange juice because the store is located on the outskirts of a city or in a remote business area to avoid high rent prices for its premises, it will be outcompeted by those stores located closer to the consumers.

The location of a retailer's facilities, either physical stores or an online distribution centre, will affect Customer Response Time. An inverse relationship exists between a facility location and the Customer Response Time: the closer the facility is to the customer, generally the shorter the Customer Response Time. In addition to distance, Customer Response Time also relates to opening or working times. A shop with opening times from 9.30 – 18.00 will miss more customers than a shop with opening times from 7.30 – 23.00. Distribution centres of online companies operating 14 hours a day to dispatch orders will have a shorter Customer Response Time than DCs that only operate for eight hours a day. Facility location decisions will be discussed in more detail in the chapter about Capacity Planning, where we will also discuss some recent trends and innovations to get the building structures and premises closer to the customer to reduce response time.

Mobile service centres: Reversed supply

In the discussion of the last-mile movement, the focus was on tangible goods, whereby the product is either taken home by the customer or it is delivered to the customer's home address. Similar initiatives have been undertaken in the service sector. Guided by the maxim *"if the customer does not come to you, go to the customer"*, a growing number of firms operating in the service industry are expanding their services and adding value for the customer by offering the service at the customer's home – or another place selected by the customer – instead of the customer going to the office building or centre where the service company is based. Although visiting the customer at home is far from new, a growing number of firms are now offer their services at the customer's spot.[21] Offering services on the spot requires adjusted production planning and staff scheduling and also transportation modes matched to the service.

A tax consultant can visit a customer using a car and bring paper and a laptop or tablet, but a plumber or carpenter must bring all kinds of tools. The appropriate transportation mode will be a van or a larger vehicle in this case. Scheduling services on the spot throws up more uncertainties than offering the same service within the

In a country with a long bicycle tradition, bike owners with a broken bike usually bring the bike to the bicycle workshop for repair. However, recently, cycle shops have begun to organize mobile repair services. When a bike breaks during a ride, the cyclist calls the mobile repair service and they will come to the place of the breakage with a van equipped with the necessary tools and instruments. The serviceperson will repair the bicycle on the spot.
Source: https://www.fixmybike.nl/.cm4all/mediadb/WhatsApp%20Image%202017-09-12%20at%2022.06.10.jpeg retrieved on January, 4 of 2022

accommodation rooms of the service supplier. Travel costs by the service person or team must be taken into consideration, and for most service jobs these *call-out costs* form an explicitly part of the price charged. Modern customized trucks and vans enable more companies to equip their vehicles with the necessary assets to offer specialized services, like mobile clinics for healthcare or childbirth facilities, especially in developing countries.

Technological trends that will affect future supply chain operations

In the 21st century, some technological breakthroughs have taken place that will almost certainly affect the way Supply Chains operate, and those trends will have an impact on Supply Chain performance. We will mention five of them without going into detail and with an emphasis on how they can transform Supply Chain operations. Supply Chain managers will monitor these developments to assess how they can benefit SC operations

1. The Internet of Things (IoT)

The Internet of Things (IoT) describes the network of physical objects —"things"— that are embedded with sensors, software, and other technologies to connect and exchange data with other devices and systems over the internet. Things have evolved due to the convergence of multiple technologies, real-time analytics, machine learning, commodity sensors, and embedded systems. Traditional fields of embedded systems, wireless sensor networks, control systems, automation (including home and building automation), and others all contribute to enabling the Internet of Things. In the consumer market, IoT technology is synonymous with products pertaining to the concept of the "smart home", including devices and appliances (such as lighting fixtures, thermostats, home security systems and cameras, and other home appliances) that support one or more common ecosystems, and can be controlled via devices associated with that ecosystem, such as smartphones and smart speakers. IoT can also be used in healthcare systems".[22]

IoT can affect SC operations is diverse ways. For example, sensors can detect that the inventory level of a product drops below a critical level and sends a signal to machinery at the manufacturing plant that starts producing new units without human intervention. A truck carrying cooled foodstuffs can send a signal to the cooling devices at a distribution centre an hour before the truck arrives and the cooling machines or refrigerators can start lowering their temperature so that the temperature is at the right level when the truck arrives.

2. Telerobotics

Telerobotics refers to remotely controlled robots or machinery. Although remote control of (toy) airplanes and cars is not new and, indeed, was already possible before World War II, the possibilities for remote control in the 21st century have expanded in scope and scale. This technique is gaining momentum for production processes, construction and engineering work in the open field, medical interventions,[23] and the repair of machinery. A consequence of telerobotics is that mechanics no longer have to be physically present on the site of operation to repair something. They can operate from a distance using a wireless or wired connection to remotely control their tools for the repair. Less travel time is needed to solve delays in production processes or elsewhere in a Supply Chain due to breakdowns. This results in a better SC performance. Telesurgery is another interesting application of telerobotics. Suppliers and demanders do not have to be in the same physical place to have interaction.

3. 3D printing and Automated Guided Vehicles (AGV)

"3D printing, or additive manufacturing, is the construction of a three-dimensional object from a CAD model or a digital 3D model. The term '3D printing' can refer to a variety of processes in which material is deposited, joined, or solidified under computer control to create a three-dimensional object, with the material being added together (such as liquids or powder grains being fused), typically layer by layer".[24] 3D printing makes it possible to, for example, manufacture spare parts of critical equipment or machinery in a manufacturing setting, thereby reducing the risk of significant production delays when a spare part or other component of a machine have broken down and must be replaced. Automated guided vehicles (AGV), such as *drones*, are already employed in some cities for last-mile deliveries, as part of logistics planning. We will discuss in more detail the last-mile delivery in a Supply Chain in Chapter 8, about asset mobility.

4. Blockchain technology

Blockchain technology will be discussed briefly in Chapter 12. It refers to a strict registration procedure in computers that allows for an easy "track and trace" of goods and services moving in a supply chain. It facilitates the reconstruction of transactions that have taken place in a Supply Chain.

5. Artificial Intelligence and Expert Systems

"Artificial intelligence (AI) makes it possible for machines to learn from experience, adjust to new inputs and perform human-like tasks. Most AI examples that you hear about today – from chess-playing computers to self-driving cars – rely heavily on deep learning and natural language processing. Using these technologies, computers can be trained to accomplish specific tasks by processing large amounts of data and recognizing patterns in the data".[25] Supply Chains can benefit greatly from AI, which can uncover and understand better the complexities that are found in elaborate supply chains.

The rapid development of the internet and its supporting infrastructure – which is discussed in more detail in the chapter about infrastructure and asset mobility – has enabled organizations to offer their services to customers whereby neither the seller goes to the home of the customer, nor the customer to the premises of the service company. Both stay at their own site and the standardized or customized service is delivered via online communication. There are abundant examples and, here, we mention a few.

1. To receive a training course the course participants can either go to the class-rooms of the firm, trainers can organize the course in-house at the customer location, or, nowadays, online training courses are offered whereby neither the trainer has to go to the customer's location, nor the participants to the supplier's site. They can join the course interactively, sitting behind a computer screen, and see and listen to the trainer online. The increasing number of Massive Online Open Courses (MOOCs), some of them free of charge, attended by anyone in the world, are examples of this new way of supplying digital services.

2. People faced with defective software on their computer no longer have to bring the notebook to the seller's workshop and the mender does not have to come to the customer's spot. A remote online connection can be established whereby the mender gets access to the customer's computer, enabling him to repair or reinstall the software while chatting with the customer. Some PC manufacturers put videos online to assist users in the step-by-step repair of frequently occurring hard- or software errors.

3. Remote vigilance with cameras connected to the internet overlooking private and public places, both indoors and outdoors, are steadily replacing on-site security guards. Watching online movies instead of going to the cinema or renting a DVD at a shop are all examples of digitalized services where neither the customer nor the supplier moves.

Digitalized services where no physical movement by either supplier or customer is needed, reduce passenger traffic and relieve road congestion, resulting in a more ecologically friendly footprint. Information flow in a Supply Chain is discussed in one of the later chapters of this book.

Online Meetings and Teaching Skyrocket during the Covid-19 Pandemics

From March 2020 until mid-2021, a significant number of schools and universities in many European countries were shut down due to the Corona crisis. In particular, knowl-edge workers and clerical staff had to work from home. Although teaching and school exams continued, the only way that teachers could communicate with their pupils and students was through online communication. Both teachers and students operated from home, sitting behind their computer screens. Many meetings were scheduled online in virtual meeting rooms. Demand for software offering these services, like Microsoft Teams, Zoom, and several others, flourished. The demand for supporting tangible assets like cameras, microphones, and loudspeakers also peaked to unprecedented levels for videoconferencing and digital meetings. Datacentres and the internet network were operating in their highest gear and congestion on the network occurred several times. In Chapter 8, about information, we discuss in more detail the necessary infrastructure for efficient information exchange in Supply Chains.

Notes

1-21   See Instructor's Manual

22   Source: https://en.wikipedia.org/wiki/Internet_of_things retrieved on February 1 of 2021

23   See Instructor's Manual

24   Source https://en.wikipedia.org/wiki/3D_printing retrieved on February 1 of 2021

25   Source: https://www.sas.com/nl_nl/insights/analytics/what-is-artificial-intelligence.html retrieved on February 1 of 2021

2   Forecasting in a Supply Chain

Forecasting as a valuable tool to optimize Supply Chain planning

Some of the most successful entrepreneurs started with a bright idea in which they invested much effort, resources, and time in order to transform their idea into a business success. Not all of them conducted any form of market research in advance, resorted to a structured decision process, or forecasting. Convinced of the potential of their idea or product, they simply started and worked many hours a day and many days a year to transform their idea into a flourishing business. Sometimes, they did not even spend money on advertising, aware that there was a demand for their product. However, in all cases, one notion was clear: *"No demand, no business, no future."*

Any business will irrevocably dive into a process of bankruptcy if there is no demand for its products. A company that starts production without demand will incur costs, but no revenues. And this truth also holds for any Supply Chain. Demand is the red thread that justifies any Supply Chain operation and gaining knowledge about demand means improving Supply Chain efficiency. Demand, however, is not something static over time or a given fact of business life. When a company starts to grow and enters a new phase of its life cycle or sales expand geographically, the company will seek structured methods to estimate demand before making any subsequent decision about capacity, production, procurement, inventory, logistics, and other Supply Chain activities.

Demand is a first and indispensable prerequisite for a well-functioning Supply Chain: NO demand and the Supply Chain will sooner or later collapse (in most cases, sooner). Companies therefore resort to some form of demand forecasting before starting operations and planning. There are many different forecasting methods, and different phases in the product life cycle require different forecasting methods.

When a company launches a new and innovative product, it has no historical track record for that product. In this case, the company will resort to qualitative forecasting methods. Some of them are:
- *Substitute approach*: the company will look at their product and consider it as a close substitute for an existing product. The demand for the existing product becomes a frame of reference for the forecast of the new product.
- *Buyer's or consumer's view*: the company will ask a panel of potential consumers to rate their new product and to issue an opinion about it.

- *Experts opinion*: experts or sales representatives in the product category in which the new product is subsumed, are asked to express an opinion about the feasibility of the new product.
- *Market test method*: the new product is freely distributed at a small scale during a fixed time to customers who are asked if they would buy it. The sample results provide input for making forecasts.
- *Scenario approach*: sales scenarios are constructed and calculated based on assumptions and parameters to estimate demand under different scenarios.

Forecasting for products with a sales record[1]

Products already on the market for some time build up a track record of sales. If the firm has a well-developed sales registration system, in which detailed sales information is recorded, e.g. when, where, and to which customer group products are sold, the product acquires an established sales record. Past sales data can be used as input data for demand forecasting for the near or long-term future. Forecasting based on quantitative data is called *quantitative forecasting* and this leads us into the domain of statistics and econometrics.

Quantitative demand forecasting methods are diverse, ranging from relatively simple to highly sophisticated and complex models.[2] Most of these models are beyond the scope of this book. Here, we focus on *time series models*, which are frequently used among business consultants for demand forecasting. We focus on demand forecasting for consumer products and historical sales data that originates from Point of Sales transactions for brick-and-mortar shops, but also from online retailers. With the necessary assumptions, they can also be applied to Business to Business (B2B) sales.

Forecasting and exploring sales data patterns

A basic property of statistical demand analysis is *pattern recognition*. This means trying to uncover structural patterns over time by looking at past sales data. A pattern could be, for example, a sales increase in the first six months of the year and a decline over the last six months. A pattern could be a substantial sales upswing just after a weekly price promotion, while sales in the two weeks after the promotion drop more significantly than in average circumstances. This points to possible *forward buying* by consumers, discussed in Chapter 4.

One way to observe patterns is by charting past sales data. Sales charts can point to micro-patterns – like the distribution of sales during the day or during a week – or macro-patterns like sales distribution over a year or a couple of years. Charts can also be applied to detect the geographical distribution of sales (by country, by region, or by city) or patterns linked to the social and economic background of consumers. If patterns repeat themselves over many cycles and show structural traits, the forecaster has good grounds to assume that these patterns will continue in the future. They can be incorporated into the demand forecasting process. In time series forecasting, statistical sales data are decomposed into four constitutive building blocks:

1. *Level* of sales
2. *Trend* in sales
3. *Seasonality* in sales or *periodicity*
4. *Random component* in sales (also called *noise*)

The *level* refers to a constant sales volume that will continue over time if there are no upward or downward trends or any form of seasonality. The demand forecast is then based on the level of sales adding a random component.

Trend refers to structural changes over a relatively long period of demand and can be upward or downward. In this situation, demand forecasts are based on the sales level plus the trend plus a random component. *Seasonality* refers to upward and downward swings in demand that depend on the time of the year and that repeat themselves sales cycle after sales cycle. The name *seasonality* stems from the fact that sales of some products are strongly dependent on the season of the year. However, time series can contain other forms of seasonality, for example by month or even by week. The basic characteristic is that the data show repetitive or recurrent patterns. Seasonal sales data displayed in a chart often appear as wavelike patterns, going up and down. But these up and down movements are not a necessary prerequisite for seasonality. What makes data seasonal is that the pattern repeats itself each sales cycle. The standard time unit for a cycle is a year. Repetitive patterns can also be, for example, four consecutive months going up, then two months down, then three months up again, and the last three months going down.

The last time series component is the random component, also called *noise*. This component is the unpredictable part of the forecasting method. Any part of the demand that cannot be explained by the previous three structural components is part of the random component. The random component is the major cause of demand variation and, above all, affects the reliability of the forecasts. If there was no random component present in the data, forecasts would be perfect. Some graphical examples of time series patterns are shown below. The horizontal axis shows the time and the vertical axis sales in units. The pattern classification is based on a visual inspection of the chart.

Graph A

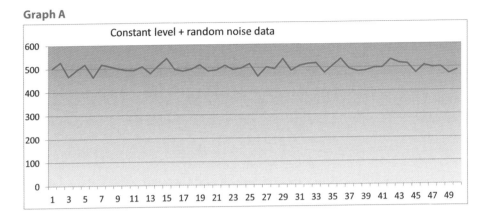

The chart above seems to have a small unpredictable variation around a fixed level (approximately 500). This graph indicates a constant level and random noise. Although it is difficult to say which products in real-life follow this pattern, we suggest it represents a product that is in the maturity phase of its life cycle and has a stable customer group. The forecast for the next period will be level plus a random component.

Graph B

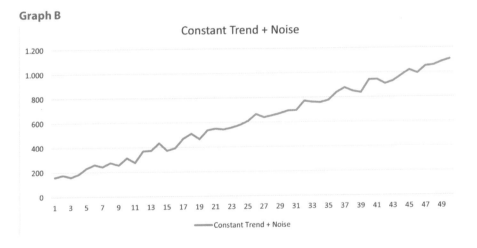

The data displayed above show an upward sloping trend with a starting level of approximately 100 at the first observation and random variation around the trend line. The trend can be calculated as the slope of the line using linear regression. Forecasting sales for the next period is done by taking the level plus the slope coefficient multiplied with the forecasted period number plus a random component. This pattern is shown by products showing steady growth as part of their life cycle.

Graph C

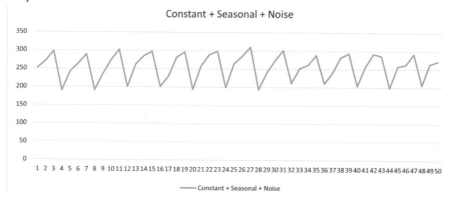

The data displayed above show a repetitive variation (ups and downs) with a cycle of three months around a constant level (approximately 250) and a random variation. The forecast for the next period will be level plus the seasonal adjustment for the forecasted period plus the random variation. Holiday bookings of hotels at a beach resort often exhibit this kind of sales patterns.

Graph D

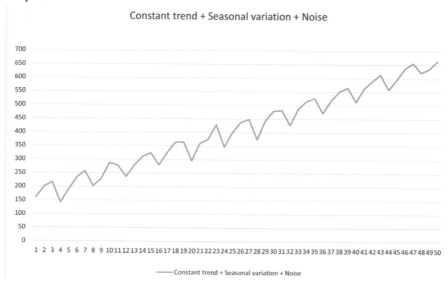

The data displayed above show a repetitive variation (ups and downs) every three months around an upward sloping trend line and a random variation. The forecast for the next period will be: level plus slope coefficient multiplied by the forecasted period number plus a seasonal adjustment for the forecasted period plus the random component.

Graph E

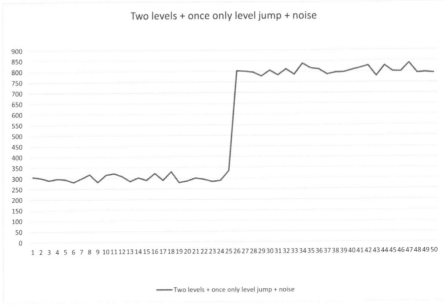

The data displayed above show a low level around ±300 up to period 25 and then a sudden jump to ±800, after which it continues around this level plus a random variation over the entire time range. If we assume that no second sudden jump will occur in the forecasted period, the forecast will be calculated as a high level plus random component. Jumps occur often when unexpected information is released about a product, like newly discovered health effects of food or a new store is opened in another country boosting sales in that country.[3]

Combining level, trend, and seasonal components in a single demand

A forecast is an outcome of combining the four components in a single mathematical model. We define Y_t as the demand in period t, L_t the level at period t, T_t the trend in period t, and S_t the seasonal index in period t. The symbol e_t will be used for the forecast error in period t. We discuss three ways to combine the structural components:

   Additive: $Y_t = L_t + T_t + S_t$

The *additive* model is only applicable when all components are expressed in absolute numbers and not in percentages or indices.

Multiplicative: $Y_t = L_t * T_t * S_t$

The *multiplicative* model is only reliable if the level is expressed in absolute numbers and T_t and S_t in relative numbers, such as percentages or indices.

Mixed: $Y_t = (L_t + T_t) * S_t$

The mixed model is only reliable if level and trend are expressed in absolute numbers and S_t as a percentage or index. The mixed model is the one that is used most often. Incidentally, it must be noted that the trend in data does not have to be linear. Non-linear trends, like those stemming from learning effects or other factors that do not behave linearly, can also be incorporated into the forecasting model. If data contain a non-linear trend, it can only be detected either by decomposing the sales data or by solid theoretical support to assume a non-linear functional trend. A visual inspection of the plotted data gives a first clue to the existence of a non-linear trend.

An important issue is how to uncover the three components when only raw sales data per period are available. The solution is *decomposition* of the sales data Y_t. In the mixed model, we can derive S_t for each season. If we can divide the sales data by S_i, the outcome is $(L_t + T_t)$. These are called *deseasonalized* data.

The first method we will discuss for identifying the seasonal element in sales is calculating a centred moving average. The initial step in this method is a visual inspection of the plotted sales data to see if any seasonality is observed. That means looking for a repetitive pattern by week, months, or seasons in each data cycle, usually a cycle of a year. If the repetitive pattern is weekly and the sales cycle is one year then the seasonality pattern repeats itself every 52 weeks. If the repetitive pattern is monthly and the cycle is one year then the seasonality pattern repeats itself every 12 months. If the repetitive pattern is given per season, the pattern repeats itself every four seasons. Once we observe seasonality in the data per month, we calculate a moving average over 12 consecutive observations. We start in period 12, because we need a minimum of 12 observations to calculate the first 12-month moving average.

An example of deseasonalized data presented in Excel using a twelve-month moving average is shown in Graph F, which displays sales data from 24 months in red. The green line is the associated centred moving average of these data. The actual data for this graph are in Table 1.

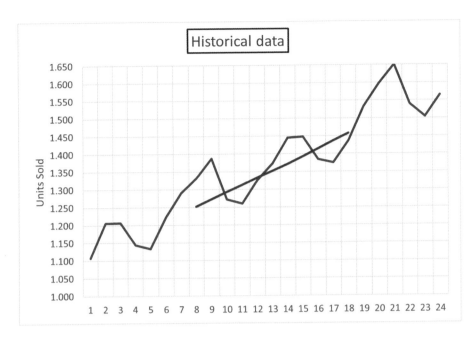

A visual inspection of the red-coloured data indicates a seasonal pattern based on a twelve-month cycle. The upward and downward moves observed in month t and month $t+12$ are similar. To remove the seasonal effect – i.e. to deseasonalize the data – we calculate the 12-month moving average (MA). We need 12 observations before we can calculate the first moving average. Our first MA is calculated in month 12 and is the average value of the months 1 to 12 inclusively.

The second MA in month 13 is the average value of the months 2 to 13 inclusively; the third MA in month 14 is the average value of the months 3 to 14 inclusively, etc. We end up with 12 moving average values. However, these MAs are not well centered over the 24-month period.[4] We would like to place the middle value of the MAs in the same row as the middle value of all months. We grab the 12 MAs and shift the values six months upward, so that there are <u>no</u> MAs for the first six months or for the last six months. Shifting data in a column upward in Excel rows does not change the values in the cells. After this operation, the 12 moving averages are not yet fully centred. There are 24 months in the data series and the middle period is the month $[24 + 1]/2 = 12\frac{1}{2}$. Data for month $12\frac{1}{2}$ are not available, only for months 12 and 13. To enable placement in the middle of the time range, we centre the MAs at month $12\frac{1}{2}$ and therefore we must determine the average value at month $12\frac{1}{2}$. We calculate this average using the MA of months 12 and 13 – an average of an average – to obtain the MA for month $12\frac{1}{2}$. Likewise, centring the remaining MAs from the first to the last is done as it was for month $12\frac{1}{2}$.

As a result of taking the moving average from two data points, we lose one more observation and end up with 11 moving averages of moving averages. The middle

Table 1

	A	B	C	D	E	F	G	H	I
1	Month	Month number	Sales	Moving Average	Centered MA		Month Index	Forecast Model	Formula view forecast
2	January	1	1,107				1.00	1,130	(20,484+1107,6*B2)*F2
3	February	2	1,206				1.04	1,192	(20,484+1107,6*B3)*F3
4	March	3	1,207				1.02	1,197	(20,484+1107,6*B4)*F4
5	April	4	1,144				0.96	1,146	(20,484+1107,6*B5)*F5
6	May	5	1,133				0.94	1,141	(20,484+1107,6*B6)*F6
7	June	6	1,223				0.97	1,197	(20,484+1107,6*B7)*F7
8	July	7	1,291		1,252	AVERAGE(D13:D14)	1.03	1,290	(20,484+1107,6*B8)*F8
9	August	8	1,332		1,273	AVERAGE(D14:D15)	1.05	1,331	(20,484+1107,6*B9)*F9
10	September	9	1,387		1,293	AVERAGE(D15:D16)	1.07	1,386	(20,484+1107,6*B10)*F10
11	October	10	1,272		1,313	AVERAGE(D16:D17)	0.97	1,272	(20,484+1107,6*B11)*F11
12	November	11	1,260		1,333	AVERAGE(D17:D18)	0.95	1,260	(20,484+1107,6*B12)*F12
13	December	12	1,326	1,241	1,352	AVERAGE(D18:D19)	0.98	1,327	(20,484+1107,6*B13)*F13
14	January	13	1,373	1,263	1,371	AVERAGE(D19:D20)	1.00	1,376	(20,484+1107,6*B14)*F14
15	February	14	1,445	1,283	1,392	AVERAGE(D20:D21)	1.04	1,447	(20,484+1107,6*B15)*F15
16	March	15	1,448	1,303	1,414	AVERAGE(D21:D22)	1.02	1,449	(20,484+1107,6*B16)*F16
17	April	16	1,384	1,323	1,436	AVERAGE(D22:D23)	0.96	1,383	(20,484+1107,6*B17)*F17
18	May	17	1,375	1,343	1,458	AVERAGE(D23:D24)	0.94	1,373	(20,484+1107,6*B18)*F18
19	June	18	1,437	1,361	1,478	AVERAGE(D24:D25)	0.97	1,436	(20,484+1107,6*B19)*F19
20	July	19	1,533	1,381			1.03	1,544	(20,484+1107,6*B20)*F20
21	August	20	1,598	1,403			1.05	1,588	(20,484+1107,6*B21)*F21
22	September	21	1,651	1,425			1.07	1,650	(20,484+1107,6*B22)*F22
23	October	22	1,540	1,448			0.97	1,510	(20,484+1107,6*B23)*F23
24	November	23	1,504	1,468			0.95	1,492	(20,484+1107,6*B24)*F24
25	December	24	1,565	1,488			0.98	1,569	(20,484+1107,6*B25)*F25
26	Januari	25					1.00	1,622	(20,484+1107,6*B26)*F26
27	Februari	26					1.04	1,703	(20,484+1107,6*B27)*F27
28	Maart	27					1.02	1,700	(20,484+1107,6*B28)*F28

value is the 6th MA, which has become the centred moving average at month 12½. The middle of the centred moving averages is now aligned with the middle of the month's numbers, as shown in column 5 of Table 1.

A remarkable feature of the centred MA line is its relatively linear shape in which all seasonal variations have been virtually removed. We end up with deseasonalized sales data containing only the level and the trend and a random element: $Y_{deseasonalized,t} = L_t + T_t + \varepsilon_t$.

Finding the level and the trend boils down to a straightforward linear regression of the deseasonalized data. When using Excel, either the Add-in *Data Analysis*, the *LINEST*-function in the Excel function library, or the trendline option available among the Chart options will do the job.

Each of the three will yield the same result. The equation of the line is $Y_{deseasonalized}$ = 20.48*t + 1,107.6. This is the deseasonalized trend line containing level and trend. The symbol t in the equation represents the month number. Therefore, the level of the sales data L = 1,108 units, and the trend equals the slope of the line 20.48.[5]

For forecasting purposes, applying the mixed model $Y_t = (L + t{*}T) {*} S_t$ we convert the S_t to a percentage or index because the moving averages are expressed in absolute values. There are several ways to achieve this goal, but a common one is calculating a seasonal index using the *ratio-to-moving average*. To do this, we divide the actual sales data by the centred moving average in the same month, starting in the month with the first centred MA, and repeat this calculation for each subsequent month up to and including the month with the last centred MA.[6] The results can be found in the column *Seasonal Index* in Table 1.

From time series decomposition to forecasting

To make a forecast based on the centred moving average and seasonal indices, we will tweak the model slightly. We copy the seasonal indices in Table 1 to the cells with like months but still without a seasonal index. Each of the 12 months will be assigned the same seasonal index: month 1 and 13, month 2 and 14, month 3 and 15, and so on.

To make a forecast for January, February, and March of the *third* year, we add the month numbers 25, 26, and 27 after the last row as well as the seasonal indices for these three months in the corresponding column. Then, we compute the sales data using this centred moving average model. The model predicts in month t: $(1{,}107.6 + 20.48{*}t){*}S_t$ with S_t calculated in column *Seasonal Index* Table 1.

Graph G

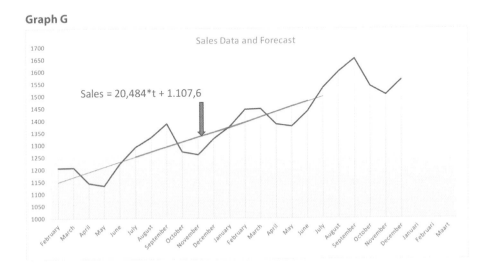

We can extend this formula to forecast the first three months of the third year and then plot the model forecasts in the same graph with the historical sales data and the centred moving average. The outcome can be found in Table 1 and the plotted data in Graph G. The red line in Graph G shows the original sales data and ends in December year 2, and the blue data are the model forecasts continuing up to March of year 3. A visual inspection reveals that the model functions well and fits the original data. The pattern of the first 3 months of year 3 mimics the patterns of the same monthly range of year 1 and year 2.

Assessing the reliability of the model and calculating forecast errors

A visual inspection of our model indicates a good fit between the model output and the original data. Critically, however, a visual inspection depends on the scale of the graph and the order of magnitude of the data and can be delusive. What is needed is a more quantitative benchmark that tells us something about the reliability of the model data and the forecast error. The closer the values produced by the model are to the actual observation, the better the model is, and the more reliable the forecast will be. In the statistical literature, one can find different indicators to quantify the forecast error. Here, we will discuss some that are frequently used in business forecasts.

The first indicator is the *Mean Absolute Deviation (MAD)*. The Mean Absolute Deviation is computed by taking the absolute deviation or error between the calculated value and the actual observation in each month t: $|A_t - F_t|$. We take the *absolute* value to avoid positive deviations in one month cancelling out negative deviations of other months. Once we have calculated the deviations for 24 months, we take the mean of all these values, which results in the Mean Absolute Deviation.

The MAD is not very informative as an absolute value. The order of magnitude of the MAD is a function of the order of magnitude of the observed sales data. If we multiply the observed sales data by a factor of 1,000, the absolute deviations will be inflated with the same order of magnitude as the MAD.

An equivalent reliability measure is the *Mean Squared Error (MSE)*. The MSE is calculated by taking the difference between the observed and forecasted model value of each month t squared:

$$[A_t - F_t]^2$$

Squaring has the same effect as taking absolute values; it gives all deviations positive signs and there are no cancellations of positive with negative deviations. Finally, we take the *mean* value of all squared errors. The order of magnitude of the MSE is considerably higher than the MAD due to the squaring. Moreover, the MSE is not very informative: the value is fully dependent on the order of magnitude of the original sales data.

The third indicator for measuring the forecast reliability is the *Mean Absolute Percentage Error (MAPE)*. MAPE is calculated as

$$\frac{1}{N}\sum_{t=1}^{N}\left|\frac{(A_t-F_t)}{A_t}\right| * 100\%.$$

We multiply by 100 to convert the fraction to a percentage, and take the absolute value to avoid months with a positive percentage being cancelled out by months with a negative percentage deviation. The advantage of MAPE is that it is not dependent on the order of magnitude of the original data as it expresses the forecast error as a percentage. This allows us to compare the forecast errors of a small company with those of a large company. A potential drawback of MAPE arises when the values of A_t are small compared to the error in the numerator $[A_t -F_t]$. This inflates the quotient and overstates the real forecast error. Several authors have searched for better measurements of the forecast error, but it is beyond the scope of this book to go into the technical details. The interested reader is referred to the paper mentioned in footnote 7.[7] The three forecast errors applied to the data in our example are:

MAD	MSE	MAPE
6.9	120	0.52%

Forecasting using binary regression

Another forecasting method that is appropriate for making forecasts when seasonal data are present is *linear regression with binary variables.* This involves introducing binary variables after visual inspection of the plotted data seasonality has been observed in order to account for the seasonal effects.[8] The number of binary variables (X_t) we introduce is one less than the number of seasons: in our example of a cycle of 12 months, we need to assign 11 binary variables for 11 months. The month that is *not* assigned a binary variable will become the base month and all seasonal effects are calculated as differences with respect to the base month. The choice of the base month is arbitrary and does not affect the results. We take January as the base month and the months February until December will be assigned a binary variable. The regression equation using the standard symbols used in regression has the following functional form:

$$F_t = \beta_0 + \beta_1 * t + \sum_{t=2}^{12}\beta_i * X_{i,t}$$

F_t represents the forecasted sales in period t with t running from month 1 until 24; β_0 is the intercept that represents the level component; β_1 is the coefficient representing the trend; and t is the corresponding month number. β_i is the seasonal coefficient of month i and $X_{i,t}$ the corresponding binary variables for the i months.

For example, $X_{2,t}$ will take on the value 1 for February (months 2 and 14) and the value 0 for all other months; $X_{3,t}$ will take on the value 1 for March (month 3 and 15) and the value 0 for all other months, and so on.[9] Now, we can run the regression in Excel using either the Add-in *Data Analysis* → Regression, or the function LINEST from the Excel Function Library. The regression equation becomes:

$$F_t = 1{,}096 + 20.6*T + 64.9*X_{feb} + 46.3*X_{mar} - 37.8*X_{apr} - 68.4*X_{may} - 13*X_{June} + 48.5*X_{July} + 80.9*X_{aug} + 114.3*X_{sep} - 19.3*X_{oct} - 63.9*X_{nov} - 21*X_{dec}$$

We are now able to make forecasts for the first three months of the third year:

$F_{25} = 1{,}096 + 20.6*25$ $= 1{,}611$ units for January
$F_{26} = 1{,}096 + 20.6*26 + 64.9*1$ $= 1{,}696$ units for February
$F_{27} = 1{,}096 + 20.6*27 + 46.3*1$ $= 1{,}698$ units for March

The original sales data and the model forecast are plotted in Graph 2 below.

Graph II

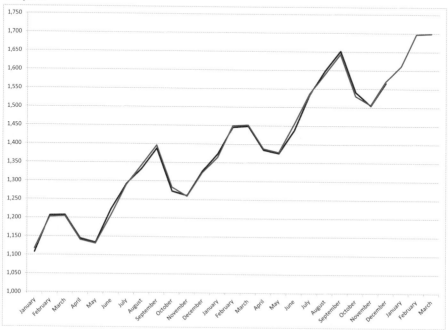

The two curves fit so closely to each other that it is hard to distinguish the blue and red curves. NB: the last three months only show the forecasted values. The table below shows the numerical data:

Month	Sales data	Forecast
January	1107	1116
February	1206	1202
March	1207	1204
April	1144	1140
May	1133	1130
June	1223	1206
July	1291	1288
August	1332	1341
September	1387	1395
October	1272	1282
November	1260	1258
December	1326	1322
January	1373	1364
February	1445	1449
March	1448	1451
April	1384	1388
May	1375	1378
June	1437	1454
July	1533	1536
August	1598	1589
September	1651	1643
October	1540	1530
November	1504	1506
December	1565	1569
January		1611
February		1696
March		1698

The three forecast errors applied to the binary regression forecast are:

MAD	MSE	MAPE
6.31	58.6	0.47%

All three forecast errors are lower than the centred moving average forecasting method. We can conclude that the binary regression gives a more reliable forecast than the centred moving average for our data.

The third forecasting method: Holt-Winters exponential smoothing[10]

The two forecasting methods discussed above assign equal weights to all data points from the past. Sales forecasts are equally influenced by the historical sales from 23 months ago as by the sales from last month. Many empirical studies show that, in many cases, recent sales have more impact on sales in the near future than sales that occurred a long time ago. It is therefore possible to improve a forecast by assigning higher weights to recent data and less weight to data from the past. This category of forecasting methods, where recent data is weighted differently from data further in the past, is part of the *exponential smoothing* method. This method uses a parameter called the smoothing coefficient and is indicated by the Greek letter α under the condition: $0 < \alpha < 1$.[11]

Depending on the choice of α by the forecaster, the combination is either closer to A_t or closer to F_t.

The Holt-Winters forecasting method uses a time series approach with three default systematic components: *Level* (L); *Trend* (T); and *Seasonality* (S). For each component, exponential smoothing with three different smoothing coefficients is applied. The symbol α for the level smoothing, β for the trend smoothing, and γ for the smoothing of the seasonal effects. Calculating the forecast using the mixed model gives:

$$F_{t+1} = (L_t + 1^*T_t)^*S_{t-p}.$$

The three exponential smoothing equations for calculating each component of period *t+1* are done in the current period *t* looking forward to the period [*t+1*]:

[I] $T_{t+1} = \alpha * \left(\frac{A_{t+1}}{S_{t+1}}\right) + (1 - \alpha) * \left(L_t + T_t\right)$ to calculate the updated value of the level.

[II] $T_{t+1} = \beta * (L_{t+1} - L_t) + (1 - \beta) * T_t$ to calculate the updated value of the trend.

[III] $S_{t+1} = \gamma * \left(\frac{A_{t+1}}{L_{t+1}}\right) + (1 - \gamma) * S_{t-p+1}$ to calculate the updated value of the seasonal index.

Equation [I] shows how the model calculates the level for the next period $t+1$ by taking the observed value in $t+1$ (A_{t+1}) and dividing it by the seasonal index of $t+1$ (S_{t+1}). This removes the seasonal deviation from the observed value A_{t+1}. What remains is the level and trend, which are hidden in A_{t+1}. The second part of the equation is the sum of the level and trend value of the previous period – also deseasonalized. The α assigns the weight to each of the two parts in the equation.

Equation [II] shows how the model calculates the trend for the next period [$t+1$] as the difference between the level of the forecasted period minus the level in the previous period. Take into account that L_{t+1} is calculated in equation [I]. The trend can be considered as the slope to jump from one data point to the next one and ($L_{t+1} - L_t$) gives the most up-to-date information about the trend. The second part of this equation is taking the trend value of the previous period. The β is the weight assigned to recent and previous data to find the value of T_{t+1}.

Equation [III] shows how the model calculates the seasonal index of [$t+1$]. For the seasonal index, we need to know how many seasons there are in one cycle. The model contains *p* seasons. (for example, p = 12 for months and p = 4 for seasons). A seasonal index can only be updated with previous indices from the *same* season. Therefore, we must go back to *p* seasons to get the latest information about the same season. The formula tells us that the updated seasonal index corresponding to the period [$t+1$] is found by taking the actual data from $t+1$ and dividing it by the level of the same period [$t+1$]. This division removes the most recent level from the actual data so that only trend and season remain. The second part of the equation takes the last available seasonal index, which is *p* seasons back in time. The two parts are linked with the smoothing coefficient γ.

Notice that we need equation [I] to find L_{t+1} to use it in equation [III], but we also need S_{t+1} in equation [I]. We have an interdependent relationship between the two equations, and they must be solved simultaneously as a system of equations.

In the Holt-Winters model, we make a forecast of the next period $t+1$ when we find ourselves in (at the end of) period t. As long as we have not arrived at the last month with actual data we have information about data point A_{t+1} as well as the previous values of L_t, T_t, and S_{t-p+1}. We want to calculate L_{t+1}, T_{t+1}, and S_{t+1}, so we have three unknowns for each month, but also three equations per month and therefore the model has a solution.

Once we have calculated the forecasted values of L_t, T_t, and S_t up to the last month with actual data, we proceed to the model forecast $F_{t+1} = (L_t + t^*T_t)^*S_{t+1}$ for which we have NO actual data. The problem is that there are no observed or actual data for the forecast for future periods. If we have, for example, 24 observed data up to and including December 2017, and we want to forecast for January, February, and March 2018, the forecast calculation can only use *observed and calculated* data. The most recent data come from December 2017. The forecast for January becomes:

$$F_{25} = (L_{24} + 1^*T_{24})\ ^*S_{13}$$

Our last seasonal index for January is the one of January a year ago [t = 13].

$$F_{26} = (L_{24} + 2^*T_{24})\ ^*S_{14}$$

Our last seasonal index for February is from February a year ago [t = 14]. We multiply the T_{24} with a scalar 2, because we are forecasting two periods ahead, so we move two units to the right on the time axis and therefore take 2 times the slope coefficient for the vertical distance on the trend line

$$F_{27} = (L_{24} + 3^*T_{24})^*S_{15}$$

Our last seasonal index for March is from March a year ago [t = 15]. We multiply the trend with a scalar 3 because we move three periods to the right on the horizontal time axis and therefore take 3 times the slope coefficient for the vertical distance on the trend line.

A complication arises when making the model forecast for period 1. All three equations need input data from the previous period and there are no data available for period 0 in our problem. We must resort to other calculations to find the initial values L_0 and T_0, as well as the initial values for the first *p* seasons S_t.

One option is to copy these initial values from the moving average forecasting method as starting values. We will apply the Holt-Winters forecasting model using the same sales data as the previous example.

Graph III and Table 2 with the values and Table 3 with the formulas are shown below. The blue line represents the observed sales data and the red line is the model forecasts, including the forecasted values for the third quarter of the third year.

Graph III

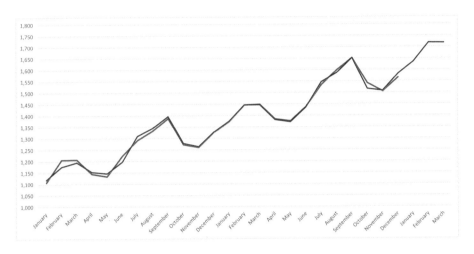

Table 2

Month	Observed sales	Level	Trend	Season	Forecast
Start values	Month #	1088	20		
January	1	1107	1104	19	1,01	1118
February	2	1206	1135	23	1,05	1175
March	3	1207	1162	24	1,03	1194
April	4	1144	1183	23	0,97	1152
May	5	1133	1201	21	0,95	1146
June	6	1223	1233	25	0,98	1197
July	7	1291	1251	23	1,04	1309
August	8	1332	1269	21	1,05	1343
September	9	1387	1287	20	1,08	1396
October	10	1272	1306	20	0,98	1277
November	11	1260	1325	19	0,95	1263
December	12	1326	1344	19	0,99	1327
January	13	1373	1362	19	1,01	1375
February	14	1445	1381	19	1,05	1445
March	15	1448	1401	19	1,03	1445
April	16	1384	1422	20	0,97	1380
May	17	1375	1444	20	0,95	1371
June	18	1437	1466	21	0,98	1434
July	19	1533	1482	19	1,04	1545
August	20	1598	1506	21	1,06	1585

Month		Observed sales	Level	Trend	Season	Forecast
September	21	1651	1527	21	1,08	1651
October	22	1540	1558	24	0,98	1515
November	23	1504	1581	24	0,95	1506
December	24	1565	1598	22	0,99	1582
January	25					1634
February	26					1717
March	27					1716

The formulas in the cells in the columns *Level, Trend, Season,* and *Forecast* are shown below.

Table 3

Month	Level	Trend	Season index	Forecast
	1088	20,4		
January	=$I$2*(C3/F3)+(1-$I$2)*(D2+E2)	=$J$2*(D3-D2)+(1-$J$2)*E2	1,00894060012247	=(D2+E2)*F3
February	=$I$2*(C4/F4)+(1-$I$2)*(D3+E3)	=$J$2*(D4-D3)+(1-$J$2)*E3	1,04634322954381	=(D3+E3)*F4
Mach	=$I$2*(C5/F5)+(1-$I$2)*(D4+E4)	=$J$2*(D5-D4)+(1-$J$2)*E4	1,03195153818743	=(D4+E4)*F5
April	=$I$2*(C6/F6)+(1-$I$2)*(D5+E5)	=$J$2*(D6-D5)+(1-$J$2)*E5	0,971114489533388	=(D5+E5)*F6
May	=$I$2*(C7/F7)+(1-$I$2)*(D6+E6)	=$J$2*(D7-D6)+(1-$J$2)*E6	0,949913644214162	=(D6+E6)*F7
June	=$I$2*(C8/F8)+(1-$I$2)*(D7+E7)	=$J$2*(D8-D7)+(1-$J$2)*E7	0,978993982059725	=(D7+E7)*F8
July	=$I$2*(C9/F9)+(1-$I$2)*(D8+E8)	=$J$2*(D9-D8)+(1-$J$2)*E8	1,04056958624395	=(D8+E8)*F9
August	=$I$2*(C10/F10)+(1-$I$2)*(D9+E9)	=$J$2*(D10-D9)+(1-$J$2)*E9	1,05477101755312	=(D9+E9)*F10
September	=$I$2*(C11/F11)+(1-$I$2)*(D10+E10)	=$J$2*(D11-D10)+(1-$J$2)*E10	1,08127070746443	=(D10+E10)*F11
October	=$I$2*(C12/F12)+(1-$I$2)*(D11+E11)	=$J$2*(D12-D11)+(1-$J$2)*E11	0,976333631828067	=(D11+E11)*F12
November	=$I$2*(C13/F13)+(1-$I$2)*(D12+E12)	=$J$2*(D13-D12)+(1-$J$2)*E12	0,952500944941414	=(D12+E12)*F13
December	=$I$2*(C14/F14)+(1-$I$2)*(D13+E13)	=$J$2*(D14-D13)+(1-$J$2)*E13	0,987341772151899	=(D13+E13)*F14
January	=$I$2*(C15/F15)+(1-$I$2)*(D14+E14)	=$J$2*(D15-D14)+(1-$J$2)*E14	=$K$2*(C15/D15)+(1-$K$2)*F3	=(D14+E14)*F15
February	=$I$2*(C16/F16)+(1-$I$2)*(D15+E15)	=$J$2*(D16-D15)+(1-$J$2)*E15	=$K$2*(C16/D16)+(1-$K$2)*F4	=(D15+E15)*F16
March	=$I$2*(C17/F17)+(1-$I$2)*(D16+E16)	=$J$2*(D17-D16)+(1-$J$2)*E16	=$K$2*(C17/D17)+(1-$K$2)*F5	=(D16+E16)*F17
April	=$I$2*(C18/F18)+(1-$I$2)*(D17+E17)	=$J$2*(D18-D17)+(1-$J$2)*E17	=$K$2*(C18/D18)+(1-$K$2)*F6	=(D17+E17)*F18
May	=$I$2*(C19/F19)+(1-$I$2)*(D18+E18)	=$J$2*(D19-D18)+(1-$J$2)*E18	=$K$2*(C19/D19)+(1-$K$2)*F7	=(D18+E18)*F19
June	=$I$2*(C20/F20)+(1-$I$2)*(D19+E19)	=$J$2*(D20-D19)+(1-$J$2)*E19	=$K$2*(C20/D20)+(1-$K$2)*F8	=(D19+E19)*F20
July	=$I$2*(C21/F21)+(1-$I$2)*(D20+E20)	=$J$2*(D21-D20)+(1-$J$2)*E20	=$K$2*(C21/D21)+(1-$K$2)*F9	=(D20+E20)*F21
August	=$I$2*(C22/F22)+(1-$I$2)*(D21+E21)	=$J$2*(D22-D21)+(1-$J$2)*E21	=$K$2*(C22/D22)+(1-$K$2)*F10	=(D21+E21)*F22
September	=$I$2*(C23/F23)+(1-$I$2)*(D22+E22)	=$J$2*(D23-D22)+(1-$J$2)*E22	=$K$2*(C23/D23)+(1-$K$2)*F11	=(D22+E22)*F23
October	=$I$2*(C24/F24)+(1-$I$2)*(D23+E23)	=$J$2*(D24-D23)+(1-$J$2)*E23	=$K$2*(C24/D24)+(1-$K$2)*F12	=(D23+E23)*F24
November	=$I$2*(C25/F25)+(1-$I$2)*(D24+E24)	=$J$2*(D25-D24)+(1-$J$2)*E24	=$K$2*(C25/D25)+(1-$K$2)*F13	=(D24+E24)*F25
December	=$I$2*(C26/F26)+(1-$I$2)*(D25+E25)	=$J$2*(D26-D25)+(1-$J$2)*E25	=$K$2*(C26/D26)+(1-$K$2)*F14	=(D25+E25)*F26
January				=($D$26+$E$26)*F15
February				=($D$26+2*$E$26)*F16
March				=($D$26+3*$E$26)*F17

The cells $L$2 contain the smoothing constant $\alpha = 0.4$, cell $M$2, in the trend column the smoothing constant $\beta = 0.3$ and $N$2 in the seasonal columns $\gamma = 0.2$ (they are not visible in the screenshot). Column C contains the actual sales data, column D the calculation of the Level, Column E the calculation of the Trend, Column F the calculation of the Seasonal Index and the last column are the forecasts. The three forecast errors applied to the Holt-Winters forecast model are:

MAD	MSE	MAPE
9.72	166.5	0.738%

Comparing these errors with the other two methods, we see that the three forecast errors above fall between the equivalent errors of the centred moving average method and the binary regression. For our example, the Holt-Winter method ranks number 2 as a forecasting method!

When discussing the structure of the Holt-Winters method, we said that the three smoothing constants were arbitrarily chosen: in this example $\alpha = 0.4$, $\beta = 0.3$, and $\gamma = 0.2$. Our goal is to look for the most reliable forecast; or, in other words a model forecast that fits the sales data best and has the lowest forecast error. Because α, β, and γ are arbitrary parameters, we can choose those values in such a way that they minimize the forecast error. Excel has a powerful optimization Add-in called *Solver* that can minimize the error term by entering the α, β, and γ values as variables under the constraint that all three are smaller or equal to 1 and by selecting *GRG Nonlinear* as the solving method. If we select the MSE as the objective function, the solution to the Solver minimization gives the following values:

α	β	γ	MSE	MAD
0.235	0	1	93.69	4.42

By optimizing the smoothing constants, the MSE has dropped from 166.5 to 93.69 and MAD from 9.72 to 4.42. Both indicate a better forecast than using arbitrary smoothing constants.[12]

Forecasting with the aid of regression analysis

All the forecasting models discussed up to now are based on time series analysis. The future is predicted using the past. There is no reference to the main drivers of demand; that is to say, there is no causal analysis of demand. What drives consumers to buy a specific product or service? Making forecasts using cause-and-effect relations would bring us to the domain of regression analysis, where demand as a dependent variable is explained using a set of demand drivers as independent variables. Although evidence from empirical studies shows that better forecasts are obtained using regression analysis, there are some reasons why this method is not always feasible for demand forecasting. The first is that demand for many products is affected by many different causes, like sales price, prices of competitive products, the company's market share, the preferences and purchasing power of consumers, products that serve basic human needs (food and medicines), or luxury products, advertising and marketing efforts, the popularity of the product, and many more factors. In practice, it is very difficult to quantify all the causes influencing demand and to find all necessary data to run a regression. Moreover, even if the forecaster has access to all information, a demand forecast also requires forecasting the values of the independent variables before being able to forecast the future sales as the dependent variable.

The discussion of regression is beyond the scope of this book and the interested reader is referred to the extensive literature as well as many other forecasting techniques like neural networks, ARIMA [Autoregressive Integrated Moving Average], panel data forecasts, and spectral analysis.

Main Point: no forecasting method is the best under all circumstances. Finding the best method depends on, among other things, the data patterns. More sophisticated forecasting models do not necessarily yield better forecasts than simpler models. When selecting a forecasting method, the forecaster will also take into account whether the improvement in forecast reliability, measured in a lower MAD or MSE, outweighs the costs of the new method in terms of investment in new software and fees paid to expensive forecasting consultants. An improvement in the order of magnitude of 1000 units when global sales oscillate around hundreds of millions is not sufficient to justify spending much more money on forecasting.

Collaborative forecasting and planning in a Supply Chain

A Supply Chain is only economically viable if there is demand for its product. There-fore, demand forecasting focuses on consumer demand. Consumer demand can be decomposed into different levels of aggregation, ranging from long-term macro demand to time-specific local demand (e.g. the demand for electric bikes in April 2021 in a local bicycle store in a Polish town). The outcome of the forecasting becomes the input for other Supply Chain activities. If the forecasting is applied at an aggregate level, with data from several years hindsight and forecasting for several years in the future, it serves as a first step in a company's decision-making process with respect to capacity planning. Long-term capacity planning will be discussed in more detail in the next chapter.

Where are historical sales data coming from? For many products, the basic source is the registration of Point of Sales transactions at the checkouts of local stores, and for some products also in vending machines. Online transactions are registered in the web retailer's computer system. If all POS-registered transactions are connected to a global computer system, then all sales data are saved at one central point, often in real-time, and can be used for making global forecasts as well as regional and local forecasts.

If the computer systems of distribution centres, manufacturers, and suppliers of raw materials to the manufacturer are also linked to this digital network, all partners in the Supply Chain share access to up-to-date sales information at the lowest disaggregated level in the Supply Chain (POS), within the limits set by the digital information rights of each SC partner. Not all Supply Chain partners will have access to all information, usually only to the information that is relevant for their activities.[13] The diagram below shows important elements of a collaborative joint forecasting and planning process.

Collaborative planning, forecasting and replenishment

- **CPFR Model**

Planning {
1. Develop front-end agreement
2. Create joint business plans

Forecasting {
3. Create individual sales forecasts
4. Identify exceptions to sales forecasts
5. Resolve / collaborate on exception items
6. Create order forecast
7. Identify exceptions to order forecast
8. Resolve / collaborate on exception items

replenishment
9. Generate orders

Source: https://image3.slideserve.com/6688981/collaborative-planning-forecasting-and-replenish-ment1-l.jpg retrieved on 2nd December 2021

Besides having access to digital data for good forecasting and planning in a Supply Chain, sales representatives and managers also have joint meetings – on-site or via videoconferencing – to discuss the reliability of the forecasts. These forecasts are used to: set up production and distribution planning; design delivery contracts; information exchange about unforeseen demand changes; coordinate price promotions; plan lead times; standardize order sizes and shipping documents; and many more demand-related issues. The outcome of this huge and complex coordination process is a joint forecast and planning. If the forecasts are accurate, it will reduce the bullwhip effect.

Another feature of good forecasting is its ability to update forecasts as soon as new data become available. When partners in a supply chain have access to real-time information, forecasters can update forecasts and plans as soon as the previously forecasted demand drifts away from *real* and *observed* demand.

As said before, there are many more, and more complex, statistical forecasting models. Discussing all these models is beyond the scope of this book and belongs to a course on statistical forecasting.[14]

Chapter summary

Forecasting has been practiced for centuries. Forecasting is step one in every Supply Chain's planning and policy. Forecasts, both long- and short-term, form the quantitative basis for all other Supply Chain activities: capacity planning; production planning; inventory planning; logistics planning; and even financial planning. Errors in forecasts will propagate throughout the Supply Chain, reducing SC performance and wasting resources. There are qualitative and quantitative forecasting methods. With the increasing availability of data, quantitative forecasting methods have seen a rapid development, mainly triggered by the increased power of modern computers. In this chapter, we discussed three quantitative forecasting methods that are commonly used in business and demand forecasting. They all belong to the class of time series. Comparing different forecasting techniques requires reliability indicators: three common indicators were discussed, MAD, MSE, and MAPE. In general, one cannot say that one method is always better and more reliable than other forecasting methods. It depends on the specific data on which the forecast is based. Comparing the outcomes of several forecasting methods on a historical dataset and then selecting the most reliable one is a sound way of working. In a Supply Chain, forecasting transcends the narrow limits of individual forecasting by one company. By sharing data, the process will become a collaborative forecasting process in which information contributed by all SC partners serves as input for making more accurate and more reliable forecasts for the Supply Chain as a whole.

Notes

1-14   See Instructor's Manual

3   Capacity Planning and Facility Location

Capacity Planning and Facility Location Decisions

Source: By Cygnusloop99 – Own work, CC BY-SA 3.0, https://commons.wikimedia.org/w/index.
php?curid=15445642

At the beginning of the project, the hotel was called the Lifestyle Hotel. The tower was
planned to have 400 hotel rooms and approximately 207 condominium residences from
74 m² to 269 m² on 49 floors. The hotel's pool deck was to be on the roof high above the
Las Vegas Strip. The exterior of the building was finished in 2009, but interior work to correct construction issues extended into 2010. […] On 11 July 2011, Weidlinger Associates,
an engineering firm hired by MGM Resorts International released a report indicating that
the building was likely to collapse in a major earthquake and that remedial work would
take at least a year. On 15 August 2011, MGM announced plans to demolish the hotel. This
plan was approved by a judge in August 2013, as the building represented a threat to
public safety due to the risk of collapse in an earthquake. Due to its proximity to other
buildings, the hotel was taken apart floor by floor. Dismantling of the hotel began in
June 2014 and was completed in 2015. The estimated costs were $11.5 million.
Source: https://en.wikipedia.org/wiki/The_Harmon retrieved on 1 December 2021

Hyundai Motors Ulsan Plant is the world's largest single plant. It is made up of five independent factories, with approximately 32,000 personnel producing an average of 5800 vehicles per day. A surprising feature of this complex is the 600,000 trees planted within the area, making the plant a factory surrounded by a forest. Visitors to the plant can tour the vehicle manufacturing plant and the port that houses 76,000-ton ships. This factory is so huge that it has its own road network and infrastructure, complete with hospital, fire services, and a sewage treatment plant. **Source**: http://tong.visitkorea.or.kr/cms/resource/95/1845795_image2_1.jpg

The above-mentioned case of the Las Vegas casino is not the only example of a major investment failure.

They occur in all industries. The causes of major investment collapses vary and range from fraud and scandals to construction errors in buildings, complete overestimation of forecasted demand, cost overruns, and many more. A positive element of analysing investment failures is the learning potential. The knowledge gained from uncovering the causes of an investment failure can be considered a critical success factor in decision-making processes for future investment – indeed, sometimes they become case studies in MBA courses.

There is a common aphorism, which states: *"people don't plan to fail, they just fail to plan"*. Although planning is no guarantee of success, it at least reduces the risk of investment failure. Planning is an art and a science requiring intellectual, strategic, and practical skills complemented with social and operational skills of the planner or planning team. Capacity investment is a *strategic decision* made by corporations and public organizations. Capacity refers to the highest production rate or output rate (number of products, goods, or services per time unit) that an organization can achieve. Capacity planning in the context of a Supply Chain structure adds a new dimension to capacity, i.e. the ability to get the units produced at the right place and at the right time to move on to the next stage in the Supply Chain and, finally, to meet customer demand. The optimal capacity of one member in the Supply Chain is not necessarily the capacity that optimizes the Supply Chain capacity.

Capacity is made up of a combination of tangible assets,[1] intangible assets, or resources (technical know-how, software, patents), the availability of human resources in quantity and quality expressed in job skills, and other production factors, like raw materials, storage space. Institutional, legal, and ethical factors also affect capacity. They require that the targeted production level must be achieved by complying with labour laws, health, safety, and environmental regulations.[2] Some of these regulations are discussed later in this chapter as *Location Decisions*. Engineers, business analysts, and accountants distinguish different capacity concepts, each concept having a different impact on how capacity costs are calculated:

- *Theoretical Capacity*
  This is the capacity whereby production is running at full technical efficiency without interruptions due to maintenance or breakdowns during the economic life of the asset.
- *Practical Capacity*
  Practical capacity reduces theoretical capacity by deducting unavoidable operating interruptions, like scheduled maintenance, shutdowns during Sundays and holidays for employees, and others.
- *Normal Capacity*
  This capacity concept measures capacity in terms of demand and is linked to capacity utilization set by the average demand over a given period.

The first two capacity concepts are based on supply, the last one on demand. To maintain a sustainable capacity, neither too small nor too large, which leads to structural underutilization, the practical capacity concept is the most relevant one.

Another consideration in capacity decisions is the question of whether capacity planning must be based on peak demand or a *smoothed average demand?* Consumer demand is volatile and unpredictable over time. This last option is, in practice, nearly always the guideline for capacity decisions, because investing in peak demand capacity drives up capacity costs considerably and leads to long periods of idle capacity.

Many textbooks about microeconomics discuss the theory of the firm by exclusively focusing on cost considerations. They claim that the optimal capacity of a firm is achieved when the *average capacity costs per unit* are at a minimum. However, this least average cost production level does not always align with the production volumes needed to meet demand in a Supply Chain.

A typical characteristic of many capacity investments is that capacity cannot be built or acquired on a per-unit basis. It can only be scaled up or down based on orders of magnitude.[3] Consequently, all firms exploiting their production capacity face spells of overcapacity and idle capacity. Instruments for hedging against under- and overcapacity due to demand uncertainty and peak demand will be discussed later.

Capacity Investment, Capacity Costs, and Capacity Classification

Investing in capacity – either building new capacity from scratch, expanding existing capacity, upgrading existing capacity, or reducing existing capacity – usually requires huge sums of money. Most companies conduct *feasibility studies* to obtain a quantitative indication of the expected profitability of a capacity investment. Many of these feasibility studies are commissioned by consultancy offices and management scientists who charge big fees for this job. This means that even if the investment results in a *no*-go decision, the company has already incurred a loss on the fees paid to the consultants. Over many decades, management scientists have developed a toolkit of decision support systems and tools (DSS), which they use to make their recommendations about the desirability of investments. There are too many DSS to discuss here without going beyond the scope of this book and therefore we will discuss only a few, which are helpful for making capacity decisions in a Supply Chain setting.[4]

Capacity investment is a long-term decision, requiring large sums of money, and if, the investment does not yield the expected return, it can be very difficult, if not impossible, to reverse the investment or, if the reverse is technically possible, only at very high expense. Investing and later disinvesting usually doubles the costs of a project. Unexpected cost overruns have been reported during the execution phases of major public and business projects. Decision-makers, deciding on major investments, not only take into account the building costs involved in getting the new asset in place, but also all the costs associated with operating the new asset. This includes periodic maintenance costs, costs of breakdowns and repair, set-up costs, cleaning costs, insurance and security costs, fees to acquire permits from the local administration, etc.

Often, the first thing that comes to mind when hearing about capacity investment is investments in tangible assets, so-called *Plant Property, and Equipment* (PPE). PPE refers to factories, distribution centres, machinery, installation, vehicles, and physical facilities, and all these are certainly elements of capacity investments. But an organization can also expand and improve its capacity by investing in people, i.e. sending them on training programmes or hiring new, qualified staff with necessary skills. In many cases, these two asset categories are complementary: investing in sophisticated tangible assets implies that the skills of the employees who use those assets must be improved or upgraded.

Investment in human resources is important for all kinds of companies, but in particular for companies whose core business is in the service sector. Nowadays, many organizations invest considerable sums of money in *Information Technology*, including hardware, software, and network devices to meet corporate information needs. These are key investments to achieve optimal digital information exchange in a Supply Chain, especially for online sales.

Investments are also made in *Research and Development (R&D)*, in the search for more efficient production processes (automation and robotization), new products, and for product improvements that will generate higher customer satisfaction and added value. Some corporate investments are mandatory by law to comply with quality and regulatory standards regarding safety, health, and environmental aspects of products and production processes. In these cases, the basic decision is not so much whether the investment will be made, but rather how to invest at the lowest possible cost while complying with the established standards.

Main Point: Capacity investments are part of the corporate strategy and Supply Chain structure and refer to the highest production rate a company wants to achieve. They have a long-term horizon, require large monetary outlays, and are rarely reversible when they do not yield the expected return. They are usually preceded by feasibility studies using Decision Support Tools to minimize the risk of partial or complete failure.

Instruments for hedging supply against unexpected demand change

As previously discussed, consumer demand is volatile, exceeding existing capacity during peak periods and generating idle capacity in periods with little demand. Companies have access to a large toolkit of instruments to make capacity flexible during those periods. We list a few of them:

- Sharing production and storage facilities with other companies, especially warehouses and distribution centres, or hiring storage space from third parties.
- Offshore or outsource part of the production to companies equipped with adequate production facilities.
  The outsourcing company will select *preferred suppliers* and sign long-term contracts with them.
- If a company deploys more than one geographical facility or has several production lines in a plant to make the same product, they can spread production over the different facilities or production lines.
- Production can be smoothed over time by producing not only to meet the demand of that period, but also to build up inventory for future periods with peaking demand.

–   Creating economic incentives, such as price promotions, to persuade (business) customers to place their orders in months with idle capacity (forward buying) or backlogging orders, whereby customers will receive products later than ordered.[5]

–   Increasing practical capacity closer to theoretical capacity in peak periods by deploying overtime labour during evenings and weekends, hiring temporary workers, and using tangible assets like machinery and equipment more intensively than under normal demand conditions. This option is not without risk: regarding labour, it can affect labour productivity, increase the risks of production errors and asset breakdowns, and increase production costs (overtime wage rates are higher than normal wage rates).

–   Companies with several production lines for different but similar products can reallocate production to lines with a higher production rate.[6]

Mass customization and capacity

Advanced production technology and modularization, as discussed in the first chapter, have made it easier to customize products to the preferences and tastes of individual customers. For example, the number of smartphone *models* on the market in 2022 is very large. The number of protective cases to cover such phones is virtually unlimited: many users have similar smartphones but with different protective cases. If a manufacturer planned production based on the demand for each smartphone model and the corresponding demand for protective cases, he would certainly make too many of some cases and models and too few of others. By producing smartphones and phone cases separately – or by subcontracting the production of the protective cases – it is much easier to fulfill customer orders quickly, by assembling the phone model and placing them in one of the many protective cases. Many manufacturers store lots of components that can easily be assembled to make the end product without incurring extra marginal costs and which can simultaneously be fine-tuned to customer preferences. *Mass customization* is one of the main causes of the incredible range and variety of similar products (heterogeneity) on the market today.

Capacity planning and geographical location decisions

Aggregate long-term forecasts can be disaggregated into smaller time units to obtain forecasted values for the medium- and short term. Aggregate forecasts can also be disaggregated geographically in forecasts per market and region, for example per continent, or even per country. Production can be organized as fully centralized mass production in one single large plant or as decentralized production in several smaller production plants. An advantage of the first option is the economies of scale achieved by the centralization of mass production, which means decreasing production costs per unit. The disadvantages include potential troubles in upstream relations with suppliers and downstream relations with customers. Suppliers must be able to supply raw materials, parts, and subassemblies in large quantities and aligned to the production planning of the central manufacturing plant of the company. This requires important suppliers to be geographically close to their major customers, shortening shipping distances and lead times. If the product is sold worldwide, then the company must organize a complex distribution network and shipment to meet customer demand spread over the lower echelons of the Supply Chain.

The larger the distance, the longer the lead time – depending on the mode of transportation – and also increasing uncertainty about the lead time due to congestion and other shipment interruptions like border controls or vehicle breakdowns. With centralized production, response time is often longer than that of decentralized production. Feasibility studies for selecting the optimal geographical site to open new plants and facilities take into account many aspects of business processes and socioeconomic standards and we will discuss some of them without the pretension to be exhaustive. We distinguish *hard, socioeconomic*, and *legal* factors as selection criteria for a geographical location for capacity investment. It is not only impossible, but also quite useless to go into the details of each consideration mentioned above. Each country, each region, and even each city is different and therefore location decisions are case-specific. Even within the European Union, which strives for harmonization among its member states and for a reduction of differences, the daily reality remains a long way from the intended goals.

Among the group of **hard** factors to be considered when making location decisions are:
- the availability in quantity and quality of infrastructure: access to highways, railways, and (air)ports
- the availability of data networks: access to (high-speed) optical glass fibre for internet connections, coverture of wireless communication devices
- access to basic services: availability of drinking water, electricity, sewage systems, and so on
- geological features of the location: soil quality, weather conditions, earthquake-prone areas

Under the group of **socioeconomic** factors are:
- Labour market conditions, the ratio of skilled to unskilled workers, labour costs: this includes both direct wage rates and indirect labour costs (social security premiums)

Labour market conditions also include labour regulations regarding overtime, worker safety, and other regulations applicable to employees.
– Proximity to customers and suppliers
– Living conditions for expatriate managers and employees, e.g. house prices, crime rates, leisure facilities, school facilities, and others
– Political situation: political stability, the proximity of war zones.

Under the group of **legal** factors are:
– Taxes at all administrative levels: national, regional, and municipal, both direct and indirect taxes
– Rules regarding transfer pricing between company divisions located in different countries
– Regulations regarding permits required for building, safety, health, and environment
– Zoning plans and land use plans
– Other bureaucratic and administrative burdens determined by (inter)national law

Decision Support Tools

Several scientific tools have been developed to support management location decisions. A frequently used tool is the *decision tree*, which we will describe in general terms. A decision tree is a structured and quantitative approach to decision-making. It consists of decisions, displayed as *squares,* and events displayed as *circles*. Decisions and events are connected by arrows and to each event corresponds a financial pay-off (or profit) together with the probability of the occurrence of an event. The easiest way to understand a decision tree is by using a simple example:

Example decision tree

A supermarket chain is studying the possibility of opening its first supermarket store in Lithuania, on 1 January 2018. Two locations are a candidate: the capital of Vilnius or the city of Kaunas. Information published by incumbent supermarkets in these cities shows that, under good economic conditions, the forecasted payoff at the end of 2018 for a supermarket location in Vilnius is +€500,000, with a probability of 15% (good economic conditions), +€200,000 with a probability of 55% (expected economic conditions), and a loss of -€160,000 with a probability of 30% (bad economic conditions).

The forecasted payoff in Kaunas at the end of 2018 is +€400,000 with a probability of 10% (good economic conditions), +€180,000 with a probability of 75% (expected economic conditions), and -€60,000 with a probability of 15% (bad economic conditions). The layout of the decision tree for this problem is shown in Graph I. From the blue rectangle sprout two arrows, one for the decision to open a location in Vilnius and the other arrow for a location in Kaunas. At the end of 2018, the event circle is shown with three possible and mutually exclusive events, represented by an arrow coming from the event circle and ending in the payoff column.

In the payoff column, the forecasted payoff is shown per event, and next to each arrow is the probability of event occurrence. At the end of 2018, there are six possible payoffs. We calculate the expected payoff for each city by multiplying the payoff by its probability and sum these values for Vilnius and Kaunas, respectively.

The outcome for Vilnius is €137,000 and for Kaunas €166,000. If the objective of the supermarket chain is to select the highest expected payoff, it should choose to invest in Kaunas.

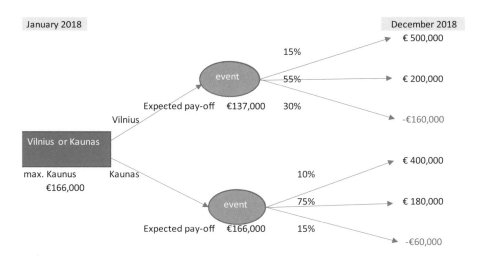

The decision tree can be extended by adding follow-up decisions for 2019. If the municipal permit allows store expansion in Vilnius, the forecasted payoffs at the end of 2019 are estimated at +€650,000 with a probability of 40%, a payoff of +€200,000 with a probability of 45%, and a negative payoff of -€150,000 with a probability of 15%.

The municipality of Kaunas has *not* granted an extension permit, so the situation in 2019 will not change compared to 2018: 2019 will have the same payoffs for the single store with the same probabilities as 2018 with an expected payoff of €166,000.

Having already decided to open a location in Vilnius in January 2018, a question arises in December 2018 about in which of the three economic scenarios the supermarket should decide to expand the floor space. We will solve this expansion decision problem below, assuming that the company started in Vilnius in 2018.

At the end of 2018, the supermarket management has to decide about expansion in 2019 in Vilnius, or whether to continue as in 2018. If they decide to expand, the expected payoff in 2019 equals 0.4 *€650,000 + 0.45*€200,000 − 0.15*€150,000 = €327,500. This outcome is independent of the three economic conditions that might occur at the end of 2018. If they do not expand in 2019, and continue with the same single storage space in 2019 as in 2018, this will generate the same expected revenues of €137,000 in 2019 as in 2018.

In a scenario where the supermarket chain decided to open in Vilnius in 2018, the best decision is to expand the storage space in 2019, generating higher than expected revenues of €327,500. This is independent of the economic situation at the end of 2018. This means that the option to continue with the old store space in 2019 is no longer relevant. However, we still have to calculate the expected payoff for Vilnius for 2018 and 2019 and compare this value with the payoff for Kaunas over the two years. First, we sum the payoffs in 2018 for each economic situation and add the expected payoff for 2019.

(1) Economic conditions 2018 *good*: €500,000 (2018) + €327,500 (2019) = €827,500. The probability of good conditions is 15% → the expected payoff for both years is 0.15 * €827,500 = €124,125

(2) Economic conditions 2018 as *expected*: €200,000 (2018) + €327,500 (2019) = €527,500. The probability of economic conditions as expected is 55% → the expected payoff for both years 0.55 * €527.500 = €290,125

(3) Economic conditions 2018 *bad*: -€160,000 (2018) + €327,500 (2019) = €167,500. The probability of bad conditions is 30% → the expected payoff for both years 0.30 * €167,500 = €50,250.

So, the expected payoff at the start of 2018 for opening a store for 2 years in Vilnius is €124,125 + €290,125 + €50,250 = €464,500.

Investing at t=0 in Kaunas yields an expected payoff equal to 2 years * €166,000 = €332,000. This is less than the expected payoff for Vilnius. Opening a location in Vilnius in January 2018 and expanding this store in 2019 offers the highest payoff. If we *exclude* the expansion option in 2019, Kaunas has the highest expected payoff for a single year.

Designing a production and distribution network

Finding the best location to set up new production plants and distribution centres is an important element in the Supply Chain configuration. Responsiveness increases the closer a company is to its customers, but if customers are spread over the globe a large network of plants and DCs are needed at the cost of losing economies of scale. Setting up plants and DCs further away from major customers decreases responsiveness, but the company can look for locations with lower production costs, while shipment costs will increase because of the larger shipment distances to customers.

Using linear programming for capacity planning

We will now discuss a linear programming model to find the lowest cost solution for a combined production and distribution network consisting of N plants or factories and M distribution centres with storage space for that product. The plants are labelled i = 1,2, . . . , N and the distribution centres serving M different markets are labelled j = 1, 2, . . . , M.

The production cost per plant is different due to the differences in wage rates and other costs: the unit production cost is p_i with i = 1, 2, . . . , N, and the annual capacity per plant is indicated as Cap_i. Annual market demand is aggregated at the level of the DCs as D(j) with j = 1, 2, 3 . . . , M. Transportation costs per product from each plant to each DC are given as c_{ij} with index i and j the same interpretation as before. The variables are labelled X_{ij} and stand for the number of units produced in plant i and shipped to DC_j. The objective of the firm is to *minimize* the sum of all production and shipment costs per year (TC) under the condition that each DC receives what they order, and that production does not exceed plant capacity. The objective function is formulated as:

$$\text{Minimize } TC = \sum_{i=1}^{n} \sum_{j=1}^{m} (p_i + c_{ij}) * X_{ij}$$

Subject to the constraints:

Demand $\quad \sum_{i=1}^{N} X_{ij} \geq D(j) \qquad$ for j = 1, 2, 3 . . . . , M

Supply $\quad \sum_{j=1}^{M} X_{ij} \leq Cap(i) \qquad$ for i = 1, 2, 3 . . . . . N

$X_{ij} \geq 0$ for all i and j

The demand constraint states that the sum of all units received from all production plants by distribution centre *j* must be greater than or equal to the demand of distribution centre *j*.The supply or capacity constraint states that the sum of the units sent from plant *i* to all DCs must be smaller than or equal to the capacity of plant *i*. We will illustrate the model with an example using Excel's add-in *Solver*. Car manufacturer *People's Car plc* has four plants: in Sweden, in Russia, in Portugal, and in Sicily. It operates five DCs in Poland, Bulgaria, Italy, Jordan, and the United

Kingdom. All data about costs, demand, and capacity are shown in the table below, displayed in an Excel worksheet. The table below shows the shipment cost table as well as the combined production + shipment costs.

	A	B	C	D	E	F	G	H
1								
2	Shipment Cost table	Poland	Bulgaria	Italy	Jordan	United Kingdom	Plant capacity	Production cost per unit
3	Sweden	€ 57	€ 42	€ 45	€ 40	€ 57	13,397	€ 147
4	Russia	€ 60	€ 50	€ 44	€ 43	€ 48	14,756	€ 175
5	Portugal	€ 40	€ 49	€ 53	€ 53	€ 41	13,418	€ 138
6	Sicily	€ 52	€ 40	€ 43	€ 51	€ 42	14,138	€ 146
7								
8								
9	Production + shipment	Poland	Bulgaria	Italy	Jordan	United Kingdom		
10	Sweden	€ 204	€ 189	€ 192	€ 187	€ 204		
11	Russia	€ 235	€ 225	€ 219	€ 218	€ 223		
12	Portugal	€ 178	€ 187	€ 191	€ 191	€ 179		
13	Sicily	€ 198	€ 186	€ 189	€ 197	€ 188		

The screenshot of the sheet in formula view is shown below. The yellow cells are the variables that will be calculated by Solver.

	A	B	C	D	E	F	G	H
16	Quantity table	Poland	Bulgaria	Italy	Jordan	United Kingdom	Units sent	Plant capacity
17	Sweden	0	0	0	0	0	0	13,397
18	Russia	0	0	0	0	0	0	14,756
19	Portugal	0	0	0	0	0	0	13,418
20	Sicily	0	0	0	0	0	0	14,138
21	Units received	0	0	0	0	0		
22	Demand DC	10,701	11,661	10,161	10,163	12,600	Total capacity	55,709
23							Total demand	55,286
24								
25	Objective	€ 0						
26	Function							

Explanatory note

Cells B17:F20 are the quantity cells and are the variables in this problem. The row *Units Received* [17] is the sum of all units that each distribution centre receives from each of the four plants. This amount must be greater than or equal to the demand of the DC in the row below. The penultimate column [G] is the sum of units that each plant sends to each of the 5 DCs and this value cannot exceed the capacity of the plant shown in the column to the far right of the table [H]. The Objective function is shown as the *SUMPRODUCT* function from the Excel function library. It takes each cell from the *total cost* table (B10:F13) and multiplies it with the corresponding cell in the quantity table (B17:F20) and then sums all those products. In other words, this is the calculation for the total variable costs of the joint production and distribution plan. Once the data have been entered in Excel in this format, we can use Solver to find the optimal plan.

The objective cell refers to the cell containing the *SUMPRODUCT* function for the total costs (B25). The objective is to minimize the total costs in this objective function → we check in Solver *Min*. The first block of constraints (B21:F21) in the constraint box instructs Solver that the sum of units received per DC must be greater than or equal to the demand of each DC (B22:F22). The second block of constraints (G17:G20) instructs Solver that the sum of the units sent to the DCs may not exceed the plant capacity (H17:H20). The entire problem is linear, both in its objective function and in its constraints, and therefore the Solving method selected is *Simplex LP*. Finally, we instruct Solver that all variables must be non-negative and then click on OK. The result of the optimization is shown in the table below.

	A	B	C	D	E	F	G	H
						United		Plant
16	Quantity table	Poland	Bulgaria	Italy	Jordan	Kingdom	Units sent	capacity
17	Sweden	0	7,406	0	5,991	0	13,397	13,397
18	Russia	0	0	10,161	4,172	0	14,333	14,756
19	Portugal	10,701	0	0	0	2,717	13,418	13,418
20	Sicily	0	4,255	0	0	9,883	14,138	14,138
21	Units received	10,701	11,661	10,161	10,163	12,600		
22	Demand DC	10,701	11,661	10,161	10,163	12,600	Total capacity	55,709
23							Total demand	55,286
24								
25	Objective	€ 10,695,361						
26	Function							

If we take a look at the solution table, we notice the following: The units received per DC are the same as the demand. This is a direct effect of the cost minimization: each unit sent more than demanded pushes total costs upward, straying from the minimum. The plants in Portugal, Sicily, and Sweden work at full capacity, while Russia has some idle capacity, which is calculated as the difference between plant capacity and actual units sent. The total cost to achieve this least-cost plan is €10,695,361. At the bottom right there is a cell labelled *Capacity*, which is the sum of the capacities of the four plants; the cell labelled *Demand* is the sum of the demand of the five DCs. It is always a good preliminary check to see if total capacity is greater than total demand. If that is not the case, Solver will give an error message and there is no feasible solution.

Example 2

Company Melie AG manufactures washing machines at one plant in Munich, and they manage five major distribution centres in Europe – Stockholm, Maastricht, Warsaw, Vienna, and Sofia. The washing machines are shipped from the distribution centres to a network of retailers in Europe. Distribution costs include freight, handling, and warehousing costs. Demand (i.e. orders) is aggregated at the DC level.

To meet increased demand, the management of Melie AG has decided to build new plants, each with a capacity of 40,000 washing machines per month. After several feasibility studies, they must choose from three new potential plant locations: Malmö, Budapest, and Barcelona. The study also includes the option to shut down the plant in Munich. Data about the plant in Munich and the three potential new plants are given in the table below, together with shipment costs per washing machine from each plant to each DC.

In this example, the total demand is 62,000 machines and a total capacity of 147,000, which is far beyond the total expected demand. One of the options is to shut down one or two production plants and to centralize production in only two plants. In this decision problem, both fixed costs and total variable costs, consisting of production and distribution costs, are relevant in the cost minimization.[7]

This decision problem can be modelled by using *binary* variables (also called decision or dummy variables). Binary variables can only take on the values 0 (No) and 1 (Yes). In this example, we introduce four binary variables, one for each plant. If a plant is *not* used, Melie will *not* incur the fixed costs or have access to the capacity of that plant. By multiplying the fixed costs of each plant as well as its capacity with the associated binary variable only two solutions are possible: if Solver sets the binary variable to 0, there are no fixed costs and zero capacity. If Solver sets the binary to 1, Melie will incur the full fixed costs of that plant and has full access to its capacity.

	A	B	C	D	E	F	G	H	I
1	Plant Location								
2	Data				DC Locations				
3	Possible Plant	Fixed Costs	Stockholm	Maastricht	Warsaw	Vienna	Sofia	Capacity	Production cost per unit
4	Munich	€ 7,000	€ 0.42	€ 0.36	€ 0.41	€ 0.39	€ 0.50	27,000	€ 2.70
5	Malmö	€ 4,000	€ 0.46	€ 0.37	€ 0.30	€ 0.42	€ 0.43	40,000	€ 2.64
6	Budapest	€ 6,000	€ 0.44	€ 0.30	€ 0.37	€ 0.38	€ 0.45	40,000	€ 2.69
7	Barcelona	€ 7,000	€ 0.48	€ 0.45	€ 0.43	€ 0.46	€ 0.27	40,000	€ 2.62
8	Demand		10,000	15,000	16,000	19,000	12,000		
9									
10	Production and Distribution		Stockholm	Maastricht	Warsaw	Vienna	Sofia		
11	Munich		€ 3.12	€ 3.06	€ 3.11	€ 3.09	€ 3.20		
12	Malmö		€ 3.10	€ 3.01	€ 2.94	€ 3.06	€ 3.07		
13	Budapest		€ 3.13	€ 2.99	€ 3.06	€ 3.07	€ 3.14		
14	Barcelona		€ 3.10	€ 3.07	€ 3.05	€ 3.08	€ 2.89		

We will now discuss how to set up this problem in Excel and solve it with *Solver*. First, we recalculate the table with the shipment costs to a table with all variable costs by adding the production costs to shipping costs. In the table below we introduce *binary variables*, which are the cells in the column labeled "*In use*" while the shaded cells are the variable cells representing the units produced at each plant and shipped to each DC.

	A	B	C	D	E	F	G	H	I
19	Shipment	in use	Stockholm	Maastricht	Warsaw	Vienna	Sofia	units shipped	Capacity
20	Munich							=SUM(C20:G20)	=H4*B20
21	Malmö							=SUM(C21:G21)	=H5*B21
22	Budapest							=SUM(C22:G22)	=H6*B22
23	Barcelona							=SUM(C23:G23)	=H7*B23
24		Received	=SUM(C20:C23)	=SUM(D20:D23)	=SUM(E20:E23)	=SUM(F20:F23)	=SUM(G20:G23)		
25		Demand	=C8	=D8	=E8	=F8	=G8		

The column labelled *units shipped* is similar to that in the previous example and sums all units shipped from each plant to the five DCs. The column labelled *Capacity* is calculated by multiplying the cell with the binary variable (B-cells) with the cell containing the associated plants capacity (Column H).

The objective function is formulated as follows:

Objective	Costs
Fixed costs plants	=SUMPRODUCT(B20:B23;B4:B7)
Variable costs	=SUMPRODUCT(C11:G14;C20:G23)
Total costs	=C28+C29

The total fixed costs are computed using the *SUMPRODUCT* from the Excel function library by taking the binary variables as the second array (B4:B7) and the fixed costs per plant as the first array (B17:B20). The total variable costs are the *SUMPRODUCT* of each unit cost in the variable cost table (C11:G14) multiplied with the corresponding cell in the variable cost table (C17:G20). The last step is to sum the total fixed costs and variable costs. Now we enter all information into the Solver window, as shown in the screenshot below:

In the Objective line, we enter cell B27, which is the cell with the total costs and select *Min(imize)*. In the Variable Cells line, we enter all blank shipments cells plus the binary cells (B17:G20).[8] In the Constraint box, the third constraint H17:H20 is the supply constraint and tells Solver that this value must be smaller than or equal to the decision-linked capacity (I17:I20).

The second constraint is the demand constraint (C21:G21), which imposes the condition that each DC receives at least what they demand (C22:G22). The first constraint defines the variables (B17:B20) as binary. We require all variables to be non-negative and select the *Simplex LP* as Solving method. Clicking on <u>S</u>olve gives the optimal plan, as shown below.

	A	B	C	D	E	F	G	H	I
16	Shipment table	in use	Stockholm	Maastricht	Warsaw	Vienna	Sofia	units shipped	Capacity
17	Munich	0	0	0	0	0	0	0	0
18	Malmö	1	0	15,000	16,000	9,000	0	40,000	40,000
19	Budapest	0	0	0	0	0	0	0	0
20	Barcelona	1	10,000	0	0	10,000	12,000	32,000	40,000
21		Received	10,000	15,000	16,000	19,000	12,000		
22		Demand	10,000	15,000	16,000	19,000	12,000		
23									
24		Objective	Costs						
25		Fixed costs plants	€ 11,000						
26		Variable costs	€ 216,210						
27		Total costs	€ 227,210						

The solution shows that the Munich and Budapest plant will not be used and are assigned zero capacity and zero fixed costs. The entire production is concentrated in Malmö and Barcelona and from there is shipped to the five DCs at the lowest total cost of €227,210. The capacity in the Malmö plant is fully used and Barcelona still has an idle capacity of 8,000 units. All DCs receive exactly the number of washing machines they demanded. The example of Melie is an all-or-nothing example: either use the facility or do not use it. In the chapter exercises, you are invited to solve a more involved problem whereby the capacity of the facilities can be scaled down by a certain percentage instead of shutting it down completely.

Main Point: Decisions about investment capacity – whether to invest in new capacity, or to expand, shut down, or reduce capacity – can be modelled by using either decision trees or binary variables. Decision trees contain payoffs and probabilities linking decisions to events in order to model uncertainty about future outcomes. The other model is applying linear programming. In non-probabilistic situations, each possible capacity level is assigned a binary variable indicating that this capacity level is either chosen or not. This binary variable is then linked to capacity as well as to the fixed costs associated with that capacity level.

A general model for optimizing capacity decisions

We can extend the example above to a more general case. Let us assume that a company has N factories with capacity F_i and annual fixed costs of FC_i. They have divided their market into M regions and each region is supplied from one DC, where the demand D_j is regionally aggregated. Production and shipment costs from each factory i to each DC j are given as p_{ij}. The units shipped are indicated by X_{ij}. The binary variable to keep factory i open next year or to close it is called b_i. The problem is to find the lowest cost solution using linear programming. The model has the following structure:

Minimize $\sum_{i=1}^{N} FC_i * b_i + \sum_{i=1}^{N} \sum_{j=1}^{M} p_{ij} * X_{ij}$ First part is fixed and second part is variable costs

Subject to the constraints:

$\sum_{j=1}^{M} X_{ij} \leq F_i * b_i$ the supply constraint for each factory i = 1 up to N.

$\sum_{i=1}^{N} X_{ij} \geq D_j$ the demand constraint for each DC j = 1 up to M

$X_{ij} \geq 0$ for all i and j and b_i binary for all i.

This general model can easily be extended to also include Open-or-Close decisions for the distribution centres. New binary variables will then be assigned to the DCs to incorporate them in the distribution plan.

Location decisions based on gravity models[9]

Another quantitative model for selecting a plant location is the application of gravity models, whose main purpose is to minimize total transportation costs. The basic model uses geo-coordinates for a plant and the distribution centre location and calculates the geometric distances to either the customer location or from the location of suppliers of that facility, or both. The following symbols are used for each supply facility of market j: (L_j, W_j) are the map coordinates. C_j is the shipping cost per unit per kilometre between the plant and its customer or between the plant and its supplier j. Q_j is the quantity shipped *from* supplier j or *to* customer j coming from the plant location. The coordinates of the optimal plant location (L, W) are unknown and calculated. N facilities are served *from* the plant or send goods *to* the plant.

The Euclidean distance D_j between the plant and facility j
is $D_j = \sqrt{(L - L_j)^2 + (W - W_j)^2}$

The total transportation costs are $\qquad TC = \sum_{j=1}^{N} D_j * Q_j * C_j$

The solution of this gravity-based location model can easily be found with the aid of Solver. Select the cell containing the *Total Cost equation* as the objective function that has to be minimized. The cells containing (L, W) are the two variable cells of the optimal plant location. All data about the geo-coordinates, the unit shipment cost per kilometre, and the quantity data have to be stored in the cells of the Excel sheet. There are no further constraints except for selecting the GRG-nonlinear solving method and clicking on OK.

The gravity model provides only a good approximation when the shipments of goods can be done in a straight line, because that is how the distance D_j is calculated. That is seldom the case for road transport. For air transport, the model is a better approximation if the plant location is close to an airport and all facilities that are served are also located close to an airport. For maritime transportation, the model provides approximately good decisions in the case of open waters where marine vessels can sail in a straight line from A to B. For example, when the plant is located close to the seaport of an island and all customers and suppliers are also located in the proximity of seaports, so that the cargo ship can sail in a straight line from the island to the destination seaports. The model gives more weight in the objective function to large-volume customers than to small-volume customers or suppliers (Q_j).

Location decisions and geographic concentration of competitive suppliers.

Looking at a map displaying the dispersion of retail stores, one will notice that, in many cases, firms are located in densely populated areas that form their customer base – also called catchment area – but are also close to their competitors. Shopping malls and shopping centres are good examples of geographically concentrated retailers, but also firms operating in the service industry tend to locate their premises close to their competitors, creating clusters of competitive firms in concentrated areas.

Although it is not difficult to explain why retail stores establish themselves in their customers' neighbourhoods, it is not immediately evident that being close to your competitor is an efficient decision. A seminal paper published by the economist H. Hoteling[10] shows how competition among suppliers drives them to concentrate their firm's locations close to each other. We will illustrate his view with a simple numerical example of two ice cream vendors A and B, who have permission to locate themselves every summer day on a one-kilometre-long, straight stretch of beach. The beach tourists are evenly spread over the beach (equal people density or the same number of beach visitors per square metre) and every beach visitor is assumed to buy one ice cream every day from the vendor who is closest by. In other words, they minimize the walking distance to the vendor. Let us assume that this stretch of beach can accommodate 1,000 evenly spread beachgoers.

On the first day, the permit allows vendor A to places its ice cream stall on the far-left side of the beach (Location point 0) and the vendor B on the far-right side (Location point 1.000). Given the equal spread of all beachgoers, those from the extreme left up to the middle of the beach will go to vendor A (500 persons) and all beachgoers from the middle to the far-right side (500 persons) will go to vendor B. The market shares of both ice cream vendors are 50%. The minimum walking distance is approximately 0 for the visitors who are just next to the ice cream booth. The maximum is 500 metres for visitors in the middle of the beach. The *average* walking distance is

$$\sum_{i=1}^{500} i \ = \ 2*(\tfrac{1}{2}*500*499)/1,000 \ \approx 250 \text{ metres.}[11]$$

On the second day, vendor A moves its stall to the right, to the location point 250 metres, while vendor B remains on the same site. Consequently, all beach visitors lying between points 0 and 250 will go to vendor A. The distance between vendors A and B is now 1,000 − 250 metres = 750 metres. All beachgoers lying from 250 metres (location A) to location 250 + 750/2 = 625 metres will also go to vendor A.

All visitors from location point 625 to 1,000 metres, equal to 375 visitors, will go to vendor B. The market share of A is now 625/1,000 = 62.5% and for B 37.5%. A has won an additional market share of 12.5% at the expense of B (moving positions is a zero-sum game). The average walking distance for the beachgoers going to A has become

$$\frac{\sum_{i=1}^{250} i \ = \ \tfrac{1}{2}*250*249 + \sum_{i=1}^{375} i \ = \ \tfrac{1}{2}*375*374 + \sum_{i=1}^{375} i = \tfrac{1}{2}*375*374}{1.0000} \approx [31,125 \text{ (left of A)} + 70,125 \text{ (right}$$

of A) + 70,125 (left of B)]/1,000 visitors ≈ 171 metres.

Divided over A and B, the average walking distance of the beachgoers to vendor B is $(\tfrac{1}{2}*375*374)/375 \approx 187$ metres. On average, therefore, beachgoers must walk more in the new situation. The average walking distance to vendor A is approximately 162 metres.

On the *third* day, vendor B reacts to the movement of A by moving its stall from location point 1.000 to location point 750 metres. Consequently, all visitors lying on the stretch from 0 – 500 will go to A and all visitors from 501 – 1.000 will go to B. Market shares are back at 50%:50%. However, the average walking distance for the buyers from A has dropped to [½ *250*249]*2)/500 ≈ 125 metres, and this also holds for the average walking distance for the people going to B (the situation is again symmetrical). So, the overall average walking distance for all beachgoers is approximately 125 metres.

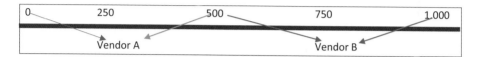

The optimal location is A at 250 metres and B at 750 metres. Market shares are 50%:50% and customers have the shortest average walking distance (125 metres) with a minimum distance of 0 and a maximum distance of 250 metres! Any other distribution of the locational of A and B, as long as it is symmetrical, will give equal market shares to A and B, but longer average walking distances for the consumers. If this shifting of locations continues, every metre that vendor A moves to the right, closer to the beach centre, will increase his market share at the cost of the market share of B. In response, B will move to the left, in the direction of the beach centre, to recapture its lost market share.

The process ends up in equilibrium when both vendors locate their stalls in the middle of the beach. All beachgoers will walk to the centre to buy ice cream and, assuming that they have no preference for either A or B – except the waiting time in the queue before the stall – market shares will be 50%:50%. However, the walking distances have changed. Given the symmetry of the situation whereby the distribution of beachgoers from 0 to 500 is the same as for beachgoers 501 to 1,000, we obtain an average walking distance of [½ * 500 * 499] / 500 ≈ 250 metres, which is the same as the day-one situation! However, this distance is more than the optimal situation with A located at 250 metres and B at 750 metres. The market shares were also 50%:50%, but the average walking distance for the beachgoers achieved its lowest value, namely, 125 metres.

Applying this centripetal settlement process to (urban) shopping centres, competition creates an incentive to locate retail stores in a concentrated shopping centre. In such a situation, equilibrium is achieved when none of the retailers has any further incentive to move to another location. However, as the example shows, this is not necessarily the optimal location for the customers, who are better off insofar as it affects their travel time due to the dispersed location of similar stores.

By looking at this concentration tendency from the perspective of urban planning purposes, to achieve an optimal retail store spread that minimizes the overall movement of city residents who want to buy their basic necessities, competing retailers, e.g. supermarkets, drugstores, DIY, clothing, restaurants, household, and electronic stores, will improve the situation for city residents by spreading these stores over multiple locations in a city, instead of concentrating all stores in one single central point, i.e. a shopping mall. This is a useful insight for urban planners in charge of issuing permits to establish retail stores in their city.

The theory of the dynamics of geographical concentration has many more applications. It has also been applied to explain the incredible range of product diversity in shops. Let us assume as an example that, initially, three retailers have a specialized product assortment. The first retail store sells sports shoes, the second retailer hiking shoes, and a third one skates. When the first retailer starts adding hiking shoes to his assortment, customers can go to the same place for sports and hiking shoes. The retailer selling hiking shoes will lose market share to the sports shoe retailers. In response, he will add sport shoes to his assortment to recapture his lost market share. When, later, the sports shop adds skates to its assortment, it will gain market share at the cost of the skates retailer. The skates retailer will add sports shoes to his assortment to recapture lost market share. The retailer with the hiking shoes will join the game and, in the long run, competition will drive all three stores to sell sports shoes, hiking shoes, and skates. *Specialization* evolves into *generalization* driven by competition. This phenomenon is also the major explanation for the growth of warehouses, super- and hypermarkets, Do-It-Yourself stores that combine a wide range of different products under the same roof, outcompeting stores that remain specialized in only one or a few products.

Location decisions and Geographic Information Systems (GIS)

A Geographic Information System (GIS) is a computer-supported system designed to store, map, integrate manipulate, and display spatial or geographic data. One of its many applications is finding an optimal location for building a plant or distribution centre, and for other planning purposes. Digital maps at the country level, regional level, or smaller spatial units, like cities or urban neighbourhoods, are the starting point of a GIS. These maps are composed using satellite images, aerial pictures, and other techniques used in cartographic and topological science. The maps often consist of several layers. A first map can consist of a basic layer with standard geographic data, like a street map, or a road map. A second layer can consist of population density data displayed on top of that map. A third layer can consist of socioeconomic data, such as the average income per capita.

Another GIS example is the first layer with basic geographic data with another layer on top displaying the distribution of retail stores on the map, so that the user sees in a bird's-eye view of the spatial density of, for example, food retailers in a certain area. Some countries make maps with zoning and land use plans, which enables a company to see quickly which sites are available as potential locations for building a plant, distribution centre, or opening a retail store. It is now also possible for GIS users to create their customized maps by placing self-collected data as a new layer on top of other layers. There are many software packages on the market to enter and manipulate data in a GIS.[12]

Capacity planning in a Supply Chain setting

Optimal capacity planning within a Supply Chain requires more sophisticated models than those previously described. The main goal in SC-setting is not to minimize the costs of a single firm and not even a group of firms in the SC, but to minimize the total costs of the capacity investment for the entire Supply Chain. Therefore, the consequences of a capacity decision on the costs of all other SC partners must be taken into account in the decision model. Due to the complexity of these models, they are beyond the scope of the book, and the reader is referred to specialized papers about this topic.[13]

Customer response time and location decisions for DCs: upcoming trends

In the first chapter, we discussed the inverse relation between customer response time and facility location. The closer a physical store or webshop distribution centre is to the customer, the shorter, in general, the customer response time, both in the case of a customer going to a physical store to buy a product and in the case that the product is shipped to the buyer location by an online retailer.

Many distribution centres and large stores, such as Do-It-Yourself stores, are located in suburban areas, business districts of cities, or even further away, where rental rates for premises are lower than in the densely populated, crammed, congested sprawling urban centres of the world's major cities. Urban planners and real-estate developers are seeking solutions to make more efficient use of the available industrial space in urban areas. Municipal administrations in charge of urban zoning plans can adjust the zoning areas to make new city land available for business areas. Existing industrial zones can be used more efficiently by building multistorey distribution centres, something that, up to now (2022), is seldom observed in business areas in most European countries and in the US, where land outside city centres is in relative abundance and is relatively cheap. Multistorey distribution centres, either built from scratch or by adding a new floor to existing distribution centres, are still in their infancy, but they bring facilities closer to the urban customer, reducing customer response time.

Notes

1-13   See Instructor's Manual

4 Production Planning in a Supply Chain

Production Planning in a Supply Chain

In the previous chapter, we discussed capacity planning as a strategic decision with a long-term scope. Production planning, by contrast, has a shorter horizon, ranging from medium- to short term, and is more detailed. Production planning is done by manufacturing companies and companies operating in the distribution sector, as well as in the service industry, where labour is the most important resource. The planning scale of the production volume can descend to the level of individual units. In business practices, the most common horizon for production planning is one year, normally disaggregated into months, but planning can also be done with a time horizon of a month, disaggregated into weeks or even days, and some companies even use a daily planning horizon divided into hours. The basic input data for each planning consists of demand forecast for the planning period under consideration, corporate inventory policy regarding safety and cycle stock levels, constraints imposed by regulations, and the external environment.

In microeconomic textbooks, production is described at an abstract level as a firm's output as a function of input factors, which are corporate resources or the production factors labour and capital. More recently, many economists add information such as Information Technology, market information, and other information as an input resource for companies. In business practice, there is less flexibility in adopting many combinations of input resources than assumed by production theory, due to all kinds of production constraints. There is a greater flexibility in the 21st century in terms of deploying resources, especially human resources, with the hiring of part-time and temporary workers, the relaxation of hiring and firing procedures for employees working under a permanent contract, and more.

The deployment of the asset *Plant, Property and Equipment (PPE)* – the main component of the capital resource – in the 21st century offers more flexibility than in previous times. Legal constructions like renting, leasing, outsourcing, and other business practices are drivers of this augmented flexibility. This flexibilization trend is not only seen in manufacturing environments, but also in the service sector. Flexibility allows for increased combinations of a company's resources allowing the management to select the lowest cost production from among all possible resource combinations while, at the same time, addressing the constraints. In this chapter, we will restrict ourselves to a discussion of a monthly planning model with a time horizon of one year. The different models we will discuss start with simple versions and are further developed into models of intermediate complexity. All models will be built and discussed first in algebraic relations and equations and then converted to Excel format for solving numerical examples.

Production Planning Model I

The following assumptions are made in the production planning model:
- the company has monthly demand forecasts;
- the production is labour-intensive, i.e. labour is the bottleneck in terms of either quantity or job qualifications, and all workers have a permanent employment contract.
- Workers always come to the manufacturing plant or factory and produce, even if demand is much lower than the planned production rate.
- Units that are produced but not sold in a particular month are added to the inventory.
- Wages are expressed on an hourly basis and are the same for all workers in the production plan.
- Labour regulations, set out in law or in collective labour agreements, constrain the maximum hours of overtime work. Overtime wage rates are higher than rates for regular working hours.
- The labour policy of the company is to maintain a fixed labour force in the planning year and will match peaks in demand by deploying overtime work.
- Machine capacity is sufficient and does not form a production bottleneck. For each unit produced the unit production costs given consist of all production cost categories except labour.
- Management wants to avoid stock-outs and all production takes place in-house.

Production and demand do not have to be synchronized over the months and inventory forms the buffer to meet monthly demand. The objective is to establish an annual production plan that meets demand at the lowest possible costs. The following symbols are used, with the index i for month i with i running from 1 to 12.

W_i = number of workers available in month i. With a fixed labour force $W_1 = W_2$ = W_3 = ... = W_{12}

wd = number of working days per month. It is constant for all months

wh = number of working hours per day. It is constant for all working days

S_{hr} = wage rate per hour during regular working time

S_{ho} = wage rate per hour during overtime

I_i = inventory level in month i

s = inventory cost to keep one unit in inventory for one month

Pr = productivity rate. The number of hours needed per product. The Pr is the same for all workers in all months.

mc = average production cost per product, excluding labour costs

P_i = the production volume in month i

D_i = the demand forecast for month i

O_i = the number of *hours* worked in overtime in month i

OT = the maximum number of overtime hours per worker, per month, in accordance with labour regulations

The model has three cost categories: labour; inventory; and production costs.
- monthly total labour costs are wd*wh*S_{hr}*W_i during *regular* working time plus O_i*S_{ho} during *overtime*.
- monthly inventory costs are s*I_i
- monthly production costs are mc*P_i

The planning model uses three monthly variables: the production rate per month; the monthly inventory; and the hours of overtime work. There are twelve months per year, so the total number of variables in the annual plan is 36. All other information is given with the parameters. The basic model has three monthly constraints yielding 36 constraints per year.
- The easiest *one* is the overtime (maximum) constraint: $O_i \leq OT$
- The *second* one is the capacity constraint (a maximum). This constraint states that no more units can be produced than the capacity per month. Given that labour in this model is the only bottleneck, capacity can be split into labour capacity during regular working time and labour capacity during overtime. During regular working time in month I, W_i workers work during wd days times wh hours per day. With a productivity rate of Pr labour hours per product, this translates to (W_i*wd*wh)/Pr *products per month* in regular working time. Monthly capacity in month i can be expanded with O_i/Pr units using overtime work. Total capacity in both regular working time and overtime becomes [W_i*wd*wh + O_i]/Pr
- The *third* constraint refers to inventory levels and is formulated as a balance constraint to keep consistency in the inventory flow from month to month. It starts with the beginning inventory at the start of the month and then adds the units produced, which, in this model, is only the monthly variable production P_i. The units leaving inventory are then subtracted, which equals monthly demand D_i plus ending inventory in that month. Expressed in symbols, the constraint equation reads: $I_{i-1} + P_i - D_i = I_i$

It is important to note that there is no inventory change in the transition from the end of month i-1 to the beginning of month i: the ending inventory of the previous month I_{i-1} automatically becomes the beginning inventory of the next month. We can rewrite the inventory equation as $I_{i-1} + P_i - D_i - I_i = 0$ for month i. I_i is always the inventory at the *end* of month i. We can now convert the monthly data and constraints into an annual planning model.

Objective function

$$\sum_{i=1}^{12}(wd * wh * S_{hr} * W_i) + \sum_{i=1}^{12}(S_{ho} * O_i) + \sum_{i=1}^{12}s * I_i + \sum_{i=1}^{12}mc * P_i$$

Constraint Overtime $O_i \leq OT * W_i$ for i = 1 until 12

Constraint Production capacity $P_i \leq \left[\frac{(W_i * wd * wh + O_i)}{Pr}\right]$ for i = 1 until 12

Inventory constraint $I_{i-1} + P_i - D_i - I_i = 0$ for i = 1 until 12

The planning variables are O_i, P_i, and I_i, together 36 variables, and they are used to achieve the lowest cost production plan. By looking at the objective function and the constraints, we note that they are all linear and that this planning problem is a *linear programming* problem that can be solved in Excel using Solver. The table below is an example with data about the Workforce, Demand, and total costs.

	A	B	C	D	E	F
1		**Workforce**	**Overtime**	**Inventory**	**Production**	**Demand**
2	t = 0	240		300		
3	January	240				3,816
4	February	240				3,842
5	March	240				2,240
6	April	240				3,662
7	May	240				3,496
8	June	240				3,256
9	July	240				7,840
10	August	240				3,730
11	September	240				3,254
12	October	240				3,970
13	November	240				3,472
14	December	240				3,818
15						46,395
16	**Cost table per cost category**					
17		**Workforce**	**Overtime**	**Inventory**	**Production**	
18	January	€ 760,320	€ 0	€ 0	€ 0	
19	February	€ 760,320	€ 0	€ 0	€ 0	
20	March	€ 760,320	€ 0	€ 0	€ 0	
21	April	€ 760,320	€ 0	€ 0	€ 0	
22	May	€ 760,320	€ 0	€ 0	€ 0	
23	June	€ 760,320	€ 0	€ 0	€ 0	
24	July	€ 760,320	€ 0	€ 0	€ 0	
25	August	€ 760,320	€ 0	€ 0	€ 0	
26	September	€ 760,320	€ 0	€ 0	€ 0	
27	October	€ 760,320	€ 0	€ 0	€ 0	
28	November	€ 760,320	€ 0	€ 0	€ 0	
29	December	€ 760,320	€ 0	€ 0	€ 0	
30	Annual Cost	€ 9,123,840	€ 0	€ 0	€ 0	
31						
32	**Objective**	**€ 9,123,840**				

	G	H	I	J
1		Constraints		
2		Overtime	Inventory	Capacity
3		3,360	-3,516	4,224
4		3,360	-3,842	4,224
5		3,360	-2,240	4,224
6		3,360	-3,662	4,224
7		3,360	-3,496	4,224
8		3,360	-3,256	4,224
9		3,360	-7,840	4,224
10		3,360	-3,730	4,224
11		3,360	-3,254	4,224
12		3,360	-3,970	4,224
13		3,360	-3,472	4,224
14		3,360	-3,818	4,224
15	Total Demand			50,688
16				Total Capacity
17	Input data			
18	Workforce 1/1	240		
19	Workdays per month	22		
20	Work hours per day	8		
21	Wage rate regular time	€ 18	per hour	
22	Wage rate overtime	€ 24	per hour	
23	Inventory cost	€ 150	per month per unit	
24	Production cost	€ 56	per unit	
25	Productivity rate	10	hours per unit	
26	Beginning inventory 1/1	300	units	
27	Targeted ending inventory 31/12	300	units	
28	Maximum overtime per worker	14	per month	
29				
30				
31				
32				

The input data are shown in the Excel screenshot above. The upper-left block contains the variables used in this problem. The lower-left block in the screenshot is the cost table, in which each variable cell is multiplied by its unit costs. The upper-right part of the screenshot contains the three constraints for overtime, inventory, and total capacity. The lower-right block contains the input parameters for the planning. The formulas in the constraint cells and the cost table cells are shown in the screenshots *below*: Cell H18 contains the workforce; cell H26 is the cell with the beginning inventory; cell B3 is the fixed workforce; cell H19 is the # of workdays; cell H20 is the # of work hours; and cell H21 is the hourly wage rate during regular working time. C3 is the variable monthly overtime and H22 is the hourly wage rate during overtime. Cell D3 is the monthly inventory and H23 is the monthly inventory cost per unit. Cell E6 is monthly production and H24 unit production cost per unit. The inventory balance constraint reads for each month: Beginning inventory + Production – Demand – Ending inventory and will be set in Solver equal to 0.

	A	B	C	D	E	F
1		Workforce	Overtime	Inventory	Production	Demand
2	t = 0	=$H$18		=H26		
3	January	=$H$18				3816
4	February	=$H$18				3841,6
5	March	=$H$18				2240
6	April	=$H$18				3662,4
7	May	=$H$18				3496
8	June	=$H$18				3256
9	July	=$H$18				7840
10	August	=$H$18				3729,6
11	September	=$H$18				3254,4
12	October	=$H$18				3969,6
13	November	=$H$18				3472
14	December	=$H$18				3817,6
15						=SUM(F3:F14)
16	Cost table per cost category					
17		Workforce	Overtime	Inventory	Production	
18	January	=B3*$H$19*$H$20*$H$21	=C3*$H$22	=D3*$H$23	=E3*$H$24	
19	February	=B4*$H$19*$H$20*$H$21	=C4*$H$22	=D4*$H$23	=E4*$H$24	
20	March	=B5*$H$19*$H$20*$H$21	=C5*$H$22	=D5*$H$23	=E5*$H$24	
21	April	=B6*$H$19*$H$20*$H$21	=C6*$H$22	=D6*$H$23	=E6*$H$24	
22	May	=B7*$H$19*$H$20*$H$21	=C7*$H$22	=D7*$H$23	=E7*$H$24	
23	June	=B8*$H$19*$H$20*$H$21	=C8*$H$22	=D8*$H$23	=E8*$H$24	
24	July	=B9*$H$19*$H$20*$H$21	=C9*$H$22	=D9*$H$23	=E9*$H$24	
25	August	=B10*$H$19*$H$20*$H$21	=C10*$H$22	=D10*$H$23	=E10*$H$24	
26	September	=B11*$H$19*$H$20*$H$21	=C11*$H$22	=D11*$H$23	=E11*$H$24	
27	October	=B12*$H$19*$H$20*$H$21	=C12*$H$22	=D12*$H$23	=E12*$H$24	
28	November	=B13*$H$19*$H$20*$H$21	=C13*$H$22	=D13*$H$23	=E13*$H$24	
29	December	=B14*$H$19*$H$20*$H$21	=C14*$H$22	=D14*$H$23	=E14*$H$24	
30	Annual Cost	=SUM(B18:B29)	=SUM(C18:C29)	=SUM(D18:D29)	=SUM(E18:E29)	

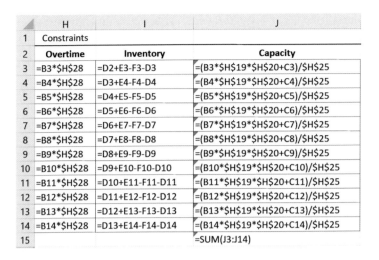

	H	I	J
1	Constraints		
2	Overtime	Inventory	Capacity
3	=B3*$H$28	=D2+E3-F3-D3	=(B3*$H$19*$H$20+C3)/$H$25
4	=B4*$H$28	=D3+E4-F4-D4	=(B4*$H$19*$H$20+C4)/$H$25
5	=B5*$H$28	=D4+E5-F5-D5	=(B5*$H$19*$H$20+C5)/$H$25
6	=B6*$H$28	=D5+E6-F6-D6	=(B6*$H$19*$H$20+C6)/$H$25
7	=B7*$H$28	=D6+E7-F7-D7	=(B7*$H$19*$H$20+C7)/$H$25
8	=B8*$H$28	=D7+E8-F8-D8	=(B8*$H$19*$H$20+C8)/$H$25
9	=B9*$H$28	=D8+E9-F9-D9	=(B9*$H$19*$H$20+C9)/$H$25
10	=B10*$H$28	=D9+E10-F10-D10	=(B10*$H$19*$H$20+C10)/$H$25
11	=B11*$H$28	=D10+E11-F11-D11	=(B11*$H$19*$H$20+C11)/$H$25
12	=B12*$H$28	=D11+E12-F12-D12	=(B12*$H$19*$H$20+C12)/$H$25
13	=B13*$H$28	=D12+E13-F13-D13	=(B13*$H$19*$H$20+C13)/$H$25
14	=B14*$H$28	=D13+E14-F14-D14	=(B14*$H$19*$H$20+C14)/$H$25
15			=SUM(J3:J14)

In the Solver window cell B32, which contains the objective function, is selected for minimization. The variables are cells C3:E14, which are the 12 overtime cells, 12 inventory cells, and the 12 monthly production cells.

In the Constraints box, the first line says that the variable hour's overtime (C3:C14) must be smaller than or equal to what is allowed (H3:H14). The second line says that the ending inventory (D14) must be equal to its targeted value (H27).

The constraint in line three says that the monthly production (E3:E14) must be smaller than or equal to the total monthly capacity (J3:J14). The fourth line is the inventory constraint and says that the balance equation (I3:I14) must be equal to 0, as discussed in the description about inventory in the production plan.

The optimal production planning is shown in the screenshot below:

	A	B	C	D	E	F
1		Workforce	Overtime	Inventory	Production	Demand
2	t = 0	240		300		
3	January	240	0	0	3,516	3,816
4	February	240	0	0	3,842	3,842
5	March	240	0	350	2,590	2,240
6	April	240	0	912	4,224	3,662
7	May	240	3,360	1,976	4,560	3,496
8	June	240	3,360	3,280	4,560	3,256
9	July	240	3,360	0	4,560	7,840
10	August	240	0	0	3,730	3,730
11	September	240	0	0	3,254	3,254
12	October	240	0	0	3,970	3,970
13	November	240	0	0	3,472	3,472
14	December	240	0	300	4,118	3,818
15						46,395
16	Cost table per cost category					
17		Workforce	Overtime	Inventory	Production	
18	January	€ 760,320	€ 0	€ 0	€ 196,896	
19	February	€ 760,320	€ 0	€ 0	€ 215,130	
20	March	€ 760,320	€ 0	€ 52,560	€ 145,062	
21	April	€ 760,320	€ 0	€ 136,800	€ 236,544	
22	May	€ 760,320	€ 80,640	€ 296,400	€ 255,360	
23	June	€ 760,320	€ 80,640	€ 492,000	€ 255,360	
24	July	€ 760,320	€ 80,640	€ 0	€ 255,360	
25	August	€ 760,320	€ 0	€ 0	€ 208,858	
26	September	€ 760,320	€ 0	€ 0	€ 182,246	
27	October	€ 760,320	€ 0	€ 0	€ 222,298	
28	November	€ 760,320	€ 0	€ 0	€ 194,432	
29	December	€ 760,320	€ 0	€ 45,000	€ 230,586	
30	Annual Cost	€ 9,123,840	€ 241,920	€ 1,022,760	€ 2,598,131	
31						
32	Objective	€ 12,986,651				

	G	H	I	J
1		Constraints		
2		Overtime	Inventory	Capacity
3		3,360	0	4,224
4		3,360	0	4,224
5		3,360	0	4,224
6		3,360	0	4,224
7		3,360	0	4,560
8		3,360	0	4,560
9		3,360	0	4,560
10		3,360	0	4,224
11		3,360	0	4,224
12		3,360	0	4,224
13		3,360	0	4,224
14		3,360	0	4,224
15	Total Demand			51,696
16				Total Capacity
17	Input data			
18	Workforce 1/1	240		
19	Workdays per month	22		
20	Work hours per day	8		
21	Wage rate regular time	€ 18	per hour	
22	Wage rate overtime	€ 24	per hour	
23	Inventory cost	€ 150	per month per unit	
24	Production cost	€ 56	per unit	
25	Productivity rate	10	hours per unit	
26	Beginning inventory 1/1	300	units	
27	Targeted ending inventory 31/12	300	units	
28	Maximum overtime per worker	14	per month	

Explanatory notes

First, we inspect to see if all constraints are met: all monthly inventory balance constraints are indeed 0, the production column is smaller than or equal to the capacity in regular plus overtime for all months. The variable overtime for all months is smaller than or equal to the allowed overtime hours. The ending inventory in December is 300 units, as required.

A closer look at the production plan shows that, in January, 3,516 units are produced in regular working time with a demand of 3,816 units. The difference comes from the beginning inventory and, consequently, the ending inventory is 0. In May, for example, 4,560 units are produced, of which a maximum of 3,360/10 = 336 units in overtime. Demand is 3,496 units the balance equation gives 912 +

4,560 – 3,816 = 1,976 units in ending inventory. The build-up of inventory, partly in overtime, can be explained by the forecasted demand peak of 7,840 units in July, when capacity is far too low to meet this monthly demand. Therefore, capacity in the months before July is used to build up inventory to meet the July demand. The total cost of production and storage is €12,986,651. There is a trade-off in costs in months with peak demand: either move production from regular time to overtime at incremental costs of 10 hours * (€24 – €18) = €60 per unit; or, produce a month earlier during regular working time and then store it in inventory at €150 per month. Inventorying units is much more expensive, so Solver will first look to shift production from the cheaper, regular working time to overtime. When overtime reaches its maximum, it will shift production to preceding months and store them in inventory until needed to meet demand.

Extending the model with subcontracting and deploying a flexible workforce

We now introduce two new options in the planning example in order to reduce the costs of the production plan. The first is *subcontracting.* In the case of subcontracting, the company will search for another company that can manufacture the product according to the standards established by the commissioning firm. The subcontractor will charge the company a price, but the company will save variable production costs. The units produced by the subcontractor are *added* to inventory and be sold in months with high demand. The new inventory constraint will be modified to include units subcontracted, indicated by the symbol S_i.

Inventory constraint: $I_{i-1} + P_i + S_i - D_i - I_i = 0$ for $I = 1$ until 12

We also insert a new column in the variables table with the monthly variable units subcontracted (S_i). In the cost table, we insert a column with monthly subcontracting equal to $S_i {}^* s$, with s the price the subcontractor charges for producing one unit.

The next option to smooth monthly production and reduce production costs is the flexibilization of the workforce. During the economic crisis in the early 21st century, several European companies wanted to lay off part of their employees, but rigid labour laws protected the position of workers, making it difficult to fire them. Consequently, a labour construction contract was designed, whereby former employees converted their labour status to the category of *self-employed without staff* (Dutch: ZZPer) or freelancer. They then offered their job services again on the labour market as a freelancer, but now they were able to set their hourly wage rate.

The employer, who, in the old situation, paid fixed salaries with the concomitant social premiums, now paid the worker a wage rate based on hours worked.[1] In many cases, the employer also had to pay for mediation costs to a job broker to contract a suitable freelancer, as well as to end the freelance contract once the job had been completed. To incorporate this labour flexibility into the production planning, the monthly workforce now becomes variable and two new monthly variables are introduced: workers hired for month I (H_i) with a fixed *hiring* fee and workers fired during month I (F_i) with a fixed *firing* fee. The hourly wage rate paid to the flexible workforce is the same for regular working time as it is for overtime, as in the case of a fixed workforce. Monthly overtime restrictions are the same for all workers and all months. Using a flexible workforce policy requires a new workforce constraint to maintain consistency over the months. This workforce constraint is similar to the inventory constraint. It says that the workforce at the start of the month plus workers hired minus workers fired equals the workforce at the end of the month.

Expressed as a formula:

Workforce constraint: $W_{i-1} + H_i - F_i - W_i = 0$ for $I = 1$ until 12

We return to our example and add the two new features into the model shown in the Excel screenshots below.

	Persons hired	Persons fired	Workforce	Overtime	Inventory	Production	units subcontracted	Demand		Constraints			
											Overtime	Inventory	Capacity	Workforce
t = 0			240		300						0	-3,516	0	240
January								3,816			0	-3,842	0	0
February								3,842			0	-2,240	0	0
March								2,240			0	-3,662	0	0
April								3,662			0	-3,496	0	0
May								3,496			0	-3,256	0	0
June								3,256			0	-7,840	0	0
July								7,840			0	-3,730	0	0
August								3,730			0	-3,254	0	0
September								3,254			0	-3,970	0	0
October								3,970			0	-3,472	0	0
November								3,472			0	-3,818	0	0
December								3,818						0
								46,395					Total Capacity	

Cost table per cost category

	Hiring costs	Firing costs	Workforce	Overtime	Inventory	Production	Subcontracting		Input data	
January	€ 0	€ 0	€ 0	€ 0	€ 0	€ 0	€ 0		Workforce 1/1	240
February	€ 0	€ 0	€ 0	€ 0	€ 0	€ 0	€ 0		Workdays per month	22
March	€ 0	€ 0	€ 0	€ 0	€ 0	€ 0	€ 0		Work hours per day	8
April	€ 0	€ 0	€ 0	€ 0	€ 0	€ 0	€ 0		Wage rate regular time	€ 18 per hour
May	€ 0	€ 0	€ 0	€ 0	€ 0	€ 0	€ 0		Wage rate overtime	€ 24 per hour
June	€ 0	€ 0	€ 0	€ 0	€ 0	€ 0	€ 0		Inventory cost	€ 150 per month per unit
July	€ 0	€ 0	€ 0	€ 0	€ 0	€ 0	€ 0		Production cost	€ 56 per unit
August	€ 0	€ 0	€ 0	€ 0	€ 0	€ 0	€ 0		Productivity rate	10 hours per unit
September	€ 0	€ 0	€ 0	€ 0	€ 0	€ 0	€ 0		Beginning inventory 1/1	300 units
October	€ 0	€ 0	€ 0	€ 0	€ 0	€ 0	€ 0		Targeted ending inventory 31/12	300 units
November	€ 0	€ 0	€ 0	€ 0	€ 0	€ 0	€ 0		Maximum overtime per worker	14 per month
December	€ 0	€ 0	€ 0	€ 0	€ 0	€ 0	€ 0		Subcontracting price	€ 280 per unit
Annual Cost	€ 0	€ 0	€ 0	€ 0	€ 0	€ 0	€ 0		Cost hiring	€ 500 per person
									Cost firing (severance payments)	€ 700 per person

Objective   € 0

All shaded cells are variables with the first two columns and the column *Subcontracting* inserted. In the cost table, each variable is multiplied by its corresponding unit costs: *Persons Hired* with the hiring cost; *Persons Fired* with the firing cost; and

Subcontracting with the subcontracting price. The cell in the *Inventory* constraint is modified to =F2+G3+H3-I3-F3 in January. This formula is then copied to the other months: F2 is beginning inventory; G3 is production in January; H3 is units subcontracted in January; I3 is January demand; and F3 is January's ending inventory.

The cell in the *Workforce* constraint for January reads =D2+B3-C3-D3 with D2 the starting workforce, B3 persons hired in January, C3 persons fired in January, and D3 the ending workforce of January.[2] The objective function is the sum of all annual cost categories. The screenshot of the Solver window is shown below:

The cell with the adjusted objective function is still B32 and will be minimized. The variable list is B3:H14 and contains all shaded cells. The first line in the Constraint box says that Overtime (E3:E14) must be smaller than or equal to what is allowed K3:K14.[3] The second line says that the ending inventory for December (F14) must be equal to the targeted value (K27). The third line says that the in-house production (G3:G14) must be smaller than their in-house capacity. (M3:M14). The fourth line says the monthly inventory balance constraint must equal 0 and the last line, the workforce balance constraint, must equal 0. The problem is linear in its objective function and all its constraints and therefore *Simplex LP* is selected. The screenshot of the Solver window and the least-cost production plan is shown below.

	A	B Persons hired	C Persons fired	D Workforce	E Overtime	F Inventory	G Production	H subcontracted	I Demand
2	t = 0			240		300			
3	January	0	40	200	0	0	3,516	0	3,816
4	February	0	0	200	0	0	3,516	326	3,842
5	March	0	72	127	0	0	2,240	0	2,240
6	April	71	0	199	0	0	3,496	166	3,662
7	May	0	0	199	0	0	3,496	0	3,496
8	June	0	14	185	0	0	3,256	0	3,256
9	July	27	0	212	0	0	3,730	4,110	7,840
10	August	0	0	212	0	0	3,730	0	3,730
11	September	0	27	185	0	0	3,254	0	3,254
12	October	12	0	197	0	0	3,472	498	3,970
13	November	0	0	197	0	0	3,472	0	3,472
14	December	37	0	234	0	300	4,118	0	3,818
15									46,395

16	Cost table per cost category							
17		Hiring costs	Firing costs	Workforce	Overtime	Inventory	Production	Subcontracting
18	January	€ 0	€ 28,159	€ 632,880	€ 0	€ 0	€ 196,896	€ 0
19	February	€ 0	€ 0	€ 632,880	€ 0	€ 0	€ 196,896	€ 91,168
20	March	€ 0	€ 50,750	€ 403,200	€ 0	€ 0	€ 125,440	€ 0
21	April	€ 35,682	€ 0	€ 629,280	€ 0	€ 0	€ 195,776	€ 46,592
22	May	€ 0	€ 0	€ 629,280	€ 0	€ 0	€ 195,776	€ 0
23	June	€ 0	€ 9,545	€ 586,080	€ 0	€ 0	€ 182,336	€ 0
24	July	€ 13,455	€ 0	€ 671,328	€ 0	€ 0	€ 208,858	€ 1,150,912
25	August	€ 0	€ 0	€ 671,328	€ 0	€ 0	€ 208,858	€ 0
26	September	€ 0	€ 18,900	€ 585,792	€ 0	€ 0	€ 182,246	€ 0
27	October	€ 6,182	€ 0	€ 624,960	€ 0	€ 0	€ 194,432	€ 139,328
28	November	€ 0	€ 0	€ 624,960	€ 0	€ 0	€ 194,432	€ 0
29	December	€ 18,341	€ 0	€ 741,168	€ 0	€ 45,000	€ 230,586	€ 0
30	Annual Cost	€ 73,659	€ 107,355	€ 7,433,136	€ 0	€ 45,000	€ 2,312,531	€ 1,428,000
31								
32	Objective	€ 11,399,681						

	J	K	L	M	N
1		Constraints			
2		Overtime	Inventory	Capacity	Workforce
3		2,797	0	3,516	0
4		2,797	0	3,516	0
5		1,782	0	2,240	0
6		2,781	0	3,496	0
7		2,781	0	3,496	0
8		2,590	0	3,256	0
9		2,967	0	3,730	0
10		2,967	0	3,730	0
11		2,589	0	3,254	0
12		2,762	0	3,472	0
13		2,762	0	3,472	0
14		3,275	0	4,118	0
15				41,295	
16				Total Capacity	
17	Input data				
18	Workforce 1/1	240			
19	Workdays per month	22			
20	Work hours per day	8			
21	Wage rate regular time	€ 18	per hour		
22	Wage rate overtime	€ 24	per hour		
23	Inventory cost	€ 150	per month per unit		
24	Production cost	€ 56	per unit		
25	Productivity rate	10	hours per unit		
26	Beginning inventory 1/1	300	units		
27	Targeted ending inventory 31/12	300	units		
28	Maximum overtime per worker	14	per month		
29	Subcontracting price	€ 280	per unit		
30	Cost hiring	€ 500	per person		
31	Cost firing (severance payments)	€ 700	per person		

We can draw some conclusions by taking a look at the solution. The first conclusion refers to the total cost. We used the same input data in this extended model as in the restricted model, but by adding the options of a flexible workforce and subcontracting we offer Solver a larger solution set. This implies that the optimal solution of the extended model can never be worse than the restricted model I, keeping all other circumstances equal. Indeed, the total costs of €11,399,681 are less than €12,986,651. We also notice that no overtime or inventory build-up is used. Making use of the flexible workforce and subcontracting is cheaper than producing in overtime or keeping products in stock.

Adding more variations to the production planning model

The model used in the previous examples is relatively simple and uses aggregate data as input and output. For the planning of day-to-day operations, aggregate numbers relating to the workforce have to be converted into individual workers with names, to scheduling hours per day, and all kinds of personalized restrictions and preferences, such as vacation days, part-time or full-time workers, leave days, etc. must be taken into account for each worker. Some of the assumptions, for example, that all workers earn the same hourly wage rate and have the same productivity rate, are rather naïve and should be differentiated at the individual level.

Personnel scheduling software – called staff planning or human resource scheduling – can schedule production activities per hour, per person, and location. However, the production planning model is very flexible, and all kinds of restrictions can be incorporated into the planning. In our second example, the number of units subcontracted is not limited. If the subcontractor has limited capacity, it is very easy to introduce a new constraint that takes into account limited subcontracting facilities, even broken down per month: $S_i \leq C_i$ putting a cap on S_i for $I = 1$ until 12.

Another feature refers to the inventory. In the examples, the company only targeted a fixed number of ending inventory in December. If the inventory manager wants to maintain a minimum stock each month to keep safety inventory, this restriction can be added by introducing $I_i \geq I_{safety}$ in the Constraint box in Solver.

The two examples were applied to a single product, which is a rather simplistic situation, because most companies produce a range of similar products on the same production line, e.g. a car manufacturer may produce four different car models on the same line, or a clothing manufacturer may use the same production line to produce trousers with ten different waist- and length sizes and ten different colours. Multiproduct planning can also be included in the production model without sophisticated model adjustments.

Production planning in a competitive environment

Up to now, we have focused on planning using production costs and demand forecasts. We have not taken into consideration the selling price to calculate the revenues and the profits of the least-cost production plan. Now, we will discuss a profit-maximizing – and not a cost-minimizing – production plan. To achieve this, we outline the price setting of the company. In a situation where the company does not have serious competition, the sales manager can fix the selling price for all forecasted demand during the year.

Most companies, however, operate in a competitive environment and they cannot set a price without taking into consideration the selling price of competitors. Demand forecasts in competitive markets are based on an individual company's selling price, but also on the market prices of competitors. This is especially the case for consumer products sold in many different stores, ranging from food retailers, electronic retailers, drugstores, and many more. Besides facing competition from other store chains with a physical presence, they also face competition from online stores selling the same product. Changing a price for a price promotion or by offering a discount can sometimes have unexpected positive or negative effects, but a price discount by a competitor can also critically impact the sales of the company that does *not* change its price. The responses to a price discount – and the same holds for price increases, as a mirror image – can be summarized in three potential market reactions:

The *first* reaction is that a price discount creates a *larger market size*: by lowering a price, consumers who were previously unwilling to pay for the product may now be willing to buy it. Total market demand goes up and this upswing in demand will benefit all suppliers of the same product selling at the lower price.

The *second* effect is called *stealing market share*. If retailer A drops its price, some customers of retailer B selling the same product will reject their old retailer and go to the cheaper competitor B. These customers planned to buy the product anyhow, but select the cheapest supplier. Sales of retailer A will go up to the detriment of the sales of retailer B. Stealing market share is a zero-sum game among competitors operating in the same industry.

The *third* effect is *forward buying*. A customer who planned to buy the product, e.g. an electric bike, in September from retailer A being informed that retailer A has a price discount in July will shift his purchase forward to July. The total demand of retailer A will go up in the month with the price discount and drop in later months. On average, the demand will remain constant over the year but is only reallocated over the months. Forward buying is a zero-sum game over time for a single company.

We can illustrate a profit-maximizing production planning using the same input data as in the first example. We call our firm *Ilda* and assume that she has only one main competitor, called *C4*. The market price for their common product is €410 – the base price – and if one of the two firms engages in a price promotion, the sales price is discounted to €390 for one month. After that month, the price returns to the base level. We set up a game-based payoff table to mimic the effect of the price discount and to consider possible price reactions by the competitor. The percentages given refer to the demand forecast of the month of the price discount and show the impact on *Ilda*.

Units sold in discount month	C4 discounts in month X	C4 does NOT discount
Ilda discounts in month X	+4%	+5,5%
Ilda does NOT discount	-5%	0%

In addition to the sales changes in the table, Ilda also knows from their sales records that a discount in month X will trigger forward buying: in month (X+1) +18% demand shifts to month X. In month (X+2) +4% of the demand shifts to month X. In month (X +1) demand drops by 18% and in month (X+2) by 4%.

In summary, if Ilda engages in a price discount in month X her sales will go up, due to either total market growth and/or increased market share, depending on the reaction of C4, plus 2 months of forward buying. The list with variables and constraints is the same as in Example I. The Objective function is adjusted to convert it into a profit cell by subtracting total production costs from total revenues (price times demand). Total revenues are calculated in Excel as the *SUMPRODUCT* of the demand column times the price column. Total annual production costs are calculated in the same way as in the first example. The Excel formulas of the Objective function are shown below. (F3:F14) is the demand column and (G3:G14) the price column and (B30:E30) the sum of the annual production costs.

Objective

Annual Revenues	=SUMPRODUCT(F3:F14;G3:G14)
Annual Production Costs	=SUM(B30:E30)
Annual Profit	=B33-B34

If we instruct Solver to maximize the Profit cell in the situation that neither of the two firms will discount the price, Ilda's total profit becomes €19,022.032 and the total production cost €12,986,651. This €12,986,651 is the same number we obtained in the total production cost minimization of Example I. The production variables also have the same values as in Example I. Maximizing profit or minimizing cost under the condition of fixed selling price during the year yields the *same* outcome.

Scenario II

Ilda discounts her price to €390 in June (= month X) and C4 does NOT discount. In the Excel sheet, we change the price cell of June to €390. The demand of June becomes [100% + 5,5%]*3.256 units of June + 18% of 7.840 units of July + 4% of 3.730 units of August= 4.735 units. The demand for July becomes [100 – 18%) * 7.840 units

= 6.429 units and the August demand [100 − 4%]*3.739 = 3.581 units. A screenshot of the profit-maximizing plan is shown below in the Excel formula view.

	A	B	C	D	E	F	G
1	Ilda	Workforce	Overtime	Inventory	Production	Demand	Selling price
2	t = 0	=$I$18		=I26			
3	January	=$I$18	0	0	3516	3816	=$I$29
4	February	=$I$18	0	0	3841,6	3841,6	=$I$29
5	March	=$I$18	0	418,695999996333	2658,69599999633	2240	=$I$29
6	April	=$I$18	0	980,295999996333	4224	3662,4	=$I$29
7	May	=$I$18	3360	2044,29599999756	4560,00000000122	3496	=$I$29
8	June	=$I$18	3360	1868,79999999878	4560,00000000122	=3256*(1+0,055)+F9*I30+F10*I31	390
9	July	=$I$18	3360	0	4560,00000000122	=(1-I30)*7840	=$I$29
10	August	=$I$18	0	0	3580,8	=(1-I31)*3730	=$I$29
11	September	=$I$18	0	0	3254,4	3254,4	=$I$29
12	October	=$I$18	0	0	3969,6	3969,6	=$I$29
13	November	=$I$18	0	0	3472	3472	=$I$29
14	December	=$I$18	0	300	4117,6	3817,6	=$I$29
15							

	I	J	K
	Constraints		
	Overtime	Inventory	Capacity
	=B3*$I$28	=D2+E3-F3-D3	=(B3*$I$19*$I$20+C3)/$I$25
	=B4*$I$28	=D3+E4-F4-D4	=(B4*$I$19*$I$20+C4)/$I$25
	=B5*$I$28	=D4+E5-F5-D5	=(B5*$I$19*$I$20+C5)/$I$25
	=B6*$I$28	=D5+E6-F6-D6	=(B6*$I$19*$I$20+C6)/$I$25
	=B7*$I$28	=D6+E7-F7-D7	=(B7*$I$19*$I$20+C7)/$I$25
	=B8*$I$28	=D7+E8-F8-D8	=(B8*$I$19*$I$20+C8)/$I$25
	=B9*$I$28	=D8+E9-F9-D9	=(B9*$I$19*$I$20+C9)/$I$25
	=B10*$I$28	=D9+E10-F10-D10	=(B10*$I$19*$I$20+C10)/$I$25
	=B11*$I$28	=D10+E11-F11-D11	=(B11*$I$19*$I$20+C11)/$I$25
	=B12*$I$28	=D11+E12-F12-D12	=(B12*$I$19*$I$20+C12)/$I$25
	=B13*$I$28	=D12+E13-F13-D13	=(B13*$I$19*$I$20+C13)/$I$25
	=B14*$I$28	=D13+E14-F14-D14	=(B14*$I$19*$I$20+C14)/$I$25
			=SUM(K3:K14)

Notice that the optimal production plan is not the same as in Example I, but nor are there large differences. If we optimize profit for the four different interaction strategies between Ilda and C4 we get the following payoff table, shown below:

Profit Ilda	C4 discounts	C4 does not discount
Ilda discounts	€6,068,627	€6,093,119
Ilda does not discount	€6,051,151	€6,035,522

If Ilda decides to discount in June her expected profits depend on the reaction of C4: €6,068,627 if C4 also discounts, or €6,093,119 if C4 does NOT discount. If Ilda decides NOT to discount, her expected profit is €6,051,151 if C4 discounts and it becomes €6,035,522 as long as Ilda remains passive. Given that the first two payoffs are both higher for Ilda than the last two there is a *dominant* strategy for Ilda and that is to discount the price in June and then wait and see C4's reaction.[4]

Materials Requirement Planning (MRP) as part of production planning

Once a production plan has been approved by management, the company has to arrange for orders of raw materials from its suppliers, as well as other items needed for production and personnel planning. Ordering raw materials is part of *Materials Requirement Planning* (MRP). It was later embedded into the more comprehensive *Manufacturing Resource Planning* as a method of effective planning for all needed resources of a manufacturing company. Around 1990, an even more comprehensive planning tool became popular in the business world: *Enterprise Resource Planning* (ERP). Nowadays, ERP includes the planning and evaluation of Finance and Accounting, Budgeting and Management Accounting, Order Processing, Human Resource Management, e-business, and it integrates virtually all business functions, areas, and activities in one system. ERP is almost impossible without a full-fledged IT system, including a database for systematic storage of corporate information emerging from all divisions and departments, and the option to operate in real-time within the company, with stakeholders and supply chain partners connected to the IT system.[5] ERP supports the company's *Customer Relation Management* (CRM), *Supplier Relation Management* (SRM), and *Internal Supply Chain Management* (ISCM), discussed in the first chapter.

In the context of production planning, this paragraph will focus on Materials Requirements Planning, which aims to manage and control the flow of raw materials, subassemblies, intermediate components, and other parts, which are needed to execute the master production planning. A basic component of MRP is the Bill of Materials (BOM).[6] Every product has a Bill of Materials that consists of a layered structure with a top-level containing the main components, a second deeper level with subcomponents making up the main component, a third even deeper level with sub-sub-components, etc. The BOM contains the number of all components needed to make an end-product and also includes the replenishment of all those items for inventory purposes. A production plan can fail if even one critical component is not in stock when needed for production. Production planning is directly linked to inventory planning. A simple BOM example of a consumer product A is displayed in Diagram I. The numbers between parentheses indicate the numbers of that part going into the part one level higher. Five parts, G, are going into Component B, three units of which go into Product A → 15 units of G go into product A.

Diagram I

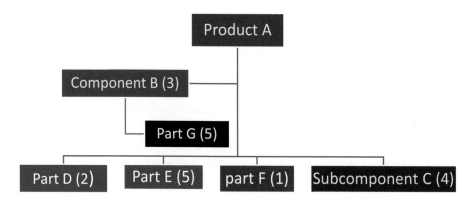

The amount of safety inventory a company keeps of an item used in a production process depends on how critical the item is. An item that can obstruct the progress of the production process if it is missing and that cannot be postponed, is stocked in higher numbers than items that can be added at a later stage of the process of manufacturing the main product. The leading manufacturing company will arrange supply contracts detailing all component requirements. If the leading company targets high-quality end-products, all parts from the suppliers must meet high-quality standards, which requires, for example, a Total Supply Chain Quality Management plan. However, this topic is beyond the scope of this book.

Lean production and just-in-time (JIT) processes

For several decades, a new production philosophy has established a position in the library of management tools of manufacturing companies. Known as *Lean Production*, it is closely related to *Just-in-Time* inventory management. Just-in-time and lean production refer to a *manufacturing* policy that has its roots in post-war Japan, and one of its pioneers was the Toyota Car Company, which called it the Toyota Production System. Its principal aim is to minimize waste generation without compromising productivity and quality. It directs the business processes, especially with respect to reducing Work in Process inventory to the absolute minimum.

Lean production focuses on features of a product that meet customer preferences, which, in turn, means that the customer is willing to pay for it. It omits all activities and services that do not add value for the customer. Nowadays, an increasing number of global companies, e.g. Nike and Intel Inc., have implemented lean production processes, sometimes with amazing results. Lean manufacturing is often coupled to a corporate *quality* policy, such as Six Sigma Quality control, as well as to just-in-time production management. Just-in-time aims at reducing safety inventories and its associated holding costs, as well as minimizing cycle inventory of raw materials, components, and parts not directly needed in the production process. When a company adopts a JIT policy, lot sizes are reduced, because ordering large lot sizes increase inventory costs to store them. A number of business resources and processes that are the subject of lean production standards and improvements are referred to as the seven wastes of lean manufacturing. Those seven wastes are:

-   transport (the internal movement of products from one location to another, like work in process, from the machining shop to the painting bath, or from a production facility in India to the assembly line in Brazil).
    This internal transportation adds no value to the product, does not transform it, and customers are not happy to pay for it.
-   inventory (all components, work in process, and finished product not being processed)
-   motion (people or equipment moving more than required to perform their tasks in a process)
-   waiting (the time spent on inactive waiting for work to arrive or to be told what to do)
-   overproduction (production ahead of demand and inventoried)
-   overprocessing (adding more value to a product than the customer requires, such as painting areas of a car that will never be seen or be exposed to corrosion)
-   the waste of resources through inefficient use of electricity, gas, water, and any other resources

The image on the next page is a visual representation of the seven wastes (an 8th one, employees skills, is included).

A prerequisite for optimal performance of lean production is that major suppliers are geographically close to the customer. Bridging large distances for order shipment, sometimes daily, drives up transportation costs and can contribute to low and inefficient vehicle load factors (truck, ship, plane, or train). Major suppliers of large manufacturing companies sometimes set up a warehouse or a plant located in the proximity to its major customer(s) to keep transportation costs low.

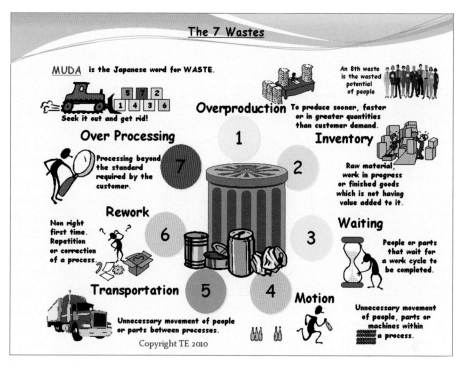

Source: http://leanmanufacturingtools.org/wp-content/uploads/2011/06/7-wastes2.gif

Main point: lean production is a production philosophy whereby excess resources are reduced to a minimum. Lean production policy is closely coupled to just-in-time inventory management, which aims to have all production input resources available only when they are needed and no more than needed. The scope of lean production covers materials, logistics handling, inventory, and the deployment of human resources.

Notes

1-6   See Instructor's Manual

5 Inventory Management in a Deterministic Scenario

One of the distribution centres of the English supermarket chain Sainsbury's located in Waltham point, Hertfordshire, United Kingdom.
Source: By Nick Saltmarsh – flickr.com, CC BY 2.0, https://commons.wikimedia.org/w/index.php?curid=10637658

In previous chapters, we have scratched the surface of inventory management, but now the moment has come to go deeper and offer a more systematic and detailed discussion of inventory management. There are different definitions of inventory, one of which defines it, rather generally, as *the storage of resources to satisfy a current or future need of the organization*. In financial accounting terms, inventory is one of the current assets shown on a company's balance sheet. More specifically, organizations distinguish between different forms of inventory that they keep. A common distinction based on the *nature* of these current assets or resources is:[1]

1. Finished Goods Inventory
2. Work-in-Process inventory
3. Raw Materials, Components, and Parts Inventory

4. Spoilage Inventory
5. Maintenance, Repair, and Operating Supplies (MRO)

More forms of inventory can be distinguished depending on the company and the nature of the production process.

1. Finished Goods Inventory is goods whose production has been completed, has undergone the necessary quality inspections, and, in many cases, is already packaged and ready for sale. In manufacturing plants, finished goods enter the sales and distribution channels and are shipped to the distribution centres of major customers. Distribution centres store finished goods temporarily and ship them to retail stores or other Points of Sale. Distribution centres and retail stores are the largest holders of finished goods inventory. The total amount and the variation over time of this form of inventory depend primarily on the often-unpredictable and volatile demand patterns. Managing finished goods inventory uses sophisticated quantitative models to optimize inventory levels.

2. Work-in-Process inventory (WIP) refers to products whose production extends over a longer period. This refers not only to large products, like airplanes, marine vessels, trucks, construction works, and high-tech machinery, but also to products with a long processing time, like the ripening process of wine and beer. Work-in-Process inventory is important for financial accounting purposes. WIP is always tagged with a degree of completion, which reveals the stage of the production process that the product is at every moment. This information about progress helps the inventory manager to plan for products that will become available as a finished product for sale, on different time scales, e.g. within one day, one week, or one month.

3. Raw materials, components, and parts are inventory items needed for the continuity of the production process to make end-products. This inventory is part of the inbound inventory, whereby the manufacturing plants receive the raw items from suppliers. The need and demand for this kind of inventory are directly related to the production planning of the company and indirectly to the demand for end-products. The flow of this kind of inventory is easier to manage and control than end-products, because of its link with production planning, which is a tool under management control.

4. Spoilage inventory is all units that do not comply with technical or quality specifications or do not meet customer expectations. Their production has already started but they are withdrawn either during or just after completion and before entering the distribution channels when disconformity with or deviation from the specifications are detected. What happens after deviations or other errors are detected depends on the product and the kind of error. Some product defects can be reworked at additional costs to restore the product to the necessary standards,

after which they are sold and generate revenue. Other products have to be discarded, generating costs but no revenues, and some products with minor imperfections can either be sold at a discounted price or on a secondary market.

Another factor with a significant impact on spoilage costs refers to the stage in the business process when the error or failure is detected. The worst-case scenario occurs when the product is already on the market and customers detect the error. Then, a public product recall will be set in motion by the company whereby customers can return the product. Product recalls create high costs for the company and a loss of corporate reputation.[2] If the error is detected before the product leaves the manufacturing site, the products can be taken out of production to avoid them moving to the next stages in the Supply Chain. Special provisions are needed when finished products produced for export enter a country and, on arrival in the importing country, but before sales to consumers, it is discovered that they do not meet national legal standards, like safety, health, or environmental standards.

Dealing with and avoiding spoilage belongs to a company's quality policy. A number of major companies have adopted so-called *Total Quality Management* (TQM). Part of a quality policy consists of setting the frequency and moments of internal inspection to discover potential product failures and errors as soon as possible. However, company and Supply Chain quality management is beyond the scope of this book.

5. MRO includes all assets needed to keep the production process smoothly running, and, in the case of a production discontinuity, having all the necessary MRO assets available to restore or repair the production process as soon as possible.

Classification based on inventory purpose

Inventory can also be classified based on the reason for keeping it. Here, we restrict ourselves to a common classification that is especially useful for Supply Chain purposes:

A. *Cycle* inventory
B. *Safety* inventory
C. *Seasonal* inventory

A. Cycle inventory is the average inventory an organization maintains, because companies produce or purchase in order sizes larger than those necessary to meet immediate consumer demand during an inventory cycle. An *"inventory cycle"* is defined as the time elapsing between the receipt of a product batch in inventory and its replenishment by the next batch. When discussing the Economic Order

Quantity model later, we will go into more detail about the costs and benefits of cycle inventory.

B. Safety Inventory (also known as buffer inventory). The prime reason for keeping safety inventory is to meet demand during the lead time before new stock arrives. The level of safety inventory mainly depends on the degree of demand uncertainty, lead time uncertainty, and the Cycle Service Level pursued by the company. Safety inventory will be discussed in the next chapter.

C. Seasonal inventory is the stock kept to meet seasonal demand. Seasonal primarily refers to low demand during off-peak seasons and high demand during peak seasons. A major difference with the first two inventory concepts is that demand is not evenly spread over a standard period, such as a year, but experiences strong recurrent fluctuations across seasons.

Inventory accounting, information technology, and inventory costs

Inventory Information supplied by large companies in public financial statements is presented as very aggregate data and is usually short on information content. A large stock-listed food retailer like the French Group Carrefour SA, published a total inventory value of €5.942 billion in their first half 2021 consolidated balance sheet.[3] This number is an aggregated number and includes all inventories in all their approximately 1,462 store outlets worldwide and their consolidated subsidiaries. This inventory figure is the outcome of multiplying all units in their product portfolio with a unit cost, which, in turn, depends on the inventory accounting method of the company. This aggregated inventory figure does not give relevant information about the performance of Carrefour's inventory policy, nor is it an appropriate figure for Supply Chain analysis. The most common inventory accounting method in the European Union applied by stock listed companies, used especially for fast-moving consumer goods, is the *First-In-First-Out* (FIFO) method.

For Supply Chain analysis, more detailed information is needed about the distribution of all products among all stores, turnover data for each product, the number of products discarded due to exceeding shelf life, and other inventory features. Carrefour SA does have this information, but, like much corporate information, it is not publicly available and is protected behind strong digital firewalls. Carrefour SA, like most medium-sized and large companies in the world, uses advanced database systems, which keep track of almost all their transactions, keeping information about inventory levels in real-time and up to date. Thus, we touch on a crucial prerequisite for any inventory policy: the need for a global, well-functioning IT system that connects (virtually) all decentralized stores to a centralized database system of the parent company to support inventory decisions. Any change in inventory must be recorded as soon as possible – nowadays real-time – allowing managers in charge of inventory policy and its associated processes, such as procurement, to intervene quickly. In a Supply Chain setting, data exchange about inventory levels and turnover at each level of the Supply Chain is necessary to achieve the best performance of an SC inventory policy.

Another dimension of inventory management is the cost categories associated with keeping inventory. Although some inventory costs are company- and product-specific the following cost categories are valid for virtually all inventoried merchandise and form part of most inventory policies:

1. Carrying or holding costs
2. Ordering costs
3. Cost of capital tied up in inventory
4. Stock-out costs
5. Purchase prices based on lot sizes ordered

1. The first prerequisite for keeping inventory is that it needs storage space and the cost per m² or m³ of space is one of the components of the carrying or holding costs.[4] Specific product storage requirements, such as maintaining internal climate conditions for fresh food with temperature and humidity control, increase carrying costs. For other products, special safety precautions are taken, like storing chemicals and fossil fuels. Many products are insured during storage. All costs of internal climate control, safety, and insurance premiums are included in the carrying or holding costs.

2. When inventory levels are low, the stock will be replenished by the supplier. All costs related to ordering a new lot, up to the arrival moment and moving it to the designated place in the distribution centre, are subsumed under *ordering costs*. They include administrative costs, shipment costs from the supplier to the distribution centre that places the order, and internal handling costs within the facility once the products arrive at the incoming docking station of the distribution centre. [see a picture of a docking station below]. Ordering costs and carrying costs have an opposite relation. By ordering more units carrying costs go up, while the number of orders, and thereby total ordering costs, will go down. We come back to this point in the discussion about the EOQ model.

Source: https://en.wikipedia.org/wiki/Loading_dockretrieved on 5 January 2022

3. Any unit in inventory and not yet sold has money invested in it, namely, the price the company paid to acquire the unit or the costs to manufacture it. Any euro invested in inventory and not yet sold does not earn a financial return that could otherwise be earned by investing the same euro in a savings account or in financial securities. This is called the *cost of capital* embodied in inventory and is calculated as a percentage of the purchase price and during the time the units remain in inventory. For this percentage, many companies use their corporate cost of capital, i.e. the return the company earns on using their total assets for the operational business activities.

A company pursuing a just-in-time inventory policy with a minimum of inventory will have low costs of capital tied up in inventory. Cost of Capital is often included in holding costs and the holding costs are then expressed as $C = h*P$, with h the holding cost % and P the purchase price (cost) of a unit in inventory.

4. Stock-out costs are the cost a company incurs when a customer places an order and the company is not able to deliver it at the moment the customer wants it. Stock-out costs consist of, among others, the cost of *backlogging*, sending the product later using urgent shipment modes (by plane instead of by ship) at higher

costs than ordinary shipment. In some delivery contracts for B2B transactions, penalties are included if the supplier does not deliver on time. A customer noting the non-availability of a product can go to a competitor for the same product, and, in this case, the company misses the revenues of that order. In the worst case, the customer can cancel all future business relations with the company and switch to the competitor for current and future purchases. Losing a regular customer means losing a sequence of orders and revenues from this customer. If stock-out costs occur frequently the company can, additionally, suffer a loss of goodwill and reputation.

5. Quantity-based lot prices mean that the supplier adapts his selling price to the amount ordered by the customer. If the purchase price is independent of order size the price does not matter for finding the least-cost ordering policy. It does not matter, then, if the company orders 100 units each month or 1,200 units only once a year. The two order policies will only affect the total holding cost and ordering cost, but not the annual purchasing cost of the goods. If the supplier has a price policy based on quantity ordered, price *does* affect the total annual purchase costs, and the number of units ordered, and purchase price becomes a relevant variable in calculating the optimal order size. We return to the impact of quantity-related purchase prices on the optimal order size in the discussion on the extended version of the EOQ model.

Economic Order Quantity model: cradle of scientific inventory management

In 1913, R.H. Wilson published a seminal and pathbreaking paper describing a quantitative model to calculate the order size that minimizes overall inventory cost.[5] The model has become known as the *Economic Order Quantity* model (EOQ). His model continues to form the basis for many inventory decisions and it is used all over the world and has seen many extensions and adaptations over the years to address more complex inventory scenarios. This seemingly simple model builds on a set of assumptions, of which the most important are:

I.   Demand and sales of the inventoried products are evenly spread over time and are certain
II. Lead time is zero (instantaneous or overnight) delivery
III. Purchase price is *in*dependent of the order size
IV. The holding cost is €H per unit for a whole year
V.   The ordering costs are €O per order

A sale of one unit equals a drop in inventory by one unit. If demand is evenly spread over time, this implies that inventory decreases proportionally to sales.

The assumption of evenly spread sales does not sound very realistic for finished goods, because the demand for many consumer goods is often erratic, volatile, and unpredictable. For the inventory of raw materials, parts, and subcomponents needed for the production process, this assumption can be a reasonably good approximation of reality. The production department is the demander of all raw materials needed to execute the production planning. If, for example, the production of e-bikes is a continuous production process on a production line and one battery per bike is needed, then every new e-bike taken into production requires a new battery out of inventory. The drop in the inventory level of batteries over time keeps an equal pace with the production rate of e-bikes. The drop in the inventory levels of bicycle wheels and bicycle pedals is twice as fast as the production rate of e-bikes given that one bicycle has two wheels and two pedals. But, even then, inventory is still declining linearly. The Bill of Materials for an e-bike indicates how fast inventory levels drop for each part and component used in the production of an e-bike.

A linear decline in inventory levels creates a sawtooth pattern, shown in Graph A, whereby daily demand is two units and, every Monday morning, replenishment takes place with 12 units, the same as the order size. The inventory cycle – the time between two replenishment moments – is one week. An important indicator in the EOQ model is the average inventory over the period under consideration – in this example, seven days – needed for calculating the holding costs. The average inventory is six units and can be explained as follows. Average inventory = total inventory per week/number of days. Average inventory per week is $12 + 10 + 8 + 6 + 4 + 2 = 42/7$ days per week = 6 units. This pattern repeats itself week after week, so the average cycle inventory is six units the whole year-round.[6] The total holding costs are equal to the *average* inventory ($Q_{average}$) multiplied by the holding costs per unit per year (€H). The fact that inventory drops to 0 on Saturday (evening) at the end of the cycle and is replenished on Monday morning reflects the zero-lead time.

Graph A

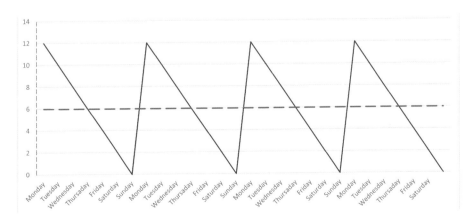

The second part in the EOQ is the total annual ordering costs, that are equal to the number of orders placed per year times the ordering cost per order. In the EOQ, the annual demand is assumed to be known and certain and is calculated as 52 weeks times weekly demand. The number of orders, when demand is evenly spread over the year – i.e. that inventory drops in a linear way – is the annual demand divided by the order size. We now cast this in some formal equations and calculate the order size Q_{EOQ} with the lowest inventory cost. We use the following symbols: D *annual* demand; H annual holding cost per unit; O ordering cost per order. From the inventory graph above, we can calculate the average inventory as $[Q – o]/2$, with Q the maximum level occurring after replenishment with order size Q and the lowest inventory o at the end of the cycle. Given the linear decline due to the evenly spread demand, the average annual inventory equals ½*Q. The number of orders per year to meet demand D is demand divided by the order size: D/Q. Total carrying cost is the average inventory times annual carrying cost per unit: ½*Q*H. Total ordering cost is the number of orders per year times ordering cost per order: [D/Q]*O

Total Inventory cost   TIC = ½*Q*H + [D/Q]*O

The next step is to calculate the order size Q_{EOQ}, which minimizes TIC by taking the derivative of TIC to the variable Q and setting this derivative equal to o: d(TIC)/d(Q) = 0.

$$D(TIC)/d(Q) = ½*H – (D*O)/Q^2 = 0 \rightarrow ½*H = \frac{D*O}{Q^2} \rightarrow Q^2 = \frac{2*D*O}{H} \rightarrow Q_{EOQ} = +\sqrt{\frac{2*D*O}{H}}$$

units per order.[7]

By replacing the formula of Q_{EOQ} in the equation of total holding cost and total ordering costs we get:

the total *holding* cost at Q_{EOQ} of $\sqrt{\frac{1}{2}*D*O*H}$

the total *ordering* cost at Q_{EOQ} of $\sqrt{\frac{1}{2}*D*O*H}$

Total inventory cost $TIC = \sqrt{2*D*O*H}$

Notice that in the lowest cost situation of Q_{EOQ} the annual holding cost and annual ordering cost are the same. Any deviation of the order size from the optimal value Q_{EOQ} increases total inventory cost. Increasing the order size Q_{EOQ} increases average inventory and thereby the annual carrying costs, but at the same time decreases the order frequency and thereby the annual ordering costs. However, the marginal increase in carrying costs is more than the marginal decrease in ordering cost and, consequently, annual inventory costs go up. For a small decrease in order size Q_{EOQ} the arguments go the other way around: the marginal decrease in carrying cost is less than the marginal increase in order cost and therefore annual inventory costs go up as well. The annual *purchase cost* is calculated as the annual demand times the unit purchase price P: $D*P$. Given that the purchase price is fixed and independent of the order quantity, $D*P$ will be the same for all possible order sizes Q and does not affect the optimal order quantity. We can therefore omit it from the EOQ model calculation.

The Reorder Point (ROP)

In the EOQ model the lead time is instantaneous – or, at least, very short – and the moment of placing the order and receiving the goods coincide. If goods are ordered when the inventory drops to 0 and the facility opens the next day the inventory is replenished and sales or production continue. This is seldom the case in daily business processes, and lead time is nearly always greater than 0 and can range from less than a day to several months if the supply comes from the other side of the globe and production at the supplier only starts once orders are received.

Let us assume that the lead or delivery time is L days. If the company places the order as soon as inventory drops to 0, they will have to wait L days before replenishment arrives. Demand during lead time cannot be satisfied or production will be halted due to a lack of parts. If the lead time is known and certain, the company will issue the purchase order to the supplier at the moment when the remaining inventory is sufficient to continue sales or production during the lead time. When the new batch of goods *arrives*, inventory has dropped to 0. The inventory level whereby the company issues a new order to its supplier is called the *reorder point* (ROP) and equals the lead time times the demand per time unit: $L*D_{day}$.[9]

If we return to the example of Graph A and we assume a lead time of $L = 2$ workdays the demand during 2 workdays is 4 units. The reorder point is achieved when the inventory level is 4 units, and the order will be issued on Friday morning. The new batch of 12 units will arrive on Sunday evening or Monday morning, just before sales or production continues.

Optimal Economic Order Quantity with quantity or volume discounts

Many suppliers are willing to discount their selling price to boost sales if the buyer is willing to buy in order quantities exceeding certain preset critical values. This applies to consumer products but even more to B2B transactions, where price negotiations between seller and buyer are more common.[9] The selling price becomes a variable while the annual purchase cost is determined dependent on the order quantity Q. Although annual demand is still D units, the purchase costs become $D*C_i$, whereby C_i is the unit cost for ordering an amount falling in the ith price/ quantity range. The annual cost of inventory in case of quantity discounts become:

$TIC = D*C_i + \frac{1}{2}*Q_i*H + [D/Q_i]*O$ with the last two terms the annual holding and ordering costs.

We will first illustrate the calculation of the cost-minimizing order quantity using an example and then discuss the general formulas. A coffee roaster company, called Brightwhite, offers weekly packages of coffee to restaurants, bars, and other organizations in the hospitality industry. They have the following price scheme:

Orders less than 1,000 packages	€6.00 per package [C_1]
Orders between 1,001 and 1,500 packages	€5.50 per package [C_2]
Orders between 1,501 and 2,000 packages	€5.00 per package [C_3]
Orders of 2,001 packages or more	€4.80 per package [C_4]

The more packages the customer orders the higher the average inventory of coffee packages, but the ordering costs, including the shipment costs, will be less. Restaurant *Parrot* wants to have Brightwhite, their preferred coffee supplier, as a partner. The ordering costs for Parrot are O = €80 per order and the holding costs of storing the coffee are set as a percentage of the purchase cost per package at h = 20%. This percentage is related to the capital cost of Parrot. Parrot's annual demand D = 22,000 packages of coffee.

If we apply the standard EOQ formula to these data to find the optimal order quantity we are not sure whether the Q_{EOQ} falls inside or outside the associated price range. Therefore we apply a step by step approach. The first case is where Parrot orders less than 1000 packages when the unit cost is €6.00. Calculating the Q_{EOQ} for the first price range of €6.00 yields

$Q_{EOQ} = \sqrt{\frac{2*22.000*80}{0.2*6}} \approx 1713$ packages.

This optimal value of 1,713 packages is outside the range for a price of €6.00 ($\leq$ 1,000) and therefore this order size is no candidate for optimization. Calculating the Q_{EOQ} for the second price range of €5.50 yields

$Q_{EOQ} = \sqrt{\frac{2*22.000*80}{0.2*5.50}} \approx 1789$ packages.

This order quantity is still outside the price range of €5.50, which ends at 1,500 sheets. Calculating the Q_{EOQ} for the third price range of €5.00 yields

$$Q_{EOQ} = \sqrt{\frac{2 * 22,000 * 80}{0.2 * 5.00}} \approx 1,876 \text{ packages}$$

This falls within the selected range [1,501 – 2,000] of €5.00 per package.

We can now evaluate the annual inventory plus annual purchase cost at this order size as:
TIC = 22,000*€5.00 (buying) + [(1,876/2)*(0.20*€5)] (holding) + (22,000/1,876)*€80 (ordering) = €111,876

There is still one alternative we have to consider and that is the lowest price range of €4.80. The associated Q_{EOQ} for this price is 1,915 units and that is less than the minimum required amount of 2,000 packages to qualify for this price. But we must also account for the boundary value where the price drops from €5.00 to €4.80 by placing an order of exactly **2,001** packages. That does not result in the lowest carrying and ordering costs, but it does save €0.20 per package over 22,000 packages and affects annual total inventory costs.
TIC = 22,000*€4.80 (cost) + [(2,000/2)*(0.20*€4.80)] (carrying cost) + (22,000/2,000)*€80 = €107,440

Because €107,440 is less than €111,876 the optimal lot is 2,000 sheets per order. (NB: for computational simplicity, we have taken the boundary value at 2,000 sheets instead of 2,001!)

From an example to a general calculation of the economic order quantity with all-unit quantity discounts

A supplier offers a product for a price of C_i with $C_i < C_{i-1}$ in different price breaks and quantity ranges. Each range encompasses q_i units with $i = 0$ until n. The starting quantity $q_0 = 0$. The buyer orders in lots of Q_i, with $q_i \leq Q_i < q_{i+1}$ and the price to be paid per unit is C_i.

We want to find the value Q_i of the buyer, which minimizes total inventory costs including the purchase costs using the following symbols: D is annual demand; O is the ordering cost per order; h is the constant holding cost percentage. The annual holding cost is h*C_i per unit. The solution is found stepwise:

Step 1:
Evaluate the Q^*_i for each price range C_i using $Q_i = \sqrt{\frac{2 * D * O}{h * C_i}}$

The following outcomes can occur:

- $q_i \le Q_i < q_{i+1} \rightarrow Q_i = Q_i^*$, the optimal order quantity is **in** the targeted price range C_i
- $Q_i < q_i \rightarrow Q_i$ is outside the targeted range for which price C_i holds. If the buyer wants to have the price C_i he will set the order size equal to the boundary quantity for this price $q_i \rightarrow Q_i^* = q_i$
- $Q_i > q_{i+1} \rightarrow$ this case is considered in the next price range of the different order quantities

Step 2:

Calculate the annual inventory cost, plus purchase cost for _each_ price range using the Q_i^* from step 1

$$TIC_i = D^*C_i + \tfrac{1}{2}^*Q_i^* *[h^*C_i] + [D/Q_i^*]^*O$$

Step 3:

Select the Q_i^* with the lowest TIC. This one will become the optimal Q_{EOQ} for the buyer.

A less common variation of the All-Unit Quantity Discount is the _Marginal Unit Quantity Discount._ In this pricing policy, the seller sells all units in one price range for the price associated with that range. This leads to the following annual purchase costs if the order size is Q_i^*

For all units up to q_1, total purchase cost become – assuming the value

$q_0 = 0$ $\qquad\qquad\qquad\qquad\qquad\qquad\qquad\qquad\qquad [q_1 - q_0]^*C_0$

For all units between q_2 and q_1 purchase, cost becomes $\qquad [q_2 - q_1]^*C_1$

For all units between q_3 and q_2 purchase, cost becomes $\qquad [q_3 - q_2]^*C_2$

. . . .

For all units between q_{i-1} and Q_i^* purchase cost become $\qquad [Q_i^* - q_{i-1}]^*C_{i-1}$

and then sum all those purchase costs to obtain the total purchase cost *PC*. In formula with Q_n the number of units ordered:

$$PC = [Q_n - q_{n-1}]^*C_{n-1} + \sum_{i=1}^{n-1} + [q_i - q_{i-1}]^* C_i)$$

Because there are discontinuities in the purchase prices for different quantities, the calculation of the optimal order quantity Q_{EOQ} as well as for the purchase dependent holding cost h^*C_i is a little more complex than for the all-unit quantity discount. We leave the mathematical derivation of this Q_{EOQ} and the calculation of the total annual inventory cost for the mathematical appendix.

Quantity discounts and supply chain optimization

In the first chapter, we discussed the overall objective for a supply chain, which was to maximize the supply chain profits instead of the profit maximization of individual SC partners. The question arises, whether quantity discounts set by a selling partner benefit the supply chain as a whole, and the answer is generally **not**. We first describe why independent decision-making does not lead to an optimal supply chain outcome and then illustrate it with an example. The EOQ is the optimal order size set by the *buyer*. However, the supplier also incurs inventory and/or production costs for every unit ordered by the buying party. In some cases, suppliers keep inventory to fulfil orders proceeding from many different buyers and incur their holding costs and costs for executing the buyer's order including shipment costs. If the buyer placing the order is his only customer, then the annual demand exercised by the buyer is equal to the total annual demand received by the seller. If the supplier has N customers or buyers, then the seller's demand equals the sum of the demands exercised by all buyers: with D_i the annual demand from buyer *i*. If the supplier is a manufacturer and keeps inventory levels low, any new order means that the units ordered must be produced or assembled. This process causes machine set-up costs and other production-related costs.

A supplier also has an optimal order size, which minimizes inventory and production costs. The optimal value of the EOQ of the supplier and the EOQ of the buyer are seldom the same and therefore the party that sets the order size can benefit, at the cost of the other party. In most cases, the buyer sets the order size, and the supplier has to accept it, or faces not selling at all to this customer. In exceptional cases, when the seller has a monopoly position, the seller sets the order quantity and the buyer has to accept it, otherwise they will not receive any supply. In this case, the supplier benefits, at the cost of the buyer.

Product aggregation combined in a single order

Hypermarkets and Do-It-Yourself stores (DIY) have an enormous assortment of products purchased from many different suppliers. If, for store replenishment, each product or family of products (like lawnmowers and electric drills) requires a truck to stop at the hypermarket, the shipment costs, as part of the ordering cost, will be unnecessarily high.[10] To make more efficient use of truck space logistics companies use *merge-in-transit* shipments. A truck will visit several suppliers during one trip to collect ordered products and bring all of them together to the same destination. Orders for several different products are combined in one **joint** shipment order.

Combining separate orders into one affects the ordering costs. In addition to the administrative order procedure, the truck will drive more kilometres to collect items from several suppliers and deliver these to the customer location. Let us assume that five products are combined into a joint order. The fixed ordering costs related to the order as a whole are **O** and we add the individualized shipping cost per product s_i. This gives $O_{joint} = O_{fixed} + s_1 + s_2 + s_3 + s_4 + s_5$.

The problem now is that we cannot calculate directly an optimal order quantity for the products jointly, because each of the five products has its Q_{EOQ} and associated optimal order frequency. In a joint order situation, we <u>first</u> calculate the optimal annual order frequency N^*, which gives us the number of times the truck will come to the stores delivering the different goods. With this N^*, the optimal order quantity for each product $Q^i_{EOQ}{}^*$ can be calculated. With these five Q^i_{EOQ} annual carrying costs for each of the five products can be calculated as well as total ordering costs. We set N as the variable representing the number of orders per year, which we optimize to find N^*. The annual demand for the product i is D_i. The derivation of the optimal order quantity for m different products follows similar steps as the derivation of the standard EOQ.

- Annual ordering costs: $O = N * O_{joint} = N * [O_{fixed} + \sum_{i=1}^{m} s_i]$

- Annual holding costs: $H = \sum_{i=1}^{m} \frac{D_i * h * C_i}{2 * N}$ with h the constant holding cost % of purchase cost C_i.

- Total annual inventory costs: TIC = O + H

- Purchase costs are independent of order size and can be excluded from the EOQ calculation!

If we minimize TIC the variable is now the order frequency N, and we take $d(TIC)/d(N) = 0$ to find N^*. After some algebraic tweaking, we obtain

$$N^* = \sqrt{\sum_{i=1}^{m} \frac{D_i * h * C_i}{2 * O^*}}$$ with $h*C_i$ holding cost

The optimal order size for product i becomes

$$Q_i{}^* = D_i / N^*$$

All other calculations for each product are straightforward.

Main Point: combining orders for several products or product groups into one single joint order can save ordering costs, especially the shipping cost from the supplier to buyer destination using merge-in-transit shipment. The EOQ model can be easily adapted to calculate the economic savings of combining orders into a single joint order.

Notes

1-2   See Instructor's Manual

3   Source: https://www.carrefour.com/en/finance/financial-publications, retrieved on 6 December 2021

4-10   See Instructor's Manual

6   Inventory Management under Uncertainty

Inventory Management under Uncertainty

The effect of <u>under</u>stocking: empty shelves at a supermarket.
Source: https://upload.wikimedia.org/wikipedia/commons/thumb/d/d6/Dried_pasta_shelves_empty_in_an_Australian_supermarket.jpg/1280px-Dried_pasta_shelves_empty_in_an_Australian_supermarket.jpg

The effect of <u>over</u>stocking: unsold food ready to be dumped on the garbage heap.
Source: https://foodtribute.com/latin-america-food-waste-can-feed-37-worlds-hungry/

In the previous chapter, we discussed inventory management with the Economic Order Quantity (EOQ) model, where all parameters, in particular demand and lead time, are certain. Inventory models under certainty, especially the EOQ model, can be applied effectively for the Bill of Materials inventory needed as input for production. Production planning is easier to control by management than the demand for finished goods and therefore inventory planning for raw materials is generally easier to manage. The focus of these models is on cost minimization under *certainty* conditions.

Finished Goods inventory depends primarily on the demand for it and the demand for consumer goods is often volatile and unpredictable. In the chapter about forecasting, we saw that forecasts refer to expected future demand and that any forecast is surrounded by uncertainty margins measured by Mean Absolute Deviation (MAD) or Mean Squared Error (MSE) metrics.

Matching inventory to uncertain demand is an art and a science. The art is in the skills and experience of managers in charge of procurement and inventory; the scientific part is introduced in this chapter. The most common sources of uncertainty in inventory management originate from unpredictable demand, uncertain lead times, and uncoordinated price promotions.[1] Uncertain lead times have an impact on the reorder point (ROP) and replenishment time; uncertain *demand* leads to the introduction of *safety inventory* or *safety stock* (ss); and uncoordinated price promotions can lead to overordering.

Costs associated with understocking and overstocking

The table below shows the most important costs linked to too much (overstocking) and too little inventory (understocking).

Costs related to *over*stocking	Costs related to *under*stocking (stock out costs)
Purchase costs of buying stock that is not sold and generate no or much less revenue	Profit foregone for units demanded (ordered) but not sold
Unnecessary holding costs of excess units of stock	Loss of customer goodwill
Costs to get rid of excess stock	Very high shipment costs for fulfilling urgency orders
	Penalties imposed by customers, linked to overtime delivery, especially in B2B transactions.

In the service industry, inventory of services hardly exists, because consumption and production coincide. However, a mismatch between supply and demand manifests itself in queues or waiting lines, e.g. at a helpdesk or in public transportation. In physical stores, inventory shortage sometimes leads to long waiting *lines* and long waiting *times* for online webshops.

Quantifying uncertainty: Probability scenarios

It is one thing knowing that a future event is uncertain or exhibits random characteristics, a different and much more difficult problem is being able to tell *how* uncertain the event is, other words, to quantify uncertainty. Uncertainty has been studied for many centuries and belongs to the science of probability and statistics. The field is fully in progress, not least due to the advent of incredible computing power, the enormous amount of data available, and the specialized software that has been developed to analyse so-called Big Data. This is not a book about statistics and we will restrict ourselves to the application of a few probability density functions commonly employed for inventory management: the *Normal probability distribution,* the *Poisson distribution,* and the *Exponential* distribution.

The normal probability distribution function is the most important in statistics and is the backbone of many other derived distribution functions like the F(isher)-distribution, the Student-t distribution, Chi-square distribution, and the lognormal distribution. Normal distribution is closely linked to other statistical laws, like the *Law of large numbers* and the *Central Limit Theorem.* It possesses some salient features: it is completely and uniquely identified by two parameters – its average value (μ) and its standard deviation (σ) – and it is a continuous function that can take on all values (positive and negative). The average value, the modus, and the median coincide, and the graph has a symmetric bell-shaped form. It is a very good description and approximation of many real-world random phenomena, ranging from physical, social, and economic events, traffic accidents, biological phenomena, weather patterns, and more.

Another important function is the Poisson distribution, commonly used in queueing problems and the management of waiting lines. Waiting lines arise when service capacity is insufficient to meet demand, and examples include calling a helpdesk, people waiting at a bus stop for public transportation, customers queueing at the checkout in stores, etc. The Poisson distribution function is *discrete* and has only one parameter (λ), which is both the mean value and the variance of the distribution. The Poisson distribution is frequently used to model the number of events occurring during a fixed time interval, whereby arrivals occur independently of each other. Arrivals can be the number of customers entering a shop during a day buying a specific product. It also refers to events, such as the number of retail stores in a country where the daily sales of a product exceed Y units.

Closely related to the Poisson distribution is the Exponential distribution. If random variable X representing the number of events during a fixed period follows a Poisson distribution, then the random variable Y representing the *time that elapses between two consecutive events*, the *interarrival* time between event *i* and *i+1*, e.g. customers entering a store's premises, follows an exponential function. Both the Normal and the Poisson distribution can be extended, with one random variable, from a *univariate* distribution to a *multivariate* distribution function with several interdependent random variables.[2] The mathematical equations of the three probability density functions (PDF) with random variable X are:

Normal Distribution:

$$f(X) = \frac{1}{\sigma * \sqrt{2\pi}} e^{\frac{(X-\mu)^2}{2\sigma^2}}$$

with μ and σ defined as the mean and the standard deviation. Also written as $X \sim N(\mu, \sigma)$

The *cumulative* normal distribution function (CDF):

$$P[X \leq z] = \int_{-\infty}^{z} f(X) dX$$

with f(X) the normal distribution function. Also denoted as F(z)

The probability density function of the *Poisson* is:

$$P[X = N] = \frac{\lambda^N}{N!} * e^{-\lambda}$$

with λ the parameter of the PDF for N = 0, 1, 2, 3 etc.

The *cumulative* Poisson distribution is

$$P[X \leq N] = \sum_{i=0}^{N} \frac{\lambda^i}{i!} * e^{-\lambda}.$$

The PDF of the *exponential probability density* function is

$$f(Y) = \mu * e^{-\mu * Y}$$

for random variable $Y \geq 0$ and equals 0 for Y < 0. Its mean value is $\frac{1}{\mu}$ and its variance is $\frac{1}{\mu^2}$.

The *cumulative* exponential distribution function is

$$P[Y \leq y] = F(y) = 1 - e^{-\mu * y}$$

Before examining the applications of the probability density functions, we will first define the *standard* normal distribution function. To standardize a random variable, we subtract its mean value and divide it by its standard deviation. If $X \sim N(\mu,$

σ) distributed then the variable $Z = \frac{(X - \mu)}{\sigma}$ follows the standard normal distribution with a mean value $\mu = 0$ and standard deviation $\sigma = 1$: $f(Z) = \frac{1}{\sqrt{2\pi}} * e^{-\frac{1}{2}*z^2}$

Safety inventory – or safety stock (ss)

If the demand for and lead times of finished goods are certain (a highly exceptional situation in business practice) then the inventory at the reorder point (ROP) will be exactly sufficient to meet demand during lead time. Just before the replenishment takes place, the inventory drops to 0 and after replenishment it increases by the amount Q, the order size that is delivered by the supplier.

If demand is uncertain and lead time certain, inventory at the moment of replenishment can be greater than 0 or equal to zero. If demand during lead time is greater than the ROP, some customer demand will not be fully satisfied, leading to backlogging (unfulfilled orders that are sent later to the customer). The firm has to send the goods later, at a higher cost, or it will lose the order and, in the worst case, the customer. The associated costs are called the *stock-out* costs.

The chart below shows inventory decline when the demand follows a normal distribution with daily mean sales $\mu = 20$ units and standard deviation $\sigma = 8$ units. Demand is displayed as the red dotted line in the chart. The lead time between order placement and the arrival of the goods (inventory replenishment) is two days and the ROP is set at a level of 40 units (horizontal line). The chart shows three cycles of one week each. The demand uncertainty reflects itself in the jerky and bumpy decline of the inventory levels, keeping in mind that one unit sold equals an inventory decline of one unit.

A new order size of Q = 120 units is released when the inventory level has dropped to 40 (ROP) and arrives two days later. Compared to the EOQ model discussed in the previous chapter, the inventory at arrival is no longer always 0. At the replenishment, at the end of week 1, the ending inventory is 10 units, and, by adding Q = 120 units, the firm starts the new cycle with 130 units. At the end of week 2, the ending inventory is -15 (this means either 15 back orders or 15 units of sales foregone as stock-out costs). After replenishment, the starting inventory is again 120 units and sales continue in week 3. If backlogging occurs, 15 out of the 120 replenished units are set aside for the customers with the outstanding orders of the previous cycle and the remaining units are available for sale in the current cycle. At the end of week 3, ending inventory is approximately +15 units and after replenishment, the fourth week starts with 135 units.

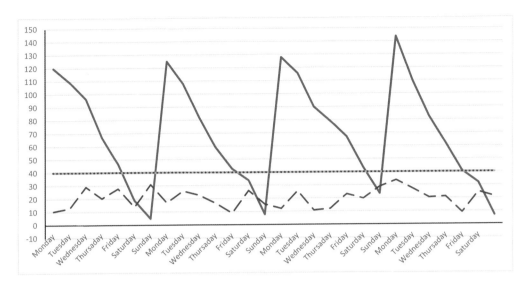

If the profit margin on the product is high and inventory costs relatively low, the sales manager may want to avoid any stockout during lead time. In the situation that the company releases the order at 40 units ROP, it runs the risk of insufficient cycle inventory during lead time, when demand during the two days exceeds 40 units. One way an organization can hedge stock-out is by building *safety inventory*. This means keeping more than 40 units in inventory to meet demand during the lead time above 40 units.

Safety inventory, Cycle Service Level, and fill rate

The higher the safety inventory the lower the probability of running into a stock-out situation, but at the price of higher holding cost.[3] There are different metrics for calculating stock-out levels. One of them is the Cycle Service Level, or CSL for short. The CSL is expressed as the fraction of inventory cycles during which an organization does not experience any stock-out, in other words, that actual demand during this cycle is smaller than or equal to the inventory.[4] If, for example, the inventory cycle – the time between two replenishment moments – is one week and during one year, the demand was higher in five weeks than inventory, then the CSL equals $(52 - 5)/52$ weeks = 90.4%.

Another and even better metric for stock-outs is the *fill rate*, which measures the *percentage* of demand that has been fulfilled during a cycle. In formula: (Inventory / demand) met during the inventory cycle. In the table below, we show the two stock-out metrics for 12 weeks. We will explore the relation between CSL and fill rate in more detail later in this chapter.

Inventory Cycle	Inventory available	Demand during cycle	CSL	Fill rate
1	400	308	1	100%
2	400	404	0	99%
3	400	421	0	95%
4	400	402	0	99,5%
5	400	335	1	100%
6	400	459	0	87%
7	400	514	0	78%
8	400	391	1	100%
9	400	443	0	90%
10	400	355	1	100%
		Cycle Service Level	40%	
		Average Fill Rate	94,896%	

Main Point: The Cycle Service Level is an indicator of how many inventory cycles the company was able to meet all demand or orders. The fill rate calculates the fraction of demand or orders that have been fulfilled with the inventory on hand. Fill rates are usually much higher than CSL and are a much more important indicator of customer satisfaction for business organizations than CSL.

In the following sections, we will mainly use CSL, because it simplifies the calculations considerably. At the section end, we will discuss how to convert a fill rate to a CSL, and vice versa, so that, at any moment, equivalence between the two metrics can be found. We start with an example before turning to the general formulas for the optimal safety inventory. We assume that weekly demand D for a product follows a normal distribution with a mean value μ = 400 units and a standard deviation of σ = 25 units. In technical notation D ~ N(400, 25). If the inventory is replenished with 400 units in each cycle the probability of stock-out in that cycle is $P[D \geq 400]$ = 50%. This is the same as saying that, over many inventory cycles, the CSL is 50%. When the profit margin of products is much higher than the holding costs, many companies want to cash in on demand keeping more inventory than the expected sales. They will therefore target a higher CSL using safety stock.[5] If management has preselected a CSL and demand is normally distributed, we use the Z-value of the standardized normal distribution with the random variable Z = . This Z-value has an expected value μ = 0 and standard deviation σ = 1 and will enable us to find the safety stock level needed during the lead time. The graph and data table of the standardized normal function are shown below.

Standard normal distribution		
Z	p[Z = z]	P[Z ≤ z]
-4	0.013%	0.003%
-3.5	0.087%	0.023%
-3	0.443%	0.135%
-2.5	1.753%	0.621%
-2	5.399%	2.275%
-1.5	12.952%	6.681%
-1	24.197%	15.866%
-0.5	35.207%	30.854%
0	39.894%	50.000%
0.5	35.207%	69.146%
1	24.197%	84.134%
1.5	12.952%	93.319%
2	5.399%	97.725%
2.5	1.753%	99.379%
3	0.443%	99.865%
3.5	0,087%	99.977%
4	0.013%	99.997%

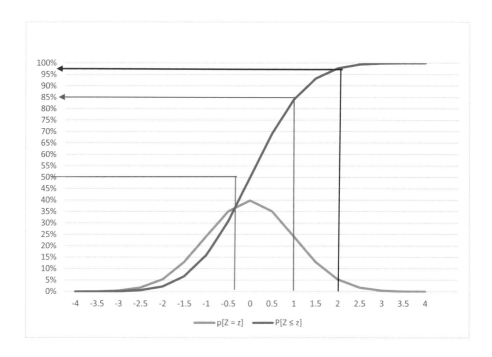

If we set z = 0, the data table and the graph show that we capture 50% of the probability density area to the left, which translates into a CSL of 50%. If we set z = 1 we capture 84.13% of the left area. This percentage for z = 2 is 97.725% and for z = 3 the area covered is 99.865% CSL. These percentages are the CSL.

In practice, management targets a CSL and then looks for the corresponding Z-value. If the *targeted* CSL is 80%, we *first* look for the Z-value corresponding to 80% CSL probability. In Excel, the function NORM.S.INV in the function library will do the job and gives the outcome of z ≈ 0.84.

If the lead time is one week and the demand *D* during lead time follows an N(200, 35) distribution, the safety stock equals $z^* \sigma$ = 0.84 * 35 ≈ 30 units. The expected demand during lead time is 200 units and therefore the ROP is set at 200 + 30 = 230 units to obtain an 80% CSL.

We will now derive the general formula to calculate the safety inventory and the corresponding reorder point using the following symbols:
- z = F^{-1}(CSL), where F^{-1} is the inverse standard cumulative normal distribution[6] and CSL the targeted CSL.
- $\overline{D}_L$= expected demand during the *lead* time and σ_L the standard deviation of demand during the *lead* time.

The reorder point becomes
$$ROP = \overline{D} + z^* \sigma_L \text{ and the safety stock}$$
$$ss = z^* \sigma_L \text{ with } z = F^{-1}(CSL).$$

If demand is known per base period (days, weeks, months) to be normally distributed N(μ, σ) and the lead time is *L* periods, we first have to compute the expected demand and the standard deviation during lead time. The expected demand during lead time is straightforward:
$$\overline{D}_L = L^* \mu. \text{ The standard deviation during a (multiperiod) lead time } \sigma_L = \sigma * \sqrt{L}.[7]$$

The next scenario will add a more realistic element to the safety stock calculation by allowing for both *un*certain lead time *L* and uncertain demand. One of the prime reasons for lead time uncertainty is congestion during transportation or production delay, topics discussed extensively in Chapters 8 and 11. Assuming that the uncertainty of the lead time also follows a normal distribution,[8] with an expected lead time of $\overline{L}$ and a standard deviation S_L, the two elements contributing to possible stock-out are:
1. the demand in excess of the expectation during the scheduled or expected lead time. This is the same uncertainty as in the fixed lead time situation.
2. the extra demand during the time that replenishment arrives later than the scheduled date – or, in a situation where the freight arrives before the scheduled date, a period less of expected demand per cycle.

The standard deviation of uncertain demand over uncertain lead time becomes
$$\sigma_L = \sqrt{\overline{L}^* \sigma^2{}_D + \overline{D^2}^* S^2{}_L}.$$

$\sigma^2{}_D$ is the variance of demand during the expected lead time and $S^2{}_L$ is the variance of the lead time itself. $\overline{L}$ is the expected or scheduled lead time and $\overline{D^2}$ is the expected demand squared during lead time.

Example
The lead time for spare part XYZ coming from Japan to the United Kingdom follows a normal distribution with $\overline{L}$ = 20 days and a standard deviation S_L = 4 days. The demand in the UK for these spare parts follows an N(200, 24) distribution per day. The targeted CSL is 90%. Calculate the safety stock and the reorder point for spare parts XYZ.

Solution
The expected demand during a planned lead time of 20 days is 20 * 200 = 4,000 parts. The standard deviation of demand during the expected lead time σ_D = $\sqrt{20^* 24^2 + 200^{2\,*} 4^2} \approx 807$ parts.
The z-value of a CSL of 90% is $F^{-1}(0.9) \approx 1.28$.
The safety stock is 1.28 * 807 = 1,033 spare parts and the reorder point $[\overline{D} + z^* \sigma_L]$ is 4,000 + 1,033 = 5,033 spare parts XYZ.

Main point: two major causes of uncertainty in inventory policy are demand and lead time. If both of these random variables follow a normal distribution function one can calculate the safety inventory and reorder point for each Cycle Service Level. The total standard deviation is composed of both the standard deviation of demand and that of the lead time.

The impact of aggregating and centralizing safety stock

The case described at the beginning of Chapter 1 shows the number of stores and distribution centres of the major food retailers in the Netherlands. One salient feature of these data is that operating more stores does not always correlate proportionally with more DCs. The question arises of whether there is an optimal ratio between the number of stores and the number of distribution centers. We will focus the discussion on the impact on safety stock by aggregating demand or orders in fewer DCs. In a fully disaggregated or decentralized situation demand arrives at the store level, or even at a lower level at the Point of Sales.

Each store is faced with its demand variability and calculates its safety stock and associated holding costs at the store level. The orders received one level higher, at the distribution centre, are the sum of all orders issued by the individual stores, which are supplied by that distribution centre. If demand is aggregated at the level of the distribution centre[9] and the DC keeps the safety stock of all stores, substantial savings in safety stock and associated holding costs can be achieved, particularly if demand between the individual retail stores is *pairwise correlated*.

When the network of retail stores is geographically close, correlation can be a consequence of customers who do not find what they are looking for in store A, go to store B next door. This creates a *negative* correlation between A and B. Correlation can also be a consequence of a promotion campaign initiated by the company controlling all stores. A price discount implemented in all stores will see an increase in demand in most, if not all, of the stores, so that demand and orders surge for all stores simultaneously. This is a positive correlation. We use an example to illustrate the impact of demand correlation. A chain operates four Do-It-Yourself (DIY) stores A, B, C, and D, all acting independently of each other. Each of the stores sells the same product (foldable ladders). The sales of foldable ladders over 20 days follow four different normal distributions displayed in the second row of the table, while actual sales data in weeks 1 to 20 are displayed below.

Week	Store A	Store B	Store C	Store D	Total Sales
	N(60, 4)	N(50, 8)	N(110, 40)	N(70, 12)	
1	55	35	157	60	307
2	57	63	134	71	326
3	58	63	-9	64	176
4	61	55	115	80	312
5	58	45	121	56	279
6	62	50	126	51	289
7	53	62	160	73	347
8	58	49	154	67	328
9	66	41	186	64	356
10	56	41	110	59	266
11	55	54	124	81	314
12	54	40	134	51	278
13	65	50	96	93	304

Week	Store A N(60, 4)	Store B N(50, 8)	Store C N(110, 40)	Store D N(70, 12)	Total Sales
14	61	50	106	72	289
15	47	61	87	72	266
16	54	51	105	78	288
17	64	45	147	64	320
18	62	48	100	73	282
19	59	44	119	73	295
20	63	31	88	64	246
Average	58	49	118	68	293
Variance	20,4	80,1	1,483.5	103.0	1,445
Std Dev.	4,5	9,0	38,5	10,2	38,0

The table above calculates the average daily sales over a period of 20 days, the variance, and the standard deviation for each store. We also need to know the pairwise correlation of demand among the four stores. Instead of using correlation coefficients $\rho(X, Y)$, we replace them with covariances. The relation between covariance and correlation coefficient is $Cov(X, Y) = \rho(X, Y)^* \sigma_X {}^* \sigma_Y$. The covariance matrix over the 20 days yields the results in the table below.

Covariance matrix

	Store A	Store B	Store C	Store D
Store A	20.4	-14.0	16.2	3.1
Store B	-14.0	80.1	-108.9	38.7
Store C	16.2	-108.9	1,483.5	-55.9
Store D	3.1	38.7	-55.9	103.0
Sum all covariances		1,445		
Standard Deviation DC		38.0		

Explanatory notes about the tables above

The fourth column shows the daily demand aggregated at the DC level and is the sum of the daily sales of all four stores. The variance of the demand for the DC is, rounded, 1445 foldable ladders and that is less than the sum of the variances of each store separately. In the covariance table, the diagonal entries are the variances of each store $Cov(X, X) = \sigma^2_X$.

The off-diagonal elements are the covariances complying with the rule that $Cov(X, Y) = Cov(Y, X)$ and therefore always appear twice. Some covariances are negative and other positive. But the primary finding is that the sum of *all* cells in the covariance table *equals* the variance of the daily demand of the DC and that this variance is *lower* than the sum of the four variances of each store. The mean demand of the DC is the sum of the mean demand of each store (293 foldable ladders per day). The DC serves as a kind of cushion where positive and negative deviations of mean demand per store partially cancel each other out due to the correlation among the stores.

Main Point: by aggregating uncertain demand and orders at a higher level in the Supply Chain, demand at this level is the sum of the demand of all lower-level units (stores). In other words: by aggregating demand and inventory at a higher level no demand is lost, but the variance and, the standard deviation for the higher level is lower than the sum of the variances and standard deviations of the lower-level units. Consequently, both safety stock and concomitant holding costs are less with aggregation.

We will now derive a general formula to calculate the safety stock in case of aggregating demand and orders starting with the demand experienced by the POS and then moving upward to a higher echelon in the Supply Chain.
- $D_i \sim N(\mu_i, \sigma_i)$, the demand at each POS i follows a normal distribution with known parameters for $i = 1$ to N.
- Lead time is fixed at L periods (days, weeks, months).
- The covariance between demand at POS i and POS j is $Cov(D_i, D_j)$
- CSL is the Cycle Service Level set by the sales manager

The expected demand with aggregation is $D^A = \sum_{i=1}^{N} D_i$ and the variance per period with aggregation is
$$\sigma^2_A = \sum_{i=1}^{N} \sigma^2_i + 2 * \sum_{i<j} Cov(D_i, D_j)$$
$$\text{and } \sigma_A = \sqrt{\sigma^2_A}.$$

The first sum in the equation of σ^2_A refers to all diagonal elements in the covariance matrix (= variances) and the second to all off-diagonal elements. The number 2 before the Σ-sign is a consequence of the symmetry of the covariance matrix: $Cov(D_i, D_j) = Cov(D_j, D_i)$, and, consequently, all covariances appear two times in the matrix.

The Reorder Point at the aggregated level becomes ROP = F^{-1}(CSL) * $\sqrt{L}$ * σ_A with F^{-1}(CSL) the inverse standardized normal distribution function at the given CSL. The reorder point ROP = $[D^A + ss]$.

An interesting characteristic is that if all demand functions for each POS have an identical N(μ, σ) distribution function and are pairwise *un*correlated, aggregation over N yields $\mu^A = N^*\mu$ and $\sigma_A = \sqrt{N}^*\sigma$.

Calculating holding costs for cycle inventory, safety inventory, and shipment[10]

The computation of holding costs is different for cycle inventory and safety stock. Cycle inventory is kept for sales and follows the sawtooth pattern, described in the chapter about the EOQ, with an average level of ½*Q. Safety stock (ss) is not intended for daily sales and serves as a buffer against stock-outs during lead time. The variability of safety stock is usually significantly less than for cycle inventory and, if safety stock is used, it will be replaced as soon as possible, immediately after the next replenishment. Therefore, if holding cost per unit per year is €H, total annual holding cost for cycle inventory is approximated by [½*Q]*H, but for the *safety* stock is €H*ss – not the average value of safety stock.

Although aggregation reduces the holding costs of inventory, it comes with a side effect. By centralizing inventory, the distance to the stores or final customer will be greater and therefore the logistics costs higher, and it will also affect the response time before products arrive at the customer's location.[11] There is a trade-off between more aggregation and larger shipment distances and most companies will look to strike an optimal balance between the two cost factors: higher logistics costs for longer shipments and lower holding costs for reduced safety stock.

Reviewing inventories: Continuous and periodic policy

In this digital era, when Enterprise Resource Planning (ERP) software keeps instantaneous track of transactions, managers in most medium-sized and large companies have access to real-time information about the inventory levels and, in some cases, suppliers also have access to this information. Replenishment can take place at any moment. This is an example of *continuous review.*

For some smaller firms, which are not equipped with fully automated inventory systems, inventory is periodically checked manually, and replenishment orders are sent to the supplier based on the inventory at hand. The manager in charge of inventory sets the order size to target an inventory level of X units *after* replenishment has arrived. This form of inventory review is called *periodic review*. The mean demand and its standard deviation in periodic review will be calculated over the review period (T) plus the lead time (L): T + L. Consequently, the periodic review will lead to higher safety stock and therefore higher holding costs.

A third inventory policy is *just-in-time* inventory (JIT). JIT originated in Japan and means that inventory arrives when needed, mostly for manufacturing activities and sometimes for sales. JIT keeps the average cycle inventory and the associated holding costs low, but shipment costs and order-processing costs are high. JIT inventory policy is closely linked to JIT manufacturing, whereby replenishment of raw materials and components fits as well as possible into the production planning. JIT is closely linked to *lean* production, discussed in Chapter 4.

Another replenishment policy issue is the physical storage and economic ownership of inventory. Storing goods requires the availability of adequate storage facilities and space. For, say, a store located in a downtown area with little free space in its premises, or for storage requiring special conditions, like cooling systems for fresh food or safety systems for fireworks, a supplying DC can be better equipped than a smaller physical store. The local store can make arrangements regarding buying and paying for goods directly from its supplier's DC. The DC keeps the items stored on behalf of the store and cannot sell them to third parties because the ownership rights belong to the store. The store will pay a fee to the DC for this external warehousing or will compensate it in another way for this service, which results in the DC incurring the costs of physical storage.[12]

Postponement as a tool to reduce inventory in a manufacturer setting

Production planners of, for example, clothing manufacturers producing a specific model of trousers must take into account a variety of waist sizes and lengths and many different colours, so the company can end up with several hundreds of varieties of the same trousers. Even if the company can make a reliable consumer demand estimate for this model of trousers for the upcoming year, the company will seldom have a reliable estimate of every variety. A manufacturer targeting a high CSL will have to produce large numbers of each variety before the sales season starts. The probability of overproducing some varieties and underproducing other varieties is high.

Postponement means that a manufacturer is able to differentiate the varieties to the last possible phase of the production process. By arranging special machine set-ups, they can produce initial basic components, like weaving the yarn and fibres for trouser legs, for trouser pockets, for zippers, and other parts. When customer orders arrive, specified by colour and sizes, the manufacturer can customize the trousers faster by putting the preproduced parts into one single trouser and then dyeing them with the ordered colour. If, for example, the manufacturer does not receive an order for trousers with size XXL, waist 28, and in the colour dark brown, then none of this model will be produced. If the manufacturer does not use a postponement policy and chooses to make all variations in advance of orders, they are likely to produce at least some units of each variety. Postponement moves the moment of customization closer to the moment when orders arrive and demand becomes more visible. It can save the manufacturer considerable quantities of unsold, semi-finished trousers.[13] This broad range of variations of the same product also impacts production planning, especially the set-up of machines for each new variation. However, nearly all varieties are made on the same production line and require marginal machine adjustments.

Cycle Service Level and fill rate

Up to now, all the formulas are based on a targeted Cycle Service Level, the metric indicating in how many inventory cycles demand was not met – even if it was only for one unit. Much more realistic is a targeted fill rate, which indicates what *percentage* of demand was met during an inventory cycle. As discussed at the beginning of this chapter, the formulas are much simpler with CSL than with fill rate. Fortunately, there is a way to convert the CSL into fill rate, and vice versa, and that is what we will explore now in more detail.[14]

If a company targets a given fill rate, we first convert this fill rate to the corresponding CSL, and then use the calculated CSL in the formulas to compute safety stock. Therefore, we must first explore fill rate and the related concept of stock-out in more detail. Stock-out occurs when demand during lead time is higher than the reorder point, because lead time starts when orders are released at the ROP. We introduce a new metric: the *expected shortage per replenishment or inventory cycle* or ESC. We set the ordered lot size Q equal to the expected demand during lead time $\overline{D}$ + safety stock *ss*. In formula Q = $\overline{D}$ + *ss* and Q is also the inventory level for the reorder point. Stock-out occurs during the lead time which starts with the order release to the supplier at the reorder point *ROP*. Demand is assumed to follow a normal distribution function with a mean value $\overline{D}_L$ and standard deviation σ_L both during the lead time. Stock-out occurs when demand D > Q = ROP. The expected shortage per replenishment cycle (ESC) in *units* is defined as ESC = D – Q. If we express this stock-out as a *rate*, we take the percentage ESC/Q = (D – Q)/Q = D/Q – 1.

The fill rate is the *complement* of the ESC, namely 1 – ESC/Q = (Q – ESC)/Q, and is expressed as a percentage of demand per inventory cycle. By taking the normal density function f(D) of demand D during the lead time the *expected* (or average) *shortage* ESC is calculated over *all* values for which [D – ROP] > 0 times the probability of each shortage occurring. In formula:

$$ESC = \int_{D=ROP}^{\infty}(D - ROP)^*f(D)d(D).$$

After some awkward operations, this integral can be rewritten as:[15]

$$ESC = -ss^*\left[1 - F_S\left(\tfrac{ss}{\sigma_L}\right)\right] (part\ 1) + \sigma_L{}^*f_S\left(\tfrac{ss}{\sigma_L}\right) (part\ 2)$$

ss = safety stock, $\left(\tfrac{ss}{\sigma_L}\right)$ is the safety stock per unit of standard deviation during lead time, $F_S()$ is the *cumulative* standardized normal distribution, and $f_S()$ is the standard normal *density* function.

The formula of the ESC allows us to calculate the ESC in units, the fill rate fr = $1 - (ESQ/Q)$, and the Cycle Service Level (CSL). Recall that the CSL and the safety stock are related to each other: ss = $F_S{}^{-1}(CSL)^*\sigma_L$. This can be rewritten as $F_S{}^{-1}(CSL)$ = ss/σ_L. If we overlay the standard cumulative distribution function at the left and right side we obtain $F_S[F_S{}^{-1}(CSL)]$ = $F_S[ss/\sigma_L]$. Because the inverse function of its inverse $F_S(F_S{}^{-1})$ is the argument of the function (CSL) we get CSL = $F_S[ss/\sigma_L]$.

The CSL is implicitly in part 1 of the formula

$$-ss^*\left[1 - F_S\left(\tfrac{ss}{\sigma_L}\right)\right] \qquad [A]$$

By rewriting formula [A] we get

$$F_S\left(\tfrac{ss}{\sigma_L}\right) = CSL = -\left(-ss^*\left[1 - F_S\left(\tfrac{ss}{\sigma_L}\right)\right]/-ss\right) + 1$$

We illustrate these relations with an example, where safety stock is given based on historical data and other parameters are given. The Expected Shortage per Cycle and the Cycle Service Level are shown in the Excel screenshot below:

	A	B	C	D	E
1	Safety Stock is given. ESC and CSL are computed based on ss!				
2	Lot Size Q = ROP = Exp Dem + ss	Expected Demand	Std. dev. Demand	Lead Time	Safety Stock ss
3	175	150	32	1	25
4					
5	Expected Shortage per Cycle	Fill Rate fr	CSL		
6	3.975	97.73%	78.3%		
7					
8	Calculated values				
9	Part 1 formula	-5.43			
10	Part 2 formula	9.41			
11	Expected Shortage per Cycle ESC	3.98			

The input formulas in the cells are shown in the screenshot table below:

	A	B	C	D	E
1	Safety Stock is given. ESC and CSL are computed based on ss!				
2	Lot Size Q = ROP = Exp Dem + ss	Expected Demand	Std. dev. Demand	Lead Time	Safety Stock ss
3	=B3+E3	150	32	1	25
4					
5	Expected Shortage per cycle	Fill Rate fr	CSL		
6	=B11	=1-(A6/A3)	=NORM.DIST((E3+B3);B3;C3;1)		
7					
8	Calculated values				
9	Part 1 formula	=-E3*(1-NORM.DIST((E3/C3);0;1;1))			
10	Part 2 formula	=C3*NORM.DIST((E3/C3);0;1;0)			
11	Expected Shortage per Cycle ESC	=SUM(B9:B10)			

The parameters in the model are the expected demand during lead time (cell B3), the standard deviation of demand (cell C3), the Lead time (cell D3), and the Safety stock (cell E3). Q in cell A3 equals the reorder point. The expected shortage per cycle equals four units after rounding in cell B11, the fill rate 97.73% in cell B6, and the Cycle Service Level 78.3% in cell C6. All these values are calculated based on a *preset* safety stock of 25 units. We get the same CSL by using the equation as discussed above: $- (5.433/-25) + 1 = 78.3\%$!

More common business practice is that management sets a *targeted* fill rate and based on this fill rate calculates the associated safety stock and CSL. We use the same data as in the table above and make the safety stock cell E3 a variable. To find the value of the safety stock and the CSL we need *Solver* using the data shown below. The goal is to achieve a targeted fill rate of 95%. The objective function is in cell B6 and we want to obtain the value of 0.95 indicated in the Solver line "*Value of:*". The variable is cell E3, which contains the safety stock. After clicking on Solve we get the outcome cells shown under the Solver screenshot.

	A	B	C	D	E
1	Safety Stock is given. ESC and CSL are computed based on ss!				
2	Lot Size Q = ROP = Exp Dem + ss	Expected Demand	Std. dev. Demand	Lead Time	Safety Stock ss
3	161	150	32	1	11
4					
5	Expected Shortage per cycle	Fill Rate fr	CSL		
6	8.046	95.00%	63.3%		
7					
8	Calculated values				
9	Part 1 formula	-4.00			
10	Part 2 formula	12.05			
11	Expected Shortage per Cycle ESC	8.05			

Safety stock is rounded to 11 units, CSL is 63.3%, and ESC is eight units after rounding.[16]

Management recommendations to reduce costs of safety stock

The example discussed above points to the managerial levers to reduce costs of holding safety stock and also offers some management suggestions. The main driver of safety stock is the level of demand uncertainty measured by the standard deviation during lead time. Any reduction in this uncertainty will lead to a lower safety stock and therefore to lower safety stock costs. Given that safety stock is the standard deviation during lead time L and equals $\sigma^*\sqrt{L}$, any reduction in lead time is an effective way of safety stock reduction.

Lead time reduction can be accomplished by negotiating with the supplier more accurate delivery times or selecting a faster mode of transportation. The next lever is σ itself. σ is often the outcome of the forecasting process. Improving the forecasting method and implementing collaborative forecasting over the entire supply chain and not compartmentalized for each partner firm in the SC separately, will improve forecasting and thereby reducing σ.[17]

Before we end this chapter, we will devote a few words about a topical issue in supply chain inventory management and that is *multi-echelon cycle inventory*. In a SC, any stage or echelon keeps an inventory of products, from the manufacturing level at the top, down to the individual store level. The models discussed up to now focused on individual companies and did not take into account the impact that keeping safety stock has on other echelons in the SC.

A multi-echelon inventory optimization (MEIO) policy, sometimes also referred to as *multilevel or multi-stage inventory optimization*, is an integrated inventory policy to find the lowest cost inventory plan for the supply chain as a whole. The inventory coordination and synchronization not only refer to relations between the different stages in the SC for single products, like matching order frequency from retailer to distribution centre and the associated order frequency between the distribution centre and manufacturer, but also extend to the broad range of combinations of inventory aggregation. Some MEIO models also include the supporting logistics process to move all items at the right time in the right quantity to the different SC destinations. The planning models for MEIO are considerably more complex and usually tested by using computer simulation, which is beyond the scope of this book. A reference to the scientific literature about MEIO can be found in the Instructor's Manual.[18]

Notes

1-5   See Instructor's Manual
6   In Excel, the inverse standard normal distribution is the function NORM.S.INV in the function library and its argument is the CSL.
7-18   See Instructor's Manual

7 Optimal Customer Service Level, Sourcing Policies, and Risk-Sharing

Optimal customer service level, sourcing policies, and risk-sharing

In the previous chapter, we discussed the fill rate and the Cycle Service Level as metrics for the level of demand satisfaction. We concluded that a higher level of safety stock will reduce expected stock-outs, but simultaneously increases total holding costs. The question arises of whether a company can strike a balance between the marginal holding costs of keeping one unit more in safety stock and the expected profit of selling that unit. In this chapter, we will explore this topic in more detail and go deeper by giving an economic foundation for the optimal number of products stocked for sale to customers. A company always faces the trade-off between large amounts of inventory to increase responsiveness and to satisfy (peak) demand on one side and increased holding costs on the other side.

We will first translate physical stock levels into their associated costs and revenues. Any unit sold earns a selling price (P_{sales}), but also has to be purchased from a supplier at a purchase cost ($C_{purchase}$). When the supplier is a manufacturer, the product has to be produced and the manufacturer will incur production costs, which are the equivalent of the purchase cost for a merchandise company.[1] When the company has products inventoried and is not able to sell them at the regular selling price (P_{sales}) during the inventory cycle due to a lack of demand, it has several options:[2]

- Drop the selling price before the product becomes unmarketable during the final sales days of the inventory cycle. This is a common option in the retail sector and especially for products with a short shelf life, such as fresh food and flowers. This process of lowering prices is not necessarily restricted to a once-only price drop but can be done gradually: the company can, for example, drop the price by 10% two weeks before replenishment, by another 10% one week before replenishment, and by 50% two days before replenishment.
- Sell the products to a factory outlet at a discount. We call this price P_o, and this price is usually lower than the purchase cost C_p. If it is higher, the outlet store is better advised to buy the product immediately from the manufacturer for the lower C_p.
- If the product cannot be sold in anyway it can be donated to a charity.[3] In this case, the company does not earn revenue and P_o = €0.

–   In the worst-case scenario, it will be discarded and thrown away, or made available for recycling.
The downside is that if this practice becomes known to the general public, it can hurt the company's reputation.

What are the basic calculations of the cost of overstocking C_o and understocking C_u?

1. Any unit that is sold at the regular price earns a *profit* of $[P_{sales} - C_{purchase}]$
2. Any unit that is overstocked creates a loss equal to $[C_{purchase} - P_o]$
3. Any unit that is understocked incurs a cost equal to the profit margin *foregone* due to non-availability and this profit margin is the same as in bullet 1.

If a company targets a high Cycle Service Level, the probability of units unsold will rise and therefore will encounter expected overstocking costs. Ordering too few units means that the probability of understocking increases. We will illustrate this with an example with the data displayed in the table below showing *un*certain demand.

	A	B	C	D	E	F	G	H	I
1	Order size in unit	Selling price	Purchase cost	Sale to outlet					
2	500	€ 24.00	€ 14.00	€ 11.00					
3									
4	Cycle Demand	Probability of demand	Cumulative probabilities	Probability exceeds given demand		Profit on units	Loss on unsold units	Probability occurrence	Expected profit
5	200	1.0%	1.0%	99.0%		€ 2,000	€ -900	1.0%	€ 11
6	250	3.0%	4.0%	96.0%		€ 2,500	€ -750	3.0%	€ 53
7	300	5.0%	9.0%	91.0%		€ 3,000	€ -600	5.0%	€ 120
8	350	8.0%	17.0%	83.0%		€ 3,500	€ -450	8.0%	€ 244
9	400	12.0%	29.0%	71.0%		€ 4,000	€ -300	12.0%	€ 444
10	450	15.0%	44.0%	56.0%		€ 4,500	€ -150	15.0%	€ 653
11	500	18.0%	62.0%	38.0%		€ 5,000	€ 0	18.0%	€ 900
12	550	14.0%	76.0%	24.0%		€ 5,000	€ 0	14.0%	€ 700
13	600	11.0%	87.0%	13.0%		€ 5,000	€ 0	11.0%	€ 550
14	650	7.0%	94.0%	6.0%		€ 5,000	€ 0	7.0%	€ 350
15	700	5.0%	99.0%	1.0%		€ 5,000	€ 0	5.0%	€ 250
16	750	1.0%	100.0%	0.0%		€ 5,000	€ 0	1.0%	€ 50
17								Sum =	€ 29,681

The input data are given in row 2 in the Excel screenshot. The order quantity is set at Q = 500 units, which can be based on past practice or by using the EOQ formula. The consumer selling price is €24 and the purchase price is €14. If the product is not sold for the standard price, it will be sold at the end of the sales cycle to a factory outlet for a price of €11.

Any unit sold generates a profit of €24 – €14 = €10 and any unit purchased and not sold (overstocked) generates a loss of €11 – €14 = -€3. Demand per cycle varies between a minimum of 200 units and a maximum of 750 units and is given in steps of 50 units. Based on historical sales data, the probabilities at each demand level are shown in the second column. Columns F, G, H, and I of the table below show the underlying formulas.

	F	G	H	I
			Probability	
4	Profit on units sold	Loss on unsold units	occurrence	Expected profit
5	=IF(A5<=$A$2;A5;$A$2)*($B$2-$C$2)	=IF($A$2>=A5;($A$2-A5);0)*($D$2-$C$2)	=B5	=H5*(F5+G5)
6	=IF(A6<=$A$2;A6;$A$2)*($B$2-$C$2)	=IF($A$2>=A6;($A$2-A6);0)*($D$2-$C$2)	=B6	=H6*(F6+G6)
7	=IF(A7<=$A$2;A7;$A$2)*($B$2-$C$2)	=IF($A$2>=A7;($A$2-A7);0)*($D$2-$C$2)	=B7	=H7*(F7+G7)
8	=IF(A8<=$A$2;A8;$A$2)*($B$2-$C$2)	=IF($A$2>=A8;($A$2-A8);0)*($D$2-$C$2)	=B8	=H8*(F8+G8)
9	=IF(A9<=$A$2;A9;$A$2)*($B$2-$C$2)	=IF($A$2>=A9;($A$2-A9);0)*($D$2-$C$2)	=B9	=H9*(F9+G9)
10	=IF(A10<=$A$2;A10;$A$2)*($B$2-$C$2)	=IF($A$2>=A10;($A$2-A10);0)*($D$2-$C$2)	=B10	=H10*(F10+G10)
11	=IF(A11<=$A$2;A11;$A$2)*($B$2-$C$2)	=IF($A$2>=A11;($A$2-A11);0)*($D$2-$C$2)	=B11	=H11*(F11+G11)
12	=IF(A12<=$A$2;A12;$A$2)*($B$2-$C$2)	=IF($A$2>=A12;($A$2-A12);0)*($D$2-$C$2)	=B12	=H12*(F12+G12)
13	=IF(A13<=$A$2;A13;$A$2)*($B$2-$C$2)	=IF($A$2>=A13;($A$2-A13);0)*($D$2-$C$2)	=B13	=H13*(F13+G13)
14	=IF(A14<=$A$2;A14;$A$2)*($B$2-$C$2)	=IF($A$2>=A14;($A$2-A14);0)*($D$2-$C$2)	=B14	=H14*(F14+G14)
15	=IF(A15<=$A$2;A15;$A$2)*($B$2-$C$2)	=IF($A$2>=A15;($A$2-A15);0)*($D$2-$C$2)	=B15	=H15*(F15+G15)
16	=IF(A16<=$A$2;A16;$A$2)*($B$2-$C$2)	=IF($A$2>=A16;($A$2-A16);0)*($D$2-$C$2)	=B16	=H16*(F16+G16)
17			Sum =	=SUM(I5:I18)

Explanatory notes on the table above

If the demand is lower than the order size – evaluated by the IF-statement in cell A5 and below in the table – the full demand is sold for a profit of (B2 – C2). The remainder (A2 – A5) is sold to the factory outlet at a loss of -€3 (D2 – C2) displayed in column G. Both values are summed in column H and then multiplied with the probability that this demand will occur. The outcome is the expected profit in column I. For all rows where demand is higher than Q = 500 units, the entire inventory of 500 units will be sold at a profit margin of €10 and there is no loss on overstocked units.

The profit foregone due to understocking is not part of the profit calculations. They are opportunity costs that are not accounted for in a corporate *profit-and-loss statement*. The expected profit is the sum of the columns *Profit on units sold* and *Loss on unsold units*. The outcome gives an expected profit of €29,681 per cycle. The Cycle Service Level with an order size Q = 500 can be read as 62% in the column *Cumulative probability*.

To see if the expected profits will go up by ordering quantities greater than 500 we use a marginal approach and increase the order size Q stepwise with 50 units – in line with demand, which also uses steps of 50 units to keep the table readable.[4] We start with a new order size Q = 550. Adding 50 units to the cycle inventory adds a marginal profit of 50 * (€24 – €14) = €500 only if demand is 550 or *higher*. The probability of P[D ≥ 550] can be read in the fourth column of the table and is 24%.

If demand is 500 or lower, the 50 units will remain unsold via the usual sales channel and sold to the outlet at a loss of 50 * (€11 – €14) = -€150. The probability P[D ≤ 500] = 76%. The expected change in profit by adding these 50 units to the order size is 24% * €500 + 76% * -€150 = +€6 and total expected profit becomes €29,681 + €6 = €29,687. So, ordering Q = 550 units is marginally more profitable than ordering 500 units and increases the CSL to 76%.

Now we add another ΔQ = 50 units to obtain 600 units and follow the same line of reasoning as with the first increment of Q. If these 50 units are sold they contribute a marginal profit of €500 only when demand is 600 or higher with an associated probability of 13%. With a probability of 87%, the additional 50 units are sold at a loss of -€150 to the outlet. Expected incremental loss is 13% * €500 + 87%*-€150 = -€65. So, by ordering 600 units a loss is incurred. We conclude that the optimal order size Q = 550 units with a CSL of 76%.

We now derive the optimal Cycle Service Level based on the costs of under-stocking C_u = $(P_{sales} - C_{purchase})$ (profit foregone) and the cost of overstocking C_o = $(P_{outlet} - C_{purchase})$. Because this is a negative number, we write $C_{purchase} - P_{outlet}$ to make it positive costs. We define the optimal order size by adding an asterisk Q^* and the optimal CSL as CSL^*, whereby CSL^* is the probability corresponding to a demand less or equal to Q^*. This implies that the entire demand is fulfilled with Q^*. We use the marginal approach by adding, at each step, one unit to the optimal order size $Q^* = Q^*+1$. This marginal unit will be sold only if demand is larger than Q^* and that probability is $(1 - CSL^*)$ and earns a profit margin of $(P_{sales} - C_{purchase})$. It will not be sold when demand is lower than the demand associated with CSL^* and generates a loss of $(C_{purchase} - P_{outlet})$.

Adding more units to Q^* increases total profit as long as the expected profit of this unit is higher than the expected loss of selling it to the outlet. An optimum is reached when the two expected values are equal.

In formula: maximization of the expected profit is reached when:

$$(P_{sales} - C_{purchase})^*(1 - CSL^*) = (C_{purchase} - P_{outlet})^*CSL^*$$

Removing brackets on both sides:

$$P_{sales} - C_{purchase} - P_{sales}^*CSL^* + C_{purchase}^*CSL^* = CSL^* * C_{purchase} - CSL^* *P_{outlet}$$

Rearranging terms moving all terms with CSL^* to the right

$$P_{sales} - C_{purchase} = CSL^* * P_{sales} - CSL^* * P_{outlet} \rightarrow$$
$$P_{sales} - C_{purchase} = CSL^* *(P_{sales} - P_{outlet}) \rightarrow$$
$$CSL^* = [P_{sales} - C_{purchase}]/[(P_{sales} - C_{purchase}) + (C_{purchase} - P_{outlet})].$$

We recognize the numerator as C_u and the denominator as $(C_u + C_o)$, where, for convenience, we have added in the denominator, the zero term $-C_{purchase} + C_{purchase} = 0$!

Putting pieces together we get:

$$CSL^* = \frac{C_u}{C_u + C_o}.$$

Referring to the previous chapter, the corresponding optimal Order Size is found as
$Q^* = F^{-1}(CSL^*, \mu, \sigma)$.

Applying this formula to our example above, we obtain CSL = €10 / (€10 + €3) = 76.9%.
This is approximately the same as the 76% we found in the table with $Q^* = 550$.
The small difference is because the table is set up in steps of 50 units and not as a
continuous range. If the table is set up in single units the optimal CSL would be even
more accurate.[5] We can then convert the optimal CSL to the optimal corresponding
fill rate by following the steps described in the previous chapter.

Expected profits under optimal CSL

Now that we have found the optimal CSL^* and order size Q^* we can calculate the
corresponding expected profit for the retailer in the optimal situation. The formula
for the expected retailer profits consists of *four* parts.[6] For simplicity, we replace
P_{outlet} with P_{Res} where the index *Res* stands for residual value, Q for the order quantity,
and C_p stands for the purchase price. Demand during lead time is usually distributed
with mean μ and standard deviation σ.
  Expected profit = [1] + [2] + [3] + [4] with

[1] $+(P_{sales} - P_{Res})^*\mu^*F_S(\frac{Q-\mu}{\sigma})$ with F_S the standard *cumulative* normal distribution
    evaluated at $[(Q - \mu)/\sigma]$
[2] $-(P_{sales} - P_{Res})^*\sigma^*f_S(\frac{Q-\mu}{\sigma})$ with f_S the standard normal *density* function evaluated
    at $[(Q - \mu)/\sigma]$
[3] $-Q^*(C_p - P_{Res})^*F(Q, \mu, \sigma)$ with F the *cumulative* (non-standard) normal distri-
    bution evaluated at Q
[4] $+Q^*(P_{sales} - C_p)^*[1 - F(Q, \mu, \sigma)]$ with F the *cumulative* (non-standard) normal
    distribution evaluated at Q

An interesting feature of this expected profit equation is that, in the optimal
situation, parts [3] and [4] cancel each other and only parts [1] and part [2] suffice
to calculate the expected profit.[7]
  In addition to the expected profits, we can also calculate the *expected*
overstock and the *expected* understock for each order size Q. The respective
formulas are:

Expected overstock = $(Q - \mu)^* F_s(\frac{Q-\mu}{\sigma}) + \sigma^* f_s(\frac{Q-\mu}{\sigma})$

Expected understock = $(\mu - Q)^* \left[1 - F_s(\frac{Q-\mu}{\sigma})\right] + \sigma^* f_s(\frac{Q-\mu}{\sigma})$.

F_s and f_s in the formulas are the same functions as those used in the formula for the expected profit.

We will not give a formal mathematical proof of these two formulas because they follow the same set-up and steps as the derivation of the expected profit formula. For the interested reader this derivation is described in the Mathematical Appendix on the website. Notice that, at a given value of Q, both the expected overstock and understock are either positive or 0. If there is overstock, the value of understock will be 0 and not negative, and if there is positive understock then the value of the expected overstock will be 0 and not negative.

We point also in the overstock formula to the observation that the term $(Q - \mu)$, which is positive in the case of overstock, implying that Q > mean demand μ is weighted with the *left* tail of the cumulative distribution function $F_s[(Q - \mu)/\sigma] = P[D \leq Q]$. In the case of understock, we take $(\mu - Q)$, which is also positive in the case of understock, implying that Q < mean demand μ and is weighted with the *right* tail of the normal distribution function

$$[1 - F_s[(Q - \mu)/\sigma]] = P[D > Q].$$

Both the *expected* overstock and understock can be positive at any given order-level Q, because demand is uncertain and can end up above Q and below Q after the sales cycle. However, after demand has been materialized, there is either overstock or understock, but never both!

Main Point: finding the optimal Cycle Service Level (CSL) depends primarily on the costs of understocking and overstocking leading to $CSL^* = C_u/(C_u + C_o)$. This optimal CSL^* forms the input for the calculation of the optimal order size Q^* and, with these two parameters, the corresponding expected profit, expected understock, and expected overstock can be computed.

Backlogging and stocking-out

Stock-out costs occur when customers leave the shop, or delete their digital shopping baskets in the case of online sales, and, switch to a competitor if they cannot find their favourite product or service. In some cases, however, the customer is willing to come back later to collect or receive the wanted item. This is called *backlogging*, whereby the firm delivers the stuff later than the customer expects. The firm does not lose the profit margin of this transaction and there are no stock-out costs, although the firm possibly incurs additional ordering or shipment costs for the backlogging process. Moreover, backlogging can harm customer goodwill for the firm.

Another common problem that creates hurdles for a company in terms of orders and storing stock levels that match their optimal Cycle Service Level is the presence of capacity or storage constraints, in particular when a large variety of products is kept in inventory and each product has its optimal own order size Q^*. Finding optimal order sizes with capacity constraints can be tackled by modelling them as an optimization problem. We set the storage constraint for all products of a warehouse on A m² floor space. The warehouse stores N different products, each with its selling price, purchase cost, and salvage value. We want to calculate the order sizes Q_i for all i = 1 until N products that will maximize the overall profit of the firm. This optimization problem is described in the following model:

Maximize $\qquad \sum_{i=1}^{N} \Pr(Q_i)$

Subject to $\qquad \sum_{i=1}^{N} Q_i \leq A$ and $Q_i \geq 0$ for all i.

$\Pr(Q_i)$ is the expected profit function for product i and order size Q_i. The profit is calculated using the four-part profit formula described on the previous page. The total m² storage space for all products together cannot exceed the floor space of the company.

To insource or to outsource: That is the question!

We now make a leap from inventory management to procurement management, which explores the basic elements of optimal procurement or sourcing.[8] Procurement or sourcing refers to the decision-making process whereby raw materials, tools, subcomponents, and goods or services that support the core manufacturing and distribution activities within the supply chain are *made* or are outsourced to third-party companies.

Every organization engages in procurement activities because all need assets and resources, in the form of either tangible goods, intangible goods, and/or services, to achieve their organizational goals. There is, however, hardly any organization that has full control and all knowledge and resources to carry out every part of its business processes fully on its own, especially in the 21st century when we have sophisticated production processes, information technology, and a complex regulatory global, regional, and local business environment.

Some companies have completely outsourced their manufacturing activities to third parties – many of them to China – and often the few things they keep under their own control is marketing and sales besides collecting the profit. Many medium-sized and large companies have their own procurement departments where all know-how and skills about procurement, including sometimes global databases of suppliers for a vast range of raw materials, products, and services, are centralized and procurement strategies and policies are designed and monitored. Organizations in the European Union belonging to the public administration and government at all levels (national, regional, and local) are subject to the legal and regulatory framework of *public procurement*. As discussed in Chapter 1, this legal framework sets constraints on the group of suppliers they can select from. The most common procurement procedure for public sector companies is *public tender*.

Some business companies have centralized procurement departments that must authorize or approve all purchases by other departments exceeding a certain sum of money. Such departments keep long lists of sometimes 10,000 suppliers in many different countries, ranking from preferred to emergency suppliers. Other global operating companies have decentralized procurement departments so that every national organizational unit or division can select its own suppliers to buy what they need within the constraints set by corporate directives and procurement strategy. Decentralized procurement offers decentralized organizational divisions the option of local sourcing in the country where they are based. Between the two extremes of fully centralized and fully decentralized sourcing strategies are many intermediate ways to design sourcing processes. Nowadays, sourcing requires specialized expertise pooled in procurement teams where each team member has their own professional skills and responsibilities. Sourcing processes come in many different flavours and the selection of the right supplier depends on many factors, such as the kind products or services the company needs, the frequency of supply orders, and the price.

The *purchase requisition* is an internal company document where departments specify in detail which products and services they need to meet their organizational targets and fulfil their tasks. This document is sent to the sourcing department, which then makes a supplier selection. A traditional but still valuable classification of sourcing goods was developed by Kraljic in 1983. He distinguished the following purchase categories:

– **Strategic purchases**. These represent huge expenses (high spend) whereby the reliable performance of the supplier is very important. They are high-risk suppliers in the sense that if supply fails the company gets into trouble. An example is the supplier of brake systems or the engines to a car manufacturer.
– **Bottleneck purchases**. They have high supply risk but are low in value. A lack of these products is not critical for business activities, but delivery delays can interrupt the production and/or distribution process.

An example is the windshield wipers of a car: windshield wipers are obligatory on cars in the EU – although not for a rear window – so a car without a windshield wiper cannot be sold on the EU market.

- *Leverage purchases*. These are high-spend purchases but with low risk and typically refer to standardized goods. An example is the navigation device in a car, which is a standard accessory in many cars nowadays.
- *Non-critical purchases*. Low spend and low supply-risk items. If these items are missing, they do not cause serious problems in the production, distribution, or sales process. Examples are basic tools, which the manufacturer can also buy in Do-It-Yourself shops or order online.

For each of the four categories, a specific sourcing policy is developed.

For *strategic purchases*, selecting and building a lasting partnership with a few suppliers is the most appropriate solution. One day they may become fully qualified partners in the Supply Chain.

For the *bottleneck purchase*, it is recommended that at least two suppliers are selected – in case one of them fails to meet its delivery obligations. The company will look for alternatives in order to become less dependent on these suppliers.

For *leverage purchases* there are generally many suppliers available. Ordering costs can be reduced by standardizing supply contracts with these suppliers and using a competitive bidding process to select a low-cost supplier. Orders can be aggregated to purchase from a few suppliers in order to obtain price discounts.

For the last category of *non-critical* items, the company can use online product catalogues and electronic ordering without engaging in long and costly procurement purchase transactions. Switching suppliers is simple, and most products and services are standardized and not customized. In many cases, suppliers will be local and close to the facility that places the orders.[9]

The kind of *relationship* that a company establishes and maintains with a supplier depends on, among other things, the product categories discussed above and on the duration of the supply contract.

A sliding scale can be used to describe different supplier relationships. At one extreme is the *transactional* relationship, which consists of merely placing an order (online), receiving the product, and lodging a claim if the product does not meet the expected quality standards, or even suing the supplier if delivery conditions are not met. This relationship occurs frequently in online transactions for standardized products. The supplier hardly knows its customer, communications are scant, and the supplier does not know if there will be follow-up orders from the same customer in the future. This relationship is sometimes called an *adversarial relationship*.

Another kind of relationship is the *arm's-length relationship*, which is similar to the adversarial relationship but there is less mutual distrust between supplier and customer. It is a purely business-oriented relationship whereby each party pursues its own interests. Moving further up the relationship ladder we come to the *acceptance of mutual goals*. In this kind of relationship, there is closer collaboration between customer and supplier, but it is not as far-reaching as in a partnership. This kind of relationship is common when supplying *customized* components or services rather than standardized ones.

The last relationship is a (*full*) *partnership*, which is the strongest form of collaboration. This relationship can be compared to relations within a marriage, with characteristics such as mutual trust, flexibility, respect, and transparent information-sharing. Sometimes, both partners also engage in joint projects, such as developing better or new products.

Tesco PLA and Carrefour SA Establish A Procurement Alliance

Food retailing seems to have turned into a game of choosing a partner, or as board-rooms would see it, an exercise in high-level maneuvering. Here comes Tesco, using NATO-style language to unveil its "long-term, strategic alliance" with Carrefour of France, complete with a three-year "operational framework" to guard against corporate secrets falling into the wrong hands. All it is really talking about is combining buying clout to demand lower prices from suppliers.

Grand strategic talk is in fashion in the age of Amazon. Retail executives talk of the industry evolving into a handful of global alliances, as happened with national airlines. In the UK, Sainsbury's will also enter the orbit of the US retailer if the Asda merger is approved by the Competition and Markets Authority. Out in China and south-east Asia, there's Alibaba, the local answer to Amazon. Meanwhile, Aldi and Lidl are already global players. The Tesco/Carrefour deal creates a new sphere of influence. It is too soon to speculate about a formal merger between Tesco and Carrefour, but such a script is possible if the buyers cohabit happily.

Tesco was long ago forced to abandon its go-it-alone approach to global expansion after flopping in the US and China. Getting cozy with Carrefour, a company with which it competes only in eastern Europe sounds safer from the point of view of shareholders.

The open question is who loses from the process of organizing food sourcing into a handful of leading global chains. Big consumer goods companies such as Nestlé, Coca-Cola, Unilever, and Kraft Heinz are the official targets since they achieve 15%-plus profit margins while the supermarket trade gets by about 3%, which is the nub of why Sainsbury's thinks it should be allowed to combine with Asda. Yet the share prices of big-branded companies are not obviously trembling in fear of a retailers' revolt. The market thinks Unilever will be perfectly able to look after themselves if the fighting over prices turns rougher.

If so, the worries should be for small suppliers and providers of own-label products. Selling to a retailer that sees itself as a part of a supranational alliance, created to find supply

chain "efficiencies", sounds like a very tough gig for them. Tesco, like Sainsbury's and Asda, swears blind that local producers aren't in its sights and that small business should think fondly of the opportunities to sell to a bigger customer. Treat that claim with skepticism. Life has rarely worked out pleasantly for the little folk when the squeeze is on.
Source: https://www.theguardian.com/business/nils-pratley-on-finance/2018/jul/02/tesco-and-carrefour-alliance-sounds-like-a-tough-gig-for-suppliers

Selecting suppliers and competitive bidding

Once a list of potential suppliers meeting a company's required standards has been prepared, a definitive selection must be made. Several selection methods are in common use to make the final decision about a supplier. One is *competitive bidding*. This means that the company shares its wish list, including a description of the product and the minimum product standards, specifications, and requirements with a series of equally qualified suppliers. This is called a *request for proposal*. The supplying firms submit a bid, and the procurement department will study all submitted bids. In competitive bidding, the quoted price is often the decisive factor. A second method is *online reverse bidding* in an auction over the internet. This is sometimes called e-sourcing.

In a typical auction, the seller offers an item which she wishes to sell. Potential buyers are then free to bid on the item until the period expires. The buyer with the highest offer wins the right to purchase the item for the price determined at the end of the auction. Multiple sellers are then able to offer bids on the contract. As the auction progresses, the price decreases as sellers compete to offer lower bids than their competitors whilst still meeting all of the specifications of the original contract. Bidding performed in real-time via the Internet results in a dynamic, competitive process. This helps achieve rapid downward price pressure that is not normally attainable using traditional static paper-based bidding processes. The buyer may award the contract to the seller who bid the lowest price. Or, a buyer may award contracts to suppliers who bid higher prices depending on the buyer's specific needs concerning quality, lead-time, capacity, or other value-adding capabilities.[10]

The final method that we will discuss here is *negotiation*. Once the most promising suppliers have been selected from a list of potential suppliers, representatives of the supplying and the buying firm will meet, mostly in person. Negotiation is a bargaining process between two parties and this method is frequently applied if the buying company wants to engage in a long-term strategic partnership.[11] Suppliers possessing certificates of e.g. ISO 9000 for quality control and ISO 14000 for environmental policies, are more likely to qualify as a supplier than companies lacking such documents. Once a supplier has been selected, the established relationship must be maintained and monitored, which is part of a company's *supplier relationship management* (SRM). The supplier will be periodically assessed on Key Performance Indicators (KPI) with the aid of a *supplier scorecard* that reviews performance in areas such as delivery time, price, quality, and, nowadays, also on ethical business behaviour and sustainability.

Total Cost of Ownership

Outsourcing business activities has a direct impact on the costs of the outsourcing company. Not only the price charged by the company that carries out the outsourced activity, but also transportation costs, quality control costs, replenishment costs, and other expenses affecting the performance of the Supply Chain by selecting a sourcing company. All those costs affected by a sourcing decision are called the *Total Cost of Ownership* (TOC). The TOC is often divided into three main cost groups:

1. **Acquisition costs**
These costs refer to all expenses incurred when purchasing products and delivering them to the customer's location, up to the point that they are available in quality and quantity for use. The purchase price, import duties, and taxes are part of these acquisition costs.
2. **Ownership costs**
These costs refer to the expenses incurred from the moment that a product arrives at the customer's location until it is sold as a finished product to the final consumer, and include inventory holding costs, manufacturing costs, and quality control costs, to mention a few.
3. **Post-ownership costs**
These costs refer to all expenses incurred after the end-product has been sold to the consumer and include warranty costs, environmental costs, and product liability costs in case of product defects.

Main Point: As previously discussed, the overall goal of Supply Chain activities is to maximize the profit or minimize the cost for the entire Supply Chain. When a company in a Supply Chain plans to outsource part of its business activities it must take into account all the spillover costs to the entire Supply Chain, which arise from this outsourcing decision. This is the Total Cost of Ownership.

Risk-sharing strategies between supplier and customer

Situations in a Supply Chain where neither overstocking, nor understocking occurs are highly exceptional. Even applying common risk-reducing policies, like *"first order and pay and delivery later"*, or applying booking systems used in e.g. the airline industry, hotels, or theatres to match demand and capacity in advance is no guarantee to preventing understocking (empty seats or rooms) or overstocking. Even if customers book a flight, not all passengers will show up at the moment when the plane takes off.[12] Even if a company manufactures goods only after receiving an order and a customer's payment, it still runs the risk that the customer will return the goods if not satisfied with the product quality.

In recent decades, businesses have looked for instruments and arrangements to reduce the risk and the associated costs of under- and overstocking. These arrangements are particularly present in situations characterized by long-term partnerships between supplier and customer and we will discuss three of them. The focus of these three arrangements is on how two parties share inventory risk, how the arrangement impacts the order size Q^*, and how it impacts the supply chain profit. The three arrangements are:

1.   Return policy or buyback arrangements
2.   Revenue or sales sharing arrangements
3.   Quantity flexibility arrangements

1.   Return arrangements

A return arrangement, also called a buyback or repurchase contract, is a provision or a clause in a supply contract between supplier and customer allowing the customer, mostly a retailer, to return unsold units (up to a maximum) for an agreed-upon return price. The supplier shares in the risk in case the retailer fails to sell all ordered units to its customers. We start calculating the optimal order size Q^* in the presence of a return arrangement. The selling price of the supplier, either a manufacturer or a wholesaler, is W and this amount is simultaneously the purchase cost for the retailer. The return price is R per unit. The supplier can resell the returned units to a factory outlet for S, which is the salvage value. Production costs of the *manufacturer* are C per unit. Consumer price is P_R

The cost of overstocking by the retailer $C_o = W - R$ and the cost of understocking $C_u = P_R - W$.

The retailer's optimal Cycle Service Level is calculated using the formula described at the beginning of this chapter as $CSL^* = (P_R - W) / (P_R - R)$. The corresponding optimal order size $Q^* = F^{-1}(CSL^*, \mu, \sigma)$ assuming a normally distributed demand per period.

To calculate the *expected profit of the retailer* we use the *formula* described on *page 153*, where the P_{outlet} in this situation must be replaced by the buyback price *R*.

The expected profit for the *manufacturer* or *wholesaler* as supplier consists of two parts: the units sold to the retailer and *not* returned, and unsold units and returned by the retailer. Total units sold to the retailer are equal to the retailer's order size Q^*. All units sold and not returned generate a profit = $Q^* *(W - C)$ for the supplier. Units returned generate costs that are equal to the expected *over*stock at the retailer and are resold by the manufacturer to an outlet with a profit margin (loss) of $(R - S) \rightarrow$ total profit (loss) equals Expected overstock $* (R - S)$. The expected overstock at the retailer is computed using the expected overstock formula on page 153. Combining the two parts yields:

Expected profit manufacturer = $(W - C)^*Q^* - (R - S)^*$Expected overstock

Example

Manufacturer Huawei sells cell phones to the electronic retail chain BCC for €80. Huawei's unit production costs are €35. BCC sells the phones to the consumer for €140 and BCC returns any unsold telephones to Huawei, fetching a return price of €65 per phone. Demand for cell phones at BCC per sales cycle is normally distributed with a mean of μ = 4,000 cell phones and a standard deviation σ = 300. Huawei can resell returned phones to a factory outlet for €50.

Required

Calculate the expected profit of BCC and that of Huawei under this return arrangement.

Solution

Cost of understocking

C_u = €140 − €80 = €60 and of overstocking €80 − €65 = €15 loss.
$CSL^* = C_u / [C_u + C_o]$

The optimal CSL^* for BCC is [140 − 80] / [(140 − 80) + (80 − 65)] = 60/75 = 80%.
The associated optimal order size

Q^* = NORM.INV(0.8 ; 4,000; 300) ≈ 4,252 cell phones.

The expected profit of BCC is

$$(140 - 65) * 4,000 * F_S\left(\frac{4,252 - 4,000}{300}\right) - (140 - 65) * 300 * f_S\left(\frac{4,252 - 4,000}{300}\right) = €\ 240,000 - €6,299.14 = €233,700.86.[13]$$

The expected overstock of BCC is 286 cell phones using the expected overstock formula on page 153.

The expected profit for <u>Huawei</u> is

$$4,252*(80 - 35) - (65 - 50)*286 = €191,362 - €4,290 = €187,072.22.$$

The supply chain profit is

$$€233,700.86 + €187,072.22 = €420,773.08.$$

If there was *no* buyback arrangement between BCC and Huawei and the salvage value for BCC was the same as for Huawei, namely €50, the expected profit for BCC would be €230,812.81 and for Huawei €185,814.82 with a Supply Chain profit of €415,997.62 (this is €4,775.45 less compared to the buyback agreement). The buyback arrangement increases the profit for both companies. BCC will face a profit *decline* of €233,700.86 – €230,812.81 = €3,518.05 without a buyback arrangement. The profit decline of Huawei is €187,072.22 – €185,814.82 = €1,257.40 by eliminating the buyback clause! So, the supply chain is better off with a buyback arrangement. The worked-out calculations in Excel in the formula view of this example are shown below in two separate screenshots to get all information visible.

	A	B	C	D	E	F
1	Demand				Expected Profit BCC in 4 parts	
2	Mean μ	4000		Part 1 (+)	Part 2 (-)	
3	Std. Dev. σ;	300		=($B$4-$B$6)*$B$2*NORM.DIST(($B$8-$B$2)/$B$3;0;1;TRU	=($B$4-$B$6)*$B$3*NORM.DIST(($B$8-$B$2)/$B$3;0;1;FALS	
4	Consumer price BCC	140				
5	Purchase Cost BCC	80		Part 3 (-)	Part 4 (+)	Total
6	Buyback price Huawei	65		=$B$8*($B$5-$B$6)*NORM.DIST(B8;B2;B3;1)	=$B$8*($B$4-$B$5)*(1-NORM.DIST($B$8;$B$2;$B$3;TRUE))	=D3-E3-D6+E6
7	Residual value Huawei	50				
8	Order size set by BCC	=NORM.INV(B9;B2;B3)				
9	CSL BCC	=(B4-B5)/(B4-B6)			Expected overstock BCC	
10	Production Cost Huawei	35		Part 1	Part 2	Total
11	Cost understocking BCC	=(B4-B5)		=(B8-B2)*NORM.DIST((B8-B2)/B3;0;1;1)	=B3*NORM.DIST((B8-B2)/B3;0;1;0)	=SUM(D11:E11)
12	Cost of overstocking	=B5-B6				
13					Expected profit Huawei	
14				Part 1	Part 2	Total
15				=B8*(B5-B10)	=F11*(B6-B7)	=D15-E15
16						
17					Supply Chain Profit	
18					=F6+F15	

	F	G	H
1	Expected Profit BCC in 4 parts		
2	Part 3 (-)	Part 4 (+)	Total
3	=$B$8*($B$5-$B$6)*NORM.DIST(B8;B2;B3;1)	=$B$8*($B$4-$B$5)*(1-NORM.DIST($B$8;$B$2;$B$3;TRUE))	=D3-E3-F3+G3
4			
5		Expected overstock BCC	
6	Total		
7	=SUM(D7:E7)		
8			
9			
10	Total		Supply Chain Profit
11	=D11-E11		=H3+F11
12			420773,08
13			=H12-H11

A disadvantage of a buyback contract is that the retailer has an incentive to over order and, consequently, more units will be returned to the wholesaler at the end of the sales cycle. This increases total holding costs at the retailer level and transportation costs to bring the goods back to the supplier.

2. Revenue sharing arrangements

Another instrument for sharing risk between supplier and retailer is a revenue-sharing agreement. In this arrangement, the supplier offers the retailer a discount on the wholesale price but participates in the revenues of every unit sold by the retailer to the final consumer. Revenue sharing agreements can be combined with a buyback clause, but we will analyse the revenue-sharing agreement as a standalone provision in the contract between retailer and supplier. The consumer price is now divided in a percentage r% for the supplier and $(1 - r)$% for the retailer. We focus on the impact of these contracts on Supply Chain profit, the sum of the profit of the retailer and supplier, who can be either a manufacturing company or a wholesaler. The retailer optimizes its order size Q^* and we use the same symbols as in the buyback example. The R(eturn price) has been replaced by S_{outlet} in the formulas. We first compute the optimal CSL^* of the retailer. Cost of understocking for the retailer

$$C_u = [(1 - r)^* P_R - W]$$ and the cost of overstocking $C_o = (W - S_{outlet})$.

The optimal $CSL^* = C_u / [C_u + C_o] = [(1 - r)^* P_R - W] / [(1 - r)^*(P_R - W) + (W - S_{outlet})]$.
The optimal retail order $Q^* = NORM.INV(CSL^*, \mu, \sigma)$.
The manufacturer earns the wholesale price W per unit from selling to the retailer and $(1 - r)^* P_R$ of every unit sold by the retailer to the final consumer. Given that the retailer cannot sell more units than have been ordered, Q^*, the units *sold* by the *retailer* are, by definition, $(Q^* - $ expected overstock$) = $ unsold units.

The manufacturer profit becomes:

$$\text{Profit}_M = (W - C)^*Q^* + r\%^*P_R^*(Q^* - \text{expected overstock})$$

The retailer profit consists of three parts: [1] units sold to the consumer (Q^* − expected overstock); [2] units purchased but not sold for the regular price but discarded at salvage value (expected overstock); and [3] the purchase costs for all units purchased (Q^*). Combining the three results in:

$$\text{Profit}_R = (1 - r)^*P_R^*(Q^* - \text{expected retailer overstock}) [1] + S_{outlet}^*\text{expected retailer}$$
$$\text{overstock} [2] - W^*Q^* [3]$$

The Supply Chain profit is the sum of the supplier's profit and the retailer's profit. We will illustrate this with an example using the same data as in the buyback example. The revenue sharing percentage r = 20%. Unsold phones at the retailer are sold for S_{outlet} = €50 to the discount outlet.

Cost of understocking C_u = [(1 − 20%)*140 − 80] = €32 and of overstocking C_o = (80 − 50) = €30.

Optimal CSL^* = 51,6% and the corresponding order size Q^* = NORM.INV(51,6%, 4,000, 300) ≈ 4,012 phones.

Expected overstock for BCC – using the same formula on page 153 – is 126 phones.

Expected profit retailer BCC: Profit_{BCC} = €435,264 + €6,292.33 − €320,970.57 = €120.585,74

Expected profit manufacturer Huawei: Profit = €180.546 + €108.816 (revenue sharing) = €289.361,94

The resulting supply chain profit is €120,585.74 + €289,361.94 = € 409,947.68

The Excel solution in formula view is shown in the screenshot below.

	B	C	D	E	F	G
1				Expected Profit BCC		
2	4000		revenues sales	salvage value overstocked units	Purchase Costs	Total
3	300		=(1-B6)*B4*(B8-F7)	=F7*B7	=B8*B5	=D3+E3-F3
4	140					
5	80		Expected overstock BCC			
6	0,08		Part 1	Part 2	Total	
7	50		=(B8-B2)*NORM.DIST((B8-B2)/B3;0;1;1)	=B3*NORM.DIST((B8-B2)/B3;0;1;0)	=SUM(D7:E7)	
8	=NORM.INV(B9;B2;B3)					
9	=((1-B6)*B4-B5)/((1-B6)*B4-B7)		Expected profit Huawei			
10	35		Sales to retailer	Revenue sharing retailer	Total	
11	=(1-B6)*B4-B5		=B8*(B5-B10)	=B6*B4*(B8-F7)	=SUM(D11:E11)	
12	=B5-B7					
13						Supply Chain Profit
14						=G3+F11

Notice that the Supply Chain profit is a little lower than under the buyback arrangement, which was €420,773.08. Adjusting the revenue-sharing percentage r will change the Supply Chain profit, but, in any case, will stay below the buy-back profit level.

3. Quantity flexibility contracts

As discussed in the chapter about Demand Forecasting, short-term forecasts are usually more reliable than long-term forecasts. Some manufacturers ask their retail customers to submit an estimate of how many units they want to order long before the sales season starts. As time passes, demand for the retailer becomes more visible and accurate and the previous veil of uncertainties becomes more transparent, concrete, and certain. The order size indication released many months before can be wrong just a few weeks or days before the sales season starts. Some manufacturers therefore allow *quantity flexibility* contracts with their retailers. The retailer sets a preliminary order size Q_{base} long before the sales period starts, which gives the manufacturer input information to make better production planning. But as time passes and demand for the retailers become more visible, they can adjust the order size within limits agreed upon in advance. These limits are expressed as a percentage of the original order size Q_{base} with a maximum upward and downward delivery percentage. The *manufacturer* commits himself to delivering to the retailer upon request up to a *maximum* of $Q_{max} = (1 + a)*Q_{base}$. The *retailer* commits himself to buying at least a *minimum* amount of b% less than the original order size $Q_{min} = (1 - b)*Q_{base}$.

If the demand at the start of the sales season materializes between Q_{min} and Q_{max} the order size of the retailer will be equal to the demand with an expected value μ. The assumption is that demand in the sales season follows a normal distribution with mean μ and standard deviation σ. The manufacturer starts the production long before the sales season starts – if that fits better in his production planning – and will produce Q_{max} units, the maximum possible amount he has to supply to the retailer just before sales start. If the retailer later orders Q^*, being less than Q_{max}, just before the start of the sale season, the manufacturer will have an overstock equal to $(Q_{max} - Q^*)$ with associated holding costs. He can fetch a salvage value for selling the overstocked units at the end of the sales season to a factory outlet.

However, if actual retail demand is less than Q_{min}, the retailer has committed himself to ordering Q_{min} but now the retailer will incur an overstock of $(Q_{min} -$ demand$)$. But the manufacturer also incurs an overstock equal to $[Q_{max}$ (units produced$) - Q_{min}$ (units sold$)]$. We assume that the retailer can salvage his overstock to the factory outlet for the same salvage price as the manufacturer, although the calculations are the same if the two salvage values differ.[14] In other words, the risk of overstocked units is shared between the retailer and manufacturer. When the sales period starts the following three situations can arise:

1. Demand D is equal, or less than Q_{min} → retailer orders Q_{min} units from the manufacturer and will sell D units to the consumer. The associated probability of this scenario is $P[D \leq Q_{min}]$ or $F(Q_{min})$.

Retailer's overstock at the end of the sales season is $(Q_{min} - D)$.

2. Demand D is higher than Q_{max} → the manufacturer will supply Q_{max} units, and the retailer will sell Q_{max} units to the consumer. The associated probability of this scenario is $P[D > Q_{max}] = 1 - P[D \leq Q_{max}] = 1 - F(Q_{max})$. Neither manufacturer nor retailer have overstock. The retailer has opportunity costs due to lost sales.

3. Demand D is between Q_{min} and Q_{max} → the actual demand will be ordered with an expected value of μ units. The probability of this scenario is $P[D \leq Q_{max}] - P[D \leq Q_{min}] = F(Q_{max}) - F(Q_{min})$ and the manufacturer incurs an overstock of $(Q_{max} - D)$ units because he made Q_{max} units long before the sales season started.

There are two unknowns in these situations: the (optimal) order size set by the retailer Q^*_{Ret} (units purchased), which is the same as the quantity sold by the manufacturer to the retailer. The second one is the units *sold* by the retailer to the consumer indicated by D_{Ret}. The *manufacturer's* expected overstock is $(Q_{max} - Q_{Ret})$. The *expected* quantity **purchased** by the **retailer** Q_{Ret} is calculated in four parts:

1. $+Q_{min}*F(Q_{min})$ Demand $\leq Q_{min}$ → Q_{min} units are purchased with probability $F(Q_{min})$

2. $+Q_{max}*[1 - F(Q_{max})]$ Demand $> Q_{max}$ → Q_{max} units are purchased: probability $[1 - F(Q_{max})]$

3. $+\mu*[F_S(Q_{max} - \mu)/\sigma) - F_S(Q_{min} - \mu)/\sigma)]$ Demand between Q_{min} and Q_{max} → expected μ units are purchased with an associated standardized cumulative probability

4. $-\sigma*[f_S(Q_{max} - \mu)/\sigma) - f_S(Q_{min} - \mu)/\sigma)]$ Adjustment term

The expected quantity **sold** by the **retailer** is the consumer demand D_{Ret} and consists of three parts:

I. $+Q_{max}* [1 - F(Q_{max})]$

II. $+\mu * F_S[(Q_{max} - \mu)/\sigma]$

III. $-\sigma*f_S[(Q_{min} - \mu)/\sigma]$

Note: if demand is greater than Q_{max}, Q_{max} units are sold (part 1); otherwise, if D $\leq Q_{max}$ expected sales are μ units → μ units are sold, also when actual demand is *lower* than Q_{min}, because Q_{min} is a *purchase* quantity and the retailer orders Q_{min}

units from the manufacturer and will sell $\mu \leq Q_{min}$ to the consumers and incur overstock! We must keep in mind that units purchased by the retailer and units sold by the manufacturer are the same. Part III of the formula above has no immediate economic interpretation.

Expected overstock retailer is expected quantity *sold* minus expected quantity *purchased*: $(D_{Ret} - Q_{Ret})$

Expected overstock manufacturer is the quantity produced minus quantity sold to the retailer: $(Q_{max} - Q_{Ret})$

Expected profit **retailer** is $Profit_{Ret} = D_{Ret}*P_S + (Q_{Ret} - D_{Ret})*S_{Ret} - Q_{Ret}*C_R$

The first term in the expected retailer's profit is the revenues from units sold, the second part is the salvage value of the overstock sold at S_{Ret}. The last term refers to the total purchase cost of the retailer by ordering Q_{Ret} from the manufacturer at a cost of C_R per unit.

Expected profit **manufacturer** is $Profit_{Man} = Q_{Ret}*C_R + (Q_{max} - Q_{Ret})*S_{Man} - Q_{max}*C_{Man}$

The first term of the manufacturer's profit is the revenues from units sold to the retailer (mirror image of the purchase cost of the retailer), the second term is revenues from the overstocked units sold at the salvage price of the manufacturer. The third term is the production costs of C_{Man} per unit, which are incurred long before the sales season starts and based on the maximum order size of the retailer Q_{max}. We will illustrate the Quantity Flexibility agreement with a worked-out example in Excel format.

	A	B	C	D	E	F	G	H
2	Mean μ	4,000		Part 1 (+)	Part 2 (+)	Part 3 (+)	Part 4 (-)	**Total**
3	Std. Dev. σ;	300		12	2	3,983	-3	4,000
4	Consumer price BCC	€ 140						
5	Purchase Cost for BCC	€ 80		Expected # cell phones **sold** by BCC				
6	Initial pre-order size	4,000		Part 1 (+)	Part 2 (+)	Part 3 (-)	**Total**	
7	Maximum increase (a)	25%		2	3,998	3	3,997	
8	Minimum commitment (b)	-20%						
9	Salvage value BCC	€ 40		Expected Overstock BCC		3		
10	Salvage value Huawei	€ 50		Expected overstock Huawei		1,000		
11	Production Cost Huawei	€ 35						
12	Q_{max}	5,000		Expected **profit** BCC				
13	Q_{min}	3,200		Part 1 (+)	Part 2 (+)	Part 3 (-)	**Total**	
14				€ 559,581	€ 132	€ 320,026	€ 239,688	
15	Supply Chain Profit	€ 434,698						
16				Expected **Profit** Huawei				
17				Part 1 (+)	Part 2 (+)	Part 3 (-)	**Total**	
18				€ 320,026	€ 49,984	€ 175,000	€ 195,010	

The formula view of this solution is shown below in two parts, so that all formulas are displayed. The second screenshot below should be read as a continuation of the first one, moving the columns more to the right.

	A	B	C	D	E
1	Demand				Expected # cell phones **purchased** by BCC
2	Mean μ	4000		Part 1 (+)	Part 2 (+)
3	Std. Dev. σ;	300		=B13*NORM.DIST(B13;B2;B3;1)	=B12*(1-NORM.DIST(B12;B2;B3;TRUE))
4	Consumer price BCC	140			
5	Purchase Cost for BCC	80			Expected # cell phones **sold** by BCC
6	Initial pre-order size	4000		Part 1 (+)	Part 2 (+)
7	Maximum increase (a)	0.25		=B12*(1-NORM.DIST(B12;B2;B3;1))	=B2*NORM.DIST((B12-B2)/B3;0;1;1)
8	Minimum commitment (b)	-0.2			
9	Salvage value BCC	40		Expected Overstock BCC	
10	Salvage value Huawei	50		Expected overstock Huawei	
11	Production Cost Huawei	35			
12	Qmax	=(1+B7)*B6		Expected **profit** BCC	
13	Qmin	=(1+B8)*B6		Part 1 (+)	Part 2 (+)
14				=G7*B4	=F9*B9
15	Supply Chain Profit	=G14+G18			
16				Expected **Profit** Huawei	
17				Part 1 (+)	Part 2 (+)
18				=H3*B5	=F10*B10

	F	G	H
1	Expected # cell phones **purchased** by BCC		
2	Part 3 (+)	Part 4 (-)	Total
3	=B2*(NORM.DIST((B12-B2)/B3;0;1;1)-NORM.DIST((B13-B2)/B3;0;1;1))	=B3*(NORM.DIST((B12-B2)/B3;0;1;FALSE)-NORM.DIST((B13-B2)/B3;0;1;0))	=D3+E3+F3-G3
4			
5	Expected # cell phones **sold** by BCC		
6	Part 3 (-)	Total	
7	=B3*NORM.DIST((B13-B2)/B3;0;1;FALSE)	=D7+E7-F7	
8			
9	=H3-G7		
10	=B12-H3		
11			
12			
13	Part 3 (-)	Total	
14	=H3*B5	=D14+E14-F14	
15			
16			
17	Part 3 (-)	Total	
18	=B12*B11	=D18+E18-F18	

Notice that the risk-sharing of expected overstock is quite skewed: BCC takes an expected overstock of three units and Huawei of 1,000 units. One option to mitigate this skewness is that Huawei *postpones* production of the 1,000 phones above *expected* consumer demand and only produces the pre-order size of 4,000 cell phones early on, while booking a free time slot in its production schedule just before the definitive order from BCC arrives for an additional 1,000 units, providing that the retailer increases its order size from Q_{base} to Q_{max} – although this postponement can lead to higher production costs and crowding out production of other orders in that period.

Another mitigation strategy to reduce the skewness is to reduce the initial pre-order size of 4000 units, which in this example has been set as equal to the expected demand. A sensitivity analysis on the pre-order size shows that when this cell is set to 3898 units, the expected overstock of BCC becomes 0 and for Huawei 873 (so 127 phones less). A sensitivity analysis on a maximum order increase of 25% in the example shows that if this percentage is set at 20%, the expected overstock of BCC will be 0 and of Huawei 789 units. You can check that the Supply Chain profit with quantity flexibility contracts is the highest of the three risk-sharing arrangements.

Main Point: Three risk-sharing strategies are commonly used in Supply Chains to reduce the risk of overstocking and understocking, particularly between retailers and manufacturers or wholesalers. Return – also called buyback or repurchase – agreements allow the retailer to send back any unsold units to the manufacturer at a prespecified price. The downside is that it creates an incentive for the retailer to overorder. The second strategy is the revenue-sharing agreement, whereby the manufacturer lowers its selling price for the retailer but receives a percentage of the revenues for every unit the retailer sells to end-consumers. The third strategy is the Quantity Flexibility contract, whereby the retailer commits to buying a minimum amount and the manufacturer commits to delivering a maximum amount, if requested. This instrument is useful if demand becomes more accurate closer to the starting date for sales.

Booking systems and prepayment arrangements

The final instrument we will discuss for reducing the risk of under- and overstocking in the face of uncertain demand is the application of booking or reservation systems. Industries that commonly use these systems include the airline industry, hotels, theatres, key sports events, and many more. Although the demand remains uncertain, the company obtains a good indication of the number of customers it can expect well before the service or product has to be delivered. Companies can adjust their capacity to match the number of bookings they receive and deploy idle capacity for other products and services when demand is lower than capacity, or subcontract production in case capacity is insufficient.[15] But even booking or reservation systems are no guarantee that neither under- nor overstocking will occur. Airlines and hotels are frequently faced with customers who book but do not show up at the decisive moment. This no-show phenomenon is one of the driving forces of overbooking practices by airline companies and hotels. Applying a booking system is virtually impossible for many low-value, fast-moving consumer goods without driving up transaction costs, especially for sales in retail stores.

A *prepayment* policy reverses the classical transaction sequence from *"buy first, receive the product and pay afterward"* to *"pay first and receive later".* Prepayment is common practice among online stores and sales via websites, but it is not the most effective way to prevent under- and overstocking. The fact that customers pay in advance makes demand more visible in the short run and gives the company a brief period of relief to update inventories or to manufacture the ordered products in cases where a delivery date is promised. However, a company advertising the claim *"order in the morning, receive in the (same-day) evening"* has little time to adjust inventories to meet prepaid demand.

Notes

1-6   See Instructor's Manual

7   The corresponding Excel functions with its parameters are: $F_s[(Q - \mu)/\sigma]$ is in Excel NORM.DIST$[(Q - \mu)/\sigma;0;1;1]$. $f_s[(Q - \mu)/\sigma]$ is in Excel NORM.DIST$[(Q - \mu)/\sigma;0;1;0]$, $F(Q)$ is NORM.DIST$[Q;\mu;\sigma;1]$ and $f(Q)$ is NORM.DIST$[Q;\mu;\sigma;0]$. $F^{-1}(CSL)$ is in Excel NORM.INV $[CSL; \mu; \sigma]$ with μ the mean demand and σ the standard deviation.

8-15   See Instructor's Manual

8 Asset Mobility and Infrastructure for Supply Chains in the 21st Century

A Concise Overview of Infrastructure Assets and Its Underlying Network Structure for Asset Mobility

Source: https://upload.wikimedia.org/wiki-pedia/commons/1/1b/Truck.car.transporter.arp.750pix.jpg

Source: https://i2.wp.com/rayhaber.com/wp-content/uploads/2020/03/volvo-cars-ye-ni-otomobillerini-kamyon-yerine-trenle-tasi-yor.jpg?fit=678%2C381&ssl=1

Source: https://upload.wikimedia.org/wiki-pedia/commons/d/db/Barge_with_cars.jpg

Source: https://www.jal.co.jp/en/jalcargo/inter/service/j_solution_wheel_Y18/img/img_order_made.jpg

Although the movement of goods, persons, and information transmission is as old as mankind itself, the scale and diversity have grown exponentially over the last century. The different modes of transportation have undergone considerable transformations and innovations. From horse-drawn wagons and carts on unpaved roads in Roman and medieval times to sailing large distances over open water, new modes of transportation were developed in particular since the 17th century.

At the same time, this increase of moving assets triggered the need for a supporting infrastructure for these diverse transportation modes. Information transmission has undergone a similar development. From handwritten letters shipped in coaches, or taken by running scouts or horse riders from one place to another, the transmission of messages has evolved into its modern configuration: wired and wireless messages and communication moving at incredible speed and in staggering quantities over a digital infrastructure of internet, mobile phone masts, and satellite networks.

Globalization accelerated in the second half of the 20th century fuelled a new thrust in the international mobility of both physical goods, the movement of persons and cross-border movements of intangible and financial assets. Not only the amount of goods and persons transported grew exponentially, but also the average distances travelled per product and person continued to rise. The transmission of information skyrocketed to the unprecedented scale it has achieved today. This chapter deals with logistics and, more generally, the movement of tangible and intangible assets to keep Supply Chains running.

Logistics is a broader concept than transportation from A to B and includes, in addition to the management of the flow of goods, storage, administrative and legal procedures and documentation, in particular for the import and export of goods, and also packaging requirements. Logistics and infrastructure are mutually influential and, for this reason, our discussion of infrastructure will have a keen eye for its impact on Supply Chain operations and performance.

Let us first discuss a conceptual approach to infrastructure assets as a *system.* An infrastructure system includes more dimensions than a standalone tangible asset. A specific infrastructure asset, like a region's road network, consists of more than the road surface. It encompasses a wide range of complementary tangible and intangible assets, including: road markings and signage; the number of slip roads and exits; toll roads or free roads; the number of lanes in each direction; the presence of street lighting, crash barriers, emergency lanes, matrix boards and traffic signs; the number of car parks and filling stations along the highway; the number of ground level and non-level crossings; road maintenance planning, road clearing after accidents.

Complementary intangible and institutional regulations refer to road *usage* and include traffic rules, particularly maximum speed, bans on overtaking by trucks, driving time rules for truck drivers, prohibition of certain vehicles and goods, e.g. the transport of hazardous chemicals, police controls and road camera surveillance. There are also regulations for road usage, like different classes of driving licences, restrictions on alcohol consumption, and general controls on the driving behaviour of motorists and road users. Moreover, the financial conditions required for car usage, like vehicle tax, fuel taxes, and civil liability insurance are also part of infrastructure as a *system*.

All these elements affect, to a greater or lesser extent, SC performance and the cost of logistic operations both directly, e.g. toll road pricing, and indirectly, e.g. affecting the average vehicle lead time. In logistics, time is money. The term *infrastructure system,* then, is perhaps a more appropriate name than simply infrastructure assets. Similar conceptual interpretations apply to the railway network of a country, the waterway network, the airways, pipelines, and other infrastructure assets. To assess the performance of an infrastructure asset for Supply Chain operations, the focus is on **infrastructure as a system,** taking into account all complementary tangible, intangible, and institutional elements related to that infrastructure asset and its usage, all of which affect to a greater or lesser extent SC performance and SC costs.

As previously discussed, Supply Chain networks have treelike patterns. At the top are the suppliers of raw materials delivering their stuff to manufacturing plants, where production takes place. All those raw materials are shipped from their source location, e.g. oil fields for crude oil, or raw materials or agricultural products for the food processing industry. The shipment of raw materials shipment to their destinations is characterized by the fact that it occurs in large volumes. After being processed, raw materials leave the manufacturing plants, either as intermediate products or as end-products, and are shipped on to a larger network of distribution centres, often located outside or at the fringe of populated agglomerations or in business districts.

Large-volume shipments exhibit *economies of scale* but require the selection of appropriate transportation modes, be it cargo trains, marine vessels, or large trucks. Each transportation mode is only possible when it has access to infrastructure assets that match its typical characteristics. Once the shipment arrives in the DCs, the freight is cross-docked for further shipment in smaller volumes to supply a large network of brick-and-stone retailers. Small-volume shipment implies losing part of the economies of scale that are achieved with large volume transportation. The products must then reach the consumers via stores and points of sales (POS). Most POS are found in cities, towns, and smaller villages. This last step in the distribution pattern can be typified as many shipments to many locations in small(er) volumes. This more fine-tuned distribution requires adequate mobile transportation assets, i.e. vans instead of trucks, or small boats using city canals or small rivers as their supporting infrastructure asset. Finally, consumers either go to the store or to the pick-up point with their mode of transportation (car, bicycle, or walking to a nearby store) to buy their goods and bring them home.

For online companies, there is another stage of shipment, which consists of delivering the ordered goods to the customer's home address. This last stage is called *last-mile delivery* – although in Europe the term *last-kilometre* delivery would be more appropriate. Last-mile delivery requires a logistics network designed to reach many widely spread destinations, transporting small quantities either within cities or to more remote isolated areas, like islands. Optimizing this last-mile delivery demands matching the appropriate modes of transportation with the available infrastructure. Given the increasing number of online consumer transactions in the 21st century, we will discuss the specific infrastructure and conveyance for last-mile delivery shipments later in this chapter.

Assessment of different infrastructure assets requires appropriate benchmarks. In our discussion about different infrastructure assets we will benchmark them based on: 1) costs; 2) lead time; and 3) their impact on the performance of Supply Chain operations. All benchmarks are relative to other infrastructure systems. The following three transportation modes in a Supply Chain are discussed:

1. shipment of **goods**
2. movement of **persons** (mainly employees), especially for commuting and business travels
3. transmission of **information**

The performance of all three flows (goods, persons, and information) in Supply Chain logistics and planning depends critically on the availability, in quantity and quality, of the supporting infrastructure systems. The broad variety of infrastructure assets in the world means it is impossible to discuss each infrastructure and transportation mode in detail, hence the discussion is limited to some typical features of each asset with its advantages and disadvantages.

First, we make a practical distinction that is relevant for Supply Chain and operational logistics: the difference between internal (inside a facility, or intrafacility) and external (between facilities or interfacility) logistics.

Internal logistics refers to the way in which the movement of goods is organized *inside* a physical facility – which can be a manufacturing plant or a distribution centre -. Efficient movement from, for example, inbound to outbound docking stations is an internal movement of goods for cross-docking freight within a distribution centre. Internal logistics affects the overall Supply Chain performance. These operations within a DC or warehouse are also called *warehouse management*.

External logistics refers to the movement of goods between physical facilities in a Supply Chain network, although it can equally be applied to facilities operating outside the Supply Chain.

Second, we include a discussion about the movement of people. At first glance, passenger traffic does not seem to be part of logistics. There are, however, good arguments for including them. Our previous discussion of production planning revealed that staff or human resource planning is an integral part of the planning process in both the manufacturing and the service sectors. If all machinery and resources are set up and ready to start operations at the planned time, but the human resources – the employees – do not arrive at the scheduled time, execution of the plan will be thwarted. Staff scheduling – getting the employees with the needed job skills, in the required numbers, to the right place and at the right time, to run or maintain machines as well as their presence in logistics operations, such as the scheduling of truck drivers, airplane crew, ship crew, etc., is an essential part of logistics planning. Simply put, getting the labour force to the right place at the right time improves Supply Chain performance.[1]

Given the dynamics and the rapidly changing world of logistics, it is not feasible to discuss an exhaustive list of all transportation modes for moving goods, persons, and information. Instead, the discussion will remain general. At the individual level, each infrastructure category and asset exhibits significant variations in costs, lead time, and speed. There can even be significant differences between countries with respect to the same infrastructure asset. However, one economic rule holds for all forms of infrastructure: they are **expensive** to *build* and expensive to *maintain*. There is no such thing as cheap infrastructure if a country wants to keep its infrastructure assets sustainable and with a long economic life. Each infrastructure asset group will be assessed on the following performance indicators: cost; lead time; and congestion, complemented with a description of the institutional and regulatory framework.

Transportation and infrastructure: A classification from uncommon to common

This picture shows the world's longest (outdoor) conveyor belt, located in Western Sahara. It is 98 kilometres long and transports phosphate rocks from the mines of Bou Craa to the port city of El-Aaiun. From there, cargo vessels transport the phosphates to various countries for fertilizer production (inter-facility).
Source: http://photos.wikimapia.org/p/00/06/05/98/93_full.jpg retrieved on 6 January 2022

An (indoor) luggage-handling section with conveyor belts at Calgary International Airport.
Source: https://airportimprovement.com/article/calgary-intl-looks-forward-increasing-customer-service-decreasing-energy-consumption-new-baggage-system

An *uncommon* asset: The conveyor belt

Most conveyor belts are built and used for *intrafacility* logistics. Internal conveyor belts are, therefore, in most cases privately owned and operated. They are common equipment in distribution centres, in airports for luggage handling, and in the mining industry. An advantage of a conveyor belt is that it can handle an uninterrupted flow of goods and only needs to be shut down for maintenance and/or repair.

Ordinarily, conveyor belts rarely experience congestion, making the *internal* lead time and logistics planning predictable and reliable. Building them, however, require high investment costs. The capacity of a conveyor belt (maximum quantity shipped per time unit) depends on the width of the belts and its average and maximum speed. They are well suited for companies and industries that need an uninterrupted flow of supplies or goods. Although congestion on a conveyor belt is not a serious problem, on a multiple cross-linked conveyor belt network, like those used in airport luggage handling, suitcases and other luggage may become jammed or stuck on the belt causing delays and dissatisfied customers waiting impatiently for their luggage.[2]

Equivalent to conveyor belts: Pipelines

Source: https://www.fluor.com/projects/saudi-aramco-shedgum-gas-plant-epc

World's longest pipelines: Natural gas (year 2018)
- West-East Gas Pipeline: 8,707 km.
- GASUN, Brazil: 4,989 km.

- Yamal-Europe Pipeline: 4,196 km.
- Trans-Saharan Pipeline: 4,127 km.
- Eastern Siberia-Pacific Ocean Oil Pipeline: 4,857 km.
- Druzhba Pipeline: 4,000 km.
- Keystone Pipeline: 3,456 km.
- Kazakhstan-China Pipeline: 2,798 km.

Source: https://www.google.com/search?q=largest+pipelines+in+the+world&rlz=1C1EKKP_enN-L790NL790&oq=Longest+pipelines+&aqs=chrome.2.69i57j0i19l2j0i13i19i30j0i10i13i19i30j0i10i19i22i30j0i13i19i30j0i19i22i30j0i10i19i22i30j0i19i22i30.7143j0j15&sourceid=chrome&ie=UTF-8

Pipelines are another suitable mode of transportation when an uninterrupted supply or discharge of raw materials is needed. They are used for both internal and external movements. Unlike conveyor belts, which can only move solid products – stones or luggage – pipelines can only move liquids, gas, and small-particle solids, like sand. Most pipelines are much longer than conveyor belts and can move liquids and gas over considerably longer distances, as the statistics in the textbox above show. Pipelines can be an *intrafacility* asset, especially within oil & gas plants, but can also connect different plants where the output of a supplying plant becomes input or raw material for another plant located at an end point or at a branch of the pipeline.[3]

Pipelines can be privately or publicly owned, or a combination of the two. Long-distance pipelines, which are wholly or partially on or under public land, can only be exploited by a private firm under a *government concession*. The most extensive network of pipelines in the world is used for moving liquids, like drinking water and gas, or serves to *discharge* liquids, as in sewage systems. The costs of building and maintaining pipeline networks are less for pipelines laying on top of or just below the land surface than for submarine pipelines located on or under the seabed.[4]

In the textbox above, data are shown for the nine longest pipelines in the world. These lengths must be assessed in a correct frame of reference, however. For example, the length of underground pipeline networks in urban areas, consisting of many small, branched pipelines, can add up to a much greater length.[5] As in the case of conveyor belts, congestion in most pipelines is not a serious problem, making lead time reliable and predictable. They do, however, require interruptions for maintenance, cleaning, and repairs. Pipelines passing through countries with political instability or in war zones are exposed to terrorist attacks or physical damage. The flow of liquids passing through the pipelines can also be cut off or slowed down by government intervention in situations of conflicts with a neighbouring country who depends on the pipeline.

Freight transport by air

Cargo planes have a well-designed interior layout to optimize the storage of goods in the fuselage.
Source: https://upload.wikimedia.org/wikipedia/commons/1/1a/An-124_ready.jpg

Three major express carriers – DHL, UPS, and FedEx, operate a global network covering the entire world with a fleet of airplanes and with their own hubs at airports in order to handle the rapid shipment of a large number of packages.
Source: https://www.dhl.com/content/dam/dhl/local/de/core/images/simple-stage-2730x784/de-core-hub-leipzig-location-facts-and-figures-new.web.1365.259.jpg

Using the air space to move goods by plane is an expensive mode of transportation, but a fast one. For products for which speed is a critical factor, such as perishable items like fresh food and flowers, air transportation is a perfect mode of transportation. Transportation by plane is also an efficient option for the urgent delivery of medicines. Many airline companies operate a separate cargo division and manage a fleet of airplanes with appropriate layouts for moving goods. Planes for freight shipment can be owned or leased by an airline. The airline company itself can be privately owned, publicly owned, or a combination of the two. The main infrastructure for air transportation is not only the airspace itself, but even more importantly, the ground facilities, which are mainly the global network of airports. Many airports have special sections exclusively for freight handling and these possess the appropriate equipment for loading and unloading cargo, distribution space for temporary storage, and facilities for cross-docking.

An important airport feature for Supply Chain operations is the presence of *intermodal* transportation options. These facilitate cargo being brought in or moved out of the airport using other transportation modes, e.g. trains or trucks.

The main cost items of flying are fuel costs (kerosene), labour costs, and the depreciation costs of the aircraft fleet. In addition, an air carrier must pay the airport a fee for using its facilities. Even if an airplane flies through the national airspace of other countries without using their airports, the carrier can still be charged a fee for using foreign air space.[6] The use of the airspace and the airports is also subject to many institutional constraints that limit the degree of freedom to optimize freight flow by air. In Europe, and most other countries, operational control of the airspace is under the authority of the *Air Traffic Control Center*. They issue rules indicating which air corridors planes may use for their flights, they operate radar systems to spot planes entering and leaving the national airspace, and can even shut down air corridors for safety reasons.[7]

Airports themselves can impose additional restrictions on cargo and passenger flights. For some airports close to cities, nocturnal flights are not allowed, and, depending on the length of the runway, not all types of planes can take off or land at that airport. The European Union also has a list of banned airlines: airlines that do not meet the safety standards to land at a European airport.[8] Air traffic faces congestion and delays, in particular on or close to airports, making lead times and the planned arrival of goods and persons uncertain and less accurate for Supply Chain planning.

Freight transport by railway

The record-breaking ore train – which can be spotted in the background of this picture – belongs to BHP Billiton. It has 682 carriages and is 7,300 m long. It once carried 82,000 metric tons of ore.
It was driven by eight locomotives distributed along its length to keep the coupling loads and curve performance controllable.
Source: https://en.wikipedia.org/wiki/Longest_trains#/media/File:BHPB_long_train,_Port_Hedland,_2012.JPG

Shunting railway area for freight train (de)composition
Source: https://upload.wikimedia.org/wikipedia/commons/9/9b/MAS_6704.JPG

The history of the railway differs from country to country. Its roots can be traced to the late 18th century and are centred in Great Britain, and were soon followed by other European countries, taking off a few decades later in the United States. The technical development of locomotives and railcars is closely linked to its supporting physical infrastructure, the railway tracks. From the very beginning, trains were used both for passenger and freight transport, and even mixed trains, moving both persons and freight simultaneously, existed and are still in operation in some Asian and African countries. Although nowadays passenger and cargo rail transportation are strictly separated in nearly all industrialized countries of the world, the railway tracks are shared by both and both categories compete for space.[9]

Another distinction in rail infrastructure is the use of *electrified* or non-electrified tracks. Electrifying rail tracks requires the construction of a power network of overhead wires and supporting poles and demands huge financial investments. Electric locomotives have faster acceleration than diesel locomotives and are considered to be more environmentally friendly, although one has to keep in mind that electricity has to be generated, which, in many countries, is done by burning fossil fuels. To cover long distances in countries such as Australia, Canada, Russia, and United States most cargo transport is done with diesel locomotives. Diesel locomotives are powerful and, by combining several engines, the number of railcars they can haul can exceed the hundreds. A distinction between the sizes of track gauges, i.e. the width between to rail bars, is another differentiating feature of international railway tracks.

In Europe, most gauges are standardized, but Russia and Spain still have some tracks with different gauges. The voltage on the power cable on electrified tracks also differs between countries and even between EU member states. Railway traffic is subject to the authority of the national *Operational Rail Control Centers*, which monitor and manage the signalling devices, the railway changes, the railway crossings, and the overhead electric wires. They are the first responsible agency for the daily safety on the track network. Although, in most European countries, there are many private logistics companies supplying cargo services by train, there is usually only one public organization tasked with allocating and managing the tracks. They have a large stake and the final say in the scheduling of short-term trips and train services. These schedules can delay or hamper the planning of railway shipments carried out by private logistics companies. The table below provides statistics on the length of rail track networks in the world and Europe.

	Country/Territory	Length (km)	Electrified length (km)	% of the total electrified	Historical peak length (km)	Area (km²) per km track	Population per km track	Nationalised or private[a]	Data year	Notes
1	United States	220,480	2,025[1]	0.92%	408,833[2]	43.2	2,060	Both	2014	[3]
2	China	150,000	100,000[4]	66.67%		63.80[4]	9,570[4]	Both	2021	[4]
3	Russia	85,600	43,800	51.17%	150,000	199.98	1,678	Nationalised	2022	[5]
4	India	68,797	52,247	79.35%[6]		48.23	20,424	Nationalised	2022	[7][8][9]
5	Canada	49,422	129	0.20%		214.48	674	Private	2017	[10]
6	Germany	40,625	22,500	55.38%	64,000	9.26	2,145	Both	2017	[11]
7	Argentina	36,966	190	0.51%	47,000	77.45	1,117	Nationalised	2014	[10]
8	Australia	33,168	3,393	10.23%		231.91	742	Both	2017	[12]
9	Brazil	29,817	9,025	30.27%		299.6	7,225	Both[b]	2014	[13]
10	France	29,273	15,687	53.59%	42,500	22.78	2,374	Nationalised	2017	[11]
11	Japan	27,311	20,534	75.19%		16.10	5,451	Private	2015	[10]
12	Mexico	23,389[14]	27	0.12%	26,914[14]	114.43	6,697	Private	2020	[15]

Source: https://en.wikipedia.org/wiki/List_of_countries_by_rail_transport_network_size

In the last century, connecting the rail networks of different countries has given a boost to the international trade by railway. The longest railway transit route (2020) is the Silk Railway, part of Trans-Eurasian Railway Services (see text box).

Source: https://www.oboreurope.com/en/faster-trains-europe-china/

"Volumes of freight traveling between China and Europe by rail are rising quickly. Between 2013 and 2016 cargo traffic quintupled in weight. In the first half of this year the value of goods traveling by train rose by 144% compared with the same period in 2016. Western firms have been keen to embrace rail freight because it helps them to lower costs," says Ronald Kleijwegt, an expert on the industry.

In the case of high-tech electronics, for example, which consumers like to receive quickly, making them on China's coast and air-freighting them to Europe is extremely pricey [...]. Last year, 180.000 tons of cargo traveled on trains to western Europe from China (the remainder was destined for Russia and eastern Europe). That is a small fraction of the 52 mln tons that came by sea, but a big chunk of the 700,000 tons that came by air. Much of that air cargo could switch to rail in the future, says Mr. Kleijwegt, with one important proviso – that Russia would need to lift the retaliatory sanctions it placed in 2014 on imports of Western food. But it was only a decade ago that people thought the idea of freight trains between Europe and China was a joke, says Mr. Kleijwegt – and no one laughs at that anymore.
Source: https://www.economist.com/news/ business/16 September 2017

The common economic rule that building, expanding, improving, and maintaining a railway network is expensive – and even more expensive in populated areas than in remote areas – remains valid. The pricing of moving goods by rail is mostly expressed in ton-kilometres as a basic unit, which means that two parameters are the main cost drivers: weight of the cargo and distance travelled. Besides incurring its own costs for managing the rail cars and locomotives, a rail logistics company must pay a fee for using the track infrastructure to the entity controlling the track network. Congestion on the tracks, especially in areas with a high-density railway network, is a (nearly daily) problem. This makes lead times less reliable for Supply Chain planning and drives up costs.

Freight transport by water

Taking the number-one spot for transportation modes is the shipment of goods by water. According to conservative estimates, 90% of all tangible goods transport is waterborne. This figure includes both intercontinental maritime freight traffic on international waters and shipping traffic on inland waterways and rivers. It is the slowest mode of transportation of all, but also the cheapest. For intercontinental shipping, in particular, exploiting economies of scale and mass transport play a key role. Intercontinental maritime freight transport makes use of a broad spectrum of seagoing vessels to transport the most diverse types of goods, where economies of scale are central. The three images below give an impression of the scale of intercontinental freight transport.

On the 3 June 2020, the port of Rotterdam received what is currently the world's largest container ship, the HMM Algeciras. The ship will berth at one of the deep-sea terminals on Maasvlakte 2. The around 400-metre long and 62-metre- wide ship has a capacity of 24,000 teu (20-foot standard containers), making it the largest container giant in the world. HMM Algeciras is owned by the company HMM21 (Hyundai Merchant Marine) based in South Korea. **Source**: By kees torn – https://www.flickr.com/photos/68359921@N08/49970357017/, CC BY-SA 2.0, https://commons.wikimedia.org/w/index.php?curid=90963463

The Höegh Target, one of the largest marine car carriers in the world, was recently towed into the port of Rotterdam. The ship of the Norwegian company Höegh Autoliners can carry 8,500 cars. In total, the Höegh Target has fourteen decks where the vehicles are stored. The ship is just under two hundred meters long (199.9 meters) and 36.5 meters wide.
Source: https://www.nu.nl/overig/4110557/grootste-autoschip-wereld-in-haven-van-rotterdam.html

The Hellespont Alhambra is one of the largest oil tankers in the world to date, within the category of ships designated as ULCC (= Ultra Large Crude Carriers). The ship has a length of 380 metres and a width of 68 metres and can reach a speed of 30 km/hour. It has a capacity of 503,409,900 liters (± ½ billion!). The vessel is owned by the Antwerp-based maritime service company Euronav NV. The vessel is so large that it cannot pass through the widened Panama Canal nor the widened Suez Canal and is mainly used on the shipping routes from the Middle East to the United States and Europe.
Source: https://upload.wikimedia.org/wikipedia/commons/8/82/Hellespont_Alhambra-223713_v2.jpg

Freight transport over water is one of the oldest transportation modes for getting merchandise from A to B. One of the oldest merchant ship wrecks ever found by archaeologists on the seabed of the Mediterranean Sea dates from the 4th century BC and, according to researchers, was used for cargo transport. Over the centuries, ship quality gradually improved, and the capacity of merchant ships expanded. After the discovery of America in 1492, sea journeys became intercontinental, requiring higher standards of seaworthiness and resistance to the hardships of unpredictable oceans and weather. Nowadays, the majority of the *intercontinental* trade of goods is waterborne. It is the cheapest mode of transportation, but the slowest one. Logistics companies specialized in water transportation can select from a large and diversified supply of marine vessels suitable for (m)any kind(s) of tangible goods.

Some vessels are standardized, others customized. There are (very) large ships for mass shipment, like the vessels displayed in the boxes above, there are vessels designed for navigation over rivers, and vessels designed for intra-city waterways (canals) to supply local stores located close to the quays.[10] The supporting infrastructure is the presence of water(ways) and, despite 71% of the earth's surface being covered by water, not all water is suitable for navigation. A second element of the marine infrastructure is the global network of sea- and riverports.

Humans have long tried to redirect the flow of water masses, not only to protect themselves against flooding or other disasters, but also to shorten sailing distances. In some industrialized countries this has been done successfully by redirecting the course of a river, canalizing water streams, building barriers and locks against unwanted water level rises, and dredging river beds to create deeper water to facilitate the navigation of vessels with deeper immersion. Some global engineering waterworks have contributed significantly to shorten sailing distances and times. The most important ones are shown in the textboxes below.

One of the most important water infrastructures that made global trade more efficient has been the Panama Canal (1914): it saves vessels approximately 16,000 kilometres of sailing around South America. Based on an average vessel speed of 45 km/hour, it can reduce lead times by 15 days. After an expansion investment it reopened in June 2016.
Source: https://upload.wikimedia.org/wikipedia/commons/9/94/Ship_passing_through_Panama_Canal_01.jpg

The Suez Canal (1869), shown in the satellite image saves vessels more than 7,000 kilometres of sailing around Africa to the Indian Ocean. Based on an average vessel speed of 45 km/hour, it can reduce lead times by seven days. Recently, huge investments have been made to increase the width and depth of the Suez Canal and it reopened in august 2015.
Source: https://upload.wikimedia.org/wikipedia/commons/thumb/6/6e/SuezCanal-EO.JPG/280px-SuezCanal-EO.JPG

Source: Von Olahus – Eigenes Werk, Gemeinfrei, https://commons.wikimedia.org/w/index.php?curid=6935186

An outstanding efficiency leap in European inland waterway infrastructure is Germany's Main-Danube-Canal, which was finally completed and became operational in 1992. It connects the Rhine with the Danube, creating a navigable inland artery for ships travelling from Rotterdam to the Black Sea (approximately 3,500 kilometres), significantly shorter than the North Sea – Atlantic Ocean – Mediterranean – Black Sea route. The length of the canal is 171 kilometres; the summit elevation is 406 metres above sea level: this is the highest point on earth that is currently reached by commercial watercraft. 16 locks must be passed to overcome the water level difference. Via the different tributaries of the combined Rhine and Danube River network, many European cities can be reached by ship.

Besides global, regional, and local man-made modifications to natural waterways to accelerate shipping times, equally important is the presence of ports and port facilities, where cargo is loaded, unloaded, stored, and cross-docked. There is a worldwide network of seaports – and, in countries with rivers, also inland ports – in all countries with sea bordering coastlines. This network facilitates cross-docking and freight is further shipped to the interior of a country deploying other modes of transportation.

Expensive investments are required to expand, maintain and improve these waterways and port assets. Vessels must pay a fee for using port facilities and other water structures, such as locks. In some ports, pilots are necessary for ships to reach their mooring sites inside the port. Regulations for using waterways are diverse. Theoretically, everybody can use international waters, like oceans and open sea, at any time without paying for traversing them. International seas have no owner and are regulated by international treaties. As soon as a ship enters the territorial waters of a country, however, the vessel is subject to the regulations and laws issued by the water authorities of that country. These authorities have operational control over all ship movements within their jurisdiction and can set constraints on vessel size, cargo, setting traffic rules for navigation and others. Enforcement of maritime laws in territorial waters is done by national Coast Guards. Congestion, especially in and around ports and at locks, is a problem making lead times uncertain and increasing Supply Chain costs unpredictably. On the high seas, weather conditions, including severe storms and water turbulence, can also cause delays. Recently, a global waterway route has gained momentum due to the effects of global warming (see text box below).

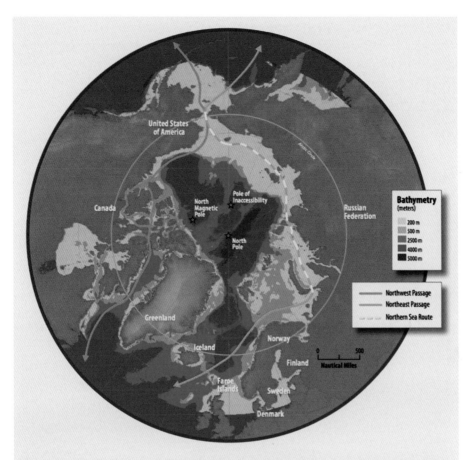

Source: https://upload.wikimedia.org/wikipedia/commons/b/bc/Map_of_the_Arctic_region_show-ing_the_Northeast_Passage%2C_the_Northern_Sea_Route_and_Northwest_Passage%2C_and_ba-thymetry.png

Although global warming has negative effects on the well-being of the world, it brings at least one economic advantage. There has been an increase in the number of months that ice thickness allows pilotage of ships in the Arctic Sea. The navigation season for transit passages on the *Northern Sea Route* (NSR) starts approximately at the beginning of July and lasts through to the second half of November. There are no specific dates for commence-ment and completion of navigation, it is entirely dependent on particular ice conditions. In 2011, the navigation season on the NSR seaways for large vessels was 141 days, i.e. more than 4.5 months. In recent years, easy ice conditions have been observed and that offers increased opportunities for operating on the NSR seaways. All NSR seaways are currently located in an area of one-year ice. In Arctic conditions, one-year ice grows to roughly 1.6 metres. In early July, at the beginning of navigation, the ice is not pressurized and so can be broken and easily moved through. Vessels can travel at the same speed as in open waters.
Source: http://www.arctic-lio.com/nsr_ice

Freight transport by road

The red line represents Australian Highway 1, which circumnavigates the entire continent. With a length of 14,500 kilometers, it is the longest national highway in the world.
Source: https://en.wikipedia.org/wiki/Highway_1_(Australia)

Very **un**common! But in case of a proper cold winter that allows for thick ice, all seven official ice roads in Estonia can be opened, thereby providing a total of more than 80 km of ice roads. The Haapsalu–Noarootsi ice road boasts the highest efficiency factor and enables a route that is 10 km shorter than the route without an ice road. Global warming is reducing the use of ice roads, however.
Source: https://www.visitestonia.com/en/why-estonia/ice-road-the-symbol-of-a-great-estonian-winter

The oldest large-scale road builders were the Romans, who started building an extensive road network in Europe already three centuries BC. The roads were built mainly of stones and intended to supply their army, encamping on the outer borders of their empire, to protect it against foreign invaders.[11] Over many centuries, the majority of roads were *unpaved*, which made travelling in periods of heavy rainfall and adverse weather conditions difficult, transforming roads into pools of mud. In the 19th and 20th centuries, the development of road networks accelerated due to industrialized mass-production, the rise of private cars, and the need for distribution networks and increased international trade. The main users of highways are trucks and private cars.

The invention of the automobile propelled by gasoline or diesel combustion engines dates from the late 19th century. The development of trucks with internal combustion engines also dates from this period.[12] Cars with combustion engines made it possible to drive over longer distances and the need for longer and adequate road pavement triggered the growth of large road networks in Europe, in the United States, and some Asian countries. This process has continued up to the scale of global, national, regional, and urban highway networks that we know today (2022).

Road travel times depend on, among other things, the average speed of freight trucks, which, in turn, depends not only on the properties of the truck engine and the cargo (weight), but even more on institutional constraints, such as traffic rules (maximum speed), traffic lights, and road congestion. Road *quality*, e.g. driving on unpaved or paved surfaces, also affects travel time.[13] A general classification of roads is *Freeways* (also called *expressways* or *motorways*, encompassing the E-roads in Europe[14]), regional highways, local roads, and special roads. The table below shows a list of countries with their total road network length, both paved and unpaved. *NB: Road length does not say anything about road quality or safety.*

Unless otherwise noted, the data is from the CIA.[1][2]

* indicates **Roads in Country/Territory** links.

	Country	Total (km)	Density (km/100 km^2)	Paved (km)		Unpaved (km)		Controlled-access (km)		Source & Year
	⬍	⬍	⬍	⬍	⬍	⬍	⬍	⬍	⬍	⬍
	World	64,285,009	47	N/A		N/A		N/A		2021
1	United States *	6,703,479	70	4,304,715	63%	2,281,895	33%	95,932	1.4%	[3] 2019
2	India *	6,215,797	189	4,266,046	69%	1,931,751	31%	2,075	0.0%	2020-21[4]
3	China *	5,198,000	54	4,943,000	95%	255,000	5%	161,000	3.1%	2020[5]
4	Brazil *	2,000,000	23	246,000	12%	1,754,000	88%	11,018	0.6%	2018
5	Russia *	1,529,373	9	927,721	61%	355,666	23%	6,768	0.4%	[6] 2019
6	France *	1,053,215	191	1,053,215	100%	0	0%	11,671	1.1%	[7] 2011
7	Canada *	1,042,300	10	415,600	40%	626,700	60%	17,041	1.6%	[8] 2014
8	Australia *	873,573	11	145,928	17%	727,645	83%	1,716	0.2%	2015
9	Mexico *	817,596	42	175,526	21%	641,986	79%	10,845	1.3%	[9] 2020
10	South Africa *	750,000	61	158,124	21%	591,876	79%	1,927	0.3%	2016
11	Thailand *	702,577	137	N/A		N/A		535.3	0.1%	[10] [11]2020
12	Spain *	683,175	135	683,175	100%	0	0%	16,205	2.4%	2011
13	Germany *	644,480	180	644,480	100%	0	0%	13,183	2.0%	[12] 2020
14	Sweden *	573,134	127	140,100	24%	433,034	76%	2,050	0.4%	2016
15	Vietnam *	570,448	172	148,338	26%	47,130	8%	1,276	0.2%	[13] 2019

Source: https://en.wikipedia.org/wiki/List_of_countries_by_road_network_size

Regarding the institutional and regulatory framework of road infrastructure, virtually all roads in the world are public property of either states, regional authorities, municipalities, or other public entities. Legal ownership does not mean that these public bodies also take care of the operational management of highways. They can commission a private company to take care of the operational management of one or more highways by granting a concession. In many cases, these companies are also responsible for road maintenance and repair.[15] This situation applies to most toll roads in the world. Later, we will discuss the theoretical framework for pricing the use of toll roads and public roads, because road prices have a direct impact on the cost of logistics and Supply Chain operations.

There is an abundant framework of regulations and institutions for managing and using national highway systems: the most important are traffic rules, especially speed limits, traffic lights, and overtaking rules, all of which affect lead times. Other rules set constraints on what cargo can be transported over a road, i.e. the transportation of designated chemicals on certain highways is prohibited in some countries and is seldom allowed within cities. In addition to highways and roads as standalone assets, there are other value-adding features of road systems. These are complementary assets such as the number and spatial distribution of gasoline stations, parking lots, emergency lanes, lighting mostly within cities, and roadside assistance for car breakdowns.

In many countries, traffic on highways is monitored by road traffic control centres that have operational control together with traffic police. They can adjust speed limits or apply other traffic rules to manage (over)crowded roads. If we focus on the main road *users*, instead of the road infrastructure, the vast majority of road freight carriers are private companies. They range from very large firms covering the entire globe, equipped with a diversified fleet of vehicles for road transportation, to small express couriers who only deliver small packages by bicycle within cities. The price of transporting goods depends on many factors: distance from source to destination; weight or volume of the product; the nature of the goods (standardized container or customized shipment); the insurance premium for the carrier's liability for damage and theft during transportation; the arrival time requested by the customer; payment of customs duties for transborder transportation, and many more. In many countries, congestion on road and highways is a serious problem, also within cities – and becoming worse in recent years – leading to unpredictable lead times and making Supply Chain planning less reliable and logistics costlier.

Freight transport by (motor)bicycle

Biking paths can have independent bridges over rivers, such as here, across the Waal, in Nijmegen.
Source: https://www.snelfietsroutes-gelderland.nl/bestanden/Afbeeldingen/Snelfietsroutes/nieuws/2021/oktober%20 2021/MaasWaal-fietsers%20op%20brug-19. jpg?hid=img;mxw=750

Food delivery to end-consumers within cities is often done by bicycle. Many countries are investing in biking infrastructure.
Source: By Môsieur J. [version 9.1] from Rouen, FRANCE – #deliveroo, CC BY 2.0, https://commons.wikimedia.org/w/index. php?curid=53481353

Although by far <u>not</u> the most important mode of freight transportation, in a few metropolitan areas the bicycle, or its motorized counterpart the *moped*, can be an efficient transportation mode. They can outperform other modes of transportation especially in intracity transportation when other road traffic is overcrowded and downtown parts of (old) cities with a narrow street grid are only accessible for (motor) bicycles. The disadvantage is their slowness, but this is partly offset by the fact that they usually ride over short distances. They can move only small cargo units and are frequently used for moving packages from a store to consumer homes, or for last-mile delivery from a pick-up point to the customer's home. An advantage is that they are cheap, at least cheaper than most other modes of transportation. An increasing number of countries are investing in the extension and improvement of the biking infrastructure, not only within cities but also between cities. In some places, the biking path is just a white line painted on the street indicating a separate biking lane.[16]

Most cycling activity is for person movement, either recreationally or for commuting, and it is expected that the growth of electric bicycles in Europe will put more pressure on the biking paths infrastructure, while some people commuting over short distances will switch from the car, which is frequently stuck in traffic jams, to e-bike riding over less congested biking paths, in particular in the inner city and peripheral areas.

Moreover, last-mile delivery of online purchases to a customer's home address in crowded cities is often more efficient by bike, moped, or scooter than by van. Of all infrastructure assets, using the cycle path network is free of both direct (no payment per kilometer) and indirect costs, because there is no bicycle tax equivalent to the tax on motor vehicles. Using accessory facilities, such as bike parking garages, can have a price tag.

Passenger service and transport

As previously discussed, production planning in a Supply Chain will only be effective if all resources are available at the right time, on the right place, in the right numbers, and with the right properties. That also holds for human resources, the employees involved in production and logistics operations. The availability of passenger transport modes and their supporting infrastructure affects planning accuracy and, consequently, Supply Chain performance. We will therefore briefly discuss several modes of passenger services and their supporting infrastructure. We distinguish movement between cities (intercity) and movement within cities (intracity). What follows is not an exhaustive list of passenger transport, only the most common modes.

For *intercity* services:
1. **Private car.** Many of the features, advantages, and disadvantages discussed for freight transport by road also apply to persons moving by car.
2. Passenger service by **train**. Besides the features discussed for freight transport by train, one important railway infrastructural asset is the presence and geographical density of railway stations along the tracks. The more stations, the more people can be transported, but at the same time more train stops make travel time longer and railway stations are a major cause of congestion on the tracks.
3. Passenger service by **public bus**. Similar features as transport by truck. Most intercity buses drive on the same highways as cars and trucks without separate lanes and face the same congestion problems as trucks. Also for buses, the number of bus stops along the route and the service frequency affect passenger travel time.
4. Passenger transport by **plane**. Many features discussed for freight transport by air also apply to passenger transport by air. Passenger air transport is mostly used for long-distance travel and seldom for daily commuting.

For *intracity* services:

1. **Subway.** Very efficient and safe mode of passenger transportation for moving large numbers of people. Very little congestion on the tracks – most congestion occurs *inside* the railcars when (too) many people jostle against each other, especially during rush hours. Travel time is reliable and predictable. Building and maintaining a subway system is very expensive, especially the tunnels for the underground part of the subway, the stations, and the track system.[17]

2. **Tram and bus.** Can be an efficient mode of passenger transport within a city if the tram or bus has separate tracks or lanes free of other traffic, thereby reducing congestion. An important asset that affects the efficiency of the system is the number and distribution of stops for boarding and alighting.

3. **Private car.** Not very efficient in cities, facing frequent congestion and parking is difficult and, in many cities, expensive.

4. **Bicycle, moped, and scooter:** shares similar features as these modes used for freight transportation.

A brief overview of the future of freight and persons mobility

Although it is hard to find reliable statistics about the hours lost and resources wasted in freight transport and passenger services due to traffic jams and congestion, congestion is a problem for all modes of transportation. It leads to the late arrival of goods and employees, it costs lots of money, and congestion continues to rise globally. Congestion is directly related to economic activity and the problem has only become worse in recent decades. Some stretches of infrastructure assets are chronically overcrowded and sometimes suffer from traffic infarcts.

Consequently, many governments and research institutions are seeking innovations to improve the efficiency of moving goods and persons. Although innovations in transportation and logistics are beyond the scope of this book, we will briefly address their impact on Supply Chain planning and organization. Any improvement in the efficiency of moving goods and of the underlying infrastructure systems adds value for the customer and, in many cases, also for the supplier, and it reduces costs.[18]

A relatively simple solution is to use better information and coordination systems to improve the load factor of moving vehicles such as trucks, cargo trains, cargo planes, and marine vessels. Empirical studies show that a substantial number of shipments have unidirectional high load factors. A truck moves loaded with products from its source A to its destination B and returns home either empty or with a very low load factor. At the same time, another truck (or plane, train, or vessel) moves cargo from B to A and returns empty from A to B. Sharing capacity and revenues can be achieved by using a two-way ride for a single truck with cargo from A to B, unloading in B, and then reloading in or close to B and driving back from B to A. If necessary, it can pass by a nearby place, C, to unload the cargo sourced at place B.

The structural existence of inefficiency in capacity usage is partly explained by competition among freight carriers. It is also a consequence of the *prisoners' dilemma* leading to a Supply Chain loss. More Information Technology coordination systems are developed to obtain a more efficient allocation of cargo orders, by making supply and demand for cargo transport more transparent and by trying to align the individual interests of logistics companies in order to share capacity and revenues. In this way, a better match of supply and demand for transportation can be achieved.[19]

Another field of continuous research is looking for increased safety of the infrastructure and its users.[20] An example is the research into self-driving vehicles and cars that automatically brake in dangerous traffic situations. Innovations in energy-saving vehicles do not directly affect Supply Chain performance, but they do affect the transportation costs and, thus, Supply Chain costs. Another line of transportation research is looking for alternative applications of existing transportation modes for cargo as well as for passengers. Two examples are shown in the box below.

Although *Unmanned Aerial Vehicle (UAV)*, the official name for drones, are a favourite toy for private and recreational uses, they are becoming competitive flight vehicles in the market for air freight transportation for small package transportation and last-mile delivery. The drone market is growing rapidly. A drone has the advantage of being able to reach remote areas as well as densely packed city neighbourhoods, making it an efficient mode for last-mile delivery in a distribution network.[22]

The institutional and regulatory frameworks for drone flights are still in development. Issues addressed in these regulations include which areas and at which height in the airspace drones are allowed to fly, what kind of licence a drone operator needs to fly a drone, what the quality and safety standards of drones should be, what package weights they are permitted to move, etc. Most countries are issuing their own, national regulations. Like many innovations, manufacturers and professional drone users are still at the beginning of the learning curve, which makes cost estimation difficult and less predictable.

Cable cars as a means of public transport. Traditionally used to move tourists upwards in ski resorts, new applications are deployed: overcoming distances in cities as a public passenger transportation mode, often built on mountain sides. Latin American cities are at the forefront of using cable cars for passenger transport[21] and a growing number of cities worldwide are studying the feasibility of using *ropes* for passenger transport. Their physical infrastructure (poles, connecting ropes, and stops) and the moving assets (gondolas) are cheaper to build and maintain than *subways*. The picture above shows the world's longest cable car connection, the La Paz – El Alto in Bolivia.
Source: By Adelina Herbas – Own work, CC BY-SA 4.0, https://commons.wikimedia.org/w/index.php?curid=67436347

Some countries are making large leaps in the development of their transportation systems. Rwanda is credited with having the first official *drone airport* in the world (picture 2016). The drones will initially be used to deliver blood, plasma, and coagulants to hospitals across rural western Rwanda, helping to cut waiting times from hours to minutes.
The aircraft is launched from a catapult and fly below 152 metres to avoid the airspace used by passenger planes. They have an operational range of 150 km but could, in theory, fly almost twice that distance.
Source: https://ichef.bbci.co.uk/news/976/cpsprodpb/7C4D/production/_91912813_5be9653f-dde5-44d9-bd42-e718a0af165b.jpg

Information and information exchange in a 21st century Supply Chain

Information[23] is sometimes called the fourth production factor in business. Some companies, e.g. news agencies, social media, Google, Reuters (mostly financial information), have managing information and selling data as their core business. However, *all* companies collect data and use information to guide their business policy, to improve products, to market new products, and to ensure consistent administrative procedures. Supply Chains are no exception to this general rule and, because a Supply Chain is a coordinated network of partner companies, the consistent collection, exchange, and communication of data and other information is a prerequisite for the success or collapse of the entire Supply Chain.

To have a better understanding of information exchange, we will first contextualize – or as it is called nowadays *frame* – our discussion about information in a more general economic, social, and institutional environment, before discussing specific information and communication features in Supply Chains.

Different faces of information and information exchange

Information is made available, stored, displayed, and disseminated in different forms. The most common and, indeed, oldest one is written text. Text can be handwritten or printed on paper, and, today, increasingly, it is digitalized, e.g. pdf-format, Word documents, webpages, and internet blogs. Audio is a second form of information display. The broadcast of news by radio, podcasts posted on the internet, telephone conversations, voicemails, and face-to-face conversations are all examples of information transmitted and stored in audio format.

A third method of information storage and display is by image, both static (photos, tables, diagrams, and graphs) and dynamic (video). Broadcast news on the television, video documentaries on the internet or television, videoconferencing, video chats on social media, and camera images are all examples of information disseminated and stored as (digital) images.

Satellite images can be used to track and trace the position of vessels for logistics planning. Although there are more ways in which information can be stored and made available, e.g. *sign language* for people with hearing impairments and *smell* indicating the presence of a certain substance – the three aforementioned methods are by far the most common. In our contemporaneous information age, these three are the main assets of the internet and social media. The information flow in Supply Chains is also dragged along at the speed of the digital evolution and will be discussed below.

Information Supply Chains and Supply Chains for intangible assets like services

Information can be considered an end-product, ready to be read and/or sold, and most information passes through one or more stages in a chain before reaching its final stage, the end-consumer (reader). Data or event information, for example about a natural disaster in a country, can be first collected by local people, or journalists on the spot. This information can be sold to an international news agency, like *Associated Press* (AP):

> "News agencies do not generally publish news itself but supply news to its sub-scribers, who, by sharing costs, obtain services they could not otherwise afford. All the mass media depend upon the agencies for the bulk of the news, even including those few that have extensive news-gathering resources of their own."[24]

Agencies sell the information to other news companies and national press agencies, like ANP in the Netherlands. ANP, in turn, sells the information to national or local newspapers, and/or other news media, e.g. local radio and television broadcasters. Every stage in this information Supply Chain transforms the information more or less, by translating, summarizing, commenting on the data, contextualizing, and, in the worst case, manipulating it. One can therefore speak about Information Supply Chains, a concept not to be confused with the information flow that is linked to and accompanies the flow of physical goods through that Supply Chain. Generally, an Information Supply Chain is smaller and less complex than Supply Chains for tangible assets.

Other intangible assets, such as services, can also be part of a Supply Chain. An example is the services supplied by the insurance industry. Many insurance companies sell insurance policies through independent brokers. An independent broker can make a deal with a client to contract one or several insurance companies. The broker earns a fee for this brokerage service.

Economic categories of information and information exchange

Economists distinguish different categories of goods and services. A common classification scheme is made between market – or private – goods, club goods, and pure public goods. This classification scheme is based on two fundamental properties: **excludability** and **rivalry.**

Excludability refers to the possibility of a supplier to exclude people from using a particular good. Rivalry means that consumption of a good by one user does not diminish the possibility for other users or consumers to use the same good or service in the same quantity and quality. In other words, *non-rivalry* implies that many users can share the same good without *degrading* its quantity and quality. A good or service that is excludable *and* rival is a private or market good. A good or service that is both non-exclusive and non-rival is a *pure public* good. *Club goods* are somewhere midway between the two and were first analysed by Nobel laureate James M. Buchanan.

> "James M. Buchanan developed club theory (the study of club goods in economics) in his 1965 paper, An Economic Theory of Clubs. He classifies club goods between pure public goods and pure private goods. Buchanan found that there was still a missing link that would cover the whole spectrum of ownership – consumption possibilities. This gap contained goods that were excludable, shared by more people than typically share a private good, but fewer people than typically share a public good.
> The whole spectrum would cover purely private activities on one side and purely public or collectivized activities on the other side. Therefore, according to Buchanan, a theory of clubs needed to be added to the field."[25]

Now, we return to information. To classify *information* as an economic resource or intangible asset we focus on the two aforementioned basic properties: excludability and rivalry. Information *content* – considered as a standalone entity abstracted from its carrier, its target group, and its mode of transmission – is **not** rival. Any person taking notice of the information content does not downgrade the content in either quality or quantity. Others can also read, hear, or see the same message. There are no letters, words, colours, or screen resolution lost when somebody views, hears, or sees the message. The message remains the same.[26] However, suppliers of information can exclude users – either persons or electronic devices – from accessing the information carrier or receiving it, thereby making the information private. If they sell the information content for a price, i.e. pay-per-article, pay-per-view, pay-per-podcast, pay-per-TV programme, or -per-movie (Netflix), the information has become a *market* good.[27]

If the information is confidential, privacy protected, or encrypted, e.g. medical files, bank account information, academic grades stored on a university server, which can only be accessed using passwords, but is not intended to be sold for money, it is a *private* good. It is excluded from unauthorized persons and is not rival. A *market* good is marketable and has economic value and a price, but a private good is not necessarily marketable. It has value for some, but no price.

If we focus on the information *carrier* and the *transmission* mode the economic assessment changes. Virtually all transmission *modes* are rival, and many are exclusive. Information, such as text and images, printed on paper, can be sold on a per-unit basis (one newspaper, one magazine, one report, etc.). A copy owned by one individual is not available for another user, although the information content is identical in all copies. If the number of printed copies is limited to, say 10, the information carrier becomes scarce: not because the information content itself is scarce, but the paper copies – the carrier – is scarce.

Identical information content can be disseminated over several carriers to reach a large, targeted audience. For example, information disseminated in press conferences held by, e.g. the prime minister of the Netherlands in 2019, 2020, and 2021 about new lockdown measures due to increased hospitalizations because of Covid-19 infections was broadcast by television and via radio. Transcription (converting speech to text) allowed for the publication of this information as text that was posted on the internet, printed in newspapers, and transmitted via social media.

The information content (the lockdown restrictions announced by the prime minister) was identical – there was only one source: the press conference. The information carriers were many. In this way, more people, managers, and business organizations were reached and informed on time about imminent new lockdown restrictions, enabling them to take appropriate actions.

Similar arguments apply to *public* digital information stored on the internet. The content of public information on a website is not rival, but if there is a massive demand for access this information at the same time, the network servers storing the information can become temporarily unavailable or very slow. In other words, it is not the information that is slow or non-existent. But the carriers and/or transmission mode – either wired or wireless – are used beyond capacity and become slow, and may even crash. When an asset is downgraded or exhibits quality reduction if *more* users access it, it is a clear indication that it is rival.

Other properties of pure public goods, from another viewpoint, are explained below, but each property is a direct consequence of its intrinsic properties of being non-exclusive and non-rival.

1. The quantity and quality of a pure public good are fully determined by the supplier of the good and not by the number of users or beneficiaries
2. the supplier cannot charge a price per user or per usage and must therefore search for alternative sources to finance the pure public good
3. A pure public good cannot be supplied or consumed in separate units. It can only be taken on an *as-is* basis (all or nothing). It cannot be *itemized* for consumption (broken down or split into parts)
4. A pure public good has 100% externality

Ad 1.
When a news event is *publicly* broadcast, anyone who owns a TV set – or just watches a news event on a TV screen in a public place – cannot be charged a price

for the news event per viewer, or per time unit, by the broadcast company (the news supplier). The quality of the programme and the time it is broadcast is fully determined by the supplier. If the supplier shortens the broadcast by 30 minutes, inserts advertisements, or uses low-quality images, all viewers (beneficiaries) have 30 minutes less viewing utility, are confronted with the advertisements, and are faced with low-quality images.

Ad 2.

Because a pure public good is non-exclusive, anyone within the influence range of the pure public good can freely benefit from it. The supplier cannot charge a price per individual. Even if they attempted to do so, the beneficiary can argue that he or she has not asked for that specific good or service and therefore does not have to pay for it. Consequently, the supplier must seek alternative sources of revenues to pay for the costs of setting up and maintaining the pure public good.[28]

Ad 3.

This is a consequence of the non-exclusivity of pure public goods. The beneficiaries can only use or consume what the supplier supplies: no more and no less. No quantity-related or individualized transactions take place between the supplier and different beneficiaries by offering some users a little more and others a little less.

Ad 4.

Externality means costs imposed on third parties (negative) or benefits received by third parties (positive) for which the third party does not receive compensating payments or does not pay for the benefits received. A beneficiary of a pure public good receives all benefits of the presence of this good without direct proportional payment, so (s)he experiences 100% externality.

Some information can be classified as *club goods*. Examples are information published on intranet sites of organizations and information shared among partners in the same Supply Chain. Only employees and participating organizations can read and share the information.

Internet forums and chat sites for specific groups are also examples of club goods. These sites are excluded from persons not belonging to the club. If club members have to pay an upfront fee to join the club and cover the costs of maintaining the club good, the more members joining the club, the lower the cost per member. Initially, the benefit per member increases with more members – assuming that the members want to be part of the group – but when a critical number is reached congestion sets in and individual benefit starts to decline.[29]

Institutional framework for information collection and dissemination

The fact that some information is public and other is private can be partly attributed to the regulations regarding information and information exchange. The main regulations in the Western world affecting the legal and economic status of information are the laws regarding the protection of intellectual property, particularly copyright, and privacy laws. Public agencies that must enforce these laws also have an impact on what degree information is private. Copyright laws impose constraints on the reproduction and dissemination of written text, animations, music, videos, and images without the approval of the author or the rightsholder. This legal protection allows the author or rightsholder to sell part or all of the information on an individual basis, thereby making the information a market good.

Privacy laws forbid publishing information in the form of photos, text, videos, or audio of individual identifiable persons without their prior consent. This prohibition not only applies to humans, but also to the protection of confidential information of organizations and even for specific tangible assets, like military sites or indoor images of private homes.[30] Typical examples of privacy-protected information are medical files of patients, bank accounts, still unpublished financial corporate statements, customer information files of companies, criminal records, and many other forms of confidential information. Privacy-protected information is not a market good, because it is not allowed to be sold for money. It is private and can only be accessed by a selected group of people who are authorized to read and use the information. Confidential digital information is usually shielded from unauthorized access with passwords or biometric identification tools, like face recognition, iris scans, or fingerprint recognition. Messages sent over social media, like WhatsApp, are encrypted to shield the information from undesired third-party reading. Confidential and private information on paper is often saved in strongboxes or locked cabinets.

Case study: MS Excel

One can question whether the spreadsheet MS Excel – or other applications of the MS Office suite like Word, PowerPoint, Access, etc. – is a market or a public good. Software is protected by copyright – in some countries even by patent protection – and is sold on an individual basis. Like most intangible assets, the highest costs are incurred in the design and development phase of the software product, but not in the sale of the copies. These are *re*production costs, and the marginal costs of selling software copies are low. However, Excel files can be shared with other Excel users who can amend, add or delete information in a sheet, or change the layout. If, for example, five persons work on the same Excel file, this file becomes a shared file. The five users can protect the file with a password so that beyond this group nobody else has access to the information in the Excel file. The Excel file has become a club good.

Information exchange within Supply Chains

After having framed information in basic economic categories, we are now ready to discuss the role of information and information flow within Supply Chains. Information flow in an SC is mostly divided into a four-way flow: downward information flow; upward information flow; horizontal information flow; and diagonal information flow. The importance of information flow in the 21st century has risen rapidly due to global digitalization. Several empirical reasons are cited below:

"The definition of supply chain management (SCM) includes information flow as one of the two major flow components of the supply chain. The need to share information across the various entities along the supply chain is definitely of paramount importance. The information serves as the connection between the supply chain's various stages, allowing them to coordinate their actions and bring about many of the benefits of maximizing total supply chain profitability."[31]

"This paper discusses the importance of information flow within the relatively complex supply chain of a communications company with centralized European production centers and national sales and service organizations. It analyses the activities within the supply chain and illustrates the importance of the relationship between goods movement and the exchange of information. Information needs to be managed before a sale is made while satisfying the sales order and during after-sales maintenance. It concludes that responsiveness to customer demand, and overall customer satisfaction, cannot be achieved without proper management of both the goods movement and information flow throughout the supply chain."[32]

A large range of documents and information sharing takes place at the different stages in an international Supply Chain. We will first discuss the main freight documentation for international shipments, particularly for B2B transactions, and between a company operating in a member state of the EU and one outside the EU. A series of documents must be exchanged between the supplier, the freight carrier, and the customer.[33]

–   The first one is a ProForma Invoice that the foreign prospect customer asks for. ProForma Invoices generally contain information about the buyer and seller in the transaction, a detailed description of the goods and the code of Harmonized System Classification[34] of the goods, the price and the currency of payment, the payment terms, delivery terms about when, where and for what cost delivery will take place. When the sales transaction has become definitive and goods are ready for shipment, the ProForma invoice is replaced by a *Commercial Invoice* and the following documents are used:

- A packing list stating what items are in the package
- Not always: an (electronic) certificate of origin. This certificate contains information about which country the product has been manufactured in and must be signed by an official organization
- Shippers Letter of Instruction. This document contains information, particularly for the freight forwarder.
- Bill of Lading, which differs between air freight, shipment over water, and by truck.

  It is a contract of carriage between the exporter and the shipper of the goods that state where the goods are going; it also serves as a receipt that the goods have been picked up and delineates who has the title (ownership rights) of a good.

Another important institutional framework for international trade transactions. and therefore also for Supply Chain partners when they operate in different countries, is the so-called *Incoterms*.[35] International freight documentation also contains information about import duties paid, about safety, health, and environmental certificates to substantiate the products' compliance with legal standards and requirements. This kind of freight information is increasingly digitalized, thereby replacing the thick paper binders used in the past (although still in use in some countries). Sometimes, it is stored on a USB stick, which a truck driver keeps in the dashboard of the truck, but increasingly freight documentation is sent over the internet or can be accessed online by authorized partners.

Another important piece of information for final consumers – especially for mechanical and electronic devices – is the multi-language *user manual*. User manuals range from just a few pages to large pdf-documents with many pages.[36] More and more of these user manuals are digitalized – saving paper and thereby trees – and can be downloaded from the internet, although many products are still accompanied with a printed user manual. For smaller items, in particular food products, the information is printed on labels attached to the packaging and more detailed product information can be found on the website of the manufacturer or the selling company of the product. All this information runs top-down. Top-down information also includes invoices sent to the receiver for the products ordered. Bottom-up information is, for example, orders placed by the customer with the supplier, either on paper, online, or via the telephone.

Other information that is gaining growing importance is the product reviews and feedback on the internet written by end consumers. These customer or product reviews are usually public and everybody, including the product supplier and manufacturer, can read them. While they can be considered bottom-up information, they also have a horizontal dimension, because other potential buyers can read these reviews and decide to buy the product or even waive a buying decision in the case of negative product reviews. Other bottom-up information includes the return forms stating the reason why customers return an ordered product, e.g. because they do not like it or the product that they received was not the one they ordered.

Other pieces of information for Supply Chain purposes are the *track-and-trace* information during shipment. This enables both supplier and customer to know the location of a product during its journey from source to destination. If any delay occurs during shipment, the customer can adjust its planning. As discussed in a previous chapter, a major added value for a Supply Chain is coordinating activities and information sharing. This information sharing among Supply Chain partners concerns, in particular, collaborative demand forecasting, production planning at the manufacturer level, and inventory levels at the DCs and the retail level. Every SC partner has access to the relevant information of other partners to achieve efficient SC coordination. This shared information flows in both directions: top-down and bottom-up. But to share data they must first be registered and processed.

In the last half-century, a range of new information carriers has emerged in the business community, specifically Barcodes (patented in 1952), QR-codes (created in 1994), and RFID-tags (patented in 1973). An ever-increasing number of products, packages, mail letters, and other assets moving through a Supply Chain, is equipped with one or more of these information carriers containing similar product information as on paper labels.[37] These information carriers contain coded information that can be read by scanners, or RFID readers. The scanners are often connected to, for example, a cash register or computer system to record each transaction in the firm's accounting system.

Today, QR-codes are also used in *digital* format and can be scanned and read with a smartphone and other electronic devices. A QR-code is an excellent tool for facilitating online payments, e.g. via iDeal. Besides saving paper to print the same information on labels, these modern information carriers, such as RFID tags, are attached to a product or package. These carriers accompany the product during a great part of their journey through the Supply Chain. They are not only excellent tools to track items during shipment between two Supply Chain stages, but also to track items *within* a facility, e.g. which worker is working on what item or product in a distribution centre or manufacturing plant.

Information stored in bar codes, QR-codes, or RFID tags is comparable to written or printed information: the content is the same, but the information carriers differ from each other, each with its advantages and disadvantages. Information stored on these carriers usually follows the same direction in the Supply Chain as the product itself, namely, top-down. If we focus on the economic categorization of information flowing through a Supply Chain, the majority of the information described above is private. It is only intended for and accessible by the supplier and the customer, and the information carrier is protected with passwords or other security controls against unauthorized access.

User manuals for consumer products and public product reviews online and on paper are exceptions, and are mostly public for consumer products. B2B information sharing within a Supply Chain about sales data, production planning, and inventory levels at the different stages can be considered as a *club good*: only SC members have access, the rest of the world is excluded.

To summarize: just as one of the main objectives of a Supply Chain is to get products and services at the right time, to the right place, in the right quantity, and be of the right quality to meet customer expectations, in the same way, information must be available at the *right time*, on the *right site* (available to those who need it, or are entitled to see it), in the *right quantity* (no more and no less than needed) and be of the *right quality* (relevant information and no fake information) available to those partners in the Supply Chain who need the information, request it, or want to access it.

Managing the information flow through a Supply Chain to meet this objective is part of the planning process and can contribute significantly to Supply Chain performance. In the next paragraph, we discuss the global and local infrastructure assets needed for an efficient transmission of data and information.

Main Points: Information **content** is non-rival: a message stays the same, irrespective of how many people take notice of or read it. Only the supplier can change the information content. Information can be classified as a market good when it is made exclusive, and the supplier sells the information at prices per unit. It can be called a club good when a selected group has access to it. Information is a pure public good if everybody can take notice of the information at no cost. It is then non-rival and non-exclusive, e.g. in the case of traffic information on signage, or radio news. Information *transmission*, however, is rival and can downgrade the quantity and quality of information once congestion sets in. Modern product information carriers used in a Supply Chain are barcodes, QR-codes, and RFID tags. Supply Chain information *shared among SC partners* can be considered as a club good.

The physical infrastructure enabling information transmission

Now, we will address the infrastructure assets that make information exchange and communication possible. Those assets refer only to the source and the transmission mode of the information and *not* to the information content. First, the sender and the receiver need tangible devices that can communicate with each other. If the message is sent by post, the physical asset or carrier is *paper and envelope,* and the transmission occurs by using the postal service and letterboxes to bring the letter to the addressee.[38]

If the communication occurs by phone, both the sender and the receiver need a mobile phone – or similar device that can receive the message -. The transmission is the connection between the phone of the sender and the device of the receiver, and the necessary infrastructure for this connection will be discussed below.

As already discussed, the need for efficient digital information transmission is great. Online shops need it for order processing, 'track and trace' of packages, fast management response to changing market conditions, navigation software to find the best route, Business Intelligence to stay up-to-date about demand and competitor's actions, video conferencing with suppliers, digital payments with credit or debit card, online product reviews, and many more applications require reliable and quickly accessible information by Supply Chain partners. Erroneous or biased information or information that arrives too late due to congestion can thwart Supply Chain planning and lead to wrong decisions.

We will therefore briefly discuss the different assets used for information storage, retrieval, and transmission together with the accompanying tangible infrastructure assets for transmission.

In the first part of the 20th century, the most common mode of information exchange was by paper mail. The supporting infrastructure was the extensive network of mailboxes spread over the country to deposit letters and the home delivery of the letters by national postal services. Although in most countries in Europe this national postal system is still operational, its market share for information transmission and communication is rapidly declining.

The oldest system for electric information transmission over a long distance was the telegraph, which transmitted written telegrams. It was first patented in 1837 but, beyond exhibitions in museums, are hardly used anymore. Closely related to the telegraph was the telex machine whereby messages were automatically typed out with a typewriter connected to the cable network.

The telephone for voice communication dates from the late 19th century and developed at a fast rate in a global network infrastructure of copper cables, creating landline connections over all continents. This network branched out to nearly all houses in most industrialized countries within cities as well as in smaller towns and villages.[39] This telecom cable network was the tangible infrastructure enabling voice and data transmission and is mostly controlled by telecom companies.

With the arrival, in the late 19th century, of radio, public audio information was broadcast wirelessly from central studios and could be received by all persons and organizations owning a radio set. Its supporting infrastructure consisted of a widespread network of radio transmitters and receiving antennas. In recent years, radio programmes are increasingly broadcast over the internet.

Information and transmission of images and video became the domain of television development using a network of wireless transmitters and reception antennas. Later, the cable network took over part of the wireless communication by radio and television, at the same time improving the quality of audio and video transmission. Radio and television use a one-way transmission, which means that, with the appropriate device, one can receive signals but not send signals back. This makes wireless radio and television technically a non-exclusive good.[40] Later, the live broadcast of international events like the Olympic Games, used communication satellites to reach all parts of the globe. As a result of the development of signal encryption, some information and programmes became private and can only be viewed after payment.

The advent and rapid development of the worldwide web have created a revolution in information and data availability and communication reaching the most remote areas in the world. In recent times, it even allows mobile communication for passengers flying at high altitudes in planes or on ships cruising the Pacific Ocean.

Communication over the internet is in most cases a *two-way direction* – a computer, laptop, or smartphone *receives* and *sends* binary coded signals containing information: text messages; images; and audio.

This gives the internet the possibilities of exclusivity and rivalry. It allows for private or encrypted information and enables companies to charge a price for viewing or listening to digital information.

Staggering amounts of information circulate nowadays over the world wide web, and it continues to increase daily. This has only been possible due to the rapid technological development of hardware, especially **data centres** for storing information content, the optical glass fibre networks for transmitting information (tangible part), and the software (intangible part) to make the hardware work.

What follows is a list of the most important infrastructure for digital communication and information transmission today:

1. The global glass fibre network, which is expanding at a fast rate. Glass fibre cables have many advantages over (existing) copper cables: they are faster; have less signal loss over long distances; have less electromagnetic interference; have a larger bandwidth; and rarely break.

The building of underground glass fibre networks has been ongoing since the beginning of the internet. Inside cities, there are widely branched networks reaching individual homes. Continents are connected via the *intercontinental submarine* cables crossing seas and oceans. The map below shows the existing network of operational intercontinental submarine glass fibre cables.[41]

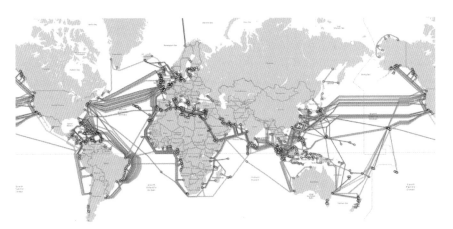

Source: https://i.redd.it/eo6248sth0pz.png

Besides the public internet, many companies and public organizations have an *intra*net. An intranet locally connects different computers at different locations, e.g. in distribution centres, and computers from corporate subsidiaries as part of closed network whereby internal and sometimes sensitive and confidential information is stored. It can only be accessed by persons authorized by the company to use the information using passwords and other security measures. Some organizations have linked their intranet to the internet, so that authorized people can access confidential intranet information from anywhere in the world. Inside buildings, Wi-Fi is a frequently used information infrastructure, composed of a network of routers connecting local computers in a building. The range of a Wi-Fi network is limited. A standard Wi-Fi has an approximate coverage of less than 100 metres.[42]

As mentioned above, *data centres* are another important physical asset for efficient data storage. A data centre is a facility used to house computer systems, servers, and associated components, such as telecommunication and data storage. Data stored in data centres are referred to as being stored in the *cloud*.[43] Glass fibre networks have similar structures to other infrastructure assets. Its *digital backbone*, which enables large-scale transmission of staggering amounts of data, is comprised of glass fibre cables, like those that connect the data centres of telecom providers with each other. The glass fibre network branches into smaller fibres with less capacity. Finally, the cable continues and splits into an extensively branched network of low-capacity underground capillaries connecting private homes and buildings to the global worldwide network.[44] However, in many cities and towns, the connection to the internet is still through copper cables that were laid in the past for landline telephone connections. To date, there is *no* global coverage with the glass fibre cable network. At the same time, radio and television devices are increasingly connected to the glass fibre network. Signals through the glass fibre network are two-way and although the network capacity is very large, during extreme peak usage signal loss and quality reduction due to congestion can and do occur.[45] Glass fibre cables also experience other forms of breakdown, like cables laid on the seabed becoming entangled in nets of fisher trawlers, but this does not depend on the number of users.

2. The global network of GSM masts[46] or cell towers for wireless microwave communication used by mobile phones, smartphones, and tablets. The majority of cell towers are connected via a glass fibre network. Wireless communication is based on electromagnetic waves with bidirectional signals. They sometimes experience signal loss during peak usage as a consequence of congestion. Usage of the electromagnetic wave spectrum is rival and subject to a pricing and allocation mechanism by public authorities. The table below provides statistics about cell towers creating cellular networks in some European countries. On a global scale, the number of cell towers approximates 6 million.[47]

Number of Owned and Operated Towers, In Number, Global, 2020

United States	27058
Uganda	3375
South Africa	2831
Peru	1935
Nigeria	5823
Mexico	9500
Kenya	2397
India	74732
Ghana	3298
Germany	2217
France	2769
Colombia	4992
Chile	3005
Brazil	16782

Source: American Tower Corporation

Source: https://www.mordorintelligence.com/industry-reports/telecom-towers-market

Are wireless connections preferable over a wired connection in offices?

Although wireless networks are rapidly gaining market share for internal information exchange and communication within offices and homes, wired and wireless networks both have advantages and disadvantages.

When configured properly, wired networks are more reliable and stable than wireless local networks, partly because signals transmitted by cable are less influenced by neighbouring connections. Two independent *wired* networks rarely interfere with each other. Another advantage is that wired networks are generally faster than wireless networks and better protected against unauthorized access.

The disadvantages are the immobility of the network: electronic devices can be moved only as far as the cable length allows. And office space can become crammed with lots of cables if many devices (telephone, computers, television, etc.) are connected to the network.

Wireless networks are easier to hack than wired networks. The probability of a loss in signal strength when many users access the network at the same time is higher for wireless networks than for wired networks.

And if the Internet of Things (IoT) gains momentum connecting heating systems, fridges, lighting, and other assets to the network, the decision between wireless, wired or a combination will become even more important.

Source: https://www.ouritdept.co.uk/wired-vs-wireless-networking-business/

3. The network of navigation satellites orbiting around the globe: Global Positioning System (GPS).

    This network of orbiting satellites is used for the navigation of airplanes, ships, vehicles, and any moving person or object equipped with a navigational device. Communication satellites are also used for live broadcasting of major events and can be used for telephone connections in areas with no cell towers, via so-called *satellite telephones*. Navigation satellites emit a unidirectional signal that is received by the receiving device, like a smartphone with GPS, or a standalone navigational device like a TomTom. Any device within the reach of the signal can capture it and receiving the signal does not rival with other receivers. It cannot be priced based on the number of hours a navigational device is receiving satellite signals for routing. According to the UCS,[48] the estimated number of operational satellites orbiting in space whose main purpose is information logistics is:

    – Communications: 742 satellites
    – Navigation/Positioning: 108 satellites

Galileo, the EU's satellite navigation system, is currently affected by a technical incident related to its ground infrastructure. The incident has led to a temporary interruption of the Galileo initial navigation and timing services, except the Galileo Search and Rescue

(SAR) service. The SAR service – used for locating and helping people in distress situations for example at sea or mountains – is unaffected and remains operational. Galileo has been providing 'initial services' since December 2016. During this initial pilot phase, preceding the 'full operational services' phase, Galileo signals are used in combination with other satellite navigation systems, which allows for the detection of technical issues before the system becomes fully operational. Experts are working to restore the situation as soon as possible. An Anomaly Review Board has been set up to analyse the exact root cause and to implement recovery actions.

Source: https://www.gsa.europa.eu/newsroom/news/update-availability-some-galileo-initial-services retrieved on 14 July 2019

4. The least important asset: the power grid for electricity transmission. Although the power grid is primarily intended and used for electricity transmission, it can also be used for data transmission and internet usage, called *Broadband over Powerlines* (BPL).[49] However, the number of providers in the world allowing the power grid for data transmission is limited. Frequently, the power grid inside a single premise or building can be used for intrafacility communication, but there it faces competition from the local Wi-Fi networks or intrafacility cable networks.

Infrastructure assets, congestion, and pricing for congestion

Mobility of goods, persons, and information in a Supply Chain is of critical importance and every combination of transportation mode and infrastructure asset has its price tag. The fastest or the shortest route is not necessarily the cheapest one. How users have to pay for the use of infrastructure assets is a hotly debated issue and, with the growing privatization of these assets, this discussion will gain impetus. Infrastructure has some characteristics, as a result of which it cannot be considered as a pure market good where supply and demand set the price for usage.

In this paragraph, we discuss the economic status of infrastructure assets and the pricing mechanism. Pricing of infrastructure usage has a big impact on logistics cost and Supply Chain performance. In the discussion of the economic classification of information, we introduced the main categories of economic goods and services: market good; club good; and the pure public good.[50] We will now apply this categorization to infrastructure systems and add a new category of semi-public goods.

The price of market goods is the outcome of a supply and demand process on the market where the good or service is traded. Most of the market goods are offered by business organizations pursuing profit. Semi-public goods are nearly always exclusive and rival but, given their importance for the well-being of persons and society as a whole, they are often supplied and managed by public institutions and are offered at relatively low prices, or even below cost, subsidized by the government or municipalities. Examples of semi-public goods are primary education, the legal system of a country, museums. Many of these institutions have a non-for-profit objective.

Another form to classify economic activity is the *externalities*. Externalities are spillovers of consumption (demand) and/or production (supply), which are not incorporated in the pricing mechanism.[51] Positive and negative externalities exist.

Let us return our attention to the infrastructure assets to determine which of the three categories they belong to. First, the exclusivity criterion. Roads, waterways, railways, airspace, and pipelines can be made inaccessible to certain user groups technically but more often by regulations. Drivers without a driving licence – e.g. the license is sequestrated after severe trespassing of the law or there is a prohibition of certain kinds of vehicles like tractors – are excluded from using part of the road system. This exclusion possibility also holds for virtually all other infrastructure assets.

The other criterion is rivalry. A car driving on a road, a ship on a waterway, a train on a railway, an airplane approaching an airstrip to land, and liquids in a pipeline, reduce the availability of the infrastructure asset for other users: usage is rival! After exceeding a critical number of users, congestion is created, up to the point that no new car, ship, train, or plane can use the infrastructure asset anymore. This rivalry is a direct consequence of the fact that all these assets have limited capacity. Externalities also emerge in the use of infrastructure.

A vehicle or vessel that is the sole user of a road on an early Sunday morning in a remote area does not create externalities for other road users. The marginal costs for driving on the road consist of the costs of this car or truck and covers fuel consumption, the truck driver's wage rate, and, if it is a toll road, the price for driving on that stretch of road. When a second truck joins the same road the impact on average speed for this car *and* the first truck on the same road is minimal and the marginal costs incurred by the second truck will be more or less the same as for the first truck.

All subsequent trucks entering the highway will have an increasing impact on the average speed of the other trucks on the highway, but costs due to externality remain low.[52] After exceeding a critical number, the impact of any new truck entering the highway lanes will reduce the average speed of the other trucks on the road as well as constrain its own average speed. If the number of vehicles joining the highway continues to increase, congestion becomes a problem and will affect the marginal costs of other road users – lower average speed means longer driving

Airspace congestion in the proximity of airports means that airplanes will line up to prepare for landing and taking off, one after the other. The more planes are queuing, the more likely delays to flight arrivals and departures, and an increase in fuel consumption. Airline regulations state the minimum time required between two arriving or departing planes.
Source: https://i.ytimg.com/vi/fgHjVvqLXV8/hqdefault.jpg

On small roads, a slow-driving vehicle, like this tractor, already causes delays for any car driving behind him. The first symptoms of congestion become visible here even with only two cars on the road. The car behind the tractor has to reduce speed and will need more time – and probably fuel – to reach its destination.
Source: https://www.mijnamstelveen.nl/runtime/images/5952/570x324/verkeer.jpg

time with concomitant higher fuel costs and higher payments for the time the truck driver is on the route.[52]

Every infrastructure asset has an optimal occupancy rate. Exceeding this rate means that all users are affected, and negative externalities arise. The marginal costs of each new vehicle entering the highway will now consist of two parts: its own marginal costs (mostly fuel plus driver's wage) and the increase in the costs of the other vehicles that have to reduce their average speed. These latter externality costs do not, however, appear in the cost calculations of the logistics company that owns the truck. Moreover, *individual* costs, and *social costs* affecting other trucks and cars, arise.

Economists claim that the optimal outcome (maximum welfare) is achieved when the marginal cost of driving equals the marginal revenue or benefit of a vehicle trip. The revenues consist of the money the logistics company earns by transporting goods for customers. Besides direct costs like fuel and driver's wages, there are cargo trips that are subject to strictly planned arrival times and the logistics company will receive less money, or pay a penalty, for every hour the cargo arrives late. If congestion and traffic jams result in many trucks arriving late, the overall lost revenues can be substantial. To optimize the number of cars on the road, the best *theoretical* price per kilometre per truck (this also holds for private cars) is a kilometre price equal to the marginal *social* costs. This means including the increase in marginal costs of fellow road users caused by this vehicle entering the highway. However, this theoretical pricing mechanism would lead to an impractical and unfeasible situation whereby each truck and car needs to pay different prices. For this reason, to date, no country has implemented a pricing mechanism with different prices depending on the number of road users.[54] However, there are pricing mechanisms in place that differentiate prices between peak and off-peak hours.

Similar analyses about congestion costs apply to pricing waterways, railways, and air space. Saying that a highway suffers from congestion does not mean that the entire length of these highways is overcrowded with cars 24 hours a day. It just means that some stretches of this highway experience suboptimal flow during some parts of the day due to too many cars and trucks. Congestion becomes a structural and not just an incidental component of vehicle flow. Congestion and rivalry are closely connected phenomena. Congestion refers to a suboptimal flow of conveyances due to the presence of too many users or over-usage. A failure to reach an optimal flow can have many different causes, including congestion (more demand than capacity allows).

A possible solution against congestion is to *reduce demand* (*use*) leading to less congestion. A suboptimal flow can also be due to a technical or a human failure. In that case, reducing demand does ***not*** solve the congestion problem, but once the failure has been solved normal flow of assets will be restored.[55] Failure can also be due to deficiencies on the side of the user or receiver. Congestion on any infrastructure asset is always linked to the characteristic of rivalry. A non-rival asset will not experience congestion and the asset can be used by everyone without affecting the availability for use by others. Only 100% pure public goods have this advantage,[56] but in the real world there hardly exists any asset that is 100% pure public.

Our discussion of congestion relating to infrastructure assets focuses on congestion caused by demand exceeding capacity and not congestion caused by technical or human failures or by deficiencies from the side of the users.

An aerial view of the entrance to the Suez Canal in Egypt, taken from an airplane during a flight on 27 March 2021. The dots in the picture are ships that are queueing due to the stranding of the Evergreen in the Suez Canal in March 2021. About 12% of world trade passes through the Suez Canal. It was expected that many Supply Chains between Asia and Europe would face disruptions because of the ripple effects after the Evergreen was freed by an incredible rescue operation carried out by tugboats of the Dutch company Smit Salvage, owned by Boskalis. **Source**: https://www.elindependiente.com/wp-content/uploads/2021/03/Canal_Suez_Estrecho_Barcos_Atasco-980x550.jpg

Main Point: infrastructure assets can best be described as semi-public goods. Up to a certain level, they are exclusive and rival, creating negative externalities. This rivalry becomes particularly visible and strong once the asset exceeds a critical flow of vehicles using the infrastructure asset. Consequently, pricing highway usage should, theoretically, also include the costs of the externality, i.e. the congestion costs created by each infrastructure user. This leads to serious practical problems with respect to implement, and has never been done.

The real value of infrastructure assets: Networks and Intermodality[57]

The picture above is the Strépi-Thieu boat lift in the *Canal du Centre* in Wallonia (Belgium). It enables a ***waterway connection*** between two stretches of a canal in Belgium. The new lift opened in 2002 and has a height difference of 73.15 meters. Until 2016, it was the tallest boat lift in the world, but has since been surpassed by the Three Gorges dam boat lift in China. **Source**: http://www.kanoroutes.nl/images/Thieu21.jpg

When discussing infrastructure assets, the first association many people make is a direct road connecting place A and place B. This is a very limited view. The economic value of infrastructure becomes especially prominent when it is part of larger, interconnected networks.[58] Historically, many road and railway connections have been built to connect two cities or towns.

With the sprawling of cities, growing urbanization, and industrial development, the need to connect different highways, railways, and waterways to reach more people and places became more pressing. Two previously separated roads, or even small networks, can be spliced to create a larger network that connects them via bridges, tunnels, dikes, and ferries to cross water masses or road hairpins to overcome height differences in mountainous areas.

This aerial picture shows the 16-km long Oresund Bridge that connects the Danish capital Copenhagen with the Swedish city Malmö. It opened in 2000.
It consists partly of a bridge (up to the island in the middle) and the second part is a tunnel. It has both a road section and a separate railway section.
Source: https://upload.wikimedia.org/wikipedia/commons/1/1a/Oresund-over-2008.JPG

One of the properties that enhances the range of an infrastructure asset, as well as its economic value, is the number of access points to the asset, like ramps and exits to enter and leave the asset. Access points enable trucks and passenger cars to easily reach towns, villages, and business property such as distribution centres and manufacturing plants, once they become integrated into a network. The number of accessible nodes can grow exponentially by constructing just a few ramps and exits on a highway.

In large cities, networks were optimized by building ring roads circumnavigating the city periphery and with many access points to enable a smoother traffic flow. Another way of road linking is the *roundabout*. The presence of ramps and exits (access points) are essential for these infrastructure assets and they serve as core nodes in a network, as will be discussed in the next chapter. Another advantage of networks, compared to single, straight-line connections from point A to B, is the existence of bypasses. If the main connection of an infrastructure asset is blocked due to an accident or reconstruction works, the user can switch to a parallel connection to continue their journey.

Infrastructure networks are studied using the theory of network economics. One of the paradigms of network economics is that the value of a network increases the more users join the network.[59] The economic value of the network increases up to the point where congestion begins to manifest itself and negative externalities appear. An optimal usage level is reached when the entrance of a new user no longer increases the utility of users of the network.

The same holds for infrastructure networks. If village A is connected, via a local road, to village B and with another local road to village C, B is *in*directly connected to village C passing through village A. Infrastructure networks consist of ***micro***-networks and ***macro***-networks. Micro-networks are small, local networks, such as the street grid of a village or the canals in a city. They consist of relatively many small and sometimes major streets with low traffic density. When micro-networks are connected, they become part of a macro-network. These connections can be intercity regional highways between villages or even expressways connecting large metropolitan districts. Micro-networks are dense and restricted to small areas while macro-networks are spread over large areas with large open spaces and with high traffic density. Infrastructure networks are sometimes compared with the human blood circulatory system.

There are *arteries* with a large diameter, which are the primary vessels for transporting blood to the main organs of the body, the macro-circulation. This macro-circulation branches into smaller veins called arterioles, which bring blood to smaller organs. The arterioles branch into even smaller capillaries, which form an interwoven network of very small or hair-fine tubes supplying even the most remote body tissues with blood. Similar models are used for networks of infrastructure assets. Major cities are connected with broad motorways, in some countries consisting of five or six different lanes for each direction, and with many access points. Connected to the motorways are smaller regional roads or road networks, often with one lane per direction, reaching smaller towns. When regional roads and motorways disembogue into towns or cities, they branch out in the municipal street grid to reach virtually every corner of the town.[60]

Intermodality

This computer image shows the Maasvlakte 2, which is the most western part of the port of Rotterdam, equipped with fully automated container terminal facilities. Large sea containerships moor here for loading and unloading containers. The unloaded containers can be placed either on a cargo train to be further transported by railway to Germany (Betuwelijn), they can be placed on trucks for further shipment by road, and can be placed on river barges bringing the containers over water to the next inland destination.
Source: https://upload.wikimedia.org/wikipedia/commons/c/c0/Toekomstbeeld_Maasvlakte_2_7_G_tcm81-32536.jpg

In downtown areas of cities that are inaccessible for trucks, but which are endowed with a capillary network of urban canals, restaurants and bars are directly replenished by ship. This picture of a beer boat was taken in the city of Utrecht (Netherlands).
Source: https://vng.nl/sites/default/files/bierboot.jpg

A very common way to ship goods from door to door is using *intermodal* freight transport, which means using multiple modes of transportation for the same product on its way from source to the final destination. Intermodal trade has been given a major boost by the standardization of containers, also known as *containerization*.[61] Even more transportation combinations have been achieved by *cross-docking.*

Cross-docking is a practice in logistics of unloading materials from an incoming semi-trailer truck or railroad car and loading these materials directly into outbound trucks, trailers, or rail cars, with little or no storage in between. This is achieved by changing the type of conveyance, sorting material intended for different destinations, or combining material from different origins into transport vehicles (or containers) with the same or nearby destinations. Large trucks, which cannot enter city centres with small streets, can cross-dock close to the municipal borders in specially constructed cross-docking stations, where the split cargo is ferried in vans that do fit into narrow downtown streets.[62]

A similar logistics operation is *Merge-In-Transit* (MIT). In a MIT operation, products from disparate sources are consolidated into a single delivery at a location in close geographical proximity to the final delivery site. In this way, more efficient use is made of the available capacity of the conveyances heading for the same destination. MIT reduces multiple shipments with multiple vehicles, each with a load factor below the optimal capacity usage.

Intermodality increases the potential number of shipment routings exponentially, allowing for more combinations by switching from infrastructure networks and transportation modes. Railway networks, road networks, waterway networks, airport connections, and even pipeline networks become a massive interconnected and interwoven infrastructure, making nearly every corner of the globe physically accessible for Supply Chain logistics, although each combination has its price tag and lead time. To give an example: If 12 cities in a country are connected to a railway network and 50 cities to a road network and none of the cities is connected to both networks, the number of combinations is as follows:

- Railway network: 12 cities each connected to 11 other cities yields 12 * 11 = 132 connections or arcs.
- Road network: 50 cities each connected to 49 other cities yields 50 * 49 = 2,450 connections or arcs.

If we connect the two networks with intermodality: a total of 62 cities are connected to 61 other cities yielding 3,782 bidirectional connections or what is the same 3782 direct combinations of sources and destinations. If we replace the 50 cities by N and the 12 cities by M then connecting the two networks using intermodality augments the number of combinations of source and destination to $(N + M)*(N + M -1)$.

Main Point: Intermodality broadens the range of possibilities to transport goods from their source to their final destination by using different interconnected infrastructure assets and transportation modes and bringing even the most remote areas in the world within the reach of Supply Chain operations. Containerization has given an enormous boost to intermodality. Due to the standardization of container sizes, one container can now be placed on several kinds of marine vessels, train cars, and trucks during its journey.

Real-time tracking of shipments

Growing importance in Supply Chain planning is given to real-time data and information about shipments, cargo movements, payments, and other business activities and processes. The information infrastructure discussed previously plays a pivotal role in facilitating real-time data exchange. An example of tracking shipments for consumers is the *track-and-trace* option managed by express couriers, whereby the customer can check where their ordered product is and when they can expect its arrival at a specified address. Real-time information is even more important for business-to-business (B2B) transactions: the business customer wants to be informed where the ordered packages or containers are and what the expected arrival time is. If there are delays, the customer can adjust the production planning and, if necessary, look for alternative emergency solutions.

Information about the global position of both freight and passengers is available via either publicly accessible sources or via private sources, or both. The most detailed and accurate information about which product or container is where on the globe is stored in databases and controlled by the logistics company arranging the shipment. These companies usually also take care of freight documentation. These data are protected with passwords and stored on servers behind firewalls. Protected private information sources usually contain more details than public data sources. Anyone consulting airport information, for example, can check when a flight arrives at the airport but only the airliner has a complete list with all passenger's names and the amount of luggage.[63] Many manufacturing companies also use intrafacility real-time locating systems to track at which stage of the production process each unit is. Real-time locating systems include tracking cars on an assembly line, locating pallets of merchandise in a DC, or tracking medical equipment in a hospital.

In manufacturing processes, products are marked with RFID- tags, optical means, or ultrasound devices for identification. They are an important tool for controlling and monitoring the progress of production and keep actual production in line with the planning.

Last-mile delivery in city centres[64]

Last-mile delivery refers to the last stage in the distribution process, usually from a retailer to the final consumer. It is characterized by shipping a few or just a single item to many individual and dispersed consumer locations.

It is a pressing issue for online companies whose customers live in city centres. Many cities continue to grow and to sprawl, leading to an increasing flow of goods inside cities. Last-mile delivery in urban centres requires logistics focused on the specific properties of inner cities, like small, overcrowded streets, congestion, streets blocked by (un)loading trucks or movers, double-parked cars, one-way streets, many traffic lights, a chronic shortage of parking, and other phenomena typical for mobility in city centres. Mobility in city centres is anything except smooth and uninterrupted. But packages ordered by city dwellers have to arrive at their destination within the time limit set by the selling firm and creative solutions are used. A solution that is gaining popularity is deploying bicycles both with and without (electric) engines, and also specifically designed cargo bikes for larger packages. (Freight) bicycle drivers can carry relatively small and lightweight freight and therefore this mode of transportation is suitable for bringing online ordered goods to individual customers and not appropriate for retail store replenishment operations. Their flexibility and agility are a big advantage: if one street is blocked, the cyclist can easily take an alternative street, an option that is more difficult for vans, let alone trucks. If a city has a well-maintained biking infrastructure, as is the case in some European countries, bike logistics is an effective and also relatively fast solution for small package transport, as the following press release testifies.

Source: https://www.kolotipy.cz/wp-content/uploads/2019/12/ups-delivery-cargo-bikeups2019.jpg

Dutch online company Wehkamp will deliver part of its parcels in 12 Dutch cities by bike thanks to cooperation with DHL and Fietskoeriers.nl.

Both couriers from DHL and Fietskoeriers.nl (bicyclecourier.nl) will deliver packages from the online shop Wehkamp to the cities of Amsterdam, Rotterdam, The Hague, Almere, Arnhem, Deventer, Hilversum, Hengelo, Eindhoven, Groningen Tilburg and Zwolle. The intention is to expand the number of cities in the coming period.

Sustainable last mile

"It shows that delivery by bicycle is serious business," says Marieke Snoek, general manager of Fietskoeriers.nl. "We observe that in the growth of our total organization. We are one of the solutions for last-mile delivery.

It is great that we now have the trust of Wehkamp and DHL to make it a joint project." According to Roelof Hofman, VP Operations at DHL Parcel, DHL is a forerunner when it comes to deploying bicycle couriers.

With the collaboration, the parties are responding to the expected mobility growth and crowding in cities. They want to contribute to the accessibility of inner cities.

"To continue to meet the customer's wishes and to keep cities accessible, cooperation is important even for the last few kilometers," says Sander Bolmer, director of warehousing & distribution at Wehkamp, in a press release. "Delivery on the bike fits well in our reputation as being a Dutch company. After all, the Netherlands is a biking country with a well-developed biking infrastructure. This way we can physically reach the customer even better and make them happy together."

Source: 27/11/2017 07:16 |. https://www.duurzaambedrijfsleven.nl/retail/26007/wehkamp-zet-in-op-duurzame-pakketbezorging-per-fiets

Another upcoming transportation mode for last-mile package delivery in cities is the deployment of drones. In 2021, these aerial delivery systems were still in an experimental phase, although they are already used in some countries for commercial logistics operations.

But many hurdles have yet to be overcome. Besides technical issues, these hurdles are mainly safety problems arising from flying in crowded urban airspace at relatively low heights, either above buildings or between large buildings, an infrastructure of suitable landing places, and a regulatory framework not yet fully developed. The following press release testifies to using drones for last-mile delivery.

Source: https://i.ytimg.com/vi/VF7aK-4r3Xs/maxresdefault.jpg retrieved 8th of January 2022

DPDgroup the international delivery network of GeoPost SA, a subsidiary of Le Groupe La Poste in France, displayed its parcel delivery drone system at a Drone Festival in Paris. DPDgroup has developed a system that incorporates a *"delivery terminal"* – which it says will *"ensure the safety of the loading, take-off and landing phases as well as the parcel release"*. DPDgroup organized a display of the system on the Champs-Elysées on Sunday 4 September 2016. In partnership with Atechsys, DPDgroup has developed a drone capable of autonomously transporting large parcels (37cm x 27cm x 12,5cm) of up to 3 kg within a radius of 20 km.

Source: https://www.dpd.com/home/news/latest_news /dpdgroup_drone_delivers_parcels_using_regular_commercial_line

Main Point: The power of infrastructure assets lies in their network configuration. Consisting of backbone connections (arteries) for large-volume shipment. Closer to the customer location, rearrangements to other transportation modes with lower capacity using smaller but more branched connections enables multiple destinations to be reached. For last-mile delivery, appropriate transportation modes to reach widely branched customer front doors are used in particular by online companies. The value of a network increases with the number of places that are connected to it, but decreases when the optimal flow through the network exceeds capacity and congestion occurs. Intermodality links the networks of one transportation mode to networks of other transportation modes, making the number of global combinations of sources and destinations virtually unlimited for every scale of transportation: from mass transportation of dairy products in large cargo ships to supplying a restaurant located on the top floor of a skyscraper with a 500-gram package of camembert cheese.

Notes

1-23   See Instructor's Manual

24   Source: https://www.google.com/news agencies

25   Source: https://en.wikipedia.org/wiki/Club_good retrieved on 21 November 2019.

26-30   See Instructor's Manual

31   Source: https://www.emerald.com/insight/content/doi/10.1108/09576059610123132/full/html retrieved on 25 November 2020

32   Source: https://www.shippingsolutions.com/blog/documents-required-for-international-shipping retrieved on 19 December 2020.

33-39   See Instructor's Manual

40   Source: https://openweb.co.za/how-far-will-your-wifi-signal-reach/

41-44   See Instructor's Manual

45   Source: https://www.quora.com/How-many-cell-towers-exist-worldwide

46   Source: https://www.pixalytics.com/sats-orbiting-earth-2017/

47   See among others: https://www.lifewire.com/broadband-over-power-lines-817450

48-62   See Instructor's Manual

9 Distribution Network Configuration and Optimal Logistics Flows

Distribution Network Models and Optimal Flows

Infrastructure as networks and its corresponding economic value

Crossover of two motorways in Flevoland, the Netherlands
Source: https://bezoekerscentrum.rijkswaterstaat.nl/SchipholAmsterdamAlmere/wp-content/uploads/2015/09/16-9K53-019.jpg

Circular cloverleaf overpass intersection of highway N261 close to Waalwijk, the Netherlands
Source: https://www.baminfra.nl/sites/default/files/domain-621/styles/slideshow_big/public/slideshow/06-01_n261-621-14438108211725924212.jpg?itok=X0hJKoak

The first picture shows a grade-separated intersection – or overpass intersection – of two highways that cross each other and where road users cannot access the other crossing highway.[1] The second picture displays a cloverleaf grade-separated intersection where motorists can access the crossing highway. Contrary to the first overpass intersection, it saves motorists and trucks a large detour to reach their destination if that destination is located on the crossing highway. The added value of the road intersection with this circular or cloverleaf node is, therefore, higher than the sum of each of the two highways separately. Road users heading for a destination on the other road can now use both roads. A cloverleaf is a good example of a typical feature of the network pattern of an infrastructure asset that significantly increases the number of combinations of sources and destinations.

Networks are an integral dimension and range from family and social to economic, and political networks. Networks trace their roots to the moment that people started to organize themselves to carry out joint activities requiring coordination, communication, and sustained relationships. The structure of these relations among various members can be called a network.

Scientists already began to analyse networks in the 18th century,[2] by abstracting from their social, geographical, or physical context and using mathematical tools to conceptualize network models to unearth underlying properties and basic structures. The field of mathematics that studies networks is *graph theory*, and we will discuss a few of its features to find optimal routings for the transportation of goods and persons within a Supply Chain network. A network consists of two sets of components: *nodes* and *arcs*. Nodes – also called vertices – can be described as a collection of distribution points. Arcs – also called edges – connect the nodes.

Applied to a Supply Chain, nodes can represent distribution centres, manufacturing plants, stores, cities, pick-up points, data centres, GSM masts, and many more. Arcs connect nodes and can represent roads, railway tracks, canals, pipelines, electricity cables, glass fibre, air corridors, telephone switchboards, and many more. Arcs are often displayed as arrows, starting at one node and ending in another or, indeed, at the same node (circle or loop). An arc can be *directed*, meaning that the flow of goods or information only goes in one direction. Otherwise, it is *undirected*, meaning that the flow of goods and information can go in both directions. Any node that has no arcs coming in or going out is out of the range of the network – it cannot communicate with the network.

This also occurs if a part of the network is not connected to the main body of the network; that is to say, it is disconnected, like a broken glass fibre cable or a tunnel temporally closed for repair. If two nodes are not connected with one single arc, but are only connected through a series of directed arcs before reaching the destination node, the path of this sequence of distinct arcs is called a *directed path*. If the entire network consists only of directed arcs the network is called a *directed network*. Some nodes are *supply* nodes (outflow or sending nodes), meaning that arcs only leave from that node. Other nodes are *demand* nodes (inflow or receiving nodes), meaning that there are only arcs coming into that node. The third group is *transshipment* nodes, meaning that the node has both incoming and outgoing arcs.[3]

A ring road around a city with five access points (vertices or nodes) to the city centre (green hexagon) can be represented as a network of 6 nodes and 10 arcs (5 of which are the pieces of the ring from one road junction to the adjacent junction, making up the complete ring.

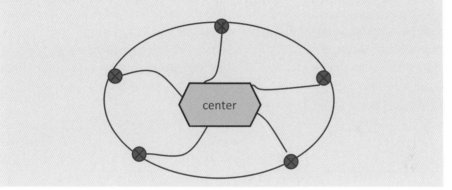

The structure of a network is uniquely identified by its nodes and its arcs, either directed (one-way) or undirected (two-way). The set of all nodes and arcs together determines how many combinations or *paths* there are to go from a supply node to a demand node in the network. They do not, however, provide information about which of all possible paths is the best one. Therefore, a metric is assigned to each arc indicating the importance of an arc within the network. The following three metrics are frequently used in logistics and route planning:

1. *Distance* of the arc
2. *Time* needed to move over the arc
3. *Costs* incurred by using an arc

Distance is the most common and relevant metric in logistics networks, if the driver or the logistics planner wants to minimize the number of kilometres to achieve the shortest distance by the truck via road or vessel over water. Data about the length of many infrastructure assets are publicly available, e.g. for roads and waterways, by consulting digital maps. All arcs in the network diagram are tagged with the number corresponding to the distance from one node to the next node.

Time metrics are relevant when meeting the arrival deadlines or agreed-upon lead times with the customer. A regional road may be the shortest distance, but because of many (red) traffic lights and lower speed limits, this route can take longer. Driving over a motorway with a length of 200 kilometres can, in fact, be much faster than driving 150 kilometres to the same destination over local or regional roads. All arcs in the network are tagged with a number representing the average time of the arc. Even if two arc distances are the same, the average driving time can be different, depending on, among other things, the congestion on each arc and other rival activities, such as maintenance work. The numbers tagged to each arc in terms of time metrics can differ for peak hours and off-peak hours, and even for days of the week or months of the year. The third dimension refers to travel costs, whose main components in logistics are fuel costs, driver wage rates, insurance premiums for the cargo and, if applicable, toll prices. If cost minimization is the management target, all arcs will become tagged with cost metrics.[4] We will now discuss two common problems in network logistics and Supply Chain planning:

1. Shortest path problem
2. Travelling salesman problem

Shortest path problem

The shortest path between two places by road is not always a straight line as this picture shows.
Source: https://upload.wikimedia. org/wikipedia/commons/9/9f/ The_Stelvio_pass.jpg

The shortest path over a river may not be a straight line, as this image of a hairpin curve on the Saar River shows.
Source: https://www.uncharted101.com/ wp-content/uploads/ saarland_foto16.jpg

Simply put, the shortest path problem is about finding the optimal path through a network, starting at the supply node (source) and ending at the demand node (destination). The *optimal path* depends on the choice of the metrics discussed above: shortest distance; least time; or lowest cost. There are several solution methods and algorithms for finding the optimal path. The most famous one is Dijkstra's algorithm,[5] but similar algorithms have been developed and some cover variations on the single-source to a single-destination path. We will not delve into the mathematical technicalities here as they are beyond the scope of a book about Supply Chain. Rather, we restrict ourselves to the Excel and Solver implementation of the shortest path, omitting a discussion of the mathematical background.[6]

An example of the shortest path algorithm in Excel

A logistics expediter has to send a freight every day by truck over a road network displayed in the graph below. The freight leaves the distribution centre at the node *Supply* and has to arrive at the node *Demand*. All arrows in the network indicate the connections and all connections are undirected. All connections are also displayed in the Excel screenshot in table format, showing the nodes with *outgoing* arcs in the left column, and nodes with *incoming* arrows in the right column.

Transshipment nodes appear both for outgoing and incoming arcs. Each row in the table corresponds to one connecting arc. The third column, *Distance*, gives the distance of each connection and the cells in the fourth column *On Route* are left blank. These cells are the binary variables of the model and can only take on the value 1, if the connection is part of the shortest path, or 0, if it is not. This column will be populated as part of the solution.

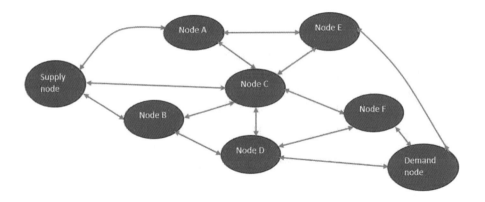

Table with the input data:

	A	B	C	D
1	**Input data for finding th**			
2	**Node_out**	**Node_In**	**Distance**	**On_route**
3	Supply node	Node A	8	
4	Supply node	Node B	15	
5	Supply node	Node C	22	
6	Node A	Node C	5	
7	Node A	Node E	24	
8	Node B	Node C	16	
9	Node B	Node D	17	
10	Node C	Node D	7	
11	Node C	Node E	13	
12	Node C	Node F	19	
13	Node D	Node F	5	
14	Node D	Demand Node	16	
15	Node E	Demand Node	18	
16	Node F	Demand Node	7	

The objective is to minimize total travel distance. To calculate total distance, we multiply each cell in the column *On route*, which is a binary variable, with the corresponding distance cell in the same row and sum over all rows. Given that the cells in the *On route* column will take on only 1's or 0's, the contribution to the total travel distance is only positive if that cell is assigned the value 1 in the solution. Excel's *Function Library* has a function called *Sumproduct,* which does this job, and it is shown in the last row of the screenshot in formula view on page 244.

The constraints are the more difficult part of the problem. The argument is as follows: the truck <u>enters</u> the network by leaving the supply node. This is modelled by assigning all outgoing arrows leaving the *Supply node* a variable, which can take on the value 0 or +1. The truck <u>leaves</u> the network after arriving at the Demand node: this is modelled by assigning all incoming arrows into the *Demand node* a variable with the value 0 or -1. All other nodes in the network are transshipments nodes, which means that, during its journey, the truck enters the node via one of the incoming arrows and leaves it through one of the outgoing arrows. This can be modelled by keeping the sum value of all incoming arrows (+1 if used and 0 if not used) in one node equal to the sum of all outgoing arcs (-1 if used and 0 if not used) leaving the same node. In other words, the sum of all incoming and all outgoing arcs in a transshipment node must be zero. To model this, we use the Excel function *Sumif* in the Excel Function Library.

Sumif has three arguments: the first argument in the Excel screenshot below is the column Node_out; the second is the specific cell containing the name of the node for which we want to find the linked values in that row; and the third column is the column labelled *On route*. The *Sumif* function does the following: it takes the name of the node in the middle cell – which is A19 for the first row – from the data table, searches in the first column *Node_Out* of the data table to the name in the middle cell. If it finds that name, it sums the values found in the third column *On route* in the data table. The second *Sumif* in the same constraint equation does the same, but instead of searching in *Node_Out,* it will look in the column *Node_In* of the data table. The last column of the Constraint box is the value assigned to each constraint equation.

As discussed above, the truck must enter the network via one of the three arrows leaving the *Supply* node. We assign the value +1 to this constraint, which means that Solver has to choose only ***one*** of the three outgoing arcs. The second part of this constraint equation in the screenshot will always be 0, because the name *Supply Node* in the *Node_In* column of the input table does not exist and is therefore always 0. For the nodes A until F, we assign the constraint value of 0. This means that if the node is not part of the optimal path, the incoming arrows will be assigned the value of 0 and all the outgoing arrows from that node will also be all 0. If the node is part of the optimal path *one* of the incoming arrows will have the value +1, but then one of the outgoing arrows must also get the value (+1) to make their *difference* equal to 0. We impose this condition in the Solver Constraint box requiring that the sum of all incoming arrows <u>*minus*</u> the sum of all outgoing arrows is zero.

The *Demand node* is the ending node, after which the truck will leave the network. We require that at least one of the arrows entering this node is equal to +1. Only the second part of the constraint equation contains the name *Demand node* in the data table, the first part does not. The *second* part of the *Sumif* function is preceded by a minus sign, converting the constraint value to -1.

	A	B	C
18		**Constraint equation**	**Constraint value**
19	Supply node	=SUMIF(Node_Out;A19;On_route)-SUMIF(Node_In;A19;On_route)	1
20	Node A	=SUMIF(Node_Out;A20;On_route)-SUMIF(Node_In;A20;On_route)	0
21	Node B	=SUMIF(Node_Out;A21;On_route)-SUMIF(Node_In;A21;On_route)	0
22	Node C	=SUMIF(Node_Out;A22;On_route)-SUMIF(Node_In;A22;On_route)	0
23	Node D	=SUMIF(Node_Out;A23;On_route)-SUMIF(Node_In;A23;On_route)	0
24	Node E	=SUMIF(Node_Out;A24;On_route)-SUMIF(Node_In;A24;On_route)	0
25	Node F	=SUMIF(Node_Out;A25;On_route)-SUMIF(Node_In;A25;On_route)	0
26	Demand node	=SUMIF(Node_Out;A26;On_route)-SUMIF(Node_In;A26;On_route)	-1
27			
28	Objective functic	=SUMPRODUCT(Distance;On_route)	

To find the optimal solution, we use the Excel Add-in Solver, as shown in the next screenshot. The first line in the Solver window asks for the cell containing the objective function, which has been labelled in the Excel sheet as Objective. In the next line, we instruct Solver to minimize the objective by checking the radio button *Min*. In the third line, Solver asks for the Variable Cells. In our example, these are all cells in the column of the data table *On route*. The white box is the place where we have to enter the constraints by clicking on <u>A</u>dd. In the left part of this window, we enter the cells of the column labelled *Constraint_equation*, in the middle part the operator equal to (=); in the right box, we enter the cells of the column with the constraint values labelled *Constraint_values*. We then click on <u>O</u>K, after which the information is copied to the Constraint box in the Solver window.[7] The next step is to tell Solver that all variables must be non-negative. The penultimate step consists of selecting the Solving method. This model is linear in its objective function as well as in its constraints and therefore we select Simplex LP. The last step is to click on <u>S</u>olve, resulting in the solution displayed in the Excel sheet. It is also possible to select first Reports → Answer to obtain more detailed information about the solution.

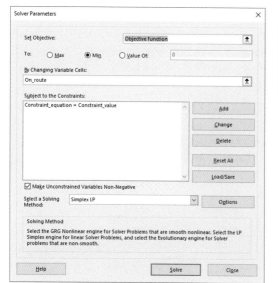

The Excel output with the optimal routing and the objective function are displayed below:

	A	B	C	D
1	Input data for finding the shortest path			
2	Node_out	Node_In	Distance	On_route
3	Supply node	Node A	8	1
4	Supply node	Node B	15	0
5	Supply node	Node C	22	0
6	Node A	Node C	5	1
7	Node A	Node E	24	0
8	Node B	Node C	16	0
9	Node B	Node D	17	0
10	Node C	Node D	7	1
11	Node C	Node E	13	0
12	Node C	Node F	19	0
13	Node D	Node F	5	1
14	Node D	Demand Node	16	0
15	Node E	Demand Node	18	0
16	Node F	Demand Node	7	1
27				
28	Objective function	32		

In other words: the shortest path is starting at the Supply Node and moving to node A. From node A move to node C, from node C move to node D, from node D move to node F, and from node F move to the Demand node where the network is left. The total distance is 32 kilometres.

Let us now focus on some variations of this model. If, one day, road DF is blocked because of road maintenance or an accident, what will the new optimal path be? Given that road DF is part of the optimal solution, we have to instruct Solver that the variable Node D to node F is *not* allowed. This can simply be done by adding a new constraint in the Solver Constraint box by setting the *On route* variable cell Node D → node F = 0. If we do so, and click on *Solve*, we obtain the following optimal path, displayed below: Supply node → node A → node C → node D → Demand node with a total distance of 36 kilometres (four more than the uncontrained DF arc).

	A	B	C	D
1	Input data for finding the shortest path			
2	Node_out	Node_In	Distance	On_route
3	Supply node	Node A	8	1
4	Supply node	Node B	15	0
5	Supply node	Node C	22	0
6	Node A	Node C	5	1
7	Node A	Node E	24	0
8	Node B	Node C	16	0
9	Node B	Node D	17	0
10	Node C	Node D	7	1
11	Node C	Node E	13	0
12	Node C	Node F	19	0
13	Node D	Node F	5	0
14	Node D	Demand Node	16	1
15	Node E	Demand Node	18	0
16	Node F	Demand Node	7	0
27	Objective function			36

Another variation. The truck leaving the Supply node has to collect additional freight (Merge-in-Transit) to bring the combined freight to the Demand node. This Merge-in-Transit can take place *either* at a distribution centre located in node B *or* at a distribution centre located in node E. What is the new optimal route? In this case, the truck has to pass either over node B or node E. We can model this by summing all incoming arcs into node B, which, in this case, is only the binary variable Supply node → B with all incoming arcs into node E – which are the variable cells AE and CE – and set this sum equal to 1. This forces Solver to find a solution where either the incoming arc in node B will be 1, or one of the incoming arcs in node E, but not both. We therefore add a new row under the last constraint, which requires the sum of the cells On route *Supply node to B* plus *Node A to E* plus *Node C to E* to be 1! The other constraints ensure that if the incoming node is +1, one of the outgoing arcs leaving that same node will also be 1. After adding this new constraint and selecting OK we get the following solution:

	A	B	C	D
1	Input data for finding the shortest path			
2	Node_out	Node_In	Distance	On_route
3	Supply node	Node A	8	1
4	Supply node	Node B	15	0
5	Supply node	Node C	22	0
6	Node A	Node C	5	1
7	Node A	Node E	24	0
8	Node B	Node C	16	0
9	Node B	Node D	17	0
10	Node C	Node D	7	0
11	Node C	Node E	13	1
12	Node C	Node F	19	0
13	Node D	Node F	5	0
14	Node D	Demand Node	16	0
15	Node E	Demand Node	18	1
16	Node F	Demand Node	7	0
28	Objective function			44

Solver has selected node E for the Merge-In-Transit operation and the optimal path is Supply node → node A → node C → node E → Demand node, a trip with a total length of 44 kilometres.

The Travelling Salesman (TSM) problem

The classic description of a travelling salesman is a salesman who plans to visit several places (customers) beginning at a fixed point (e.g. his office) and ending his trip at the same point. Each place (customer) can be visited only *once.* All distances between all places are known pairwise and the objective is to find the shortest route on the condition that all places are visited *only once* and that the travel cycle terminates at the starting point.

To translate the travelling salesman problem to a more contemporary context, we can apply it to an express courier or an online company that loads packages at a central pick-up point to distribute the packages to customers who have placed an order and who live at different addresses. When the courier has delivered his last package, he returns to the pick-up point for the next delivery cycle. Similar problems arise when a truck is loaded at a distribution centre and has to deliver its cargo passing several local stores at different locations. The key differences between the TSM and the shortest path problem are that the starting and end point are the same in the TSM and each node (customer) may only be visited once. The TSM problem can also be solved in Excel, but is more involved than the shortest path algorithm and falls beyond the scope of this book. For the interested reader, a list with references is included describing solution approaches for the TSM problem as well as its Excel implementation.[8]

Similar distribution problems based on network analysis

In addition to the shortest path and travelling salesman problems, there is another class of problems arising in Supply Chain settings that can be solved with network analysis tools. Below, we give a general description of three of these problems. They are:

1. The Minimum Spanning Tree Problem
2. The Maximum Flow Problem
3. The Minimum Cost Flow with, as special applications, the Transportation Problem and Transshipment Problem

The Minimum Spanning Tree

A characteristic of the minimum spanning tree is that the arcs between nodes have to be created and are not given, as they are in the shortest path problem. Each potential arc can be inserted in the network with a given positive length. It must establish a path so that each node is part of the connected network. The network must contain enough arcs to create paths so that *all* nodes are linked in the network. The objective is to minimize the total length of all links. A common application of the *Minimum Spanning Tree* is to set up an underground network of power cables, sewage pipelines, or drinking water pipelines in a city. This model is helpful in a Supply Chain context when there are few manufacturing plants – each with a limited production capacity – sending its products to distribution centres dispersed over several locations. However, the connections going from each manufacturing plant to the DCs have limited capacity. From the DCs, the goods are shipped to their final destination, which can be stores or final customers. In the network, all nodes (plants, DCs, and customers) must be connected to form a spanning tree. Minimum Spanning Trees can be solved in Excel with the aid of Solver.

The Maximum Flow Problem

The Maximum Flow problem can be described as getting the ***maximum*** number of products through the network when the arcs have limited capacity. Examples include getting as many vehicles through a transportation network when there are traffic jams, or getting as many new items as possible into the store network after the introduction of a new product in order to meet expected peak demand. Other applications are emergency cases such as getting as many subsistence goods, food, and medicines to the site of a natural disaster. This class of problems can also be solved with the aid of a spreadsheet and Solver.

The Minimum Cost Flow Problem

The Minimum Cost Flow problem is a frequently used network optimization model and the shortest path is a specific application of this class of optimization problems. This class of models can have multiple sources (like several plants of a company where similar products are made), many destinations (which can be the store network of a supermarket that has to be supplied), and many intermediate nodes, such as distribution centres, pick-up locations, and warehouses. It is the favourite model for designing Supply Chain networks. The problem can be applied to external networks, but is also applied to dynamic multi-product planning problems or streamlining the flow of luggage in the luggage handling section of an airport.

Designing and organizing a transportation and distribution plan

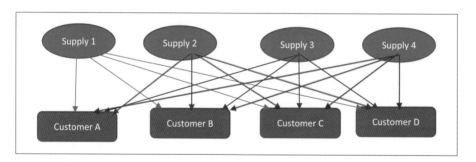

In the basic distribution model shown in the box above, each supplier sends one conveyance (train, truck, vessel, or airplane) with freight to each customer. The conveyance returns to its base camp, is reloaded, and goes to the next customer. Once arrived, the conveyance delivers the new freight and returns to reload, and then goes to the next customer. The cycle repeats itself until the truck driver returns from the last customer. Suppliers 2, 3, and 4 use the same delivery pattern. The total number of trips is 4 suppliers * 4 trips per supplier = 16 trips. This pattern can be a useful trip planning for fully loaded trucks when the entire cargo has to be delivered to a single customer location.

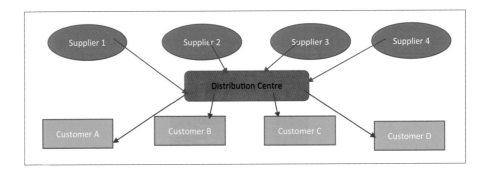

The distribution model in the box above has the same number of suppliers and destinations, but a distribution centre serves as an intermediate storage location. The cargo goes from each supplier to the DC and, is sent to each customer after cross-docking. The total number of trips made by using an intermediate DC has been reduced to 8. The DC serves as a central node with 4 incoming arcs and 4 outgoing arcs.

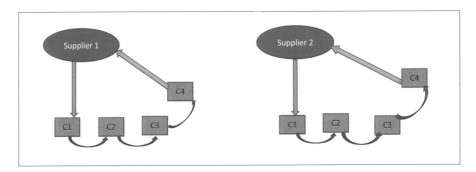

The above distribution model is called a *milk run*. The conveyance leaves the location of Supplier 1 and goes to customer location 1 (C1). There, it drops the freight for customer 1 and continues to the location of customer 2 (C2). There, it drops the cargo and continues to the location of customer 3 (C3). After dropping the cargo for customer 4 it returns to its base camp (supplier 1 location). A milk run is efficient if the load per customer is relatively small compared to the vehicle capacity – also called Less Than Truckload (LTL) – and several locations can be supplied in one run. Supplier 2 applies the same distribution pattern.

A *reversed* milk run also exists, when the supplier is replaced by one customer location and each customer location is supplied by several small supplier locations. When the customer is a large distribution centre of a supermarket chain, where thousands of different products in relatively small quantities are stored, it can be cheaper to let the truck start at the DC location. From there, it drives to the location of supplier 1 to collect products, then continues its trip to supplier 2 location, then to supplier 3 location, until the truck is fully loaded, and drives back to the DC to unload all cargo from the different suppliers. Milk runs have a pattern similar to the Travelling Salesman Problem. Milk run distribution planning is equally applicable when a DC serves as intermediate storage. The figure below contains a double milk run with a distribution centre for intermediate storage or cross-docking. The conveyance leaves the DC and visits three suppliers before returning to the DC and unloading (inbound logistics). A second conveyance loads freight for three customer locations and visits them in a milk run before returning to the DC (outbound logistics). Which distribution pattern is the best depends on many factors: the customers' order size; the shipping capacity of the supplier's vehicles; the transportation mode; the available infrastructure, the agreed upon lead time; and the transportation costs.

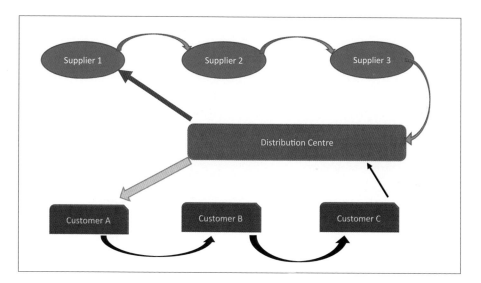

Return logistics: Products sold online and packaging returns

The load factor or vehicle utilization is a benchmark in transportation economics for measuring the *actual* occupancy versus the *capacity* of trucks and other vehicles.[9] In practice, some logistics companies decide – partly due to the competitive environment in the transportation market – to bring freight to the customer without considering the costs of empty hauling to get the truck back to its initial source, in particular for short and medium distances. Organizing an efficient return trip is part of *reverse* logistics. Besides sending freight from the supplier to the customer, shipping products back from the customer location to the source location becomes now part of the planning.

Returning goods or sending back packages with content is a frequent phenomenon in online transactions and is partly due to the consumer protection for online purchased goods at webshops. Customers who do not like the product purchased from an online company have the right to send it back to the seller at the seller's expense.[10] Another reason for returning goods is when the goods do not meet the standards expected by the customer, e.g. too many units, the wrong size, late arrival, or other errors incurred during the shipment process. Reverse logistics also occurs after the replenishment of local stores of supermarket chains and other retailers. The truck delivers the freight to the store address and reloads all kinds of packaging, crates, empty trolleys, and unsaleable items (due to defects or returned by customers to the shop, not meeting the required standards, or suffering other product deficiencies) from the retail store, bringing them back to the distribution centre.

Another development to reduce (near) empty hauling is online *freight exchange platforms*.[11] Freight forwarders publish their freight description on the demand side and carriers make known their available capacity on the supply side. The online exchange (primarily computer software) then searches for a match between demand and supply in terms of time, distance, and cargo size. A freight forwarder sending goods from Manchester to Stockholm, for example, can use these online exchanges to check for any open freight order from Stockholm to Manchester, or a location nearby Stockholm.

Main Point: At the distribution planning stage, a logistics company must consider not only optimal load factors for delivery to customer locations, but must also consider that the conveyances (truck, van, train, plane, marine vessel) have to return to their source location and will look for possibilities to increase the load factor during the return trip.

Matching distribution planning to infrastructure and conveyances

When designing a distribution network and planning for a distribution plan, a company will not only consider the size and the location of its distribution centres in terms of the outbound logistics to supply customers, on one side, and the inbound logistics for the goods received from its suppliers on the other side. It is equally important to look for the availability of infrastructure assets and networks to supply retailers and other customers, as well as the accessibility for suppliers to forward goods to the distribution centre. Two freight concepts are used in the world of logistics: *Full-Truck-Load* (FTL) and *Less-than-Truck-Load* (LTL) shipping. FTL refers to the movement of large amounts of more or less homogeneous goods to fill an entire trailer or container and deliver it usually to one destination. LTL refers to logistics companies that combine and consolidate freight from different customers in one trailer that are being sent to different destinations.

If the customer distribution centre is located close to a major motorway and orders in large quantities, full truckload shipments (FTL) in large carriers can be an economically feasible option: large volumes per ride but less frequent rides. However, the size of the road is not the only determining factor: the length and frequency of traffic jams on that road, delays due to customs control at national borders for international transport, highways where the transport of hazardous substances, like chemicals, is prohibited, and other factors, must be considered when optimizing a distribution plan.

Highway congestion is a frequent disruptor of distribution plans. If traffic jams occur mainly during rush hours, transportation during off-peak hours can be an option, providing that the receiver agrees with off-peak delivery times.

If the customer is located alongside a small road where large trucks have no access or are forbidden by traffic rules, then deploying a more frequent delivery schedule with lower volumes in smaller vehicles, like vans, can result in a lower cost distribution plan. Similar considerations are valid for transport by water and railway. Few manufacturing companies or merchandise companies operate their own fleet of vehicles. They outsource transport wholly or partially to *Third Party Logistics* (3PL), who operate a diversified fleet of conveyances and are able to achieve economies of scale. For relatively small freight packages, express carriers, like DHL, TNT, UPS, GLS, and Postnl offer acceptable shipment alternatives.

Often, standardized packaging is required, like products in corrugated card boxes, crates for transporting glass bottles, plastic or wooden boxes, and other requirements. They consolidate shipments from different sources into one full trailer for transportation to the same city or location. Some shipping companies who operate full truckload carriers also manage pick-up terminals at city fringes from where the consolidated freight is cross-docked or reloaded for further transportation in vans to its final destination in the downtown areas of a city. In practice, there is a virtually unlimited number of freight combinations possible and the availability in quantity and quality of infrastructure assets is one of the parameters for optimizing a distribution plan. Every combination has its price tag, lead time, and service level and the fastest distribution is not necessarily the cheapest one, and vice versa.

Ordering online or offline: Last-mile delivery revisited

In this section, we will discuss in more detail the major differences and similarities in logistics and distribution patterns between online purchases and purchases done in a brick-and-mortar store by the final consumer. The focus is on Business-to-Consumer (B2C) transactions and not on Business to Business (B2B) transactions. This latter category of transactions has different characteristics and generally consists of more complex transactional steps. We frame the distribution analysis from two perspectives: that of the consumer and that of the seller and discuss the concomitant configuration of the logistics process and distribution network for online and offline consumer transactions.

Although online shopping experienced a major thrust in the 21st century, home delivery of ordered goods is much older and has its roots in the first mail-order companies of the 19th century. The common business model of mail-order companies was to distribute printed product catalogues to many prospective customers. The catalogues contained an order form on which the customer indicated the desired product and the form was sent back to the mail-order company. The company dispatched the product by courier or public mail to the customer's address. From the 20th century, orders could also be placed by telephone.[12] In the 21st century, the printed catalogue has been replaced by a digital online product catalogue and payment plans have also subsequently changed.

The common starting point for a successful online business model is, as always, that consumers want to buy goods and that suppliers can sell these goods. This holds for both online and brick-and-mortar store transactions, and combinations of both. An undeniable fact is that, before the transaction, the (tangible) asset is at a location controlled by the supplier (source) and that, after the transaction, it must end up at a location indicated by the consumer (destination). This destination is usually the customer's home address, but can also be a holiday address, a hotel, or any delivery address, e.g. for products sent as a birthday present to the address of family members or friends.

The itinerary of the ordered product, from its source to its final destination, diverges between online and offline transactions. It is *either* the customer who orders and arranges the shipment to his destination address, *or* it is the selling company that arranges and takes care of the shipment to the address indicated by the customer. Combinations of both, like shipment under control of the supplier to a pick-up point, and the last mile from pick-up point to destination carried out by the customer, are also common practices.

We will now look at more detail into the differences in this matching process and the different modes of transportation with their concomitant advantages and disadvantages. First, however, we must answer a more basic question with respect to a successful online sales model, which is *whether,* and *when,* online purchases add value for consumers? Consumers and private households purchase many different goods and services ranging from daily shopping for food and drinks and other fast-moving items, to less frequent repetitive purchases such as clothing, electronic devices, and household appliances, as well as purchases done only once or a few times in a lifetime, e.g. furniture, furnishing a house, kitchen, bathroom, etc. Acquiring assets for personal mobility, like a bicycle, scooter, or car, are also examples of non-frequent repetitive purchases. The frequency cycle of purchases affects the suitability of which goods are better candidates for online or offline purchase. Online ordering can have *significant* added value for old, disabled, and sick persons who are unable to carry purchased items over the street to their home, for people purchasing assets that are too large or too heavy to be transported by one individual, such as furniture, household appliances (dishwasher), a piano, or construction materials from a Do-It-Yourself store. A van delivery of large quantities of small items, such as food for canteens in office premises and conference halls to serve the midday meals of the office staff, also adds value.[13]

Time constraints in terms of going to a brick-and-mortar store, particularly if the customer lives in a rural area and the store is far away, or when somebody is at work during the store opening hours, are also situations where online ordering can add considerable value for customers.[14] When we say *adds value* we mean that the customer is likely to buy the assets elsewhere if the option of home delivery is **not** offered by the selling company.

From the viewpoint of a company, we already mentioned that, in one way or another, the purchased asset must be transferred from the supplier location to the customer location, either under control of the supplier (online transaction) with its corresponding logistics costs, or under control of the consumer (on-location transaction), who makes the delivery with his or her transportation mode. Costs are incurred when going to the store and returning home with the product, or a combination of both. *Rational* consumer theory offers some clues for comparison between the two categories of transactions.

Among its components, this theory states that a consumer who wants to buy something of certain economic value will start searching for it and compare similar products and different suppliers of the same product. This search can be done online by consulting different websites, e.g. product and price comparison websites, or on location in a brick-and-mortar store, by walking around in the store premises, viewing items, and sometimes even touching them. *Online* searching only allows consumers to see (static images as pictures and dynamic images as videos and read product description) or to hear (audio product explanation, or hear the sound of a music instrument) a product. It does not allow for other sensory interactions between product and customer: smelling, tasting, or touching or feeling a product.[15] For products that the consumer wants to test, and when taste, smell, or touch is an important element in the supplier selection process, online selling is not excluded, but it is not always efficient. A customer can do a tentative buy of a product, e.g. a razor, clothing, bicycle, and try it out at home, once it has been shipped to his delivery address. If the product does not meet its expectations the consumer can return the product, in most cases at the expense of the online seller.

A combination of both search processes is possible and occurs. The consumer initially consults the internet and, having found something appropriate, they visit the brick-and-mortar store to get more information and buy it. Searching is a key component of consumer transactions both for online and offline purchases and the effort invested in searching in terms of time and other resources, and the results of this search process, are case-specific. It is difficult to draw generalized conclusions about whether searching on the internet yields better results (more product variation and/or cheaper products) than visiting a physical store. For foodstuffs, for example, the search process is different than for buying, say, a new kitchen furniture or a guitar.

The second dimension in a consumer transaction is the *travel dimension*. In this phase of the purchase process, differences between online and offline purchases are more evident. If the consumer is already in the brick-and-mortar store, or lives or works nearby, the purchase of the found asset will be completed at the store checkout. Two options remain at the checkout or service counter: either the consumer takes the product home using their own mode of transportation (walking, biking, public transport, car), incurring the corresponding costs and travel time. If the purchased item is a large or heavy asset (furniture, new bed, a carpet, a dishwasher, or a piano), and the store offers this option, the customer can ask the store to take care of the transportation. A date will be set when the asset will arrive at the customer's indicated address.

In one way or another, the store will charge the customer for the transportation costs, either as an explicit mark-up cost on the invoice – which is more transparent for the consumer – or the shipment cost is absorbed in the price. When ordering occurs online, the consumer has no further travel costs after completing the purchase, besides waiting and using track-and-trace to see when the ordered asset will arrive at the specified address.

Now, we take the stance of the supplier, who wants to start an online store or to extend his business model by combining sales in the brick-and-mortar store with sales online. This latter option, of combining online and offline is becoming an increasing part of the standard business model of many companies. A crucial question is whether extending a business model by adding online sales will increase revenues? If customers who previously purchased in the brick-and-mortar store now switch to the online store, there will be no revenue increase, just a zero-sum game between online sales and the sales in the physical stores. If extending the business model with an online sales website attracts new customers or leads to more frequent orders from existing customers, sales will go up. This will particularly be the case if the company ran only a few brick-and-mortar stores but caters to a broad geographical area and many of their customers are not willing to incur travel costs in terms of the time and money needed to go to the brick-and-mortar store.

Extending the business model with online sales means a significant financial investment and deploying other resources. Not only to build a website – frequently outsourced to specialized IT firms – but also to organize the distribution and logistics infrastructure to get the product from source to destination. In the business world, a wide variety of distribution configurations is observed. Some online companies manage their own distribution centres (like Bol.com and CoolBlue in the Netherlands, or Amazon at a global scale) but they do not always operate their own fleet of vehicles for logistics operations.[16] A large share of all online sales is offered by small- and medium-sized companies that do not have the resources to invest in their own DC and take care of the logistics. They keep the products either as inventory in their own retail store or they rent space elsewhere. The dispatch of the ordered products is, in most cases, outsourced to major express couriers, like DHL, Postnl, UPS, Fedex, DPD, GLS, and others. Investing in a DC and managing own logistics operations requires not only substantial investments in tangible and intangible assets, but also specific know-how, which small retail stores do not usually have.

The cost-benefit analysis of managing a few distribution centres for online transactions, on one side, versus setting up and maintaining a large network of physical retail stores – either as franchise constructions or as affiliates – for offline transactions, on the other side, is also an important trade-off for companies. Catering to customers who are spread widely over a country or even over the entire world requires a large network of brick-and-mortar stores. For many retail products, these stores are often located in city centres, where real-estate prices are high. Running these stores is part of a company's costs and will be accounted for in the selling price of the products.

Selling online requires investment in one or a few distribution centres supplying either regionally, nationally, transnationally, or even globally. The choice for a few regional DCs, or one national DC, not only depends on cost considerations, but also on the *Customer Response Time* that the company targets and advertises for their online customers. Large distribution centres are often located in the outskirts of a city, in remote areas of the country, where real estate and land prices are lower, sometimes much lower than in city centres. Another issue affecting the costs of running a network of physical retail stores and distribution centres for online sales is the make-up of the premises. Brick-and-mortar stores have window displays to showcase products and attract customers to the shop. Shops have to be clean and well decorated and maintained to attract customers. These features increase costs. DCs used for online sales do not need such properties and can be designed efficiently and soberly using steel constructions or concrete, thus keeping building costs low.[17]

Another issue is the trade-off between shipping goods to the delivery address indicated by the customer, or to other locations partnering with the supplying company. In recent decades, package couriers delivering to home addresses have experienced problems, such as delays due to congestion in narrow – and sometimes broad – city street grids and also the ‘not-at-home’ problem. Although in many European and other countries couriers can now send a text message or an email to the addressee to tell them what time the package will arrive, that does not mean that somebody is at home to open the door when the driver rings the doorbell. Until a few years ago, it was common practice to leave a message saying that the courier would come back the next day. However, this ‘double-ride’ service is very expensive. As a solution, many package couriers and online companies have discovered is setting up a network of *pick-up points*. The customer receives a text message that he or she can go to a preselected pick-up point to collect their ordered items and bring it home with using their own mode of transportation.

These pick-up points are generally located in districts that are easily accessible for courier vans. Another major advantage of using a network of pick-up points is the economies of scale. Several packages are now unloaded at the same pick-up point for different customers living in the area, instead of moving the same number of packages from one address to the next one, to deliver them one by one to single customers. The supplier saves logistics costs, although he has to pay a fee to the owner of the pick-up point. For the owners of pick-up points, it means welcome additional revenue as a business agency of a large logistics courier. Pick-up points solve the *not-at-home* problem because they have regular opening hours both for suppliers to deliver packages and for customers to collect their package. The total trajectory from source to destination can now be split into two parts: from the source to the pick-up point under the control of the selling company, and from the pick-up point to the final destination under the control of the customer. In some cases, using pick-up points is the only option if the customer address is in a rural, sparsely populated area that some online companies exclude from home delivery.[18]

They send the product to a pick-up point in a nearby city, and the customer goes to that city on a day and at a time that suits them to collect the ordered item. It is clear that in cases where home delivery adds significant value (disabled people, heavy assets) the option of a pick-up point is not realistic. If a customer is not able to bring a product (piano) from the store to home using its own transportation means, he or she is usually not able to carry it from a pick-up point either. In such cases, home delivery remains the only value-adding option. Up to now, we have discussed the distribution and logistics components of online versus offline purchases, but we have not yet discussed the corresponding payment plans. The options for payment plans are:

1. pay before receiving the product (prepayment),
2. pay when receiving the product (cash payment or payment by debit (credit) card),
3. pay after receiving the product (post-payment)
4. any combinations (e.g. partial prepayment and the remaining part in cash).

The payment plan is usually *in*dependent of the distribution plan of the product itself. Prepayment is common practice, but not exclusive, for consumers ordering online. Cash payment on receipt takes place when customers pay in a physical store at the checkout counter, or when a meal deliverer delivers the ordered meal to the door of the customer's address. Post payment is common for more expensive items like household appliances and is used both for online and offline transactions. The customer will receive an invoice containing the amount and the payment terms, e.g. the due date or how to pay in instalments.[19] Distribution from source to destination is not a free lunch and someone has to pay for it. In most cases, the customer will bear the cost burden, either as a mark-up cost, separate from the purchased assets, or the online price is higher than the offline price of the same product purchased in the brick-and-mortar store.[20] In some cases, the supplier bears the cost burden. Restaurants who have contracts with meal deliverers, like *Ubereats* or *Thuisbezorgd*, have to pay a fee to the meal delivering company. Consequently, the restaurants have lower net revenues compared to the situation in which the guests order and eat their meal in the restaurant.

Case study: Unilever sidelines supermarkets and delivers ice creams directly to your home via Deliveroo and Uber Eats.

6 Feb 2020, 11:25 Editors Foodlog

Food group Unilever, which owns more than half of the world's ice cream market, will deliver its Magnums and Ben & Jerry's ice cream directly to customer's homes. It can easily be called a 'revolution', according to the Belgian business newspaper *De Tijd*. Unilever is going to roll out its own global logistics network of more than 1,000 frozen food locations from where meal service providers such as Uber Eats and Deliveroo will take care of the 'last-mile' to the customer's front door.

As a result, the traditional distribution channel of wholesalers, retailers, and supermarkets will be sidelined. The new approach fits in the trend of producers selling directly to consumers via their own online shops and bypassing the classic retail sector. According to *De Tijd*, there is also a Flemish side to the story: the Ghent start-up Deliverect will supply the management technology for Unilever's logistics network. Deliverect will create

software that will allow managers of catering establishments to process the orders they
receive for Deliveroo and Uber Eats.
Source: https://www.foodlog.nl/artikel/unilever-zet-supermarkten-buitenspel-en-bezorgt-ijsjes-
thuis-via-deliveroo-/

As a general conclusion, there is not an unambiguous economic (dis)advantage
of online *sales* for the supplier or online ***purchases*** for the customer. The (dis)
advantages are case-specific.

Below is a diagram showing the different distribution plans used by online stores.
Double-pointed arrows indicate that the customer makes a trip in both directions.

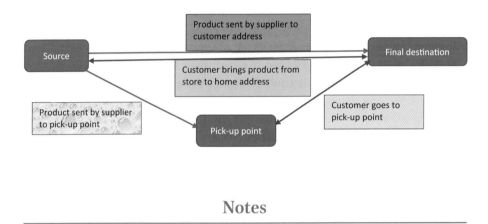

Notes

1-20   See Instructor's Manual

10 Revenue Management and Optimizing Capacity Usage

Revenue Management and Optimizing Capacity Usage

As a casual observer, you will have probably noticed that, at the end of the sales season or at the end of the year, retail stores offer sometimes substantial price discounts, particularly on perishable goods, in order to get rid of all overstocked units.[1] Similar practices are observed in the hospitality industry, where hotels offer discounted overnight stays in off-peak periods to improve the occupancy rate of their rooms. The airline industry, and many other industries in the economy, use similar pricing practices. In recent decades, using prices to increase capacity usage is part of a fast-developing field of business science called *Revenue Management,* or RM for short.[2] Because pricing decisions are aimed at influencing demand for a product, it is sometimes also called *Demand Management* or *Yield Management.*[3]

Some typical examples of demand management are: *dynamic pricing,* whereby a company charges different prices for the same product during different periods of the sales season (time segmentation); price differentiation based on categories of customers (customer segmentation like children and adults pricing); price differentiation based on geographical area (spatial or geographical segmentation); or overbooking strategies, a pricing practice common in the airline industry.

Other instruments of revenue management include reallocating capacity based on time-dependent demand, for example, deploying many connected train carriages during peak hours and fewer train carriages during off-peak hours, rearranging seats in an airplane by swapping the number of business class seats with economy class seats. Other examples are the use of multiproduct flexible production lines where several different products can be manufactured on the same production line using other machine and equipment configurations. It is not possible to discuss all sides of revenue management, for this reason we will limit the discussion here to exploring some basic components of revenue management.

The starting point of revenue management is that customer demand is *not* homogeneous and that different customers have different preferences and varying degrees of willingness to pay based on features and services added to a base product. To continue our example from the airlines, these could be: passenger preferences for a nocturnal flight or a daytime flight; for a direct flight with a traveling time of two hours or changing planes at three different airports with a total travel time of eight hours; for a seat with ample leg space close to a window or crammed into an aisle seat; paying for catering or free catering on board; and many other services affecting the passenger (dis)satisfaction of an air flight.

Dynamic pricing over time

Dynamic pricing is a policy of changing the selling price periodically in order to sell as many units as possible before the end of the sales period or the accounting year. This policy is relevant when a retailer purchases a large lot of products for a long sales period, because buying in bulk is cheaper than buying the same amount in small lots, in particular when price discounts are offered by the supplier for larger volumes. Another reason to buy in large lots can be that the supplier is located on the other side of the globe, producing private label products for the retailer. It can be quite expensive to produce and ship private label products in small lots.

Dynamic pricing can be a profitable policy for a retailer if new products are launched on the market and customer demand can be segmented. Customers making purchases in the early stage of the sales period are often frontrunners or trendy buyers who want to be the first to buy the product. In their wake, follows a customer group that can be described as 'followers', who first want to read expert reviews and user experiences from initial buyers before deciding to purchase the product. A third group can be classified as latecomers, whose maxim is *'wait and see'* before they decide to purchase. For each customer group, a (linear) demand function can be estimated either using historical data about prices and quantities or other statistical techniques.

The demand function for period i is defined as $Q_i = c_i - d_i * P_i$ with Q_i the quantity demanded and P_I the selling price in period i with $i = 1$ until N. Total revenues in period i are $P_I * Q_i$ and O is total units ordered and stored in inventory. The non-linear optimization problem is:

Max $\sum_{i=1}^{N}(c_i - d_i * P_i)* P_i$ [maximize total revenues]

Subject to: $\sum_{i=1}^{N}(c_i - d_i * P_i) \leq O$ [total units sold cannot exceed O units ordered]

              $(c_i - d_i * P_i) \geq 0$ [demand cannot be negative]

The basic version of this model assumes that demand per period is segmented. This means that each customer group only buys in the period when they planned to buy the product. No customers are swapping between the periods. Usually, customers with a high willingness to pay make their purchase in the first period and customers with a lower willingness to pay buy in later periods. This is reflected in the coefficients c_i and d_i in the demand curves. This is not always a realistic assumption, however: customers can proceed to strategic behaviour if they know that the selling price will drop over time and wait until a later period before their actual purchase. In this case, it can be advantageous for the seller to maintain a fixed price during all sales periods. We will illustrate the dynamic pricing with an example using Excel and Solver. Company GoodSleep NV sells electric blankets, which have peak demand in the winter months. They order 15,000 electric blankets in October from the manufacturer Inventum, which are sold in December, January, and February. Goodsleep has divided its customers into three groups and Inventum sells the blankets to GoodSleep for €1,100 each.

The first group in the hospitality industry buys in December with demand function $Q_{dec} = 25,000 - 8*P_{dec}$

The customer group in January are cold-sensitive consumers with demand function $Q_{jan} = 18,000 - 6*P_{jan}$

The customer group in February has a demand function $Q_{feb} = 15,000 - 5*P_{feb}$.

Goodsleep's optimization problem becomes one of a uniform price during the entire sales season

Maximize total revenue $TR = P_{dec}*Q_{dec} + P_{jan}*Q_{jan} + P_{feb}*Q_{feb}$

Subject to $Q_{dec} + Q_{jan} + Q_{feb} \leq 15,000$

$P_{dec} = P_{jan} = P_{feb}$

Below you will see the Excel screenshot with the solution, the Solver settings, and the formula view. NB: the Excel screenshot maximizes total *profit* instead of total *revenues* by subtracting the purchase price, but the resulting prices are the same!

	A	B	C	D	E
1	Order size O	15,000			
2	additional order				
3	Total Inventory				
4	Purchase cost	€ 1,100	per blanket		
5					
6		Demand (Q)	Selling Price	Purchase cost	Profit
7	December Sales	6,895	€ 2,263.16	€ 1,100	€ 8,019,668
8	January Sales	4,421	€ 2,263.16	€ 1,100	€ 5,142,382
9	February Sales	3,684	€ 2,263.16	€ 1,100	€ 4,285,319
10	Total Sales	15,000			€ 17,447,368

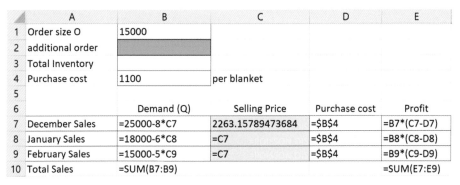

	A	B	C	D	E
1	Order size O	15000			
2	additional order				
3	Total Inventory				
4	Purchase cost	1100	per blanket		
5					
6		Demand (Q)	Selling Price	Purchase cost	Profit
7	December Sales	=25000-8*C7	2263.15789473684	=$B$4	=B7*(C7-D7)
8	January Sales	=18000-6*C8	=C7	=$B$4	=B8*(C8-D8)
9	February Sales	=15000-5*C9	=C7	=$B$4	=B9*(C9-D9)
10	Total Sales	=SUM(B7:B9)			=SUM(E7:E9)

The maximum profit during the sales season is €17,447,368 and the uniform selling price €2,263.16. If we release the condition of a single price for the entire sales period and allow price changes for each month, the only adjustment made in the Solver window is changing cells C7, C8, and C9 into *variables* and selecting S̲olve. The optimal solution is shown below.

	B	C	D	E
4	€ 1,100	per blanket		
5				
6	Demand (Q)	Selling Price	Purchase cost	Profit
7	6,605	€ 2,299.34	€ 1,100	€ 7,921,970
8	4,579	€ 2,236.84	€ 1,100	€ 5,205,540
9	3,816	€ 2,236.84	€ 1,100	€ 4,337,950
10	15,000			€ 17,465,461

The December price is €2,299.34 and for the other two months €2,236.34, achieving a total profit of €17,465,461 and that is (only) €18,093 more than the profit obtained with uniform pricing, i.e. not a substantial improvement.[4]

The last scenario that we will consider is that GoodSleep has a quantity flexibility contract with Inventum and can purchase an additional 4,000 blankets more during the sales season, achieving a maximum inventory of 19,000 blankets. The purchase price for the additional blankets is the same as for the other blankets, namely, €1,100. The Excel screenshot solution and formula view of this problem is shown below.

	A	B	C	D	E
1	Order size O	15,000			
2	additional order	3,550			
3	Total Inventory	18,550			
4	Purchase cost	€ 1,100	per blanket		
5	Maximum adjusted order	4,000	blankets		
6					
7					
8		Demand (Q)	Selling Price	Purchase cost	Profit
9	December Sales	8,100	€ 2,112.52	€ 1,100	€ 8,201,250
10	January Sales	5,699	€ 2,050.09	€ 1,100	€ 5,415,000
11	February Sales	4,750	€ 2,049.96	€ 1,100	€ 4,512,500
12	Total Sales	18,550			€ 18,128,750

	A	B	C	D	E
1	Order size O	15000			
2	additional order	3550.04624065682			
3	Total Inventory	=B1+B2			
4	Purchase cost	1100	per blanket		
5	Maximum adjusted order	4000	blankets		
6					
7					
8		Demand (Q)	Selling Price	Purchase cost	Profit
9	December Sales	=25000-8*C9	2112.51965122017	=$B$4	=B9*(C9-D9)
10	January Sales	=18000-6*C10	2050.09127971272	=$B$4	=B10*(C10-D10)
11	February Sales	=15000-5*C11	2049.95663865775	=$B$4	=B11*(C11-D11)
12	Total Sales	=SUM(B9:B11)			=SUM(E9:E11)

GoodSleep purchases an additional 3,350 blankets bringing the total inventory to 18,850. Selling prices are €2,112.52 for December, €2,049.98 for February, and €2,050.03 for January with a total profit of €18,128,750, which is more than without the option to purchase more additional blankets. To obtain this solution, two adjustments must be made in the Solver settings. Under the declaration of the variables, cell B2 must be added as a variable in addition to the three variable monthly selling prices. In the Constraint box, the sum of all units sold (cell B10) must be set as smaller than or equal to cell B3, which is the inventory including the purchasing of additional blankets. A new constraint must be added, so that cell B2 containing the additional order size is smaller than or equal to 4000, which is the maximum amount Goodsleep can buy additionally from Inventum according to their delivery contract.

Overbooking

Booking or reservation systems for attaining optimal capacity usage are a common instrument in several industries, e.g. theatres, theme parks, hotels, international train travels, and sports events.

Increased adoption of booking system in the aftermath of the Covid-19 crisis (2020–2021).

In the after effects of the global Covid-19 pandemic, when strict lockdown measures were gradually mitigated in the world, several countries enacted new regulations prescribing that many firms in the service sector (hairdressers, restaurants, bars, theme parks, zoos, fitness centre, etc.) had to implement a booking or reservation system. The new regulation initially set a maximum of 30 guests per premise. This number was well below the physical capacity of large restaurants, and to increase capacity usage and revenues, some restaurants and other branches in the Netherlands introduced shifts, whereby guests were assigned both a beginning and an end time for their dinner. Several restaurants also required a prepayment to book a table or a time slot. Where before Covid-19 guests could spend as much time as they wanted sitting and taking a meal in a restaurant, outside the strict lockdown periods where all nonessential stores were closed, this situation changed during Covid-19. A capacity usage of 60 guests eating during a period of three hours in a restaurant is, in quantitative terms, equivalent to 30 guests in one timeslot of 1,5 hours and another 30 guests in the next time slot of 1,5 hours. This system of time slots also diminishes the peak load on the capacity resources (kitchen, cooks, and waiters) leading to a better spread usage of the capacity. In terms of capacity concepts, discussed in Chapter 3, the theoretical capacity of a restaurant (maximum number of guests in one day) has been converted into a practical or institutional capacity set by public regulation to 30 guests per time slot multiplied by the number of time slots per day. As of March 2022, most restrictions on group size have been abolished in many countries.

Besides booking systems, several industries also work with a common and accepted practice of *overbooking*. Overbooking is considered a form of revenue management. Airlines are the frontrunners in this revenue management practice, but hotels, theatres, and many institutions that use booking systems apply overbooking policies to a higher or lesser degree. Overbooking aims to achieve the highest level of capacity usage given that, in the short term, capacity is fixed, e.g. the number of seats in a plane or theatre, or rooms in a hotel.

The *relevant* costs when applying an overbooking policy are the revenues (profit) foregone due to an empty seat or room (a unit of capacity), which occurs either when the unit is not booked or is booked but the customer does not show up and has the right to a refund from the firm.

The other cost of overbooking is that an *overbooked* customer does show up and there is no free seat or room available. In that case, the firm has the legal obligation to arrange for an alternative seat, flight, or sleeping place. This increases the costs for the firm, because although the customer has paid, arranging for an alternative usually implies a higher cost for the firm that made the overbooking.

We define the cost of idle capacity per unit (wasted capacity) as C_i and the cost of offering alternative capacity in case of overbooking as C_o. Furthermore, we assume that *cancellations* and *no-show* customers follow a normal distribution with mean μ_c and standard deviation σ_c cancellations. Using the same formula as we did for inventory overstocking, we calculate an optimal *percentage* of overbookings for the firm as:

$$S^* = \frac{C_i}{(C_i + C_o)}.$$

The corresponding optimal overbooking *number* is $OV^* = F^{-1}(S^*, \mu_c, \sigma_c)$, or NORM. INV($S^*, \mu_c, \sigma_c$) in Excel. The total number of bookings that the firm will accept is its capacity (# of available seats) plus OV^*.

Some companies with an extensive track record of cancellations in the past estimate an average *percentage* instead of an absolute number of cancellations ($\mu_\%$) with a corresponding standard deviation ($\sigma_\%$). Thus, the cancellation percentage is based on the number of actual bookings instead of absolute numbers for the mean and standard deviations of cancellations. If the cancellation distribution is expressed as a percentage, the method to find the optimal number of overbookings has to be modified. As an example, a firm has a capacity of $X = 200$ seats available, and the number of overbookings is the variable O. Total bookings accepted become $(X + O)$. The expected *cancellation* rate is $\mu_\%^*(X + O)$. S^* indicates the number of cancellations and is assumed to follow a normal distribution and O is the decision variable. The corresponding standard deviation of cancellations is $\sigma_\%^*(X + O)$.[5] Bringing all elements together we obtain the equation: $O = $ NORM.INV[($S^*, \mu_\%^*(200 + O), \sigma_\%^*(200 + O)$]. Notice that this is an implicit equation in O. O appears both on the left-hand side and on the right-hand side of the equation as an argument in the inverse normal distribution function. Analytically, it is not possible to solve O exactly, but Solver enables us to find an approximate numerical solution.

An example

A theatre has 400 seats for a popular performance. The cost of an empty seat is €60 and the cost of overbooking a visitor to another date for the same performance is €35. Historical data show that, on average, 12% of the customers that booked a seat do not show up at the moment of the performance, with a standard deviation of 3%. The optimal number of overbooking units O with the aid of Solver is:

	A	B	C
1	Capacity	400	seats
2	Mean % cancellations	12%	
3	Standard deviation % cancellations	3%	
4	Cost of idle capacity per unit	€ 60	
5	Cost of hiring extra capacity	€ 35	
6			
7	Optimal cancellation percentage	63%	
8	Variable with overbooking	60	
9	Probability calculation	60	
10	Difference between B8 and B9	0	

The Excel screenshot in formula view and the Solver settings are shown below:

	A	B
1	Capacity	400
2	Mean % cancellations	0.12
3	Standard deviation % cancellations	0.03
4	Cost of idle capacity per unit	60
5	Cost of hiring extra capacity	35
6		
7	Optimal cancellation percentage	=B4/(B4+B5)
8	Variable with overbooking	59.8130611500958
9	Probability calculation	=NORM.INV(B7;B2*(B1+B8);B3*(B1+B8))
10	Difference between B8 and B9	=B8-B9

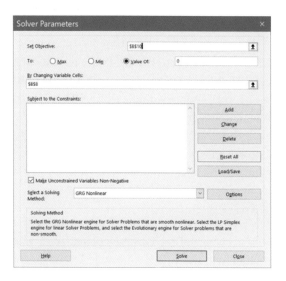

The optimal number of overbookings is 60 seats, which we obtained by setting the variable cell of overbooking *B8* equal to the formula *B9*. B9 contains the formula on the right-hand side of the equation, discussed above, and B8 the left-hand side. In Solver, the difference of B10 = B8 – B9 is set equal to 0. After clicking on *Solve*, we see that the theatre is best off by selling 400 + 60 = 460 tickets for this performance.

A binomial approach to finding the optimal overbooking rate

Another model for calculating the optimal number of overbookings – optimal in the sense of maximizing expected profits – uses a binomial approach. It is built on the following set of assumptions, which are approximately similar to the previous model. Bookings for an empty unit of capacity are *independent* of each other and the probability of an actual show-up at the designated moment is the same for all units booked. Each sold and booked unit of capacity generates a fixed revenue. Each *overbooked* customer showing up at the designated moment to claim his asset creates additional overbooking costs, which consist of finding an alternative for this customer and a loss of goodwill that manifests itself in fewer future bookings. The following model parameters are used:

- p is the probability that a customer who booked will actually show up (follows a Bernoulli distribution)
- R is the revenue earned per booking (including those earned from overbooked units)
- S is the cost the company incurs for rearranging external units for any overbooked customer that does show up.
- C = the capacity or the maximum number of units available (without overbooking)

The decision variable (N) is the number of booking requests that the company will accept. The number of overbookings will be the difference between the number of bookings minus regular capacity (N – C). The random variable $D(N)$ represents the number of customers who booked and will show up or claim their unit of capacity. The probability of showing up has a Bernoulli distribution. This implies that the probability of the number of show-ups D(N) = n when N reservations have been made follows a *binomial* distribution.

$$P[D(N) = n] = \left(\tfrac{N}{n}\right)^* p^n * (1 - p)^{N-n}$$

The mean of a binomial distribution is $\mu = N^*p$ and the variance $\sigma^2 = N^*p^*(1 - p)$. The number of *overbooked* units which will show up is

$$O(N) = 0 \text{ if } D(N) \le C$$
$$O(N) = [D(N) - C] \text{ if } D(N) > C.$$

The expected value of this variable is

$$E[O(N)] = \sum_{n=C+1}^{N} (n - C)^* P[D(N) = n]$$

The index of summation starts at (C+1), because if the # of bookings D(N) ≤ C, there are 0 **over**bookings! We use a marginal approach by incrementing the number of bookings N one by one, and look to the change (Δ) on the expected number of *over*booked show-ups ΔE[O(N)]. Two concomitant events need to happen to impact E[O(N)]: the last marginal booking must be an *over*booking and the overbooked customer must also *show up* to claim his (prepaid) capacity unit. It is easy to see that because p is the probability that the last booked show-up – a change from N to (N+1) show-ups and the number of reservations is above capacity $D(N) \geq C$

[10.1] $\Delta E[O(N)] = E[O(N+1)] - E[O(N)] = p*P[D(N) \geq C]$ using the formula for the expected value above.

Total profits with N reservations accepted will be the number of bookings N times the revenue per booking R minus the number of overbooked units who show up $O(N)$, and for whom external capacity must be arranged at a cost of S per unit

$Profit(N) = N*R - O(N)*S$

with expected value – given that only $O(N)$ is a random variable, and the rest are exogenous parameters

$E[Profit(N)] = N*R - S*E[O(N)]$.

Incrementing the # of reservations or bookings with +1 gives

$\Delta E[Profit(N)] = E[Profit(N+1)] - E[Profit(N)] =$

$(N+1) *R - S*E[O(N+1)] - N*R - S*E[O(N)] =$

$R - S*\Delta E[O(N)] = R - S*p*P[D(N) \geq C]$ applying equation [10.1]

Because $E[Profit(N)] > 0$ for small values of N and negative for large values of N and also assuming that $R > S*p$. This means that the expected cost of an overbooking $S*p$ will be smaller than the revenue R, because otherwise the firm makes a loss on this overbooked unit. We search for the value N^* that maximizes total expected profit. When C is large, the binomial distribution can be approximated by the normal distribution. This normal distribution as an approximation for the binomially distributed D(N) has a mean value $\mu = N*p$ and variance $\sigma^2 = N*p*(1-p)$. This leads to the approximated equation with R $= S*p*P[D(N^*) \geq C]$ which after some rearrangement of terms becomes:

$P[D(N^*) \geq C] = R/(S*p)$.

The NORM.S.INV of the Excel function library can be used to find the value of N^*, keeping in mind that

$P[D(N^*) \geq C] = 1 - P[D(N^*) < C] = R/(S*p)$.

If N^* is not an integer value it must be rounded to the nearest integer value.

An example

A parking garage has a capacity of 600 cars. For a weekly sports event, visitors arriving by car book a parking spot in advance for €80. Experience has shown that only 85% of all booked parking places show up to park their car during the sports match. The manager of the parking garage wants to apply overbooking and for each overbooked car showing up that lacks a parking spot the manager has to offer the car driver a very expensive parking place in a nearby private parking garage, which costs €240 for the same time.

Required

Calculate the optimal number of bookings of parking places during the weekly sports match and the expected revenues minus overbooking costs of the garage.

Solution

We will use Excel screenshots to show the solution to this problem. The left pane shows the output view, and the right screenshot shows the formula view.

	A	B	C	D
8	Mean value μ	599.1		
9	Variance σ	3.4		
10	Standardized value	0		
11	D(N*) =	0.27	NORM.S.INV(1-B7)	
12	Difference B10 - B11	0		
13	Solve for N and round	705		
14				
15	Total revenues	€56,383.55		
16	Total expected rearrangement costs	€21,378.06		
17	Total Profit	€35,005.49		

	A	B	C
1	Net Revenue per seat (r)	80	
2	Rearrangement costs (s)	240	
3	Capacity (L)	600	
4	Probability show up	0.85	
5	Number of bookings N =	704.794401929151	
6			
7	P[D(N*) ≥ L] =	=B1/(B2*B4)	[R / S*p]
8	Mean value μ	=B4*B5	
9	Variance σ	=B4*(1-B4)*SQRT(B5)	
10	Standardized value	=(B3-B8)/B9	
11	D(N*) =	=NORM.S.INV(1-B7)	NORM.S.INV(1-B7)
12	Difference B10 - B11	=B10-B11	
13	Solve for N and round	=ROUND(B5;0)	
14			
15	Total revenues	=B5*B1	
16	Total expected rearrangement costs	=IF(B5<=B3;0;B4*(B5-B3)*B2)	
17	Total Profit	=B15-B16	

The Solver settings for optimizing are cell **B12** as *Objective* function with a target value equal to 0, and the variable cell is **B5**, the number of bookings. The Solving method is GRG non-linear and the variable must be non-negative. The garage will accept 705 car parking reservations during the sports match and, with a capacity of 600 parking places, 105 cars are overbooked. The total profit is approximately €35,005.

Revenue management and consumer pricing in a Supply Chain setting

In the introductory case study of this book, about the food retail industry, we referred to pricing problems that arise in a Supply Chain. In the European Union and other countries, vertical price agreements between a supplier and a downstream (retail) company are prohibited in many cases.[6] Generally, a manufacturer cannot legally force an independent wholesaler or a retailer to sell its product to the consumers for a price that the manufacturer prefers. If, for example, a car manufacturer starts a price promotion with an 8% discount for a specific model during a month, an independent dealer selling the model to the final consumer can often ignore this price campaign. Instead, the dealer can set differentiated selling prices based on local market conditions, rather than transmitting the prescribed price by the manufacturer on a one-to-one basis. We will illustrate this pricing dilemma using an example of a car manufacturer, *Skoda*, and a local independent dealer, *Skodadeal*. The estimated demand function for Skoda automobiles is Q = 80,000 – 20*P with *Q* quantity demanded and *P* the consumer price. The *production cost* per Skoda for the manufacturer is €1,800 and Skoda sells the car to Skodadeal at a price C_{skoda}. The dealer sells the Skoda to the final consumer for P_{SD}. The local demand curve for the manufacturer is the same as for the dealer, i.e. each car sold by the dealer must be produced by the manufacturer and sold to the dealer for C_{Skoda}.

Required

Calculate the price-reaction equation between the consumer price (P_{SD}) and the dealer cost (C_{Skoda}). The dealer sets a profit-maximizing price P_{SD} and Skoda its price for the dealer at C_{Skoda}. *NB: keep in mind that the selling price of the manufacturer is the purchase cost of the dealer.*

Solution

Given that manufacturer, Skoda, cannot fix the consumer price, we first maximize the profit of Skodadeal to P_{SD}. This gives a price-reaction curve between the consumer price P_{SD} and the dealer purchase cost C_{Skoda}. We apply the standard mathematical optimization tools and set C_{Skoda} as an unknown parameter. The resulting price-reaction curve can be interpreted as the optimal price setting of Skodadeal as a function of the price charged by manufacturer Skoda. P_{SD} is the selling price set by Skodadeal. The Skodadeal profit function is: (Selling price – purchase cost) * # cars sold →

Total profit
$$TP = (P_{SD} - C_{Skoda}) * (80,000 - 20*P_{SD})$$
and after removing brackets gives
$$TP = 80,000*P_{SD} - 20 * P_{SD}^2 + 20 * C_{Skoda} * P_{SD} - 80,000 * C_{Skoda}.$$
The maximum is found when
$$d(TP)/d(P_{SD}) = 0 \rightarrow \text{price-reaction equation}$$
$$80,000 - 40*P_{SD} + 20*C_{Skoda} = 0 \rightarrow C_{Skoda} = 2*P_{SD} - 4,000$$

Now we define the profit function TP_{Skoda} of manufacturer Skoda:
$$TP_{Skoda} = (C_{Skoda} - 18,000) *Q = (C_{Skoda} - 1800) *(80,000 - 20*P) \rightarrow$$

replace C_{Skoda} with the price-reaction curve →
$$([2*P_{SD} - 4,000] - 1,800) * (80,000 - 20*P_{SD})$$
$$\rightarrow$$
$$(2*P_{SD} - 5,600)*(80,000 - 20*P_{SD})$$
$$= 160,000*P_{SD} - 40*P_{SD}^2 + 116,000*P_{SD} - 448,000,000$$
$$= -40*P_{SD}^2 + 276,000*P_{SD} - 448,000,000$$

Take the derivative $d(TP_{Skoda})/d(P_{SD}) = 0 \rightarrow -80*P_{SD} + 276,000 = 0 \rightarrow$
$$P_{SD} = €3,450 \text{ and } C_{Skoda} = 2*3,450 - 4,000 = €2,900$$

The profit of Skoda becomes €12.2 mln and the profit of Skodadeal €6.050 mln. Total SC profit equals €18.25 mln (12.2 + 6.05). The number of cars sold is 80,000 − 20*3,450 = 11,000 cars.

If the two firms *coordinate* their pricing policy by maximizing the SC profit instead of individual profits, we obtain another value of total SC profit. The wholesale price C_{Skoda} is, in this case, no longer relevant, because the SC operates as an economic unity. Only Skoda's production cost of €1,800 and consumer price P_{SD} are relevant parameters.   The Supply Chain profit function TP_{SC} reads:

$$TP_{SC} = (P_{SD} - 1,800) * (80,000 - 20*P_{SD}) =$$
$$80,000*P_{SD} - 20*P_{SD}^2 - 144,000,000 + 36,000*P_{SD} \rightarrow$$
$$TP_{SC} = -20*P_{SD}^2 + 116,000*P_{SD} - 144,000,000.$$

Taking the derivative to P_{SD} and setting this equal to $0 \rightarrow d(TP_{SC})/d(P_{SD}) = 0 \rightarrow$
$-40*P_{SD} + 116,000 = 0 \rightarrow P_{SD} = €2,900$ and $Q = 80,000 - 20*2,900 = 22,000$

Supply Chain profit is 22,000 * (€2,900 − €1,800) = €24.2 mln and this is €6.05 mln (€24.2 mln coordinated − €18.15 mln uncoordinated) more than in the situation of *un*coordinated profit maximization. Notice that this number of €6.05 mln is the same as the profit of €6.05 million of Skodadeal in the first situation. Because the consumer price cannot be fixed by Skoda, a distribution key must be agreed upon between the two firms to divide the additional coordination profit. A simple one is to take the uncoordinated profit of Skoda of €12.2 million and assign 50% of the additional €6.05 mln and add the other 50% of €6.05 million to the original profit of Skodadeal of €6.05 million. Also, notice that the number of cars sold in this situation has doubled to 22,000.

Now we can see what happens – in the case of uncoordinated pricing – if Skoda starts a price campaign by discounting his price to the dealer with €100 to €2800, in the hope that Skodadeal will discount the consumer price also with €100. Using the Excel template and entering as a constraint in Solver that the selling price of Skoda to the dealer must be €2,800 gives via the price reaction curve an incentive to Skodadeal to drop the consumer price to €3,400: a discount of €50. In other words, the campaign of Skoda to promote sales by reducing its dealer price by €100 implies that Skodadeal passes on only €50 of this discount to the consumer. In this way, Skodadeal increases its profits at the cost of both the consumer and Skoda manufacturer and thwarts the intended efforts of Skoda to offer the car buyers a discount of €100.

Let us now focus on the impact on capacity usage using price changes. Assume that Skoda has currently an idle production capacity and wants to boost the sale of cars with 500 cars, amounting to 11,500 cars, to obtain a higher occupancy rate of its production line. Using the demand function $Q = 80{,}000 - 20*P_{SD}$, sales of 11,500 cars are achieved with a consumer price per car at €3,425. The old price was €3,450, so the dealer will have to offer the consumer a discount of only €25. However, if manufacturer Skoda offers this discount of €25 it will charge Skodadeal a price of $C_{Skoda} = €2{,}900 - €25 = €2{,}875$. But the dealer will not pass along the full discount to the consumer. The Excel model shows that Skodadeal will set his selling price at €3,437.50, a discount of €12.50 instead of €25.

The car sales for €3,437.50 give, using the demand function $Q = 11{,}250$ cars, an increase of only 250 cars instead of the targeted production increase of Skoda of 500 cars. 250 cars will remain unsold and in inventory at Skoda storage space. The intended production increase of manufacturer Skoda is partly thwarted by the dealer's pricing.[7] The screenshot of this example is shown below with cell B4 the price-cost relation $C_{Skoda} = 2*P_{SD} - 4{,}000$.

	A	B
1	Production cost Skoda	1800
2	Selling price consumer	3450
3	Quantity demanded curve	=80000-20*B2
4	Selling price Skoda to dealer	=2*B2-4000
5		
6	Revenues Skoda	=B3*B4
7	Costs Skoda	=B3*B1
8	Profit Skoda	=B6-B7
9		
10	Revenues Skodadeal	=B3*B2
11	Costs Skoda deal	=B3*B4
12	Profit Skodadeal	=B10-B11
13		
14	Optimal price dealer	=B2
15	Optima price Skoda C	=B4
16		
17	Suply Chain profit	=B8+B12

We now give the general solution for the price-reaction curve between a manufacturer and a retailer in the case of a linear demand curve $Q = b - a*P_{cons}$. P_{cons} is the retailer price for the final consumer, C_{ret} is the selling price of the manufacturer or wholesaler (= purchase cost of the retailer) and C_{prod} is the production cost of the manufacturer. The fully worked out derivations of these equations can be found in the Mathematical Appendix, but the results are shown below.

- $P_{cons} = \frac{3}{4}*b/a + \frac{1}{4}*C_{prod}$
- $Q = \frac{1}{4}*b - \frac{1}{4}*a*C_{prod}$
- $C_{ret} = \frac{1}{2}*b/a + \frac{1}{2}*C_{prod}$

Main Point: If supplier and retailer set their prices independently of each other, allowing each partner to maximize its own profit, the outcome for both parties is sub-optimal (this is an example of the Prisoner's dilemma). A proposed price discount of the manufacturer will not be passed along to the consumer for the full 100%. Optimizing SC profit leads to a better outcome for all partners in a Supply Chain.

Hedging exposure to price volatility of basic commodities

Revenue is defined as the quantity sold times the selling price – net of indirect taxes like VAT. Quantity and price are linked through the demand curve. *Gross profit* is the difference between Revenues and the Costs of Goods Sold. Uncertainty in revenues stems from two interrelated factors: uncertainty about the expected *quantity sold* and about the *selling price*. Obtaining more certainty about future quantity sold has already been discussed in the chapters about forecasting, inventory management, and in this chapter.

The second parameter is the selling price. Selling prices are the outcome of supply and demand and are shaped by the market structure and price strategies, which are the topic of this chapter.

The third parameter is production costs (Cost of Goods Sold), whose main constituents are direct and indirect labour costs and the purchase prices of (raw) materials, components, and parts used for production. Market prices of virtually all raw materials and commodities can be highly volatile and unpredictable. This applies to world market prices for agricultural produce, e.g. grain, maize, potatoes, rice, vegetables, coffee, cacao, tea, fruits, cotton, etc., husbandry produces (meat, milk, wool), metals (aluminum, iron, zinc), precious metals (cobalt, gold, silver, palladium), and energy (crude oil, gas, electricity). Consequently, they also affect oil-derived products, such as plastics. If one of these basic commodities constitutes a substantial part of the procurement costs, price volatility of raw materials will create unpredictable changes in the profit margin of the end product, sometimes even on a day-by-day basis. Most companies prefer certainty over uncertainty and deploy price mitigation strategies. They are willing to pay a price to obtain purchase price certainty. In recent decades, an extensive collection of financial tools has been developed to hedge commodity prices. We will list the three most commonly used ones:

– *Forward Contracts and Future contracts on commodities.*[8]
   In a forward or futures contract, buyer and seller agree upon a forward price for a commodity that will be traded between them in the future. Whatever the market price is on the date of delivery, the commodity is sold for the fixed preset forward price. If the commodity is traded over six months and the market price on that date is higher than the preset forward price, the buyer saves the difference at the cost of the seller. If the market price is lower than the forward price then the seller gains the difference at the cost of the buyer.

– *Option contracts on commodities*
   An option is the right to buy an underlying asset, such as a commodity, at a prespecified price on or before a predetermined date. This is a *call option*. If the right consists of selling a commodity at a prespecified price on or before a predetermined date it is called a *put option*.
   A major difference between a forward contract and an option is that, in a forward contract both parties commit themselves to buying and selling, while with a call option the buyer has the *right* to buy the commodity – but can waive it – and the seller has the obligation to deliver it. In case of a put option, the

seller has the right to sell – but can waive it – and the buyer the obligation to buy the commodity at the preset price.

– *Commodity swaps*

A swap is an agreement whereby a floating (or market) price is exchanged for a fixed price, or a fixed price is exchanged for a floating price, over a specified period(s) of time. The instrument is referred to as a swap because the transaction involves buyers and sellers 'swapping' cash flows with one another.

Swaps can be customized to the needs of the trading firms. Swaps are often used as a hedging instrument in the oil and gas industry, to hedge exposure to unpredictable oil and gas prices. Swaps allow them to lock in or fix the price they receive for their oil and gas production. In addition, swaps are also utilized to hedge exposure to price volatility of agriculture commodities, metals, and others.

Discussing in detail how these hedging instruments work and their economic valuation is beyond the scope of this book, and we refer to specialized books about financial and hedging instruments. Mitigation of price volatility at the upstream level in a Supply Chain can propagate downward and also reduce volatility in the downstream area of a supply chain. More stability of input prices can lead to more stable selling prices to firms operating in the lower echelons of the Supply Chain.[9]

Notes

1-9   See Instructor's Manual

11 Managing Bottlenecks and Waiting Lines in a Supply Chain

Managing bottlenecks and waiting lines in a Supply Chain

Source: Production plant Toyota Mirai. By Bertel Schmitt – Own work, CC BY-SA 3.0, https://commons.wikimedia.org/w/index.php?curid=15352623

A38 closure causes production delay at Toyota factory near Burnaston

29 -11- 2017

A spokeswoman said staff had been held up due to heavy delays on the roads. Toyota has suffered a delay to its production as a result of a multi-vehicle crash on the A38 highway. Work on the car manufacturer's production line was put back **26** minutes this morning due to **workers being held up in traffic delays** after a section of the A38 was closed. The dual carriageway was closed overnight until 9.15 am today after a crash between 2 lorries and a car. [...] At its fastest speed, a car can come off the end of the production line approximately every 60 seconds. But the firm said it would not have an impact on the day's output.

Source: https://www.derbytelegraph.co.uk/news/local-news/a38-closure-causes-production-delays-848620

Source: https://www.telegraph.co.uk/content/dam/business/2018/02/19/TELEM-MGLPICT000154878843_trans_NvBQzQNjv4BqF17Eb5QVe68VMN2NfamVAHLAVFmfq_yKsL9AoMk-8sQo.jpeg?imwidth=680

Police Urge People to Stop Calling Them about KFC Chicken Shortage

20-02-2018

The police are urging the public to stop calling in to report that Kentucky Fried Chicken has run out of chicken. The national "KFC crisis" has seen over half of the fast-food chain's 900 UK outlets close across the country. *Last week KFC changed its delivery contract to DHL, which blamed "operational issues" for its failure to deliver the chickens.* On Tuesday afternoon KFC said over half their restaurants were open and their teams were "working flat out to open the rest". A long queue of lorries delivering supplies to the DHL warehouse in Rugby, near Coventry, was seen today as drivers waited up to 10 hours for the goods to be unloaded. In a statement, KFC said: "We anticipate the number of closures will reduce today and over the coming days as our teams work flat-out all hours to clear the backlog." Each day more deliveries are being made. (…) In the meantime, KFC has set up an online service where those who cannot wait for fried chicken, can find the nearest branch that remains open.
Source: http://www.independent.co.uk/news/uk/

One of the attractive features of both planning and computer models is that they give accurately calculated solutions and, when using random variables, also an exact range of the uncertainty surrounding the solution. In the real-world economy and many other activities of daily life, everybody – individuals and organizations – is faced with unexpected events that can thwart all the expected or planned outcomes in terms of time, money, and other resources. Supply Chains are no exception to this general rule of experience. The disconformity between planned outcomes and real outcomes is a multifaceted cause-and-effect relationship in Supply Chain operations. In Chapter 1, we discussed that Supply Chain operations aim to achieve products, services, information, and persons (see the news item in the text box above as an example of workers) arriving at their final destination: 1. at the right time (temporal dimension); 2. at the right place (spatial dimension); 3. in the right quantities; and 4. meeting the correct quality or specifications.

Any mismatch between planning and realization reduces the performance level of a Supply Chain. The mismatch can be a mismatch in time, in the sense that the product or person arrives later – or sometimes earlier – than planned, in many cases as a result of congestion and delays.

A *spatial* or geographical mismatch means that the product or person arrives at the wrong destination. This can be due to incorrect package labels, suitcases deposited on the wrong conveyor belt or luggage trolley at an airport, or other errors in the logistics process.

A *quantitative* mismatch means that the customer receives more or fewer units than ordered, an error that can have many different causes.

A *qualitative* mismatch occurs if products are sent to the customer that do not meet the agreed requirements, e.g. a different model, colour, size, or even a completely different product.

Any combination of mismatches is not only possible but occurs, although some only rarely: the wrong product arrives in the wrong quantities at the wrong place at the wrong moment. Reducing the probability of errors in quantity and quality depends partly on the quality of the supplier's administrative organization – and sometimes also that of the customer. It also depends on the supplier's corporate quality control system. Improving the administrative system by implementing, for example, a system of checks and double-checks for outgoing shipments can reduce these kinds of errors.

The risk of spatial errors can be reduced by implementing regular checks and monitoring at all levels in the Supply Chain – the manufacturer level, the logistics level, and the distribution centre – before orders are dispatched to the final customer. The widespread use of bar codes and RFID tags on containers, packages, and also letters sent by ordinary mail, makes it possible to trace the path of an item in real-time over its entire journey, and has contributed to a relative reduction in the number of misdeliveries. Finally, deviation from the scheduled arrival time, which is the main topic of this chapter, in the form of *congestion* and *delays* is a frequent cause of out-of-schedule arrival.

If we consider the Supply Chain from upstream (raw materials) to downstream (final customer) with all its intermediate stages, a delay can occur at any stage and can propagate and even amplify itself moving downward in the chain. There are countless causes of delays in a Supply Chain. To mention a few: raw materials and components arrive too late so that the manufacturer has to start production later than planned. Raw materials can be on time, but the machine set-up takes longer than expected or needs repair. When production consists of different stages, every stage faces the risk of a delay. Once the product has been completed and is ready for shipment, the carrier of the freight company can arrive too late for dispatch. Further down the Supply Chain, any kind of delay during the transit journey can take place – as discussed in the chapter about Logistics and Infrastructure – and, consequently, this results in delays at every subsequent stage downstream in the chain. Most business organizations know from experience which part or stage of the Supply Chain process has the highest probability of delays. This activity becomes a *bottleneck*. At the Supply Chain level, it is important to identify bottlenecks throughout the entire chain, and coordination of interface operations between two subsequent stages needs special attention to achieve optimal SC performance. We define a bottleneck as any event that reduces the flow of activities in the Supply Chain from its optimal performance level, expressed in time units, and that decreases customer satisfaction.

Some organizations will include the time of a bottleneck delay in their delivery calculations when there is no straightforward solution to avoid the bottleneck. They schedule a random arrival time by superimposing a probability density function on this event and informing the customer about a later delivery date and time. If, under normal circumstances, a shipment by truck, for example, can drive a distance of 200 kilometres in 2.5 hours, but the customer is located in a densely populated area, where daily morning traffic jams delay arrivals by an average of 30 minutes, the logistics route planner will include this time delay in his freight planning for the different customers. Queueing or waiting lines are simply defined as a situation where capacity is insufficient to meet demand, delaying the progress of a process or activity. In other words, queueing is a consequence of process congestion. Economically, queueing entails extra costs and, psychologically, leads to frustration, dissatisfied customers, irritation, impatience, and sometimes irrational and unpredictable behaviour. Analysing queueing problems is not a new topic[1] and belongs to the field of Management Science and Operations Research.

Over the years, management scientists have developed more complex models to quantify queues, uncover the causes of queueing, and to find solutions to effectively manage queues, and, if possible, get rid of them or at least significantly reduce their size and frequency. Queueing or waiting line models range from relatively simple to very complex, and some models are borrowed from the physical sciences. The topic of waiting lines in a Supply Chain can be considered a special application of a more general Supply Chain phenomenon, i.e. risk propagation, risk amplification, and risk mitigation in networks.

Main Point: delays can occur at any stage of a Supply Chain. Delays can propagate, amplify, and even strengthen each other throughout the chain until the bottom stage, i.e. the customer level. A major cause of Supply Chain delays is the emergence of queues at bottlenecks, which diminish the optimal flow of activities. A critical element for congestion is the <u>interface</u> between two stages in a Supply Chain. In most cases, queues are a consequence of a mismatch between (local) capacity and demand at that stage of activity. Delays increase Supply Chain costs and form a waste of valuable resources.

Basic elements and a queueing model structure

Queuing models share some common traits and features that give us a basic structure for analysing the system and that reveal the dynamics and behaviour of a queue, helping us to determine its basic characteristics and then look for potential solutions. We will give a concise description of the characteristics of queueing models with a particular focus on a Supply Chain.

Tasks, products, or persons are generated by an input source – which is usually the stage that precedes entry into a Supply Chain. They will join a queue if the service they are going to receive is not immediately available. At specific moments, a queue member is selected for service and once the service has been performed, they leave the system and move one step further down the chain.

The input source is called a *population* and refers to the activities or persons requiring service. The population can be *finite* or *infinite:* a large number can be approximated by infinity. Usually, the queue length is assumed to be limited, like the number of customers waiting at a bus stop for public transportation. For now, they are theoretically unlimited or extremely large, which can be approximated by infinite.

An important queue characteristic is the statistical *arrival* pattern at the queue. Although many statistical distribution functions are possible, the most common one is that the process of joining a queue is generated by a Poisson distribution. This arrival distribution gives information about the number of arrivals joining the queue during a specific time interval. If the arrival pattern of customers is known, one can calculate the time between two consecutive arrivals, this is called the *interarrival time.*

Another characteristic is the queue *discipline* discussed in the next section. The server or service facility is the asset or person that offers the service to the queue members. The number of servers can range from one to many. Servers are, e.g. the number of employees at the luggage check-in counters at an airport, the number of lanes at a carwash station, the number of service employees attending incoming telephone calls from customers at a helpdesk.

The time needed for a service is generally modelled as a random variable following a probability distribution. A common distribution in many queueing models is that *interarrival* times are *independent and identically distributed* and that all *service* times are independent and identically distributed both with an exponential distribution.

Queue discipline

The *queue discipline* refers to the order in which the members – persons, tangible or intangible assets – waiting in a queue are served by the server(s). We will discuss some common disciplines.

Queue discipline *First Come, First Served* [*FCFS*]
This is the most common queue discipline. FCFS means that the first person in the row is served first and the last to join the row is served last. It is not necessary for the people or assets to stand at the front of the row. A common system whereby customers draw a paper ticket with a printed serial number is also an FCFS-discipline. If the waiting time is long, they can even go out for a walk or do some shopping without losing their position in the queue.

Queue discipline based on **urgency** *or urgency declarations*
This is a common practice in the health industry. Patients who arrive by ambulance in a hospital with more severe injuries or diseases are treated before patients with lesser injuries, even if the latter ones were already waiting for a long time before the patient brought in by ambulance. Patients with an urgent referral from their general practitioner will also receive medical treatment, such as an operation, before people who are already on the waiting list.

Priority-based *queue discipline*
People who have, for example, a membership card and who have paid more money for a certain service get priority over people who are not members. A typical example is road-side assistance (Dutch: *Wegenwacht*). In bad weather conditions, drivers whose car has broken down and who have a membership card of the road-side assistance organization are served before non-members with a broken car.

Pre-emptive versus *non-pre-emptive* priority rights can be distinguished within priority-based discipline. In the pre-emptive case, the service offered to someone is temporarily interrupted if a customer with preemptive priority rights joins the queue. In the case of non-preemptive priority rights, the person who is already served will be dealt with before the person with non-preemptive priority rights joins the queue.[2] Travellers with business-class tickets boarding an airplane first, followed by the economy class ticketholders, is also an example of priority-based discipline, where the priority depends on the price paid for the tickets.

Other examples are garages. When a garage serviceman is repairing a broken truck and a logistics company with pre-emptive priority brings in its broken truck, the mechanics of the garage will stop working on the current truck and spend their time on the truck with a priority claim. If the priority is non-preemptive, the mechanics will first finish the truck they are working on and then start working on the broken truck in the waiting line with priority. All other trucks waiting for repair without priority will have to wait until all trucks with priority rights have been served.[3]

Some companies even apply a hierarchy of priority levels, the highest priority level served first, the second priority level next, the third priority level as the third group up to the items or persons without any priority in line. In most situations, high-priority customers will pay more for the same service than low-priority customers.

Queue discipline based on **grades** or merits

Some academic institutions admit a limited number of students for specific courses and they admit students in order of the grades obtained in high-school exams or grades obtained in IQ tests. Students with low scores are not admitted, even if they have already been waiting for years to be admitted.

Last Come, First served

This is not a common queue discipline in practice. An example *could* be a truck loaded with packages that embark on a milk run, visiting many customers. Packages for customers visited first in the run will be stored in the trailer closest to the trailer doors, to avoid the truck driver having to empty part of his trailer before he reaches the packages for his customer stored at the rear of the trailer.

Random selection

Order of service is based on random numbers, like in a lottery. In the past, this system was applied in the Netherlands for admitting students to courses with a maximum capacity, and all applicants were treated equally without any reference to their school exam grades.

Fixed time slots

The last queueing discipline discussed here is the fixed time slot. In this system, the organization that offers the service assigns people or assets a scheduled time slot, usually after making an appointment. This queueing discipline is applied in hospitals, general practices, maintenance services in garages, and many other forms of services. Using time slots reduces the actual waiting time once the customer arrives at the physical location for the appointment, but the time between *making* the appointment and receiving the actual service – especially in the healthcare industry – can be quite long. The waiting time is shifted from waiting in a queue of people to waiting until the date of the appointed time slot.

Queueing behaviour

In one of a series of memorable advertisements for which it has become justly famous, Federal Express (the overnight package delivery service) noted that: "Waiting is frustrating, demoralizing, agonizing, aggravating, annoying, time-consuming and incredibly expensive."[4] Queueing behaviour analyses how people who are waiting in a queue, or who plan to join a queue, behave or react when they are faced with (long) queues. We will briefly discuss four different human queueing behaviours and see the impact of each behaviour on the average queue length.

1. Balking

In queueing theory, balking occurs when a person who wants to make use of a service arrives at a queue and observes that the waiting line is too long, and then decides not to join the queue. He or she will either go to another store, come back at another moment, or look for alternatives. *Balking implies that the queue length will not grow and remain constant.*

2. Reneging

Reneging occurs when a person who is already waiting *in* the queue – or is waiting on the phone to be helped by a helpdesk – thinks that the waiting time is too long and leaves the queue, or breaks off the phone call. The effect of reneging is that the average queue length will *shorten* by one unit. Balking, *reneging*, and the combination of both contribute to the situation of *finite queue length.*

3. Jockeying

Jockeying can only take place if the queue consists of at least two lines or lanes. People standing in (the rear of) one line observing that the other line is shorter, or has less waiting time, will switch to (the rear of) another line. Jockeying is a *zero-sum game*: one waiting lane will grow and the other shorten, but the average number of people waiting for a service or for moving forward stays the same.

Jockeying is a frequently observed queueing behaviour in traffic jams, whereby motorists switch lanes.

4. *Jumping the queue*

Jumping the queue means that a person moves to a front position in the queue instead of joining the queue at the rear. This behaviour is considered very unfair and unethical, because it means other people have to wait longer. It is even more unethical if the person advances in the waiting line by offering bribes.[5] The effect of jumping the queue on the average queue length depends on the initial position of the jumper. If the jumper comes from *outside* the queue, the average queue length grows. If the queue jumper is from *inside,* already waiting in the queue, and jumps from the rear to a front position, the average queue length will remain constant. The picture below illustrates the four queueing behaviours (it omits queue jumping).

Queueing system

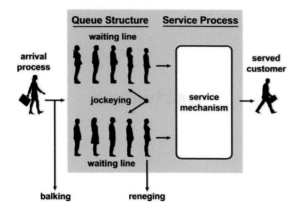

Source: https://thumbs.dreamstime.com/b/waiting-line-queueing-system-structure-process-104617427.jpg

Other dimensions of queues: Psychological and health effects, and alleviating the negative psychological impact of waiting

Many studies have been conducted on how people experience waiting, particularly waiting for a long time. Experiments have been carried out to see what measures and solutions can alleviate negative waiting experiences. It is common knowledge that the vast majority of people do not like waiting and that enduring the hardships of long waiting times requires a lot of *patience*.[6] For business organizations, *waiting* customers can lead to *lost* customers, lost orders, and a downgrading of the corporate reputation. Waiting is part of the *transaction costs* in the customer's purchase process for a good or service. It has a *negative* utility in terms of microeconomics consumer theory.

A company offering price discounts to improve its competitive position can completely undo any increased demand by letting consumers wait too long.[7] They will therefore try to minimize the negative impact of waiting and make waiting more acceptable for their customers. Two policy approaches are used to manage queues, particularly when customers have to wait often and long. A first policy is to structurally shorten the average queue length and waiting time by increasing the number of servers or improving the skills of the people offering the service, so that they spend less time per service or customer. The second is to make the waiting experience less unpleasant for the people in the waiting line. Below are a few common practices that make, particularly *unforeseen,* waiting *more acceptable.*

1. *Occupied time feels shorter than unoccupied time*
Giving people a useful activity during their waiting time makes waiting more acceptable than being bored while waiting. Offering entertainment or a useful pastime is frequently used. Examples are playing music when waiting for a phone line to be answered by a service person at a helpdesk. Or giving the menu card to guests just entering a busy restaurant, so that they can read the menu while they wait to be served by a waiter.

2. *Uncertain waits are longer than certain waits*
Offering information about how long people have to wait, approximately, makes waiting more acceptable than leaving people in the queue uninformed about how long they still have to wait. For example, announcements about train delays on the screens displayed in stations are accompanied by an indication of the duration of the delay. Electronic matrix boards above the highway give information about the expected duration of traffic jams.

3. *Unexplained waits are longer than explained waits*
Stating the reason *why* people have to wait before they receive the actual service makes the wait more acceptable than not giving them any reason for a delay or queue. As an example, railway companies not only inform travellers about the duration of a train delay, but often also state the reason for the delay.

4. *Unfair waits are longer than equitable waits*
Unfair waits, e.g. as the result of someone jumping the queue, are harder to endure and can cause considerable irritation.

The last dimension focuses on the health aspects of waiting. This applies particularly to car and truck drivers waiting frequently in traffic jams. The quote below originates from the online scientific news site Phys.org, from 25 August 2016:

> "With millions of motorists in the UK set to hit the road for the bank holiday weekend, drivers have been urged to close windows and turn off fans while in traffic jams to avoid breathing in dangerously high levels of air pollution.
> The latest research from the University of Surrey has shown that simple adjustment to your car's ventilation system while sitting in traffic jams can greatly affect your exposure to toxic fumes by up to 76%. In traffic jams, or at red traffic lights with other vehicles stationary in front, research has shown that if we close the car windows and switch off the fan, this gave us the lowest exposure to pollutants. It is also safe to put fans onto the setting where they re-circulate air within the car without drawing polluted air in from outside. In the study, scientists found that when the windows were closed but the fan was on, the exposure was usually the highest while being in traffic since the air outside the vehicle is generally much more polluted compared with the air inside the car. Switching on the fan sucks the dirty air from outside to inside the vehicle resulting in an accumulation of pollutants in the car."[8]

Although waiting in a traffic jam is not the only case that negatively affects people's health, it is a frequent one, particularly in densely populated areas and in cities. Also waiting outdoors in extreme weather conditions (too cold or too hot) negatively affects the physical well-being of people.

Queues and delays in Supply Chains

After discussing queues and queue management in general, we now focus on queues and delays in Supply Chains. Supply Chain operations consist of a sequence of activities from the upstream stage to the downstream stage. Delays can and do occur at every stage, either within facilities or while goods are moving between facilities.[9] Queues manifest themselves in the form of people lining up, the lining up of moving assets in a production process, and even in the form of information stuck or lost somewhere between the source and its destination.

At the manufacturing level, delays occur when work-in-process lines up in front of a work station; at distribution centre, when trucks are lining up at docking stations; during order execution in online distribution centres, especially during periods of peak sales; during logistics at border controls; in retail stores when customers line up in front of check-out points, and many more.

An additional characteristic of Supply Chain delays is the *cumulative effect* and *chain reactions*. A delay in an upstream activity can propagate downward and cause delays at all other lower stages in the Supply Chain. This affects, among others, *intermodality* shipments.[10] If items shipped are parts or raw materials needed in a production process, any delay can thwart the production planning and all subsequent downstream activities. Management scientists have developed mathematical models to analyse delays in networks with chain reactions and cumulative effects. One of those networks is called the *Jackson network*. But this model is mathematically too complex and beyond the scope of this text to go into the details. Planners of Supply Chain activities will, in some cases, take into account delays in their planning and assign a random duration time to an activity or shipment, instead of using a deterministic activity time. Planning models with random activity times can usually only be solved using computer simulations.

Main Point: Three dimensions of queues have been discussed in this section. The first was the queue discipline that refers to the order in which persons or items waiting in a queue are served. The second was queueing behaviours and their impact on the average queue length and waiting time. The third dimension discussed was management tools to alleviate the negative psychological experience of waiting. Waiting customers hurt business performance and customer satisfaction and can lead to lost customers and lost sales. An extra dimension to waiting in a Supply Chain is the accumulation effect and chain reactions of delays. Coordination among the different Supply Chain stages, by incorporating uncertainty due to waiting, e.g. safety inventory, in the planning process, can mitigate these accumulation effects.

The characteristics of exponential distribution

Our focus now turns to two basic models and random distribution functions frequently used in queueing analysis, namely, the *Poisson* distribution function and the *exponential* distribution function. The most commonly used distribution function in queueing systems is the *exponential function*, used to model *interarrival times* and the *service time* for service activities. This function meets one of the criteria expressed in a quote attributed to Albert Einstein, that a model should be *"as simple as possible, but not simpler."* The exponential distribution is relatively simple and has characteristics that make it suitable for queuing models. It also has reasonable predictive power, and is mathematically tractable. We will discuss some of its properties below. We define T as the *exponentially distributed random variable* of *interarrival* times and it can also be used as the random variable for the service time. t is a numerical value for which we want to find the probability. The formula of its continuous density function is:

$$f_T(t) = P[T = t] = \mu^* e^{-\mu^* t} \text{ for } t > 0 \text{ and } f_T(t) = 0 \text{ for } t < 0.$$

The cumulative probability function is

$$F_T(t) = P[T \leq t] = 1 - e^{-\mu^* t} \text{ for all } t > 0.$$

The expected value

$$E[T] = \frac{1}{\mu}$$

The variance

$$\sigma^2 = \frac{1}{\mu^2}$$

One of the properties of the exponential distribution is that the probability of the interarrival time T during a time slot of Δt minutes is higher for *earlier* time slots during the considered period than for *later* time slots of the same length. In formula:

$$P[0 \leq T \leq \Delta t] > P[t \leq T \leq t + \Delta t], \text{ with } t > 0.$$

This is a consequence of the *monotonic* decrease of an exponential function. A second property is that if the interarrival time T shifts with an additional t minutes, the new probability is independent of the time that has already passed by. In formula:

$$P[T > t + \Delta t \mid T > \Delta t] = P[T > t]$$

This property of exponential distribution is described as a *lack of memory*, whereby the remaining time until the next arrival is independent of the moment of the last arrival. This can be shown in the following steps using basic probability rules:

$$P[T > (t + \Delta t) \mid T > \Delta t] = P[T > (t + \Delta t) \cap T > \Delta t] / P[T > \Delta t] \rightarrow \text{if } T > t + \Delta t \text{ then by}$$
definition also $T > \Delta t$.

We can skip the second part of $P[T > (t + \Delta t) \cap T > \Delta t]$ and it will become $P[T > (t + \Delta t)]$. The result is $P[T > (t + \Delta t)] / P[T > \Delta t] \rightarrow$ applying the cumulative exponential distribution function:

$\frac{e^{-\mu^*(t+\Delta t)}}{e^{-\mu^*\Delta t}} \to e^{-\mu^*t} = P[T > t]$, where we used the fact that $e^{-\mu^*(t+\Delta t)} = e^{-\mu^*t} * e^{-\mu^*\Delta t}$.

Another property of exponential distribution function: if the time that elapses between two consecutive events follows an exponential distribution with parameter μ, then the frequency of occurrences X(t) during a fixed time slot of length t, like the number of customers joining a queue in one hour, follows a *Poisson* distribution with formula

$$P[X(t) = n] = \frac{(\mu * t)^n * e^{-\mu^*t}}{n!}$$

If the number of arrivals follows a Poisson distribution, then during each time slot of fixed length the probability of a new arrival is the *same* and independent of the moment of the preceding arrival.

Example

At a filling station located on a local road, the number of cars visiting the station to get fuel (indicated by the random variable X) follows a Poisson distribution function with an average of $\lambda = 12$ cars per hour. The filling station has only one petrol dispensing pump for unleaded petrol. The probabilities of 0 up to a maximum of 28 cars arriving in one hour are displayed below, together with the cumulative probabilities. They are graphed in the associated probability chart. The Excel formula view is shown in the second screenshot. The Poisson function in the Excel function library is POISSON.DIST

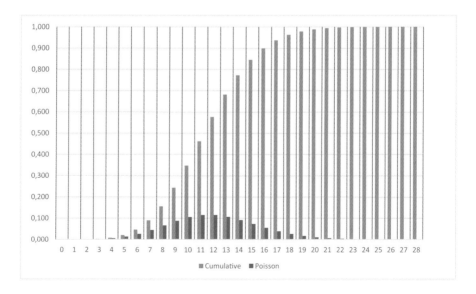

	A	B	C	D	E
1	# of arrivals	Poisson	$\lambda =$	12	per hour
2	Arrivals	Probability	Cumulative		
3	0	0.0000	0.0000		
4	1	0.0001	0.0001		
5	2	0.0004	0.0005		
6	3	0.0018	0.0023		
7	4	0.0053	0.0076		
8	5	0.0127	0.0203		
9	6	0.0255	0.0458		
10	7	0.0437	0.0895		
11	8	0.0655	0.1550		
12	9	0.0874	0.2424		
13	10	0.1048	0.3472		
14	11	0.1144	0.4616		
15	12	0.1144	0.5760		
16	13	0.1056	0.6815		
17	14	0.0905	0.7720		
18	15	0.0724	0.8444		
19	16	0.0543	0.8987		
20	17	0.0383	0.9370		
21	18	0.0255	0.9626		
22	19	0.0161	0.9787		
23	20	0.0097	0.9884		
24	21	0.0055	0.9939		
25	22	0.0030	0.9970		
26	23	0.0016	0.9985		
27	24	0.0008	0.9993		
28	25	0.0004	0.9997		
29	26	0.0002	0.9999		
30	27	0.0001	0.9999		
31	28	0.0000	1.0000		

	A	B	C	D	E
1	# of arrivals	Poisson		λ = 12	per hour
2	Arrivals	Probability	Cumulative		
3	0	=POISSON.DIST(A3;$D$1;0)	=POISSON.DIST(A3;$D$1;1)		
4	1	=POISSON.DIST(A4;$D$1;0)	=POISSON.DIST(A4;$D$1;1)		
5	2	=POISSON.DIST(A5;$D$1;0)	=POISSON.DIST(A5;$D$1;1)		
6	3	=POISSON.DIST(A6;$D$1;0)	=POISSON.DIST(A6;$D$1;1)		
7	4	=POISSON.DIST(A7;$D$1;0)	=POISSON.DIST(A7;$D$1;1)		
8	5	=POISSON.DIST(A8;$D$1;0)	=POISSON.DIST(A8;$D$1;1)		
9	6	=POISSON.DIST(A9;$D$1;0)	=POISSON.DIST(A9;$D$1;1)		
10	7	=POISSON.DIST(A10;$D$1;0)	=POISSON.DIST(A10;$D$1;1)		
11	8	=POISSON.DIST(A11;$D$1;0)	=POISSON.DIST(A11;$D$1;1)		
12	9	=POISSON.DIST(A12;$D$1;0)	=POISSON.DIST(A12;$D$1;1)		
13	10	=POISSON.DIST(A13;$D$1;0)	=POISSON.DIST(A13;$D$1;1)		
14	11	=POISSON.DIST(A14;$D$1;0)	=POISSON.DIST(A14;$D$1;1)		
15	12	=POISSON.DIST(A15;$D$1;0)	=POISSON.DIST(A15;$D$1;1)		
16	13	=POISSON.DIST(A16;$D$1;0)	=POISSON.DIST(A16;$D$1;1)		
17	14	=POISSON.DIST(A17;$D$1;0)	=POISSON.DIST(A17;$D$1;1)		
18	15	=POISSON.DIST(A18;$D$1;0)	=POISSON.DIST(A18;$D$1;1)		
19	16	=POISSON.DIST(A19;$D$1;0)	=POISSON.DIST(A19;$D$1;1)		
20	17	=POISSON.DIST(A20;$D$1;0)	=POISSON.DIST(A20;$D$1;1)		
21	18	=POISSON.DIST(A21;$D$1;0)	=POISSON.DIST(A21;$D$1;1)		
22	19	=POISSON.DIST(A22;$D$1;0)	=POISSON.DIST(A22;$D$1;1)		
23	20	=POISSON.DIST(A23;$D$1;0)	=POISSON.DIST(A23;$D$1;1)		
24	21	=POISSON.DIST(A24;$D$1;0)	=POISSON.DIST(A24;$D$1;1)		
25	22	=POISSON.DIST(A25;$D$1;0)	=POISSON.DIST(A25;$D$1;1)		
26	23	=POISSON.DIST(A26;$D$1;0)	=POISSON.DIST(A26;$D$1;1)		
27	24	=POISSON.DIST(A27;$D$1;0)	=POISSON.DIST(A27;$D$1;1)		
28	25	=POISSON.DIST(A28;$D$1;0)	=POISSON.DIST(A28;$D$1;1)		
29	26	=POISSON.DIST(A29;$D$1;0)	=POISSON.DIST(A29;$D$1;1)		
30	27	=POISSON.DIST(A30;$D$1;0)	=POISSON.DIST(A30;$D$1;1)		
31	28	=POISSON.DIST(A31;$D$1;0)	=POISSON.DIST(A31;$D$1;1)		

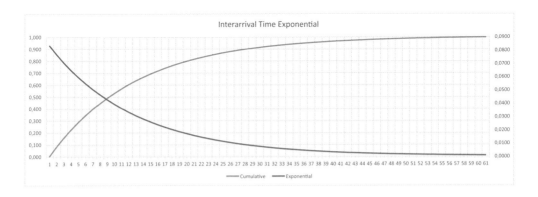

Interarrival Time Exponential

	A	B	C	D	E	F	G
37			μ =	0.0833	hour =	5	minutes
38	Interarrival per 2 minutes	Exponential	Cumulative	Formula			
39	0	0.0833	0.000	0.000			
40	1	0.0767	0.080	0.080			
41	2	0.0705	0.154	0.154			
42	3	0.0649	0.221	0.221			
43	4	0.0597	0.283	0.283			
44	5	0.0549	0.341	0.341			
45	6	0.0505	0.393	0.393			
46	7	0.0465	0.442	0.442			
47	8	0.0428	0.487	0.487			
48	9	0.0394	0.528	0.528			
49	10	0.0362	0.565	0.565			
50	11	0.0333	0.600	0.600			
51	12	0.0307	0.632	0.632			
52	13	0.0282	0.662	0.662			
53	14	0.0260	0.689	0.689			
54	15	0.0239	0.713	0.713			
55	16	0.0220	0.736	0.736			
56	17	0.0202	0.757	0.757			
57	18	0.0186	0.777	0.777			
58	19	0.0171	0.795	0.795			
59	20	0.0157	0.811	0.811		0.29	
60	21	0.0145	0.826	0.826			
61	22	0.0133	0.840	0.840			
62	23	0.0123	0.853	0.853			
63	24	0.0113	0.865	0.865			
64	25	0.0104	0.875	0.875			
65	26	0.0095	0.885	0.885			
66	27	0.0088	0.895	0.895			
67	28	0.0081	0.903	0.903			
68	29	0.0074	0.911	0.911			
69	30	0.0068	0.918	0.918			
70	31	0.0063	0.924	0.924			
71	32	0.0058	0.931	0.931			
72	33	0.0053	0.936	0.936			
73	34	0.0049	0.941	0.941			
74	35	0.0045	0.946	0.946			
75	36	0.0041	0.950	0.950			
76	37	0.0038	0.954	0.954			
77	38	0.0035	0.958	0.958			
78	39	0.0032	0.961	0.961			
79	40	0.0030	0.964	0.964			
80	41	0.0027	0.967	0.967			
81	42	0.0025	0.970	0.970			
82	43	0.0023	0.972	0.972			
83	44	0.0021	0.974	0.974			
84	45	0.0020	0.976	0.976			
85	46	0.0018	0.978	0.978			
86	47	0.0017	0.980	0.980			
87	48	0.0015	0.982	0.982			
88	49	0.0014	0.983	0.983			
89	50	0.0013	0.984	0.984			
90	51	0.0012	0.986	0.986			
91	52	0.0011	0.987	0.987			
92	53	0.0010	0.988	0.988			
93	54	0.0009	0.989	0.989			
94	55	0.0009	0.990	0.990			
95	56	0.0008	0.991	0.991			
96	57	0.0007	0.991	0.991			
97	58	0.0007	0.992	0.992			
98	59	0.0006	0.993	0.993			
99	60	0.0006	0.993	0.993			
100	Expected Valu	12					
101	Variance	125.04					

The probability chart is shown above, and the probabilities are calculated using the Exponential function EXPON.DIST. in the Excel function library. If we focus on the *interarrival* time between two cars entering the filling station, we expect that: if, on average, 12 cars per hour enter the filling station, the expected time (Y) between two arrivals is 1/12 of an hour or about five minutes. It can be shown that if the number of arrivals per fixed time slot follows a Poisson distribution, then the interarrival time follows an exponential distribution[11] with parameter $\mu = \frac{1}{\lambda}$, which, in our example, is 1/12 = 0,0833 hour. The mean value of the exponential function is $1/\mu$ = 12 minutes, and the variance is $1/\mu^2$ = 144 minutes. The probability that the owner of the filling station has to wait, for example, more than 15 minutes before the next customer arrives can be found in the table as

$$P[Y > 15] = 1 - P[Y \le 15] = 1 - 0{,}713 = 0.287 \text{ or } 28.7\%.$$

We can also calculate this probability by using the formula of the cumulative exponential distribution function $[1 - e^{-\mu * Y}] \rightarrow 1 - (1 - e^{-0{,}833 * 15}) = 0.2865 \approx 28.7\%$.

Service time distributions

Waiting in a queue before being served is only one part of a queuing system. The other part is the service or the treatment time itself, the main reason that somebody joins a waiting line. In our example above, the service is filling the car's petrol tank with unleaded petrol. Some services require more or less constant amounts of time per customer, like the time needed to fill a cup with coffee from a vending machine, standardized medical treatments like taking an X-ray at a hospital, the time spent in a rollercoaster in a theme park, or even the time a prisoner spends in prison, which is fixed by the verdict pronounced by the judge. In that situation, the only random variable is the number of people waiting for that (dis)service, calculated with the formulas listed above. The total time the person or asset spends in a such queueing system is the sum of the uncertain waiting time plus the constant service time. However, constant service time is an exception rather than the rule.

Many service activities, in particular those serving human persons, like in shops, hospitals, consultancy talks, restaurants, at the check-out counters of a store, exhibit random properties and are modelled using a probability distribution function.[12] Uncertainty regarding the service duration and the duration of production activities is often modelled with the exponential probability function, as already stated. In the analysis of queuing systems two states are distinguished: the *transient* state and the *steady-state*.

A transient state refers to the initial or starting position and an initial state strongly affects the number of people in the system. For example, a retail store opening its doors for the public at 8.00 am with a customer queue impatiently waiting outside to enter the premises to buy their stuff, shows different queue dynamics than analysing a similar queue with the initial state at 2.00 pm, when many customers have already entered and left the store, and the system tends towards a dynamic equilibrium.

A queueing system consists of the queue and its servers. The object of a queue can be people, tangible assets, like cars at a petrol station, or intangible assets, like information requests by mail waiting for a reply. Our discussion will focus on the queueing dynamics of *steady-state* conditions. To facilitate the notation of queue characteristics a standardized terminology and notation, called the *Kendall* notation, is used. This Kendall notation has three symbols each separated by a slash (/) and looks like 1/2/3. The *first* characteristic (1) refers to the arrival process. It can be M representing a Markovian[13] interarrival time, which is mostly the exponential distribution function. The other symbol is D standing for deterministic or non-random time.

The *second* characteristic (/2) refers to the service process. It can also be M for Markovian service time with an exponential distribution function, G standing for general service time (any non-exponential distribution function), or D for deterministic or non-random service time.

The *third* number (/3) refers to the number of servers available. In our previous example, the number of petrol dispensing pumps at the petrol station.

To characterize the queueing process, the following symbols with their associated meaning are used:

P_n = the probability of exactly n people in the queueing system[13]

$N(t)$ = the number of people/assets in the system at time t

s = number of (parallel) servers of the system

λ = mean arrival rate of new people/assets (mostly Poisson distributed)

μ = mean service rate of the service (measured as the # of customers completing service per unit of time)

ρ = the utilization factor of the server(s)

L_s = mean or expected system length = # people in the system (queue + service):
$\sum_{n=0}^{\infty} n * P_n$

L_q = expected length of the queue alone calculated as $\sum_{n=s}^{\infty} (n - s) * P_n$

W_s = expected waiting time in the system *in*cluding service time

W_q = expected waiting time in the queue (*ex*cluding service time)

The main queue characteristics for a model consisting of s servers and an infinite input population can be described by the following queue performance metrics:[16]

$\rho = \lambda/(s*\mu)$ and indicates the % time one or more of the joint s servers are busy.

P_0 is the probability that there are *no* items or persons in the system $\left(\sum_{n=0}^{s-1} \frac{(\lambda/\mu)^n}{n!} + \frac{(\lambda/\mu)^s}{s!} * \left(\frac{s*\mu}{s*\mu - \lambda} \right) \right)$

$L_q = \frac{P_0 * (\lambda/\mu)^{s+1}}{s!* (1-\lambda/\mu)^2}$ with L_q the expected number of persons in the queue computed as $\left(\sum_{n=s}^{\infty} (n-s)* P_n \right)$

$P_n = \frac{(\lambda/\mu)^n}{n!} * P_0$ if $0 \le s \le n$ and $P_n = \frac{(\lambda/\mu)^n}{s!* s^{n-s}} * P_0$ if $n > s$

$W_q = \frac{L_q}{\lambda}$ is the expected waiting time in the queue.

$W_s = W_q + 1/\mu$ is the expected waiting time in the *system* (queue + service).

$L_s = \lambda*(W_q + 1/\mu) = L_q + \frac{\lambda}{\mu}.$

If there is *one* server in the system with infinite (large) population and First Come, First Served (FCFS) discipline, λ the arrival rate and μ the service rate, the system properties can be summarized to:

Average queue length	$L_q = \frac{\lambda^2}{\mu*(\mu - \lambda)}$
Average waiting time in the queue	$W_q = L_q/\lambda$
Average system length	$L_s = \frac{\lambda}{(\mu - \lambda)}$
Average waiting time in the system	$W_s = L_s/\lambda$
Probability of exactly n persons in the system	$P_n = \left(1 - \frac{\lambda}{\mu}\right) * \left(\frac{\lambda}{\mu}\right)^n$

If the service time is ***constant*** the system properties become for

Queue length $L_q = \frac{\lambda^2}{2*\mu*(\mu - \lambda)}$

System length $L_s = L_q + \frac{\lambda}{\mu}.$

The formulas for the corresponding average *waiting* times with constant service time are similar to those with exponentially distributed service time.

Example

A logistics company ships goods by van from a Distribution Centre (A) to the venue of a customer (B) over a local road. The road has only one filling station, halfway between A and B, and the van fuels unleaded petrol, for which the station has only one petrol-dispensing pump available. The average driving time from A to B without fuelling is two hours. The arrival of cars at the petrol station for unleaded fuel follows a Poisson distribution with mean value $\lambda = 20$ cars per hour on a weekly day. We assume that the filling time per car is constant on $\mu = 2$ minutes per car (a filling capacity of 30 cars per hour). We must calculate the expected travel time to venue B when the van fuels during transit.

Solution

This is a M/D/1 queuing system. The time that the car stays in the petrol station is the waiting time plus the service time at the filling pump. The interarrival time at the petrol station follows a Poisson distribution with λ = 20 cars per hour. The interarrival time is 1/20 hour = 3 minutes. The maximum number of cars that can fill their tanks at the only petrol-dispensing pump in an hour is 30 cars (60 minutes / 2 minutes per car). The average number of cars waiting in the queue to fuel at the single server (petrol dispensing pump for unleaded petrol) is

$$L_q = \frac{\lambda^2}{2 * \mu * (\mu - \lambda)} = \frac{20^2}{2 * 30 * (30 - 20)} = 400 \,/\, 600 = 0.666 \text{ cars.}$$

The system length $L_s = L_q + \frac{\lambda}{\mu} = 0.666 + 20/30 = 1.33$ cars. The corresponding time spent at the petrol station $W_s = L_s/\lambda = 1.33 \,/\, 20 = 0.0665$ hour = 4 minutes. Total travel time between A and B becomes 120 (driving) + 4 (petrol station) = 124 minutes.

Queueing networks

Up to now, we have considered queueing systems with one or more servers and focused on some of the queue characteristics, like average queue length, average waiting time, and the probability to find n people or assets in the queue. In a Supply Chain network, there are several interrelated queueing systems when goods are in transit from the upstream to the downstream level of the chain. Queues in a Supply Chain can arise during intrafacility operations, e.g. in a factory where work in progress is moving from one workstation to the next one, or it can occur in distribution centres, or during one or more of the transportation stages in the Supply Chain. If a product goes from queue to queue on its way to the final customer then the analysis for calculating the expected time to reach the final customer is substantially more complex than for a single queueing system. Different models have been developed to model network queues and their common feature is that they are complex. We have already mentioned one network model called the *Jackson* network.

Another variation in the queueing model is the M/M/s model with *finite queue length*, called the M/M/s/K model. Finite queue length implies that the queue has a maximum capacity for waiting people. This can be a physical constraint, such as a waiting room in a hospital where there is only a limited number of chairs to host the arriving guests. Once the numbers of patients exceed queue capacity they are sent to another hospital or are asked to come back another day. People lining up at a bus stop can only enter the bus as long as the bus has sufficient capacity. Those waiting at the end of the queue will have to wait for the next scheduled bus. All queue characteristics discussed for infinite queue length can be adapted to meet the constraint of finite queue length.

The last variation of the M/M/s-model we will mention here is the *finite calling population*. Although there is a similarity between finite queue length and finite population, finite population means that the number of potential people that can join the queue is constrained. For example, only people who are or were members of a club, school, or other institution are allowed to join an activity or festival organized by the club, the school, or the institution. If the club has N members, the N members will still show up randomly for the activity following a Poisson distribution, creating a queue. The queue will be capped to N persons – if they all arrive at the same moment – but fewer people is, of course, possible. Having a finite calling population compared to an infinite or extremely large calling population affects the arrival process.

In the case of an extremely large calling population the mean arrival rate λ is assumed to be constant – if one person joins the queue out of, say, one million, that will not change the mean arrival rate for the remaining 999,999 persons. If the calling population is finite, especially when it is small, the mean rate is affected by the number of people who already joined the system. Let us take as an example a population consisting of N members who received an invitation to attend a meeting. The arrival rate follows a Poisson process. If *n* persons are inside the system there are *(N-n)* still outside the system who can join later. In an infinite calling population when there are *n* persons inside the system there is still an infinite – or extremely large – number of persons who can still join the queue. This means that λ in a finite calling population is not constant anymore! Consequently, the operating characteristics of the queueing system are different compared to the infinite population. The constraint of a finite population can be incorporated in the standard M/M/s model for infinite population and adjusted queue performance metrics can be computed.

A cost-benefit analysis by changing the number of servers in a queueing system

Up to now, we have discussed the properties of waiting lines (queues) in terms of its performance indicators, primarily L_q, L, W, W_q, and P_n, the probability of exactly **n** customers in the system. In the discussion about waiting times, it became clear that adding another server of service employees could significantly reduce the average waiting time. Adding a server incurs additional cost of paying that server or staff member, but reducing waiting time has the benefit that more people are willing to join the queue and wait for being served. Especially the rate of balking and reneging will go down and therefore there is less lost revenue (profit) as opportunity cost. On the other hand, adding and paying a server or service employee who has nothing to do due to a lack of customers – in other words, is idle – in the queuing system means lost productivity. This lost productivity is part of the waiting cost of the system. It is relatively simple to formulate the problem of finding the optimal number of servers as a minimization problem of the sum of the expected total cost, which means the sum of the expected service cost (server) and expected waiting cost per unit time. We use the following symbols:

$E[TC]$ = expected *total* cost per unit time
$E[SC]$ = cost of server or service per unit time
$E[WC]$ = Expected waiting cost per unit time

The objective function is formulated as

Minimize $E[TC]$ with the number of servers as variable

Next, we have to find a relation between the cost and the number of servers or services per unit time. If the servers are employees the hourly wage rate can be taken as the cost of a server per unit time (hour). If all servers have the same hourly wage rate $[C_S]$ the expected service cost $E[SC] = s*C_S$ with s the number of servers per unit time. The relation between waiting cost and the number is servers is case-specific and depends on the assumptions made and the behavior of customers. The standard performance indicators of the queue tell us that the total amount of waiting expressed as the number of people waiting multiplied with the number of waiting time has an expected value of

$$L = \lambda*W.$$

If we call the waiting cost per customer per time unit (C_w) the expected waiting cost $E[WC] = C_w*L$. If we assume the interarrival time as being exponentially distributed and the service time as well, the graphs of the three cost curve have the following shapes.

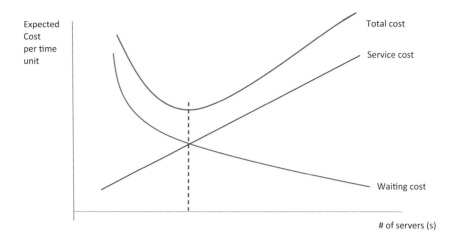

Main Points: Unexpected delays are becoming more a rule than an exception in everyday Supply Chain and business processes. These delays can be modelled using queueing systems. These queueing models have two components: the <u>queue</u> and the <u>service</u> itself. The random arrival process is modelled using a Poisson distribution and the corresponding interarrival time follows an exponential distribution. The service time can be either fixed or follow an exponential distribution. If the queueing models are built on a Markovian birth and death process the key performance metrics (indicators) of the system can be mathematically derived (see Mathematical Appendix). The standard metrics are 1) average queue length, 2) average system length, 3) average waiting time in the queue, 4) average waiting time in the system, and 5) the probabilities that there are n persons with $n = 0, 1, 2, 3, \ldots$ in the system. Finding the optimal number of servers is a trade-off between the cost of deploying more servers or server time on one side and the benefits of reduced waiting cost on the other side.

Notes

1-3   See Instructor's Manual

4   This quote is taken come from the introduction of the classical paper *"The Psychology of Waiting Lines"* by David Maister (1985).

5-7   See Instructor's Manual

8   Source: https://phys.org/news/2016-08-traffic-bad.html retrieved on 21 November 2019

9-16   See Instructor's Manual

12   Sustainability and Corporate Social Responsibility in a Supply Chain

Sustainability and Corporate Social Responsibility in a Supply Chain
The Cobalt Case in the Manufacturing of Electronic Devices

Source: http://www.miningafrica.net/wp-content/uploads/2017/03/kids.jpg

Apple has announced that it will start treating cobalt, an important mineral in the making of its devices, mined in the Democratic Republic of Congo, as a conflict mineral amid child labour allegations.[1] Furthermore, the iPhone maker is said to have instructed smelters it uses to stop buying cobalt from artisanal mines that use child labour as the owner of the accused mines, Zhejiang Huayno Cobalt, continues to investigate the allegations. Cobalt is used in the making of both Apple's iPhone and iPad batteries.

"We have been working with Huayou on a program that will verify individual artisanal mines, according to our standards, and these mines will re-enter our supply chain when we are confident that the appropriate protections are in place." Apple said in a statement to the *Washington Post*. This statement by Apple to stop buying cobalt from artisanal miners in the Democratic Republic of Congo comes after pressure from the likes of Amnesty International, who released a 2016 report on how some major international electronics brands, including Apple, source cobalt from mines that use children to mine the mineral by hand. Apple is not the only company that is guilty of sourcing cobalt from artisanal mines in the Democratic Republic of Congo, other big technology brands include Microsoft, Motorola, Dell, HP Inc., Sony, and Samsung, to name a few.[2]

Date: 13 March 2017.

News agency Reuters is reporting that a pilot of a blockchain solution is underway to track cobalt from where it is mined in the Democratic Republic of Congo (DRC) all the way until it is used in the manufacturing of electronic products, such as smartphones and electric vehicle rechargeable batteries.

The aim is apparently to ensure that the cobalt used in various electronic products is not that which is mined by children in some of the DRC's artisanal mines. Although the Reuters report does not disclose any details about who is behind the initiative and specifications of the solution; they do say, however, that "sources close to a pilot scheme expect it to be launched this year." [...]

The idea of using blockchain technology for tracking the cobalt supply chain also was highlighted in 2017 at the Cobalt Development Institute's annual conference where Core Consultants presented their proposal on how blockchain technology can be used in the cobalt supply chain starting at the mines in the DRC.

What Core Consultants propose is that artisanal miners take their cobalt to a trader in the DRC who will weigh the bag using a standard scale and using a standard spectrometer, he will identify the contained cobalt. This information will then be digitally captured on the blockchain. After that, the cobalt is allocated a barcode, which is subsequently registered in the blockchain.

"The payment to the artisanal miner is processed and that payment is recorded, and he is given an amount of money. So, we have a physical transaction, digitally recorded: Cash in exchange for goods. [...] So, the evidence is recorded, and this evidence can be viewed by everyone on the blockchain," reads a presentation that Core Consultants published at the conference.[3]

Introduction

The problems discussed in the case description about cobalt mining in the DRC is topical, but it is by no means an isolated case. Many more mining and manufacturing cases are facing similar CSR problems. *Cobalt* is a rare metal needed as raw material for the production of lithium-ion batteries. The demand for lithium batteries has been growing rapidly in recent years to power mobile devices, like smartphones and tablets, but particularly to power electric bicycles and electric cars. The second part of the case description refers to a new technology, called *blockchain technology*. This technology has the potential, at least in theory, to alleviate the opacity in the process of mining, processing, and selling of cobalt, contributing to creating a fairer market for this valuable raw material, whose market price has steadily risen in recent decades. However, blockchain technology is still in its embryonic phase and it will still be some time before it is implemented on a large scale and yields the results that experts expect of it.

What is Corporate Social Responsibility?[4]

Corporate Social Responsibility as a mainstream phenomenon in the business community traces its roots back to the 1950s, when economists and scholars started to study companies not primarily as standalone entities with a single goal *to maximize profit or shareholders value*, but refocused their business studies, framing it in a *stakeholders'* approach. The European Commission describes Corporate Social Responsibility (CSR) *"as companies taking responsibility for their impact on society. The European Commission believes that CSR is important for the sustainability, competitiveness, and innovation of EU enterprises and the EU economy. It brings benefits for risk management, cost savings, access to capital, customer relationships, and human resource management."*[5]

In the 1980s, the United Nations set up joint working groups and commissions in collaboration with corporate CEOs to study the need for and importance of global CSR frameworks, in the form of a Global Compact. They published a practical guide entitled *Supply Chain Sustainability: A Practical Guide for Continuous Improvement* as part of their Global Compact platform and framework for sustainability and Corporate Social Responsibility for business organizations. This document contains an extensive list of guidelines, goals, principles, and best practices for improving Supply Chain sustainability performance. It discusses human and worker rights, good governance, business ethics, and sound environmental practices. The document lists the following topics that must be addressed to become a socially responsible supplier.[6]

CSR extends the traditional notion of a *stockholder's* approach to a *stakeholder's* approach. A stakeholder is any party or person that has an interest in the (continuity of a) company and comprises customers, employees, suppliers, governments, local communities, and the physical environment. More recently, *corporate governance* has also been included in CSR policy. As this definition shows, CSR is a multifaceted concept that covers a broad array of activities and dimensions, not all of which are relevant for each company. Manufacturing companies face different CSR issues than service-oriented firms, and large diversified companies usually face a broader range of CSR issues than local and specialized companies, at least regarding the scale of the problems. With the proliferation of Supply Chain networks in recent decades, CSR issues are no longer effective on a stand-alone basis practiced by a single company. They must now be addressed by a commitment from all Supply Chain partners.

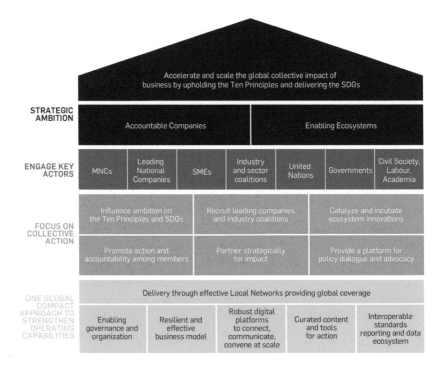

Source: https://ungc-communications-assets.s3.amazonaws.com/pics/un_images/2021%20 Strategy%20Diagrams-Figure%201.png

CSR is a container concept that covers many business practices and processes. The C means that we are dealing with companies. That does not mean that governments, not-for-profit organizations, and private households are exempt from social responsibility, but they are guided by other standards, codes, and laws specifically targeted at these groups and organizations. The *S* in CSR refers to the way the company treats people, primarily their employees, but also customers and suppliers. Many large companies have subsumed these relations in new departments with specific management policies, e.g. Human Resource Management (HRM), Customer Relation Management (CRM), and Supplier Relation Management (SRM). While at the level of individual companies there have long been examples of socially oriented enterprises – even from the time of the Industrial Revolution –at a global level CSR is still far from being common practice in the business community.

Managers who consider their employees mainly as production factors generating (high) labour costs see humans like robot, and, consequently, will try to squeeze their employees as much as possible to obtain a maximum return. For them, employee rights are a burden, rather than a source of inspiration for a good human resource policy. By contrast, managers who consider their employees – and other people – as humans endowed with dignity and the bearers of rights and duties, take another stance. In this case, they will formulate a human resource policy that makes their company more like a community, sharing common values and motivating their employees using positive tangible and intangible incentives to align employee's goals with corporate goals. They will create working conditions that make their employees feel at home in their workplace.

In most countries, the institutional framework for the working conditions of employees is highly regulated by public law. Especially in the European Union, there are extensive labour-related directives setting norms and standards regarding minimum wages, maximum number of labour hours, safe and healthy working conditions, reducing occupational hazards, career opportunities, permanent education, resting hours, severance payments, leave days, holidays, and many more. Labour laws are considered to be the minimum standards a company has to comply with to be socially responsible. Some companies, on top of the legal requirements they have to comply with, formulate their own corporate human resource policy to help their employees be more productive.

Another dimension of CSR is the *community relations* a company maintains. Companies have a physical presence in the areas where their facilities are located. They create jobs for the local population, offer a standard of living by paying decent wages to their employees, and offer career development for their workers. Some of them adopt a policy to stay on speaking terms with the people living in proximity of their facilities. Sponsoring or organizing open-house days to allow people to visit their facilities are examples of community relations management.

Another important pillar of CSR is the way a company deals with the physical environment. This is a broad pillar and addresses, among other things:
– Air pollution (sometimes health-threatening, as in the case of the smog in parts of China and India)
– Water pollution
– Soil contamination and soil depletion due to over-intensive agriculture or husbandry
– Noise nuisance
– Odor nuisance
– Seismic hazards (like quakes due to gas extraction, as in Groningen, the Netherlands, pile driving on construction sites and sinkholes)
– Impact on biodiversity (animal and plant population ecology like deforestation, overfishing, etc.)
– Visual (horizon) pollution
– Hazardous radioactive and electromagnetic radiation (GSM masts on buildings and high-voltage power pylons close to residential areas)
– Energy, water and (inefficient) raw materials usage, waste production among others
– Emission of carbon dioxide (CO_2) and other gases, such as methane, which contribute to global warming

The institutional framework of environmental protection consists of extensive environmental legislation and regulation in many countries, not least in the European Union. These laws set the minimum environmental standards that any organization has to meet in order to avoid liability for environmental damages and being sentenced to high financial fines and other penalties. In addition, some companies have their own corporate environmental goals and standards. Another CSR topic refers to the kind of products a company sells. A CSR-sensitive company will try to sell products that have a positive impact on consumer well-being, health, and safety. Selling low-quality products, narcotics, trading in endangered plants and animals, is not considered to be good CSR business practice.

Moving from an individual firm CSR policy to a Supply Chain CSR policy

In order to assess a product as *sustainable*, the entire production process – the Supply Chain of the product from cradle to grave – must be considered. This also includes the after-sales phase. The after-sales phase covers both the *consumer phase* (the moment the consumer purchases the product until he scraps it) and the *post-consumer* phase. Globalization has led to a situation whereby production, storage, and logistics have been broken down into different chain segments involving different companies, before the product reaches the globally dispersed final customers. Adding the after-sales phase (consumption and disposal by the consumer) complicates the goal of achieving a fully sustainable Supply Chain.[7]

To assess a product as sustainable it must be sustainable from cradle to grave. From the beginning of the chain, where raw materials are mined, or grown in the case of food, flowing downward to all subsequent stages. This requires production, storage, and logistics to meet the standards of sustainability, but also the after-sales phases and the product recycling options at the end of the economic life. This sustainability condition can even be extended to include product *packaging*: where will the product packaging, like PET bottles, aluminium cans, carton boxes, food packages, and paper, end up? Will it be recycled, incinerated, or put in landfill waste dumps? Or will it be dumped by the consumer on the street, in parks, forests, or local waters? Particularly the after-sales stage is beyond the direct control of the Supply Chain, whose main responsibility is producing and selling the product. Once the product has been sold, responsibility is transferred to the consumer. Therefore, in most countries, national regulations set standards on how to process and handle garbage and trash, once consumers dispose of their product.

Reporting and metrics for Supply Chain performance

Although the number of medium-sized and large companies that publish an annual CSR report is rising, the lack of binding standards about the content in these reports leads to a large diversity in lay-out and contents. At the same time, the lack of uniformity in measurement metrics for sustainable business activities makes it difficult to assess the performance of CSR policies of companies. It is rare to find a CSR report at the Supply Chain level that covers an entire Supply Chain, all its SC partners, and detailed sustainability data. This hampers a consistent and well-coordinated Supply Chain CSR report. There are many templates and metrics proposed by academics and consultants to standardize CSR reporting at a Supply Chain level. In a blog paper by the *Sloan Management Review,* the author proposes a possible measurement and reporting framework for reporting about Supply Chain sustainability. The main features of this reporting frame are shown below.[8] The author mentions three contextual considerations for this framework:

1. "Consider all key impacts
2. Set science-based goals and targets
3. Develop context-based indicators to track progress, toward goals and targets"

On top of that key players in the supply chain have to cooperate and align policies, targets, and interests. Recommendations are:

1. "Include all key supply chain players
2. Build capacity across the chain for data collection and validation
3. Align data collection and analysis systems"

Blockchain technology: A tool to improve supply chain sustainability?

Blockchain is a public record of transactions. It is also distributed, so, instead of one person controlling everything, there are many computers around the world connected to a network, and these thousands of computers together come to an agreement on which transactions are valid.

Whenever someone makes a transaction, it is disseminated in the network, and the computers run complex algorithms to determine if the transaction is valid. If it is, they add it to the record of transactions linking it to the previous transaction. This chain of linked transactions is known as the blockchain. Since the transactions all reference the one before them, one can figure out which one came first in terms of ordering transactions. This registration process is also a lot more secure than a traditional database: Since many computers are involved in validating transactions, to hack the network one needs to break into not one computer, but many computers spread throughout the world. Also, all of these computers keep records of the blockchain, so to manipulate it, one needs to manipulate it on many computers at once. This is a feat that is significantly more difficult than hacking a traditional database, and no one has managed to come close to ever hacking a blockchain.[9]

Blockchain – sometimes called *distributed ledger* – also offers new perspectives in Supply Chain operations for monitoring the entire journey of a product from raw materials up to customer sales. It allows a company to trace the origins of the product, review all transactions in the Supply Chain with respect to the ownership transfer of a product. If it is integrated with new applications like the *Internet of Things* (IoT), whereby equipment and devices are connected to the internet and are monitored and controlled online, monitoring, and control of products in a Supply Chain will be even more powerful. We previously mentioned applications such as the track-and-trace option for sending postal packages, whereby the receiver (and often also the sender) can track the path of ordered products up to the site and time of arrival. But the possibilities go much further: a supermarket selling cartons of milk could trace which cow the milk comes from. In cases where it is discovered that a certain kind of food contains contaminants and impacts consumer health negatively, the cause of the contamination can be traced to its source and adequate measures can be taken to avoid further distribution and spreading of the contaminated food. We must remember, however, that, in 2020, blockchain technology or distributed ledger is still in an incipient phase, is far from mainstream, and remains an unknown technology for many organizations in the world, and, moreover, it currently requires expertise to work with it.

Recycling and waste disposal, considered as a *reverse* Supply Chain[10]

A special point of environmental attention in a Supply Chain setting involving the last phase of a product's economic life: the moment the consumer scraps a product. This moment is the commencement of the post-consumer phase of the product as waste or recycling materials, either in its entirety, its components, and/or the raw materials from which the product is made.

We first outline where mass-produced consumer products and their packaging end up when the consumer phase has been completed and the post-consumer phase starts. Our focus is on packaging materials and solid products.

The images below show some of the places and sites where consumer waste ends up. The first three can be considered as institutionalized endpoints of consumer waste, because they are under the control of national regulatory authority and supervisory institutions.

The last three pictures are uncontrolled waste disposal, because consumers have dumped their trash – either legally or illegally – at the site where they were at the moment of disposing their garbage.

Waste endpoint: **landfills.**
This artificial hill is built on a landfill site of solid waste, called the roof of Drenthe. The landfill is managed by a private company under concession issued by public authorities. The policy is to convert solid landfills to useful applications, even for recreational purposes as shown in the picture above.
Source: https://www.rocksolidbv.nl/previews/2019/11/21/media_894_504197_w1200_fit.jpg

Waste endpoint: **Incineration plant** (Denmark)
Source: https://structurae.net/en/media/269415-amager-bakke-incinerator (Wikimedia Commons)

Waste endpoint: recycling plant (paper in this case)
Source: http://global-recycling.info/wp-content/uploads/2016/08/HSM-Smurfit_Kappa2.jpg.

Waste endpoint: urban street dumps (image Amsterdam)
Source: https://images0.persgroep.net/rcs/uR-Yk6W5yBi4IUK7QjljN6ggy_4/diocontent/131151243/_crop/0/117/1580/893/_fitwidth/763?appId=93a17a8fd81db0de025c8abd1cca1279&quality=0.8&desiredformat=webp

Waste endpoint: **rivers** (and oceans)
source: https://upload.wikimedia.org/wikipedia/
commons/5/51/Citarum_River_pollution%2C_2009.
jpg

Waste endpoint: nature. The picture shows a herd of
elephants foraging on a garbage heap in Sri Lanka.
Source: https://upload.wikimedia.org/wikipedia/
commons/7/70/A_herd_of_40_wild_elephants_at_
Ampara_in_east_Sri_Lanka_is_totally_depen-
dent_on_garbage_from_tractors_DSC8792.jpg

Waste has a lot of negative externalities, making it the object of extensive regulatory standards and legislation. Some *negative externalities* of solid waste, particularly in large concentrations, are:

1. it affects *public health*. Waste that contains organic matter, like food, attracts birds and insects, and in urban areas with canals and water also rats and other animals feeding on the waste.
   These animals can become vectors of disease.
2. Waste can generate *smell nuisance and visual pollution*, especially for people living close by.
3. Some waste particles can *enter the human food chain*, especially waste dumped in public waters, which is ingested by fish, and the fish, in turn, is eaten by people.
4. It can *disrupt and interfere with ecological processes*, e.g. contaminating underground water reservoirs (aquifers), which are used as drinking water supplies.

An organized, urban infrastructure exists for some forms of waste. It consists of litter bins located in public places, small local container parks specifically designed for this purpose for separated disposal – paper in paper containers, plastic in plastic containers, glass in glass containers, etc. From the network of local container parks, the separated discarded trash is transported to specialized sites or recycling companies who prepare and use the discarded products as raw materials for recycling.

In most cities, trash collection of solid waste disposed of by consumers is a public task of the municipality, which is done either by a specialized department of the municipality itself or is commissioned via public tenders to private companies. The price the city charges residents for waste removal may only cover the costs. In exceptional cases, the manufacturing company itself takes back its own manufactured products from the customers to reuse them completely or partly in the manufacture of new products.

Economic focus: Waste disposal and recycling described in market concepts

Many economists analyse the allocation of goods and services in the traditional framework of demand and supply interacting on a free market and the tools of consumer preferences and utility. On a market, consumers exercise demand and pay a price to acquire a good or service to which they assign a positive utility. The total utility of the consumer goes up by purchasing more of the good or service. In the post-consumer phase, when products degrade into waste, the consumer assigns a negative utility (disutility) to the product and wants to get rid of it.

The question is, who is the demander and who is the supplier? From a material point of view, it seems that the consumer is the supplier, and waste disposal or removal companies are the demanders. But this is a wrong analysis.

Consumers pay a price to get rid of their waste and the waste collector and processing company receive a price. In a normal market transaction, the supplier receives a price, and the demander pays a price. Therefore, in the case of waste, it is more in line with mainstream economic analysis that the consumer demands "waste removal services" and pays a price and the waste company supplies this removal capacity and receives the price. Total utility of the consumer increases because they experience less **dis**utility by being freed from the waste. The waste removing company earns money by selling the service of waste removal. This line of reasoning about waste analysis is consistent with other forms of consumer **dis**utility, like health problems. A patient experiences negative utility from being ill and is willing to pay a doctor as a supplier of a medical treatment to get rid of his or her illness. The patient is the demander of "health services" and the doctor (or hospital) is the supplier of these services. The total utility of the patient goes up when the patient is again healthy after the treatment.

We now focus in more detail on the post-consumer phase as part of a reverse Supply Chain. What happens to the product and its packaging when the consumer gets rid of the product once it no longer serves a purpose, or it does not meet expectations due to obsolescence, wear, or frequent technical failure? This post-consumer phase is the starting point for disposal considerations: is recycling possible? If so, how should the recycling chain be organized and integrated into existing Supply Chains?

A major problem of the after-sales phase and post-consumer phase is that as soon as a retailer has sold a packaged product to an end-user, the Supply Chain loses control of the product, because ownership and user rights have been transferred to the consumer. The retailer ordinarily does not know for how long, where, and who will use the product. The product has left the realm of control of the Supply Chain and entered the unpredictable and erratic domain of consumer behaviour. The behaviour and cooperation of the consumer in this phase is important for success. The recycling option requires research about technical feasibility as well as economic viability. Part of recycling feasibility is the design of an adequate network infrastructure for collecting, centralizing, and moving the discarded products to a recycling site.

The network structure for products discarded by consumers has similar features to those in the manufacturing and distribution network of new products. As discussed earlier, mass production is concentrated in relatively few manufacturing plants, from which the products branch into an increasingly fine-meshed global distribution network before reaching the final consumer. Discarded products, waste, and trash travel the other way around. They are generated (produced) in small quantities at many different locations by end-users, in private homes in residential areas, in offices, retail outlets, street trash bins in cities, solid trash dumped on public streets, on beaches, in public parks, etc. From there, solid trash and garbage are collected, aggregated, and sometimes physically compressed to reduce volume, by garbage trucks and similar trash removal conveyances.

These conveyances exist in a wide array of configurations so that they can reach most nooks and crannies where trash is found (dumped). The garbage trucks bring the collected garbage to dumping grounds, incinerators, or recycling plants, where large volumes of trash are consolidated for further processing. In some cases, collected solid waste is transferred in special ships and transported over water to the next link in the waste or recycling chain.

Most firms operating in this waste disposal (reverse) Supply Chain are independent businesses partnering with other companies operating in a subsequent or earlier link in the chain. Each link specializes in its activities: some firms are specialized in garbage collection; other firms in garbage logistics; others in temporary storage; others in garbage separation; and some in (re)processing or recycling garbage into valuable output materials. In this reverse Supply Chain, waste disposal starts decentralized (with many dispersed trash of end-users) and ends up in a few centralized sites.

In the Netherlands and most member states of the EU, municipalities are responsible for collecting solid household waste and retailer waste. Besides garbage bags and containers that people place at the curb to be collected and emptied by garbage trucks, municipalities are also responsible for maintaining and emptying the network of urban trash bins in the public domain and keeping public places, like streets and parks, clean. To perform these legal tasks, they have at their disposition a wide fleet of garbage and cleaning vehicles and a labour force bringing the collected garbage to centralized sites for consolidation.[11]

For recycling purposes, it can be helpful to distinguish between the product itself and the product packaging: they have different lifecycles. Packaging materials are mostly thrown away after the end-user has opened the package and starts using the unwrapped product in the packaging. The product itself ends its useful life when the consumer discards it. This implies that the collection channels for recycling or dumping the packaging and the corresponding product do not run parallel. In some cases, like for food and drinks, the lifecycle of the product and the packaging run parallel to each other: when the food has been eaten or the (soft) drink has been drunk the packaging, e.g. PET bottles, aluminium cans, glass become trash. For many other products, the package ends up in the waste stream long before the product itself ends up there.[12]

Main Point: Companies and Supply Chains designing a sustainability policy will have to account for and monitor at least two environmental dimensions: the entire production and distribution process of the product to its final destination as well as the consumer and post-consumer phase in the lifecycle – together the after-sales phase. A Supply Chain loses the control over its products once they are sold to consumers and ownership rights have been transferred. Public regulation and governments issue standards for an orderly processing of waste disposal in the post-consumer phase.

Better safe than sorry, but not always possible

This familiar saying is applicable to many human activities and also to waste management. Preventing waste means that the waste stream in the post-consumer phase is reduced to a minimum – or zero if possible – but this is not always technically possible or economically feasible. This applies particularly to packaging, which cannot always be avoided. Unpacked food sold on outdoor markets and in the open air, as is the case in many developing countries, is exposed to all kinds of external influences, like polluted air, insects landing on the food and infecting it, and other vicissitudes of (urban and rural) life, which can have a negative impact on consumer health, or reduce food quality. So, a first argument in favour of packaging is that it helps to protect food against these influences.

Another argument for packaging is that companies use it as a marketing tool. Packaging labels not only contain basic printed product information about composition and contents – which for many products, such as food and drinks, is mandatory in the EU – but much packaging is decorated with coloured images and slogans to make the content more attractive to consumers.

Another argument for using packaging is *storage*. If the end-user consumes the product in parts, like a box of chocolates stored in the refrigerator or medicines, the package life stretches over a longer period until the last piece of chocolate or last pill in the box has been consumed or withdrawn. Policies addressing waste stream abatement can be approached from the supply side, from the demand side, or both.

Starting at the supply side: The Supply Chain can reduce the waste stream increasing the economic life of a product by improving quality, avoiding unnecessary quantities of packaging, and using more sustainable raw materials. From the demand side: consumers are targeted to use packaging materials and other waste items in a responsible manner. Product user instructions supported by public campaigns can emphasize the need to not waste materials, energy, and other scarce resources. Stretching the economic life of products and packaging requirements is a trade-off between advantages and disadvantages.

Drivers of increasing waste streams: Producers and consumers

Global waste streams have increased rapidly in recent decades due to shorter product lifetimes and, consequently, higher replacement rates, as well as the increased purchasing power of consumers in many countries. The rate at which, for example, consumer electronics, like tablets, smartphones, television sets are replaced by consumers in the 21st century is much higher than the replacement rate half a century ago.

The main cause of these high turnover rates is not lower quality reducing the technical lifetime of devices, which, in many cases, has even improved. A major driver is the marketing strategy of manufacturers to boost sales by lowering prices. Mass customization,[13] discussed in the first chapter, facilitates this fast-accelerating product turnover.

Replacing just a small component or module in a major product, or giving it a new colour, is already sufficient to advertise and sell it as an apparently new product.

At a global level, the purchasing power of developing countries has increased, especially in China, India, Brazil, and from a demographical viewpoint, children and young people have more money to spend, and spend more now than they did 40 years ago.

The financial sector has also contributed by making it very easy for consumers to obtain credit from banks and other financial institutions in many countries. This triggered an accelerated rate of replacing items such as cars, household durables, and furniture.

Some companies bring out a new version or model every three or four years, supported by expensive advertising and marketing campaigns to promote sales. The added value for the consumer compared to the old model is often limited. Many new versions of electronic devices have some added or improved features, like a better camera, better audio quality, or better screen resolution, but the old versions are still perfectly usable and of good quality. Many consumers buy a new model and discard their previous model, sometimes selling it on the secondary market, but often it ends up in the garbage stream.

Consumerism

Consumerism is a social and economic order and ideology that encourages the acquisition of goods and services in ever-increasing amounts. With the Industrial Revolution, but particularly in the 20th and 21st century, mass production led to an economic 'crisis': there was overproduction — the supply of goods would grow beyond consumer demand — and so manufacturers turned to planned obsolescence and advertising to increase consumer spending. An early criticism of consumerism is Thorstein Veblen's best-known book, *The Theory of the Leisure Class* from 1899, which critically examined newly widespread values and economic institutions emerging along with newly widespread 'leisure time', at the turn of the 20th century. In it, Veblen, "views the activities and spending habits of this leisure class in terms of conspicuous and vicarious consumption and waste. Both are related to the display of status and not to functionality or usefulness. [...] In the almost complete absence of other sustained macro-political and social narratives, the pursuit of the 'good life' through practices of what is known as 'consumerism' has become one of the dominant global social forces, cutting across differences of religion, social class, sex, ethnicity, and nationality. [...]

Our enormously productive economy demands that we make consumption our way of life, that we convert the buying and use of goods into rituals, that we seek our spiritual satisfaction and our ego-satisfaction in consumption. We need things consumed, burned up, worn out, replaced, and discarded at an ever-increasing rate."

Critics of consumerism include Pope Francis, German historian Oswald Spengler (who said: "Life in America is exclusively economic in structure and lacks depth"), and French writer Georges Duhamel, who held American materialism up as "a beacon of mediocrity that threatened to eclipse civilization."[14]

Consumerism is rooted in lifestyle, status display, and *keeping up with other peer group members*, rather than in satisfying the real needs and wants of a person or social group to achieve a normal standard of living. Consumerism does not aim to consume for a living but to live for consuming.

Typical symptoms of consumerism are buying more than needed or wanted – as manifested in instantaneous impulse buying and the *"shop until you drop"* slogan

– buying unnecessary luxury products when cheaper (standard) product versions suffice,[15] purchasing frequently new and fashion-sensitive models, the nearly uninterrupted snacking by some children, and financing the acquisition of expensive assets, such as electronic devices and household appliances, with borrowed money instead of saving money to finance the acquisition. In the worst-case, consumerist buying behaviour can take on pathological forms and degrade into a compulsive buying disorder, technically called *oniomania*.

There is extensive scientific literature and research about consumerism written by economists, marketers, psychologists, sociologists, philosophers, and even theologians, describing in-depth how consumerist behaviour shapes economic structures, marketing campaigns, how it changes Supply Chains, and affects the life of people, social groups, nations, and the entire world. It is beyond the scope of this book to go into detail, but the rising global garbage heap and waste streams (solid waste, liquid waste, and gaseous waste dumped into the atmosphere) with all their concomitant social, environmental, and economic consequences can be attributed, at least partially, to *consumerism*.

In most countries, the market mechanism of supply and demand is the dominant force to explain the quantity and composition of goods and services sold on the market. Demanders (consumers) in a market economy are the ultimate actors, determining which products and in what quantity will be traded on the market. Business companies follow the preferences and tastes of the consumers and, at the same time, try to influence the consumption patterns of consumers using marketing tools and advertising. If consumerism is a major cause of the ever-increasing waste streams, consumer education is at least part of the solution.[16]

If consumers set a trend towards purchasing more sustainable products, emphasizing sustainable production processes and Supply Chains, companies and even entire Supply Chains catering to these more sustainable consumer preferences will have a stronger competitive edge and a higher probability of long-term continuity of their organization than their non-sustainable competitors. Companies and Supply Chains lagging behind, stained with a reputation of unsustainable business practices, will lose market share and have a higher probability of going bankrupt.

Many companies are very sensitive to negative product reviews posted on the internet and the way they are liked or disliked on social media. If consumers post many negative reviews about a company or its products on social media or product review sites, the pressure exerted on the company to switch to a more transparent CSR business policy and sustainable production processes can lead to changes in corporate policy. Examples of large companies that have implemented or upgraded their CSR after pressure from activist groups in recent decades are Nike Inc, Lego A/S, cosmetics company Revlon, and others.

Intergenerational natural resources usage

Renewable and non-renewable global natural resources are the basis for guaranteeing an adequate standard of living for mankind, now and in the future. Sustainability is described as using natural resources in such a way that they do not compromise the availability of resources for future generations. The way these resources are used now will affect what remains for next generations. Frequently, a distinction is made between *renewable* and *non-renewable* resources. Non-renewable resources include, among others, all mineral deposits stored in the crust of the earth (mineral assets). By their very nature, any ton of minerals extracted from a mine by the current generation will no longer be available as a raw material for future generations. Renewable resources include all vegetal and animal life (biological assets) on earth, on and under the soil, in the water, and the air. They are the prime source to feed mankind. A characteristic of a renewable resource is that it renews itself and grows by reproduction.[17]

Depletion of shared resources was first described and analysed in a seminal paper by biologist Garrett Hardin in 1968 and is known as the *Tragedy of the Commons*. The commons are common resources shared and used by many people, groups of people, and even nations where there are no restrictions on the harnessing or extraction of the resource.

Each user harnesses or extracts from the resource those quantities that will give a maximum individual benefit without considering the availability of the resource for others either belonging to the current generation or future generations. As a result, shared resources are depleted and the future availability of the resource is imperiled. Most shared resources have no individualized property rights or a governing body responsible for its sustainable use. Where such a governing body exists it does not always have the institutional and financial means to enforce sustainable use.

There are many examples of the *Tragedy of the Commons*. At a global level, international waters, large parts of the earth's atmosphere, Antarctica, many parts of the seabed are freely accessible to anyone who can harness and use it for their individual interests and goals. Harnessing natural resources takes many different forms, varying from extracting minerals or oil from geological reserves, using it as a dumping ground for garbage – even toxic or radioactive garbage – using populations for food supply, like overfishing, or excessive logging of trees in (rain) forests and many more. But even at a national level, some countries are so vast that, in remote areas, which are virtually beyond the control of institutional enforcement, people can use these areas for any activity they like. Even within some large cities surrounded by slums, e.g. in African, Latin American, and Asian countries, the few urban available resources are degrading at a fast rate in quantity and quality, causing sometimes irreparable damage to the physical environment and making these areas uninhabitable for the people living there and disrupting social harmony. Original inhabitants will move out to other parts of the city or the country. Shared resources have similar properties as semi-public goods, such as infrastructure assets. They are *rival* and, to a high degree, *non-excludable*.

A major explanation for the *Tragedy of the Commons* of shared resources is a complete or partial absence of an institutional framework to manage sustainable use, like entities responsible for an equitable allocation of property and user rights and a lack of enforcement of the regulation.[18] In many countries, combatting corruption is ineffective due to a lack of financial resources and there are inadequate countervailing powers against those who exercise economic control over the resource. Many projects and experiments have been set up to look for solutions for the Tragedy of the Commons, also referred to as common pool resource theory and common pool resource management, albeit with varying degrees of success.[19]

Sustainable use of *non-renewable* natural resources requires a different approach than renewable resources. What is extracted from a mine now, is not replaced (at least not within a foreseeable future), and, consequently, there is less stock left for future generations. For these non-renewable resources, the focus of sustainability is mainly on finding alternative materials or searching for new deposits, like minerals under the ocean bed instead of on land.

Closely related to intergenerational resource allocation is how much money the current generation is willing to spend or to set aside to provide the next generations with sufficient stocks of natural resources to maintain an adequate standard of living. In order words: how much money is the incumbent generation willing to pay both at the individual and at the collective level for activities that contribute to sustainability?[20] This willingness to contribute includes behavioral aspects, like changing excessive consumption habits, buying goods and services with lower natural resources depletion, and a better ecological footprint. This can be achieved by buying products with a longer economic lifetime, products made with a cleaner production process, less packaging, and other features contributing to a better ecological footprint.

Case: The global food Supply Chain and managing bioresources sustainably

Among the common resources, renewable biological resources are of sufficient importance that they deserve more discussion. Biological resources are at the base of the world food Supply Chain, ranging from agricultural local farms spread over the entire world in the upstream levels up to the incredibly extended downstream level encompassing the global food retail sector, restaurants, supermarkets, open markets, caterers, and many more. The way biological resources are managed will ultimately determine what food the consumer can eat, what is stocked on the supermarket shelves, and which price the consumer has to pay for it.

The global food Supply Chain is probably one of the largest and oldest in the world, not only supplying mankind with food and drink, but also offering jobs and income for an enormous number of people.

Besides direct employment, there is a very large indirect employment base consisting of organizations whose revenues depend on the performance of the food Supply Chain. Commodity traders on commodity markets, logistics companies moving the biomaterials from one stage to another in the supply chain, and companies who manufacture the tangible equipment used at all levels in the Supply Chain, like tractors and machinery used in food processing plants. Not all global bioresources are harnessed for food and drinks. Some resources have been set aside as nature sanctuaries or game reserves or used for raw materials in the construction industry, like forests for wood or bamboo plantations.

The configuration of the food Supply Chain is a little different than the architecture described in Chapter 1 for Supply Chains for mass-produced goods. They had a pyramidal structure with few, but large, production plants upstream and a widely diversified consumer base downstream. In the food Supply Chain, there is also an enormous number of producers of the raw biomaterials, which are at a more upstream stage than the food processing sector. These are farmers and growers of all kinds of agricultural, horticultural, livestock farming, forestry, and aquaculture produce. They are spread over the entire globe and their numbers run into the many millions. Their firm sizes range from very small plots of land to huge plantations controlled by large food processing companies.

The global supply of biological raw materials is fragmented in relatively small portions. The food processing companies, which are positioned more downstream in the chain, purchase large quantities of raw biomaterials. Therefore, small quantities are first aggregated, consolidated, and stored by specialized firms before they are sold to the food processing industry. Although in many countries in Africa and Asia small farmers sell directly on the open (outdoor) market to end consumers, a large amount of the farm output passes through this aggregation layer in the Supply Chain situated between the farmer's stage and food processing industry stage. In many cases, in addition to aggregation, a certain degree of preprocessing of raw agricultural produce also takes place. In this intermediate layer of the food chain, we find large globally operating companies like Cargill (US), Syngenta (Germany). In the Netherlands, examples are Avebe (potato starch), Nutreco (salmon nurseries), and ForFarmers. From this stage, partly processed raw materials find their way to the food and beverage processing industry, like Unilever, Nestlé, Douwe Egberts,

Friesland Campina, Heineken, and many thousands more with production plants all over the world.

From the food processing companies, the fully processed and mostly packaged food is channelled into the distribution system via a large, diversified network of sales channels. Part of the processed and packaged food and drinks is sold to the wholesale sector, like Vrumona in the Netherlands. Wholesalers in turn, sell to restaurants and the catering sector, and another large stream find its way to supermarkets, groceries, and the food retail sector. The basic architectural features of the food Supply Chain consist of a *broad upstream* shape (many small firms operating at this level), a relatively *small neck* (few large firms at this level), and a *broad downstream* bottom (many small firms operating at this level). This architecture is displayed below. One must take into account that this is a very simplified model of the real food Supply Chain. In the real economy, there is much overlap between the different stages in the chain. Some food processing companies manage and even own their own agricultural fields to assure themselves of a steady supply of raw materials, instead of buying the raw materials on the open commodities market or by the mediation of commodity brokers.

At the top of the food Supply Chain, the most upstream level, are the biological and ecological resources (supported by fertile soil and open waters), which are the cradle for all food, drinks, and biobased building materials. These resources are exploited by a large number of firms operating in agricultural, horticultural, livestock farming, aquaculture, and silviculture (managing forests) production.

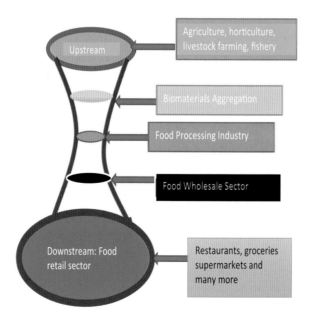

The rate at which a biological resource (population) can be harnessed for human consumption on a sustainable basis is derived from a concept used in population ecology called the *carrying capacity* of the resource. The carrying capacity is the maximum number of individuals this resource can sustain to stay in a long-run equilibrium maintaining a stable quantity and quality of the resource. The corresponding maximum harvesting rate for human consumption that does not compromise this long-term future of the bioresource is called the *maximum sustainable yield* (MSY).

The increase of a population is mainly caused by births (new members) as well as the growth of its members in size and weight, which adds to the *biomass*. Population decline is mainly caused by mortality, particularly natural mortality due to old age and diseases. Harnessing a bioresource for human consumption accelerates the decline of a population. To determine the MSY one needs to understand how populations develop over time and this is done and analysed with the aid of population models.

One of the first mathematical models of population dynamics developed to analyse population growth over time towards its carrying capacity is the *logistics equation* developed by the Belgian mathematician Otto Verhulst in 1845. The model has the following structure. We use the symbol C for the carrying capacity, $P(t)$ for the number of individuals in the population (animals or plants) at time t, $d(P)/d(t)$ – or P'- the rate of change of the population size and g the natural or intrinsic growth rate of the population under unconstrained conditions. The logistics equation reads:

$$\frac{d(P)}{d(t)} = g^*P(t)^*(C - P(t))$$

The left-hand side is a derivative of P as a function of time variable t. Consequently, the logistics equation is a first-order differential equation. The solution of this equation after some lengthy calculations is

$$P(t) = \frac{A * C * e^{g^*C^*t}}{1 + A * e^{g^*C^*t}} \text{ with } A \text{ a constant.}[21]$$

A general graph of a logistics model (sometimes called the S-curve) is shown below. This graph incorporates the fact that carrying capacity is not approached directly but with small overshoots and undershoots over time. Incorporating these under- and overshoots in the model complicates the mathematics of the logistics equation substantially and therefore we will focus on the basic structure of the logistics equation without under- and overshooting.

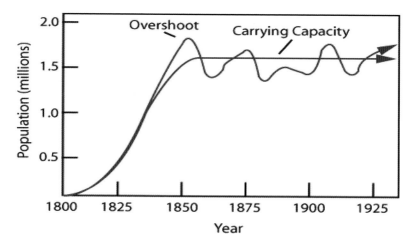

Source: https://sites.google.com/site/biologysat2/home/ecology/properties-of-populations-and-population-growth

The solution of the logistics equation tells us how the population moves towards its carrying capacity over time. Once it reaches the carrying capacity the population size will stabilize around that number. Birth rate and the natural death rate due to old age, disease, and natural enemies balance each other as long as no disrupting events occur like natural or human-induced disasters. The bioresource is in *ecological equilibrium*. The growth *rate* is geometrically represented by the tangent line (first derivative) at each point on the S-curve. If the harvest rate equals the growth rate, the population size after harvest falls back to the level of one period before and continues to grow from that point on (recover). After that period, the population will reach the size it had the period before. If the periodic – mostly annual – harvest or catch is taken when the growth rate achieves its highest value, we have the *maximum sustainable yield*. After the catch, the population size falls back with the MSY to the level of one period before and starts recovering.

One of the interesting properties of the logistics equation is that the MSY is achieved at a population size equal to 50% of the carrying capacity of the resource. At that point, the growth rate (first derivative) achieves its highest value, and the economic owner of the resource can benefit from the highest possible catch or harvest while keeping the population size approximately constant. If the harvest rate (harvest per time unit) is larger than the growth rate the population will not be able to recover to its original size and will decline after a year. If the harvest rate exceeds the growth rate year on year, the population keeps shrinking and will reach the brink of extinction and become irrecoverably lost. The population has been *un*sustainably harnessed.

The timing to catch the MSY is crucial. If, for example, population ecologists calculate an MSY of 50,000 individuals annually, but the actual population size is still _below_ 50% of its carrying capacity, then the actual growth rate will be less than 50,000 individuals per year: let us assume 30,000. If the firm captures 50,000 individuals, population size drops again with 50,000, but recovery after that year is only 30,000 individuals. Consequently, the population size after that year will be lower than the year before and the growth rate has dropped. If the year after, again, 50,000 individuals are captured, recovery after that year will be even less than 30,000 (why?) and the population size shrinks further. If this process continues every year, the population will come close to the brink of extinction, even though the annual harvest was equal to the MSY. So, harvesting the MSY is _only_ sustainable, if the population size has reached 50% of its carrying capacity.[22]

Commercial fish in breeding tanks (aquaculture)
Source: https://buwatec.com/wp-content/uploads/2018/07/WSWA-tanks-Fish-breeding-1170x554.jpg

Wild fish population
Source: Door NMFS/Southwest Fisheries Science Center – http://www.photolib.noaa.gov/htmls/fish2500.htm, public domain, https://commons.wikimedia.org/w/index.php?curid=19243291

The standard logistics model has been extended over the years to more complex population models. One of these is the so-called *Predator-Prey* model, which incorporates the more realistic position of interaction between different populations (species) inhabiting the same area either on land or in the water. These models are used to make forecasts about the growth and decline of living stocks and also support policy decisions about the maximum sustainable yield, like determining the fish quota in the European Union. There are different versions of *predator-prey* interaction models.

Some of the pioneers of these models were physicist and ecologist R. M. May with the May model, and the Lotka-Volterra equations. Both models are based on birth and death processes – not to be confused with the death and birth processes used in queuing theory – and extend the scope of the standard logistics growth pattern to more complex and realistic growth patterns. We will not discuss these models, because they belong to a class of mathematical models called *dynamic systems* that requires knowledge of systems of non-linear differential equations. Solving these models is (far) beyond the level of this book.

A second dimension of sustainability in the food Supply Chain: Food waste

The World Bank reported in 2015 some summary information about global food waste:

Global Food Loss and Waste

"Across global food systems, food loss and waste (FLW) is a widespread issue, posing a challenge to food security, food safety, the economy, and environmental sustainability. No accurate estimates of the extent of FLW are available, but studies indicate that FLW is roughly 30 percent of all food globally (FAO 2015). This amounts to 1.3 billion tonnes per year. FLW represents the wastage of resources, including the land, water, labor, and energy used to produce food. It strongly contributes to climate change because greenhouse gases are emitted during food production and distribution activities, and methane is released during the decay of wasted food. FLW also affects food supply chains by lowering income for food producers, increasing costs for food consumers, and reducing access to food. Minimizing FLW could lead to substantial food security and environmental gains. The causes of FLW vary across the world and depend on specific local conditions. Typically, FLW in low-income countries occurs at the production, postharvest handling, storage, and processing stages and is caused predominantly by managerial and technical limitations. FLW mostly occurs in the distribution and consumption stages in middle- and high-income countries, although it can happen in earlier stages such as when agricultural subsidies lead to overproduction of farm crops. These challenges re-

late to consumer behavior and government policies and regulation. Improving coordination among actors along the different stages of the supply chain could address some of
the FLW issues globally.

Measures to reduce FLW in low-income countries could involve investment in infrastructure and transportation, including in technology for storage and cooling. Small-scale
farmers could also be supported by the provision of improved financing and credit to
allow them to diversify or scale their production. In high-income countries, consumer
education for behavior change is key to decreasing FLW. In addition to decreasing FLW
along the supply chain, discarded food could also be managed productively for compost-
ing and energy recovery. Regional and international stakeholders are taking action to
address FLW. The African Union is working with 14 governments to translate the "Malabo
Declaration on Accelerated Agricultural Growth and Transformation for Shared Prosperity
and Improved Livelihoods," including food loss reduction, into proper national policy and
strategies in Africa (African Union Commission 2014). The Deputy-Secretary General of the
United Nations called on all partners to adopt a more holistic approach to food security,
one that prioritizes FLW, builds new coalitions, scales up current work, and innovates (Hel-
vetas 2018). The Food and Agriculture Organization has been working on developing new
metrics and methodologies to measure FLW, and the organization's SAVE FOOD Initiative
works with civil society to address the issue (FAO 2018). The World Food Programme is including food loss as part of some five-year country plans in Africa and launched the Farm
to Market Alliance to structure local markets and promote loss reduction technologies
among smallholder farmers (World Food Programme 2017). The World Bank is tackling the
issue through loans, such as in Argentina, and by coordinated food waste management
and the establishment of a cross-sectoral strategy (World Bank 2015)."[23]

The above report gives a more detailed description of where, how, and when food
loss and food waste take place in the different stages of the food Supply Chain.
Eliminating food waste would require, among other things, a perfect match between
food supply and food demand. This is virtually impossible given the erratic and
unpredictable demand of consumers buying food in supermarkets, online, and
taking meals in restaurants. Moreover, the bullwhip effect makes a perfect match
in the food Supply Chain very difficult. Food retailers and restaurants face two
cost items that have been discussed in the chapter about *Inventory Management
under Uncertainty*:

1. purchasing too *much* (overstocking) whereby any unsold units mean an eco-
    nomic loss equal to the purchase price (food waste has normally no residual
    value). Even if food is thrown away, it costs the retailer additional money because
    waste removal has a price tag.
2. purchasing too *few* (understocking) and losing the profit margin for unserved
    customers.

The order sizes in the food retail sector depend on these two cost items and the Cycle Service Level making a perfect match between units purchased and units sold is very improbable, leading to waste. Another factor contributing to food waste is that safety and health regulations to protect consumers against diseases caused by unhealthy food have become stricter, particularly in the Western world. This implies that food of lower quality will often be discarded, or, in the best case, be converted to animal feed.

Another cause of food waste proceeds from the fact that in many developing countries staple food (rice, corn, wheat) is often subsidized to keep food prices low and therefore affordable for lower-income households. However cheap food has a higher probability of being thrown away than expensive food. Many countries and the European Union have issued policy guidelines to reduce food waste in the member states.[24] Fortunately, some solutions can alleviate – although not fully eliminate – the problem of food waste: improving short-term forecasting; better coordination of procurement among food retailers; consumer education about (rational) food purchases; and others. These measures can contribute to food waste reduction as well as save money for consumers – who do not buy food that is later discarded – and will save precious natural bioresources, which can be used for alternative purposes, including safeguarding them as a nature reserve.

Up to now, we have used the two concepts *food loss* and *food waste* as equivalent terms of unsustainability. However, there is a difference between the two. *Food loss* is food that is lost by causes that are not under the direct control of human intervention and institutionalized policies. Failed agricultural harvests, meteorological conditions such as too dry or too wet seasons, leading to reduced yields, but also a fire in a food distribution centre can be classified as food loss.

Food waste is within human or institutional control and frequently refers to an intentional effort to make food unfit and unavailable for human consumption.

Destroying part of the commodity supply on food auctions to reduce supply and creating upward pressure on prices, overstocking because of price discounts, even when foreseeing that not all stock will be sold and will be discarded, food that is still fit for human consumption but not fresh enough and therefore dumped on the garbage heap, and excessive quantities purchased by private households and thrown away, are all examples of food waste. Sustainable management of bioresources in the upstream layers of the supply chain can be counteracted by the food waste in the lower echelons, e.g. sustainably bred fish that consumers throw away after purchase because they dislike the taste.

This brings us back to one of the principles of a sustainable Supply Chain. The food Supply Chain can only be considered sustainable if **all** actors in the chain, small and large, pursue sustainability in their business practices. As soon as one actor acts **un**sustainably, the entire Supply Chain can no longer be considered as (fully) sustainable, even if the other partners in the chain act sustainably. Given the uncountable number of entities involved in the global food Supply Chain, it is often better to pursue *acceptable* or *feasible* sustainability rather than targeting 100% sustainability. The latter can even become counterproductive. In addition, *food loss* is a phenomenon that can never be fully eliminated because it depends on exogenous natural conditions, which are not under human control.

Main points: Many environmental problems at a global, regional, and local level can be considered as examples of the Tragedy of the Commons. Shared resources without adequate and effective management lead to **un**sustainable use of these resources. These resources are mostly non-exclusive and rival. Each user tries to obtain maximum benefit from renewable or non-renewable resources. Consequently, the availability of the resource for future generations is compromised. Sustainable use of biological populations, as in the food Supply Chain, are modelled using logistics growth with carrying capacities and maximum sustainable yields, or more complex dynamic population models. Proposed solutions for abating unsustainable resource harnessing are many and varied: from one side, policies and institutions are designed to orient the behaviour of consumers and entire Supply Chains towards more sustainable production and consumption patterns. This can be achieved by issuing new regulations and legislation, but also by creating tangible and intangible incentive schemes to promote sustainability. On the other side, Research and Development efforts in the public and private sector search for alternatives to reduce the pressure on specific mineral and bioresources.

Notes

1   See Instructor's Manual
2   Source: https://www.iafrikan.com/2017/03/13/apple-to-start-treating-cobalt-mined-in-the-democratic-republic-of-congo-as-a-conflict-mineral/
3   Source: https://www.iafrikan.com/2018/02/03/blockchain-technology-to-be-used-to-track-cobalt-from-mines-to-electronic-devices/ BY IAFRIKAN NEWS ON 3 FEBRUARY 2018
4   See Instructor's Manual
5   Source: http://ec.europa.eu/growth/industry/corporate-social-responsibility_nl. Before the term CSR became common terminology, the three P's were used: People, Planet and Profit.
6-8 See Instructor's Manual
9   Source: https://medium.com/blockchain-education-network/what-is-blockchain-explained-for-beginners-5e747cea271

10-13   See Instructor's Manual

14   Source: https://en.wikipedia.org/wiki/Consumerism. Retrieved May 2018

15-22   See Instructor's Manual

23   Source: https://datatopics.worldbank.org/what-a-waste/global_food_loss_and_
         waste.html retrieved on 13 December 2020

24   See https://ec.europa.eu/jrc/en/publication/brief-food-waste-european-union
         retrieved 13 December 2020